THE POWER OF THE PRESIDENCY

THE POWER OF THE PRESIDENCY:
Concepts and Controversy
(2nd Edition)
Robert S. Hirschfield, Editor

Completely brought up to date to cover the Nixon administration and the 1972 election, this second edition of Professor Hirschfield's classic text confronts one of the most critical questions of contemporary American politics: Does the President have sufficient power to meet today's needs? Or is there a danger that the office will become a dictatorship with the growth of presidential authority? Is it possible for the presidency to remain an office of constitutional democratic leadership in the years ahead?

Selected readings (including eight new selections) from Patrick Henry to Nelson Polsby and Arthur Schlesinger, Jr., on the limits of power, on power and crisis, on the expansion of power, and on the emergence of the modern presidency show that there is no abstract or absolute view of presidential power. The reader is encouraged to formulate her or his own theory of presidential power through examples of:

- The concepts of supporters and opponents at the inception of the office

- The strong presidency and the weak presidency as conceived by the Presidents themselves from Washington to Nixon

- Majority and dissenting opinions of the Supreme Court on various aspects of executive authority

- Scholarly views of the presidency's power and limitations

ABOUT THE EDITOR

Robert S. Hirschfield is Professor and Chairman of the Department of Political Science at Hunter College of the City University of New York. He received his Ph.D. from New York University and his A.B., LL.B., and M.A. from Harvard University. He is Director of the New York Center for Education in Politics and has been an active participant in political affairs at both the national and local levels, including service as Staff Director of the first New York State Legislative Committee on Higher Education. Professor Hirschfield has taught at Harvard, Fordham, and New York universities and appears frequently on television as a political analyst and commentator on public affairs. He is the author of *The Constitution and the Court* and is a regular contributor to professional journals and other publications.

THE
POWER
OF THE
PRESIDENCY

Concepts and Controversy

Second Edition

EDITED BY

ROBERT S. HIRSCHFIELD

ALDINE PUBLISHING COMPANY
Chicago

First Edition published 1968

Second Edition published 1973 by
Aldine Publishing Company
529 South Wabash Avenue
Chicago, Illinois 60605

ISBN 0-202-24137-8 cloth
ISBN 0-202-24138-6 paper
Library of Congress Catalog Number 71-169513

Printed in the United States of America

for Muriel

PREFACE

The four years since the original edition of this book appeared span the end of Lyndon Johnson's Presidency and the beginning of Richard Nixon's second term in the White House. But the problem with which the book is concerned—definition of the scope and limits of presidential power—remains the same despite changes of party or Presidents.

That problem became a critical issue for Americans during the late 1960s primarily because Mr. Johnson conducted a "presidential war" in Vietnam. And it was not resolved by the election of Mr. Nixon. On the contrary, Nixon's exercise of independent authority in attempting to end the war turned out to be even more assertive than Johnson's was in escalating it.

The problem of presidential power is persistent. It continues to trouble observers, students, and practitioners of American Government, as it has since the beginning of the Republic. Because of Vietnam, the contemporary generation has been forced to confront it directly, but we are no more likely to come up with solutions than our predecessors. Involving as it does the delicate balance between democracy and security, constitutionality and necessity, it is a problem with which Americans will have to deal recurrently so long as our political system endures.

In revising the book I have reviewed all of the readings and tried to strengthen each section by addition, substitution, or reediting of materials. The result, I hope, is that the volume has not only been brought up to date but that it has also been made more complete and therefore more useful.

I want to thank three associates who have helped me in preparing this revised edition: Julie Nadell, Martin Rosen and Anna Goldoff.

PREFACE TO THE FIRST EDITION

The American Presidency is the most powerful political office in the world. But this impressive statement serves only to raise a whole series of fundamental questions: What is the scope of presidential power and what are its limits? Can the President use all the authority of his office or is that authority more formal than effective? Does the Presidency have sufficient power to meet today's needs or do the problems of the nuclear age demand a more powerful executive? Is there a danger of dictatorship in the growth of presidential authority or will the Presidency remain an office of constitutional democratic leadership?

This book explores such questions by presenting a wide range of views on presidential power from a variety of sources: original supporters and opponents of the office, Presidents themselves, Supreme Court decisions, and professional students of the Presidency. Throughout an effort has been made to select materials which emphasize the controversial nature of the subject, as well as its historical continuity and contemporary significance. While these readings inevitably discuss the roles and functions of the President, they have been chosen because they focus on his power, and because they stimulate serious thought about this essential aspect of the office. That the subject is important hardly needs stating. For the issue of presidential power—directly related as it is to the problems of war or peace, annihilation or survival, progress or stagnation—is among the most important political issues of our time.

I became interested in the subject of presidential power through contact with four teachers to whom I am much indebted: Carl J. Friedrich, Arthur E. Sutherland, and the late Zechariah Chafee, Jr., all of Harvard University; and Marshall E. Dimock, formerly of New York University. In preparing this volume, I had the valuable assistance of Denise Rathbun, Martin Rosen, Arthur Miltz, and Robert Laurenty, each of whom I want to thank. I am also grateful to the City University Doctoral Faculty Research Fund for a grant in support of this project. Finally, I want to express my appreciation to Mr. Charles D. Lieber and Miss Marlene Mandel of Atherton Press, colleagues and friends as well as publishers.

CONTENTS

The Emergence of the Modern Presidency

The Contemporary Presidency

III   JUDICIAL VIEWS   (195)

Presidential Power in Foreign Affairs

Presidential Power to Make War

Presidential Power in Time of War

KOREMATSU V. UNITED STATES   (216

> . . . when under conditions of modern warfare our shores are threatened by hostile forces, the power to protect must be commensurate with the threatened danger.

YOUNGSTOWN SHEET & TUBE COMPANY V. SAWYER   (221

> In the framework of our Constitution, the President's power to see that the laws are faithfully executed refutes the idea that he is to be a lawmaker.

Presidential Power Over Administrative Policy

HUMPHREY'S EXECUTOR V. UNITED STATES   (229

> We think it plain under the Constitution that illimitable power of removal is not possessed by the President.

Presidential Power to Protect the Peace

IN RE NEAGLE   (235

> Is this duty [to "take care that the laws be faithfully executed"] limited to the enforcement of acts of Congress or of treaties of the United States according to their express terms; or does it include the rights, duties, and obligations growing out of the Constitution itself, our international relations, and all the protection implied by the nature of the government under the Constitution?

IV   EXPERT VIEWS   (241)

The Scope of Presidential Power

EDWARD S. CORWIN: The Aggrandizement of Presidential Power   (245

> . . . the growth of presidential power within recent years confronts the American people with a problem of deliberate constitutional reform; otherwise what was the result of democracy may turn out to be democracy's undoing.

THE POWER OF THE PRESIDENCY

INTRODUCTION

The power of the American Presidency has been a subject of concern and controversy since the inception of the office. From George Washington's time to our own, observers have argued that presidential authority is excessive or inadequate, effective or illusory, the basis for dictatorship or the best defense of democracy. Depending on the historical period or the political orientation from which the Presidency is viewed, each of these seemingly contradictory assessments may be valid. But taken together they reflect two essential facts about presidential power: that it cannot be precisely defined, and that there are many different conceptions of its scope and limits.

The power of the Presidency—its capacity to influence or control the course of the nation and the world—is a complex phenomenon. It cannot be determined simply by reviewing the various roles and functions assigned to the President by the Constitution or by custom. Nor is it easily deduced from historical study of what Presidents have actually done, though this approach is more meaningful. To ascertain the reality of presidential power requires an analysis of many factors, including the constitutional framework which is the formal source of executive authority, the political system in which the Presidency operates, the personality and political orientation of Presidents themselves, and the circumstances, conditions, and events which confront the office and its incumbent during each period in the nation's history. For the Presidency's power is the product of interaction among all these factors.

The Constitution creates an office which is potentially, but not necessarily, powerful. Like the rest of the document, the presidential provisions are general, indefinite, and ambiguous. The basic characteristics of the Presidency—its unitary form, independent character, and national purview—are clear enough. But Article II provides at best only an outline of the President's powers. Indeed, the Constitution's executive provisions raise more questions than they answer. The President is, for example, "commander in chief of the army and navy of the United States." But does this appoint him, as Alexander Hamilton insisted, only the nation's "first general and admiral," or does it empower him to use the armed forces in such a way as to commit the nation to war? Does his authority to "make treaties" by and with the advice and consent of two-thirds of the Senate require a sharing of power in the formulation of foreign policy, or does it mean that the President is America's "sole organ of government" in the field of international relations? The very first words of Article II read: "The Executive power shall be vested in a President of the United States of America." But is this simply an introductory statement, or is it a grant of inherent power to protect the national interest? Similarly, the Basic Law is unclear with regard to matters that seem more mundane. For instance, the President must periodically inform Congress "of the State of the Union," and he may recommend measures for its consideration. But is this merely a duty to report, or is it an invitation to assume leadership of the legislative process? He is to "take care that the laws be faithfully executed," but faithful to what—the intention of Congress or his own determination of constitutional or political necessity?

Virtually every function of the Presidency may be discharged in a way that is either magisterial or ministerial. The President may be either a policy-maker or a policy-implementer, a decisive force or an ineffective participant in the political process, a leader or a figurehead. Professor Woodrow Wilson said "the President is at liberty, both in law and conscience, to be as big a man as he can," but he might have added "or as small as he chooses." For the essence of the constitutional office is its flexibility. And while this quality allows for presidential energy, resourcefulness, and creativity, it also permits passivity, indifference, or ineptitude. The absence of specificity and detail in the Constitution is that charter's most distinctive and important characteristic, and with regard to the Presidency in particular, its most valuable and necessary feature, since this indefiniteness leaves the office open to change and development, and makes it possible for the Presidency to operate as our most dynamic governmental institution.

The American political system is also amorphous and flexible, but unlike the constitutional system, it tends to limit rather than enhance executive power. The growth of democracy has made the Presidency a tribunate office, and today the President is politically as well as constitutionally, actually as well as symbolically, "the sole representative of all the people." This development, which had its beginnings in the Jacksonian era, has resulted in a popular Presidency potentially much more powerful than the monarchical office so feared by its early opponents. But because the structural components of American politics have not been redesigned to conform with the President's position of national democratic leadership, the political system imposes very real restraints on that leadership.

At the root of this anomaly is the fact that our political structure is locally rather than nationally based. Despite the quadrennial appearance of "national parties" to contest for the Presidency, politics in America is essentially local in organization, operation, and orientation. The two major national parties are themselves only federations of independent state and city political organizations, each with its own electorate, interests, and leaders. Brought together in tenuous alliance every four years to seek the substantial rewards of capturing the White House, during the remainder of the national political cycle the parties return to their more natural, fragmented condition. Their continuing concern is the satisfaction of local, not national, needs and demands; their continuing function is the selection and election, not of a President, but of their own local leaders— Governors, Senators, Representatives, state, city, county, and town officials. It is these leaders, not the President, who control the separate segments of the national party that the President ostensibly heads. Indeed, it is the magnates among them, the political chieftains of the largest states and cities, who choose the party's presidential candidate and mobilize its resources for his campaign.

Even more important is the influence of localism in the national legislature, for as a result of the political system, the individual member of Congress is relatively free to act without reference to his party's national leader. His political career is dependent not on the President, but on the local electorate; he is loyal not to the President, but to the local political organization; he is responsive not to the President's national constituency, but to local pressures and interests. His party relationship to the President does not, therefore, govern the Congressman's official behavior. He may in fact oppose the President's legislative efforts, and if he holds a position of power in Congress (such as a committee chairmanship) he may even block those efforts.

The political system is, in short, neither national nor disciplined, with the result that the President's party and legislative leadership is at best uncertain and at worst nonexistent. Moreover, all that has been said is only part of the executive's dilemma, since the system also makes it possible for one party to control the White House, while the other may control both or either of the legislative houses. Thus, an activist President must not only find ways of mobilizing congressional support among the unresponsive members of his own party, he must also gain the backing of opposition party members in order to form a majority coalition favorable to his policies or programs. All of this is difficult. In fact, leadership of party and Congress is any President's most frustrating job, whether it be John Kennedy with a legislature dominated by his own party, Richard Nixon facing opposition party control in both houses, or even such a legendary legislative wizard as Lyndon Johnson with 35 years of experience in fashioning "working majorities" on the Hill. No President who seeks to move on controversial issues can avoid these obstacles, for the party and legislative systems are rooted in the basic structural principles of American government—federalism and the separation of powers—and are uncommonly resistant to change.

Confronted with these political facts of life, a President may try to escape the problems they raise by eschewing the role of political leader. He may stand above or outside the arena of partisan conflict, and he may avoid legislative struggle by presenting Congress with only noncontroversial recommendations. A President may not have the personal qualities to act as either party or legislative leader, and he cannot be compelled to assume these roles. There are no political qualifications for the office, he need not be experienced in or familiar with the functioning of the political process, and he may not, as Dwight Eisenhower once admitted, even "like" politics. But if the President is willing and able to use the weapons at his disposal—his popularity, his prestige, his capacity to communicate with the people, all the powerful techniques, including rewards and punishments, available to him—he may also try to surmount the obstacles to his political leadership. Since in this area of activity he generally lacks the power to command associated with his constitutional roles as commander in chief or organ of foreign affairs, a President's influence or control over his party and the legislative process depends on his ability to bargain, cajole, persuade, or threaten, as well as to assert his claim as democratic leader of the entire nation by mobilizing public opinion.

Like the constitutional system, the political system allows for either a passive or an assertive approach. The structure of politics does not bend easily, but it too is flexible. Inherently it imposes limits on executive authority, especially in domestic affairs, and because it divides the American people into separate presidential and congressional constituencies representing different interests and divergent views, it raises the constant danger of dyarchy. But the political system is also resilient enough to permit change when necessary, as the

New Deal and wartime experiences demonstrate. For the executive and legislative powers have been fused, partisanship has been sublimated, and presidential leadership has been accepted under the pressure of crisis. In determining the reality of presidential power, therefore, the political system must normally be regarded as a limitational factor, but it is not an insurmountable barrier to the use of such power when events demand leadership and the President is prepared to provide it.

The third element that must be considered in attempting to ascertain the scope and limits of executive authority is not systemic but human: the personality and political orientation of the President himself. Because the Presidency is a personal office, the incumbent's own view of his power plays an important role in shaping the actual dimensions of that power. Presidents do not often indulge in theoretical exposition of their ideas, and only occasionally has one expressed himself clearly or systematically on the subject of his authority. But such formal statements are not essential, since a President's views are revealed in the way he conducts his Presidency and confronts the problems of his time. Every President has some conception of the Presidency's power. In at least one instance (Woodrow Wilson) that conception was fully developed before the office was achieved. Among the other Presidents, some (like Lincoln) formulated their views of power under the pressure of events, some (like Kennedy) modified their views in accommodating to the realities of their situations, and a few (like Buchanan) held to views which circumstances had made untenable. But however a President reaches his concept of presidential power, and whatever form that concept assumes, his own attitude and behavior are major determinants of the power he in fact possesses. Moreover, the President's conception of his functions and authority is a crucial factor in determining America's destiny, as John Kennedy pointed out in 1960 when he noted that "the history of this nation—its brightest and its bleakest pages —has been written largely in terms of the different views our Presidents have had of the Presidency itself."

Here again there are no definite rules, for the office is open to a wide range of background, experience, and temperament. But in attempting to assess the Presidents, observers have developed criteria and classifications—the "weak" and "strong" Presidents and Presidencies—which reflect the different ways that presidential power has been conceived and exercised. The categories are too simple, the standards of judgment too varied, and the connotations of "weak" and "strong" too value-laden, but as general patterns describing executive attitudes and behavior the two classifications nonetheless provide a worthwhile analytic framework.

The weak Presidents are those who regard the exercise of power as distasteful and the avoidance of decisive action as a virtue. Philosophically attuned to the credo of individualism, they are fearful of impersonal, interventionist government and distrustful of popular leadership. This view is translated into a traditionalist or literalist conception of the American constitutional and political systems, and a limitationist or strict-constructionist interpretation of the President's power in those systems. Thus the weak President believes that his office is bound by the principles of federalism and separation-of-powers. He is reluctant to advocate or enforce policies that expand national governmental control and impinge on state or local authority. He considers Congress an equal and coordinate, if not superior, organ of government, and often expects the legislature to express the public will and formulate public policy. The Presidency itself he sees as a moderative office, its influence as primarily moral; a position above partisanship, a place of honor, respect, and trust. The weak President takes a narrow view of his independent constitutional authority, even in the field of foreign affairs, and he is comfortable in the political system of widely distributed power and responsibility. Since he is not an innovator, he seldom needs or seeks policy support from his national constituency, and he does not require a disciplined congressional party to approve his limited legislative objectives. Attached to the inherited framework of economic, social, and political life, and wary of change, he can be moved only toward the refinement of existing policies and programs. Viewing Pennsylvania Avenue as a moat rather than a bridge, he does not attempt to lead Congress, and he often directs his attention instead to efficient administration of the executive branch of government.

The strong President is one who regards government as the appropriate instrument for achieving progressive change in society, and the Presidency as the mainspring of governmental activity. Associated with the development of mass democracy and the growth of social consciousness, the strong Presidency is power-oriented and attuned to assertive, charismatic, and visionary leadership. In terms of the governmental system, this Presidency reflects a latitudinarian attitude toward basic constitutional principles and an expansionist view of presidential power. National in his outlook, the strong President seeks the extension of national authority and is untroubled by the decline of localism. He attempts to join the political branches of government and to direct the legislative process. Needing widespread support to gain his policy objectives, he is both a popular and a party leader. To the strong President, the Presidency is a place of action, the only office representing the national interest, the focal position in American government and society. For him, the Presidency's essential attribute is its power, and his purposes can be achieved only through the use of that power. Thus the strong President takes a broad view of his constitutional authority, and often resorts, particularly in foreign affairs, to independent action. Faced inevitably with resistance in Congress, he uses all the techniques at his command to overcome the constraints inherent in the political system, being constantly engaged in pressuring the legislature to enact his programs and going regularly to the people to generate support for those programs. His principal concern is not the administration of an inherited office, but the use of that office to bring about change in American society.

Despite the oversimplification apparent in these descriptions, and notwithstanding the fact that there are significant gradations of strength and weakness among the Presidents in these classifications, each of the men who has held the presidential office could probably be fitted into one of the two general patterns. Those designated by history and by students of the office as "Great Presidents"—Washington, Jackson, Lincoln, Wilson, and Franklin Roosevelt—were all charismatic personalities and forceful leaders who conceived their power broadly and used it boldly. Those Presidents who are universally regarded as "Failures"—Grant, Buchanan, and Harding—all suffered from an incapacity to lead, an inability to act, and confusion in dealing with presidential authority. Caution is required in assessing the other Presidents, since most who have been regarded as weak were neither untalented nor inept. Rather, these Presidents and their administrations have almost invariably been reflective of the dominant mood of their times. Thus the succession of post-Civil War limitationist executives—including Arthur, McKinley, and Taft—must be viewed against the background of a national attitude which rejected both positive government and presidential leadership. In a period characterized by a laissez-faire economy, a developing social structure, and a commitment to isolationism, there simply was no place for a powerful executive. Similarly, circumspection is needed in judging those Presidents—like the first Adams, Hayes, and Eisenhower—who assumed office after long periods of uninterrupted crisis, since the popular desire for a "return to normalcy" (whether appropriate to the realities of the time or not) may result in, allow for, or demand a Presidency that reduces national tension and antagonism, restores administrative order and efficiency, and returns to the system of achieving political consensus through the legislative accommodation of diverse interests. Assessment of the stronger Presidents—Jefferson, Polk, Cleveland, Theodore Roosevelt, Truman, Kennedy, and Lyndon Johnson—must also take into account these considerations of time and mood. For the first four operated under conditions that permitted or encouraged at least an occasional assertion of leadership, while each of the last three, despite their broad views of executive authority, had to struggle against a national sentiment loath to accept the need for a crisis-type Presidency.

More important than rating the Presidents or adjudging their strengths and weaknesses, therefore, is the fact that the weak and strong Presidencies have generally been associated with different historical conditions—the former with periods of normalcy, of consolidation, of national reconciliation and "good feeling"; the latter with times of tension, movement, change, and crisis. Nor is this surprising, since no President operates in a vacuum, and since his own conception of the Presidency's power is not alone sufficient to determine the reality of that power. A President may conceive of his authority in the broadest terms and yet be unable to use it, or he may view his authority narrowly and still be compelled to act in a vigorous manner. Thus the history of the office demonstrates that, given the flexible constitutional and political framework within which it functions, the Presidency's actual power is the product of interaction between a President's own view of his authority and the particular circumstances of his time.

Events are consequently the final determinant of presidential power. But not events alone, since by themselves historical conditions, even critical situations, cannot guarantee an appropriate presidential response. The crisis of civil war was no less serious in December of 1860 than it was in March of 1861, but where Buchanan equivocated Lincoln acted. The Great Depression began three years before Franklin Roosevelt became President, but where Hoover waited for a return to normalcy, FDR mounted an attack on the nation's problems. The issue of presidential authority to enforce racial desegregation arose at Little Rock in 1954 and again at Oxford in 1962, but where Eisenhower was reluctant to act, Kennedy used the full power of his office. In a somewhat different way the relationship between circumstances and the exercise of presidential authority is illustrated by the examples of Theodore Roosevelt and Thomas Jefferson. TR had a broad conception of his power, but lacking a really serious national emergency with which to deal, he never had the chance to translate that conception into action; on the other hand, Jefferson's predilection for executive-legislative collaboration was overcome when circumstances provided the opportunity to purchase Louisiana and he was compelled to act independently.

It is not events or men, but the combination of events and men that defines presidential power at any given time. While circumstances, and particularly crisis conditions, can make vast authority available to the President, only he can make the decision to use it. And conversely, no presidential decision can assure the availability of ·

power without the existence of conditions to justify its use. Harry Truman was able to act on his own initiative and according to his broad view of inherent executive power when the Cold War turned hot in Korea, but when the crisis atmosphere passed he could not apply the same concept to seizure of the steel industry. John Kennedy could not move the country or Congress during a period of ostensible normalcy which he regarded as unperceived emergency, but he encountered no resistance when he alone decided the issue of national survival in the Cuban missile crisis. And while Lyndon Johnson found widespread support in 1964 for his attack on America's most critical domestic problems, by 1968 his ability to lead the nation was limited because of grave doubts regarding not only the morality but also the necessity of the war in Vietnam. Only when it is apparent that the nation's fate is at stake does power flow to the President, though when such danger is clear his authority reaches its zenith, as illustrated by Lincoln's "dictatorial" regime during the Civil War, by Wilson's highly-centralized World War I administration, and by Franklin Roosevelt's executive-dominated government during the emergencies of domestic depression and global conflict. National peril creates the conditions—psychological as well as constitutional and political—for the use of power by a power-oriented President. Partisanship and localism are sublimated, and Congress and the people alike turn to the President for leadership in time of evident emergency. It is not surprising, therefore, that all of the "Great Presidents" have held office during periods of great crisis.

That there is a direct relationship between presidential power and historical circumstances there can be no doubt. But this does not mean that strong leadership has been available at every critical moment in America's experience. If the nation's survival is the best evidence that such leadership has thus far always emerged in time, the fact remains that it was not immediately available to meet the crises of secession and depression, and there is no assurance that in the future it will always be found before crisis becomes catastrophe. Although the notion that some special Providence watches over "fools, drunkards, and the United States of America" may be a comforting thought, it is not good history. And the related idea, that the mere existence of the Presidency ensures an adequate response to the nation's problems, is dangerously unrealistic, since history teaches us that while critical circumstances may make possible the use of vast presidential power, they cannot create a President who will use it in timely or appropriate fashion. In this regard, it is important finally to note that the circumstances of the nuclear age have added a new dimension to the problem of presidential capability. The executive's control over America's nuclear arsenal gives him more naked power

than any man has ever possessed. But some future President faced
with a crisis threatening war may find that, despite the seriousness of
the emergency and notwithstanding his ability to meet it decisively,
his power cannot be fully utilized because of the consequences involved in unleashing a thermonuclear holocaust. In the Cuban crisis,
John Kennedy had to struggle with this dilemma, and he resolved
it by acting with reason and restraint, thereby demonstrating that in
the nuclear era more than ever before a President's capacity to use
his power *wisely* is the ultimate test of his leadership.

The Presidency is the most pragmatic institution in a highly
pragmatic governmental system. It is truly a mirror of our national
life, reflecting accurately the events that have made our history and
the men we have chosen, for better or worse, to deal with those
events. It is a flexible and resilient office, and though its form has
remained undisturbed for almost 180 years, its substance—that is, its
power—has constantly varied. Indeed, because the power of the
Presidency is determined by diverse combinations of men and events,
it cannot be defined abstractly and it is subject to changing interpretations. This has been true since the inception of the office, and the
contemporary acceptance of a strong Presidency does not make it less
true today. We have come to accept a powerful executive as normal
because crisis is the normal condition of our time. But the Presidency
is still a highly personal position, and it still leaves room for substantial differences among Presidents with regard to their political orientation, individual style, breadth of vision, and quality of leadership.
The pragmatic nature of the office has not been affected by the institutionalization of its authority, and its essential value—that it can
be attuned to the needs and aspirations of the nation—has actually
been enhanced by this development.

The importance of today's Presidency as a position of national
and international leadership makes it certain that the subject of presidential power will continue to be controversial. In the future, as in
the past, some will fear the Presidency because it seems too strong,
and others will be concerned because it seems too weak. But argument over the scope and limits of presidential power should not be
deplored and must not be stifled. For such debate is a sign of vitality
in American society—welcome evidence that we continue to regard
our greatest governmental institution as an experiment in constitutional democratic leadership.

I

ORIGINAL
VIEWS

Controversy regarding the scope and limits of presidential power began even before the office was established. In fact, during the struggle over ratification of the Constitution, the proposed Presidency became the major target for those who were against the creation of a stronger central government. Committed to the idea of state sovereignty and to the principle of legislative supremacy within the framework of a strictly limited governmental system, they were wary of an independent and powerful national executive. And the constitutional office was potentially strong. Its chief architects, James Wilson and Gouverneur Morris, had persuaded the Convention that effective executive power was essential to the new system's success, and the assumption that General Washington would be the first President blunted most criticism even if it did not allay all fears. Indeed, if any single factor was responsible for the strong Presidency included in the Constitution, it was this anticipation that the country's most trusted, respected, and honored citizen would be its first Chief Executive.

In a document noted for its brevity, the executive provisions of the Constitution are notably brief. Like the document as a whole, but to a greater degree than in the provisions dealing with legislative authority, Article II is simply an outline of presidential functions and powers. General, vague, and ambiguous, the language leaves much room for interpretation. The basic attributes of the Presidency are, however, manifest: the personal nature of the office, its guaranteed tenure and independence from the legislature, its national character, and its potential for leadership.

It was this conception of the Presidency that the Constitution's protagonists, the federalists, ardently supported. Merchants and traders, creditors and speculators, nationalists and elitists, they wanted a central government powerful enough to maintain law and order, protect property interests, develop the nation's resources, and make America a factor in international affairs. Seeking stable, authoritative, and vigorous rule, they regarded a strong executive as essential to the achievement of their goals. Their antifederalist opponents—individualistic, parochial farmers and tradesmen, plus some landed interests—regarded all government, particularly a distant and impersonal one, with fear and suspicion. In their view, the Constitution granted more power to the new central government than had been exercised over the colonies by Britain; in the Presidency they saw the re-establishment of monarchical rule and the specter of tyranny.

The ratification campaign was bitter. Thousands of pamphlets, handbills, editorials, and essays were published by both sides, and all the leading political figures of the time were involved in the great debate. The two crucial battles were fought in Virginia and New York, for without the participation of these important states, the new government could not succeed.

In the Great Commonwealth, Patrick Henry, George Mason, James Monroe, and Richard Henry Lee led the fight against the Constitution, while James Madison, John Marshall, and ultimately Governor Edmund Randolph supported ratification. Virginia was the most doubtful state, and the discussion in its convention the most thorough, able, and spirited. Henry, the greatest orator of his day, made an impassioned plea for individual liberty under state sovereignty, and conjured up the nightmare of a "despot" President leading his national army in "one bold push for the American throne." Madison concentrated on the dangers and deficiencies of government under the Articles of Confederation. The debate reflected a full awareness of the authority Virginia was being asked to cede, but in the end General Washington's compatriots approved the new charter 89 to 79.

Most of the antifederalists in the other states also hammered at the theme of monarchy and tyranny, with its emotional appeal to such recent events, and the Pennsylvanian who adopted the pseudonym "An Old Whig" inveighed against the Presidency because it would establish the worst kind of despot—"an elective king." But it was in New York that the opposition to the Constitution and the Presidency came closest to success. For there most of the great landowners rejected the idea of a "consolidated government," and the antifederalists were led by the Governor, George Clinton. The pro-Constitution forces not only found support among the rising mercantile interests but also had the inestimable benefit of Alexander Hamilton's brilliant advocacy and political expertise.

Out of this confrontation came the most comprehensive and valuable commentary on the Constitution—*The Federalist Papers*—a series of essays written by Hamilton, Madison, and John Jay in support of the new governmental system and designed to convince New Yorkers that it would be neither unfamiliar nor excessively powerful. Hamilton defended the Constitution's presidential provisions, emphasizing the need for "decision, activity, secrecy, and despatch" in the executive, and taking full advantage of the fact that the governorship of New York under the state constitution of 1777 had been the principal model in creating the Presidency. The battle was long and the outcome uncertain, but by the narrow margin of 30 to 27 the federalists won. Ironically, the nine state ratifications required for the Constitution to become effective were achieved before the federalist cause prevailed in either Virginia or New York, but with their approval the "great experiment" was launched, and on April 30, 1789, George Washington was inaugurated as first President of the United States.

The selections included in this section present the two opposing views of presidential power at the nation's beginning. The section opens with the various constitutional provisions related to the Presidency, for they are the source from which all conceptions of presidential power flow and to which they all refer.

THE PRESIDENCY IN THE CONSTITUTION

☆

THE CONSTITUTION: *Provisions on the Presidency*

ARTICLE II

Section 1. The executive power shall be vested in a President of the United States of America. He shall hold his office during the term of four years, and, together with the Vice President, chosen for the same term, be elected as follows:

Each State shall appoint, in such manner as the legislature thereof may direct, a number of electors, equal to the whole number of senators and representatives to which the State may be entitled in the Congress: but no senator or representative, or person holding an office of trust or profit under the United States, shall be appointed an elector.

The electors shall meet in their respective States, and vote by ballot for two persons, of whom one at least shall not be an inhabitant of the same State with themselves. And they shall make a list of all the persons voted for, and of the number of votes for each; which list they shall sign and certify, and transmit sealed to the seat of the government of the United States, directed to the president of the Senate. The president of the Senate shall, in the presence of the Senate and House of Representatives, open all the certificates, and the votes shall then be counted. The person having the greatest number of votes shall be the President, if such number be a majority of the whole number of electors appointed; and if there be more than one who have such majority, and have an equal number of votes, then the House of Representatives shall immediately choose by ballot one of them for President; and if no person have a majority, then from the five highest on the list the said House shall in like manner choose the President. But in choosing the President, the votes shall be taken by

14

States, the representation from each State having one vote; a quorum for this purpose shall consist of a member or members from two thirds of the States, and a majority of all the States shall be necessary to a choice. In every case, after the choice of the President, the person having the greatest number of votes of the electors shall be the Vice President. But if there should remain two or more who have equal votes, the Senate shall choose from them by ballot the Vice President.[1]

The Congress may determine the time of choosing the electors, and the day on which they shall give their votes; which day shall be the same throughout the United States.

No person except a natural born citizen, or a citizen of the United States, at the time of the adoption of this Constitution, shall be eligible to the office of President; neither shall any person be eligible to that office who shall not have attained to the age of thirty-five years, and been fourteen years a resident within the United States.

In case of the removal of the President from office, or of his death, resignation, or inability to discharge the powers and duties of the said office, the same shall devolve on the Vice President, and the Congress may by law provide for the case of removal, death, resignation, or inability, both of the President and Vice President, declaring what officer shall then act as President, and such officer shall act accordingly, until the disability be removed or a President shall be elected.[2]

The President shall, at stated times, receive for his services a compensation, which shall neither be increased nor diminished during the period for which he shall have been elected, and he shall not receive within that period any other emolument from the United States, or any of them.

Before he enter on the execution of his office, he shall take the following oath or affirmation: "I do solemnly swear (or affirm) that I will faithfully execute the office of President of the United States, and will to the best of my ability, preserve, protect and defend the Constitution of the United States."

Section 2. The President shall be Commander in Chief of the army and navy of the United States, and of the militia of the several States, when called into the actual service of the United States; he may require the opinion, in writing, of the principal officer in each of the executive departments, upon any subject relating to the duties of their respective offices, and he shall have power to grant reprieves

[1] Superseded by the Twelfth Amendment.
[2] See the Twenty-fifth Amendment.

and pardons for offenses against the United States, except in cases of impeachment.

He shall have power, by and with the advice and consent of the Senate, to make treaties, provided two thirds of the senators present concur; and he shall nominate, and by and with the advice and consent of the Senate, shall appoint ambassadors, other public ministers and consuls, judges of the Supreme Court, and all other officers of the United States, whose appointments are not herein otherwise provided for, and which shall be established by law: but the Congress may by law vest the appointment of such inferior officers, as they think proper, in the President alone, in the courts of law, or in the heads of departments.

The President shall have power to fill up all vacancies that may happen during the recess of the Senate, by granting commissions which shall expire at the end of their next session.

Section 3.   He shall from time to time give to the Congress information of the state of the Union, and recommend to their consideration such measures as he shall judge necessary and expedient; he may, on extraordinary occasions, convene both Houses, or either of them, and in case of disagreement between them with respect to the time of adjournment, he may adjourn them to such time as he shall think proper; he shall receive ambassadors and other public ministers; he shall take care that the laws be faithfully executed, and shall commission all the officers of the United States.

Section 4.   The President, Vice President, and all civil officers of the United States, shall be removed from office on impeachment for, and conviction of, treason, bribery, or other high crimes and misdemeanors.

ARTICLE I

Section 3. . . .   The Vice President of the United States shall be President of the Senate, but shall have no vote, unless they be equally divided.

The Senate shall choose their other officers, and also a president *pro tempore*, in the absence of the Vice President, or when he shall exercise the office of the President of the United States.

The Senate shall have the sole power to try all impeachments. When sitting for that purpose, they shall be on oath or affirmation. When the President of the United States is tried, the chief justice shall preside: and no person shall be convicted without the concurrence of two thirds of the members present.

Judgment in cases of impeachment shall not extend further than to removal from office, and disqualifications to hold and enjoy any office of honor, trust or profit under the United States: but the party convicted shall nevertheless be liable and subject to indictment, trial, judgment and punishment, according to law.

Section 7. . . . Every bill which shall have passed the House of Representatives and the Senate, shall, before it becomes a law, be presented to the President of the United States; if he approves he shall sign it, but if not he shall return it, with his objections to that House in which it shall have originated, who shall enter the objections at large on their journal, and proceed to reconsider it. If after such reconsideration two thirds of that House shall agree to pass the bill, it shall be sent, together with the objections, to the other House, by which it shall likewise be reconsidered, and if approved by two thirds of that House, it shall become a law. But in all such cases the votes of both Houses shall be determined by yeas and nays, and the names of the persons voting for and against the bill shall be entered on the journal of each House respectively. If any bill shall not be returned by the President within ten days (Sundays excepted) after it shall have been presented to him, the same shall be a law, in like manner as if he had signed it, unless the Congress by their adjournment prevent its return, in which case it shall not be a law.

Every order, resolution, or vote to which the concurrence of the Senate and the House of Representatives may be necessary (except on a question of adjournment) shall be presented to the President of the United States; and before the same shall take effect, shall be approved by him, or being disapproved by him, shall be repassed by two thirds of the Senate and House of Representatives, according to the rules and limitations prescribed in the case of a bill.

Section 9. . . . The privilege of the writ of *habeas corpus* shall not be suspended, unless when in cases of rebellion or invasion the public safety may require it.

ARTICLE IV

Section 4. The United States shall guarantee to every State in this Union a republican form of government, and shall protect each of them against invasion; and on application of the legislature, or of the executive (when the legislature cannot be convened) against domestic violence.

AMENDMENT XII
Adopted September 25, 1804

The electors shall meet in their respective States, and vote by ballot for President and Vice President, one of whom, at least, shall not be an inhabitant of the same State with themselves; they shall name in their ballots the person voted for as President, and in distinct ballots the person voted for as Vice President and they shall make distinct lists of all persons voted for as President and of all persons voted for as Vice President, and of the number of votes for each, which lists they shall sign and certify, and transmit sealed to the seat of the government of the United States, directed to the President of the Senate; The President of the Senate shall, in the presence of the Senate and House of Representatives, open all the certificates and the votes shall then be counted; The person having the greatest number of votes for President, shall be the President, if such number be a majority of the whole number of electors appointed; and if no person have such majority, then from the persons having the highest numbers not exceeding three on the list of those voted for as President, the House of Representatives shall choose immediately, by ballot, the President. But in choosing the President, the votes shall be taken by States, the representation from each State having one vote; a quorum for this purpose shall consist of a member or members from two thirds of the States, and a majority of all the States shall be necessary to a choice. And if the House of Representatives shall not choose a President whenever the right of choice shall devolve upon them, before the fourth day of March next following, then the Vice President shall act as President, as in the case of the death or other constitutional disability of the President. The person having the greatest number of votes as Vice President shall be the Vice President, if such number be a majority of the whole number of electors appointed, and if no person have a majority, then from the two highest numbers on the list, the Senate shall choose the Vice President; a quorum for the purpose shall consist of two thirds of the whole number of Senators, and a majority of the whole number shall be necessary to a choice. But no person constitutionally ineligible to the office of President shall be eligible to that of Vice President of the United States.

AMENDMENT XX
Adopted January 23, 1933

Section 1.   The terms of the President and Vice President shall end at noon on the 20th day of January, and the terms of Senators and Representatives at noon on the 3rd day of January, of the years in which such terms would have ended if this article had not been ratified; and the terms of their successors shall then begin.

Section 2.   The Congress shall assemble at least once in every year, and such meeting shall begin at noon on the 3rd day of January, unless they shall by law appoint a different day.

Section 3. If, at the time fixed for the beginning of the term of the President, the President-elect shall have died, the Vice President-elect shall become President. If a President shall not have been chosen before the time fixed for the beginning of his term, or if the President-elect shall have failed to qualify, then the Vice President-elect shall act as President until a President shall have qualified; and the Congress may by law provide for the case wherein neither a President-elect nor a Vice President-elect shall have qualified, declaring who shall then act as President, or the manner in which one who is to act shall be selected, and such person shall act accordingly until a President or Vice President shall have qualified.

Section 4. The Congress may by law provide for the case of the death of any of the persons from whom the House of Representatives may choose a President whenever the right of choice shall have devolved upon them, and for the case of the death of any of the persons from whom the Senate may choose a Vice President whenever the right of choice shall have devolved upon them.

Section 5. Sections 1 and 2 shall take effect on the 15th day of October following the ratification of this article.

Section 6. This article shall be inoperative unless it shall have been ratified as an amendment to the Constitution by the legislatures of three fourths of the several States within seven years from the date of its submission.

AMENDMENT XXII
Adopted February 26, 1951

No person shall be elected to the office of the President more than twice, and no person who has held the office of the President, or acted as President, for more than two years of a term to which some other person was elected President shall be elected to the office of the President more than once.

But this article shall not apply to any person holding the office of President when this article was proposed by the Congress, and shall not prevent any person who may be holding the office of President, or acting as President, during the term within which this article becomes operative from holding the office of President or acting as President during the remainder of such term.

This article shall be inoperative unless it shall have been ratified as an amendment to the Constitution by the legislatures of three fourths of the several States within seven years from the date of its submission to the States by the Congress.

AMENDMENT· XXIII
Adopted March 29, 1961

Section 1. The District constituting the seat of Government of the United States shall appoint in such manner as the Congress may direct:

A number of electors of President and Vice President equal to the whole number of Senators and Representatives in Congress to which the District would be entitled if it were a State, but in no event more than the least populous State; they shall be in addition to those appointed by the States, but they shall be considered, for the purposes of the election of President and Vice President, to be electors appointed by a State; and they shall meet in the District and perform such duties as provided by the twelfth article of amendment.

Section 2. The Congress shall have power to enforce this article by appropriate legislation.

AMENDMENT XXV
Adopted February 10, 1967

Section 1. In case of the removal of the President from office or of his death or resignation, the Vice President shall become President.

Section 2. Whenever there is a vacancy in the office of the Vice President, the President shall nominate a Vice President who shall take office upon confirmation by a majority vote of both Houses of Congress.

Section 3. Whenever the President transmits to the President *pro tempore* of the Senate and the Speaker of the House of Representatives his written declaration that he is unable to discharge the powers and duties of his office, and until he transmits to them a written declaration to the contrary, such powers and duties shall be discharged by the Vice President as Acting President.

Section 4. Whenever the Vice President and a majority of either the principal officers of the executive departments or of such other body as Congress may by law provide, transmit to the President *pro tempore* of the Senate and the Speaker of the House of Representatives their written declaration that the President is unable to discharge the powers and duties of his office, the Vice President shall immediately assume the powers and duties of the office as Acting President.

Thereafter, when the President transmits to the President *pro tempore* of the Senate and the Speaker of the House of Representatives his written declaration that no inability exists, he shall resume the powers and duties of his office unless the Vice President and a majority of either the principal officers of the executive department or of such other body as Congress may by law provide, transmit within four days to the President *pro tempore* of the Senate and the Speaker of the House of Representatives their written declaration that the President is unable to discharge the powers and duties of his office. Thereupon Congress shall decide the issue, assembling within forty-eight hours for that purpose if not in session. If the Congress, within twenty-one days after receipt of the latter written declaration, or, if Congress is not in session, within twenty-one days after Congress is required to assemble, determines by two thirds vote of both Houses that the President is unable to discharge the powers and duties of his office, the Vice President shall continue to discharge the same as Acting President; otherwise, the President shall resume the powers and duties of his office.

AMENDMENT XXVI
Adopted June 30, 1971

Section 1. The right of citizens of the United States, who are 18 years of age or older, to vote shall not be denied or abridged by the United States or by any state on account of age.

Section 2. The Congress shall have power to enforce this article by appropriate legislation.

ANTIFEDERALIST ATTACKS
ON THE PRESIDENCY

☆

PATRICK HENRY: *Speech Against Ratification*

This Constitution is said to have beautiful features; but when I come to examine these features, sir, they appear to me horribly frightful. Among other deformities, it has an awful squinting; it squints towards monarchy; and does not this raise indignation in the breast of every true American?

Your President may easily become king. Your Senate is so imperfectly constructed that your dearest rights may be sacrificed by what may be a small minority; and a very small minority may continue forever unchangeably this government, although horridly defective. Where are your checks in this government? Your strongholds will be in the hands of your enemies. It is on a supposition that your American governors shall be honest, that all the good qualities of this government are founded; but its defective and imperfect construction puts it in their power to perpetrate the worst of mischiefs, should they be bad men; and, sir, would not all the world, from the eastern to the western hemisphere, blame our distracted folly in resting our rights upon the contingency of our rulers being good or bad? Show me that age and country where the rights and liberties of the people were placed on the sole chance of their rulers being good men, without a consequent loss of liberty! I say that the loss of that dearest privilege has ever followed, with absolute certainty, every such mad attempt.

If your American chief be a man of ambition and abilities, how easy is it for him to render himself absolute! The army is in his hands,

Patrick Henry was a delegate to the Continental Congress (1774–1775) and Governor of Virginia (1776–1779, 1784–1786). The selection is from *Debates and Other Proceedings of the Convention of Virginia* (Richmond, 1805), p. 52. The speech was delivered on June 5, 1788.

and if he be a man of address, it will be attached to him, and it will be the subject of long meditation with him to seize the first auspicious moment to accomplish his design; and, sir, will the American spirit solely relieve you when this happens? I would rather infinitely—and I am sure most of this Convention are of the same opinion—have a king, lords, and commons, than a government so replete with such insupportable evils. If we make a king, we may prescribe the rules by which he shall rule his people, and interpose such checks as shall prevent him from infringing them; but the President, in the field, at the head of his army, can prescribe the terms on which he shall reign master, so far that it will puzzle any American ever to get his neck from under the galling yoke. I cannot with patience think of this idea. If ever he violates the laws, one of two things will happen: he will come at the head of his army, to carry every thing before him; or he will give bail, or do what Mr. Chief Justice will order him. If he be guilty, will not the recollection of his crimes teach him to make one bold push for the American throne? Will not the immense difference between being master of every thing, and being ignominiously tried and punished, powerfully excite him to make this bold push? But, sir, where is the existing force to punish him? Can he not, at the head of his army, beat down every opposition? Away with your President! we shall have a king: the army will salute him monarch: your militia will leave you, and assist in making him king, and fight against you: and what have you to oppose this force? What will then become of you and your rights? Will not absolute despotism ensue?

. . .

☆

AN "OLD WHIG": *The Dangers of an Elected Monarch*

[The] office of President of the United States appears to me to be clothed with such powers as are dangerous. To be the fountain of all honors in the United States—Commander in Chief of the army, navy, and militia; with the power of making treaties and of granting pardons; and to be vested with an authority to put a negative upon all laws, unless two thirds of both houses shall persist in enacting it, and put their names down upon calling the yeas and nays for that purpose—is in reality to be a king, as much a king as the king of Great Britain, and a king too of the worst kind: an elective king.

If such powers as these are to be trusted in the hands of any man, they ought, for the sake of preserving the peace of the community, at once to be made hereditary. Much as I abhor kingly government, yet I venture to pronounce, where kings are admitted to rule they should most certainly be vested with hereditary power. The election of a king whether it be in America or Poland, will be a scene of horror and confusion; and I am perfectly serious when I declare, that, as a friend to my country, I shall despair of any happiness in the United States until this office is either reduced to a lower pitch of power, or made perpetual and hereditary.

When I say that our future President will be as much a king as the king of Great Britain, I only ask of my readers to look into the constitution of that country, and then tell me what important prerogative the king of Great Britain is entitled to which does not also belong to the President during his continuance in office. The king of Great Britain, it is true, can create nobility which our President can-

This letter was originally published in the *Philadelphia Independent Gazeteer,* December 4, 1787.

not; but our President will have the power of making all the great men, which comes to the same thing. All the difference is, that we shall be embroiled in contention about the choice of the man, while they are at peace under the security of an hereditary succession. To be tumbled headlong from the pinnacle of greatness and be reduced to a shadow of departed royalty, is a shock almost too great for human nature to endure. It will cost a man many struggles to resign such eminent powers, and ere long, we shall find some one who will be very unwilling to part with them. Let us suppose this man to be a favorite with his army, and that they are unwilling to part with their beloved Commander in Chief—or to make the thing familiar, let us suppose a future President and Commander in Chief adored by his army and the militia to as great a degree as our late illustrious Commander in Chief; and we have only to suppose one thing more, that this man is without the virtue, the moderation and love of liberty which possessed the mind of our late general—and this country will be involved at once in war and tyranny.

So far is it from its being improbable that the man who shall hereafter be in a situation to make the attempt to perpetuate his own power, should want the virtues of General Washington, that it is perhaps a chance of one hundred millions to one that the next age will not furnish an example of so disinterested a use of great power. We may also suppose, without trespassing upon the bounds of probability, that this man may not have the means of supporting, in private life, the dignity of his former station; that like Caesar, he may be at once ambitious and poor, and deeply involved in debt. Such a man would die a thousand deaths rather than sink from the heights of splendor and power, into obscurity and wretchedness.

We are certainly about giving our President too much or too little; and in the course of less than twenty years we shall find that we have given him enough to enable him to take all. It would be infinitely more prudent to give him at once as much as would content him, so that we might be able to retain the rest in peace, for if once power is seized by violence, not the least fragment of liberty will survive the shock. I would therefore advise my countrymen seriously to ask themselves this question: Whether they are prepared to receive a king? If they are, to say so at once, and make the kingly office hereditary; to frame a constitution that should set bounds to his power, and, as far as possible, secure the liberty of the subject. If we are not prepared to receive a king, let us call another convention to revise the proposed constitution, and form it anew on the principles of a confederacy of free republics; but by no means, under pretense of a republic, to lay the foundation for a military government, which is the worst of all tyrannies.

☆

GEORGE CLINTON: *Fourth Essay of "Cato"*

I shall begin with observations on the executive branch of this new system; and though it is not the first in order, as arranged therein, yet being the *chief*, is perhaps entitled by the rules of rank to the first consideration. The executive power as described in the 2d article, consists of a President and Vice President, who are to hold their offices during the term of four years; the same article has marked the manner and time of their election, and established the qualifications of the President; it also provides against the removal, death, or inability of the President and Vice President—regulates the salary of the President, delineates his duties and powers; and, lastly, declares the causes for which the President and Vice President shall be removed from office.

Notwithstanding the great learning and abilities of the gentlemen who composed the convention, it may be here remarked with deference, that the construction of the first paragraph of the first section of the second article is vague and inexplicit, and leaves the mind in doubt as to the election of a President and Vice President, after the expiration of the election for the first term of four years; in every other case, the election of these great officers is expressly provided for; but there is no explicit provision for their election which is to set this political machine in motion; no certain and express terms as in your state constitution, that *statedly* once in every four years, and as often as these offices shall become vacant, by expiration or otherwise, as is therein expressed, an election shall

George Clinton served as Governor of New York (1777–1795) and as Vice President under Jefferson and Madison (1805–1812). This Fourth Essay of "Cato" was originally published in the *New York Journal*, November 8, 1787.

be held as follows, etc.; this inexplicitness perhaps may lead to an establishment for life.

It is remarked by Montesquieu, in treating of republics, that *in all magistracies, the greatness of the power must be compensated by the brevity of the duration, and that a longer time than a year would be dangerous.* It is, therefore, obvious to the least intelligent mind to account why great power in the hands of a magistrate, and that power connected with considerable duration, may be dangerous to the liberties of a republic. The deposit of vast trusts in the hands of a single magistrate enables him in their exercise to create a numerous train of dependents. This tempts his *ambition*, which in a republican magistrate is also remarked *to be pernicious*, and the duration of his office for any considerable time favors his views, gives him the means and time to perfect and execute his designs; he therefore fancies that he may be great and glorious by oppressing his fellow-citizens, and raising himself to permanent grandeur on the ruins of his country. And here it may be necessary to compare the vast and important powers of the President, together with his continuance in office, with the foregoing doctrine—his eminent magisterial situation will attach many adherents to him, and he will be surrounded by expectants and courtiers. His power of nomination and influence on all appointments; the strong posts in each state comprised within his superintendence, and garrisoned by troops under his direction; his control over the army, militia, and navy; the unrestrained power of granting pardons for treason, which may be used to screen from punishment those whom he had secretly instigated to commit the crime, and thereby prevent a discovery of his own guilt; his duration in office for four years—these, and various other principles evidently prove the truth of the position, that if the President is possessed of ambition, he has power and time sufficient to ruin his country.

Though the President, during the sitting of the legislature, is assisted by the Senate, yet he is without a constitutional council in their recess. He will therefore be unsupported by proper information and advice, and will generally be directed by minions and favorites, or a council of state will grow out of the principal officers of the great departments, the most dangerous council in a free country.

The ten miles square, which is to become the seat of government, will of course be the place of residence for the President and the great officers of state; the same observations of a great man will apply to the court of a President possessing the powers of a monarch, that is observed of that of a monarch—*ambition with idleness*

—baseness with pride—the thirst of riches without labor—aversion to truth—flattery—treason—perfidy—violation of engagements—contempt of civil duties—hope for the magistrate's weakness; but above all, the perpetual ridicule of virtue—these, he remarks, are the characteristics by which the courts in all ages have been distinguished. The language and the manners of this court will be what distinguishes them from the rest of the community, not what assimilates them to it; and in being remarked for a behavior that shows they are not *meanly born*, and in adulation to people of fortune and power.

The establishment of a Vice President is as unnecessary as it is dangerous. This officer, for want of other employment, is made President of the Senate, thereby blending the executive and legislative powers, besides always giving to some one state, from which he is to come, an unjust pre-eminence.

It is a maxim in republics that the representative of the people should be of their immediate choice; but by the manner in which the President is chosen, he arrives to this office at the fourth or fifth hand. Nor does the highest vote, in the way he is elected, determine the choice—for it is only necessary that he should be taken from the highest of five, who may have a plurality of votes. . . .

[A]nd wherein does this President, invested with his powers and prerogatives, essentially differ from the king of Great Britain (save as to name, the creation of nobility, and some immaterial incidents, the offspring of absurdity and locality)? The direct prerogatives of the President, as springing from his political character, are among the following: It is necessary, in order to distinguish him from the rest of the community, and enable him to keep, and maintain his court, that the compensation for his services, or in other words, his revenue, should be such as to enable him to appear with the splendor of a prince. He has the power of receiving ambassadors from, and a great influence on their appointments to foreign courts; as also to make treaties, leagues, and alliances with foreign states, assisted by the Senate, which when made becomes the supreme law of land. He is a constituent part of the legislative power, for every bill which shall pass the House of Representatives and Senate is to be presented to him for approbation. If he approves of it he is to sign it, if he disapproves he is to return it with objections, which in many cases will amount to a complete negative; and in this view he will have a great share in the power of making peace, coining money, etc., and all the various objects of legislation, expressed or implied in this Constitution. For though it may be asserted that the king of Great Britain has the express power of making peace or war, yet he never thinks it prudent to do so without the advice of his Parliament, from whom he is to derive his support—and therefore these powers, in both President and king, are substantially the same. He is the generalissimo of the nation, and of course has the command and control of the army, navy and militia; he is the general conservator of the peace of the union—he may pardon all offences, except in cases of impeachment, and the principal fountain of all offices and employments. Will not the exercise of these powers therefore tend either to the establishment of a vile and arbitrary aristocracy or monarchy? The safety of the people in a republic depends on the share or proportion they have in the government; but experience ought to teach you, that when a man is at the head of an elective government invested with great powers, and interested in his re-election, in what circle appointments will be made; by which means an *imperfect aristocracy* bordering on monarchy may be established.

You must, however, my countrymen, beware that the advocates of this new system do not deceive you by a fallacious resemblance between it and your own state government [New York] which you so much prize; and, if you examine, you will perceive that the chief magistrate of this state is your immediate choice, controlled and checked by a just and full representation of the people, divested of the prerogative of influencing war and peace, making treaties, receiving and sending embassies, and commanding standing armies and navies, which belong to the power of the confederation, and will be convinced that this government is no more like a true picture of your own than an Angel of Darkness resembles an Angel of Light.

FEDERALIST DEFENSE OF
THE PRESIDENCY

☆

ALEXANDER HAMILTON: *The Federalist, No. 69*

To the People of the State of New York:
I proceed now to trace the real characters of the proposed Executive, as they are marked out in the plan of the convention. This will serve to place in a strong light the unfairness of the representations which have been made in regard to it.

The first thing which strikes our attention is that the executive authority, with few exceptions, is to be vested in a single magistrate. This will scarcely, however, be considered as a point upon which any comparison can be grounded; for if, in this particular, there be a resemblance to the king of Great Britain, there is not less a resemblance to the Grand Seignior, to the khan of Tartary, to the Man of the Seven Mountains, or to the governor of New York.

That magistrate is to be elected for *four* years; and is to be re-eligible as often as the people of the United States shall think him worthy of their confidence. In these circumstances there is a total dissimilitude between *him* and a king of Great Britain, who is an *hereditary* monarch, possessing the crown as a patrimony descendible to his heirs forever; but there is a close analogy between *him* and a governor of New York, who is elected for *three* years, and is re-eligible without limitation or intermission. If we consider how much less time would be requisite for establishing a dangerous influence in a single State, than for establishing a like influence throughout the United States, we must conclude that a duration of *four* years for the Chief Magistrate of the Union is a degree of

Alexander Hamilton was a delegate to the Constitutional Convention and the leader of the Federalist Party in New York. This essay by "Publius" was originally published in the *New York Packet*, March 14, 1788.

permanency far less to be dreaded in that office, than a duration of *three* years for a corresponding office in a single State.

The President of the United States would be liable to be impeached, tried, and, upon conviction of treason, bribery, or other high crimes or misdemeanors, removed from office; and would afterwards be liable to prosecution and punishment in the ordinary course of law. The person of the king of Great Britain is sacred and inviolable; there is no constitutional tribunal to which he is amenable; no punishment to which he can be subjected without involving the crisis of a national revolution. In this delicate and important circumstance of personal responsibility, the President of Confederated America would stand upon no better ground than a governor of New York, and upon worse ground than the governors of Maryland and Delaware.

The President of the United States is to have power to return a bill, which shall have passed the two branches of the legislature, for reconsideration; and the bill so returned is to become a law, if, upon that reconsideration, it be approved by two thirds of both houses. The king of Great Britain, on his part, has an absolute negative upon the acts of the two houses of Parliament. The disuse of that power for a considerable time past does not affect the reality of its existence; and is to be ascribed wholly to the crown's having found the means of substituting influence to authority, or the art of gaining a majority in one or the other of the two houses, to the necessity of exerting a prerogative which could seldom be exerted without hazarding some degree of national agitation. The qualified negative of the President differs widely from this absolute negative of the British sovereign; and tallies exactly with the revisionary authority of the council of revision of this State, of which the governor is a constituent part. In this respect the power of the President would exceed that of the governor of New York, because the former would possess, singly, what the latter shares with the chancellor and judges; but it would be precisely the same with that of the governor of Massachusetts, whose constitution, as to this article, seems to have been the original from which the convention have copied.

The President is to be the "Commander in Chief of the army and navy of the United States, and of the militia of the several States, when called into the actual service of the United States. He is to have power to grant reprieves and pardons for offences against the United States, *except in cases of impeachment;* to recommend to the consideration of Congress such measures as he shall judge necessary and expedient; to convene, on extraordinary occasions, both houses of the legislature, or either of them, and, in case of disagreement between them *with respect to the time of adjournment,* to adjourn them to such time as he shall think proper; to take care that the laws be faithfully executed; and to commission all officers of the United States." In most of these particulars, the power of the President will resemble equally that of the king of Great Britain and of the governor of New York. The most material points of difference are these: *First.* The President will have only the occasional command of such part of the militia of the nation as by legislative provision may be called into the actual service of the Union. The king of Great Britain and the governor of New York have at all times the entire command of all the militia within their several jurisdictions. In this article, therefore, the power of the President would be inferior to that of either the monarch or the governor. *Secondly.* The President is to be Commander in Chief of the army and navy of the United States. In this respect his authority would be nominally the same with that of the king of Great Britain, but in substance much inferior to it. It would amount to nothing more than the supreme command and direction of the military and naval forces, as first general and admiral of the Confederacy; while that of the British king extends to the *declaring* of war and to the *raising* and *regulating* of fleets and armies—all which, by the Constitution under consideration, would appertain to the legislature. The governor of New York, on the other hand, is by the constitution of the State vested only with the command of its militia and navy. But the constitutions of several of the States expressly declare their governors to be commanders in chief, as well of the army as navy; and it may well be a question, whether those of New Hampshire and Massachusetts, in particular, do not, in this instance, confer larger powers upon their respective governors, than could be claimed by a President of the United States. *Thirdly.* The power of the President, in respect to pardons, would extend to all cases, *except those of impeachment.* The governor of New York may pardon in all cases, even in those of impeachment, except for treason and murder. Is not the power of the governor, in this article, on a calculation of political consequences, greater than that of the President? All conspiracies and plots against the government, which have not been matured into actual treason, may be screened from punishment of every kind, by the interposition of the prerogative of pardoning. If a governor of New York, therefore, should be at the head of any such conspiracy, until the design had been ripened into actual hostility he could insure his accomplices and adherents an entire impunity. A President of the Union, on the other hand, though he may even pardon treason, when prosecuted in the ordinary course of law, could shelter no offender, in any degree, from the effects of impeachment and conviction. Would not the prospect of a total indemnity for all the preliminary steps be a greater temptation to undertake and persevere in an enterprise against the public liberty, than the mere prospect of an exemption from death and confiscation, if the final execution of the design, upon an actual appeal to arms, should miscarry? Would this last expectation have any influence at all, when the probability was computed, that the person who was to afford that exemption might himself be involved in the consequences of the measure, and might be incapacitated by his agency in it from affording the desired impunity? The better to judge of this matter, it will be necessary to recollect, that, by the proposed Constitution, the offence of treason is limited "to levying war upon the United States, and adhering to their enemies, giving them aid and comfort"; and that by the laws of New York it is confined within similar bounds. *Fourthly.* The President can only adjourn the national legislature in the single case of disagreement about the time of adjournment. The British monarch may prorogue or even dissolve the Parliament. The governor of New York may also prorogue the legislature of this State for a limited time; a power which, in certain situations, may be employed to very important purposes.

The President is to have power, with the advice and consent of the Senate, to make treaties, provided two thirds of the senators present concur. The king of Great Britain is the sole and absolute representative of the nation in all foreign transactions. He can of his own accord make treaties of peace, commerce, alliance, and of every other description. It has been insinuated that his authority in this respect is not conclusive, and that his conventions with foreign powers are subject to the revision, and stand in need of the ratification, of Parliament. But I believe this doctrine was never heard of, until it was broached upon the present occasion. Every jurist of that kingdom, and every other man acquainted with its Constitution, knows, as an established fact, that the prerogative of making treaties exists in the crown in its utmost plentitude; and that the compacts entered into by the royal authority have the most complete legal validity and perfection, independent of any other sanction. The Parliament, it is true, is sometimes seen employing itself in altering the existing laws to conform them to the stipulations in a new treaty; and this may have possibly given birth to the imagination that its cooperation was necessary to the obligatory efficacy of the treaty. But this parliamentary interposition proceeds from a different cause: from the necessity of adjusting a most artificial and intricate system of revenue and commercial laws, to the changes made in them by the operation of the treaty; and of adapting new provisions and precautions to the new state of things, to keep the machine from running into disorder. In this respect, therefore, there is no comparison between the intended power of the President and the actual power of the British sovereign. The one can perform alone what the other can do only with the concurrence of a branch of the legislature. It must be admitted, that, in this instance, the power of the federal Executive would exceed that of any State Executive. But this arises naturally from the sovereign power which relates to treaties. If the Confederacy were to be dissolved, it would become a question whether the Executives of the several States were not solely invested with that delicate and important prerogative.

The President is also to be authorized to receive ambassadors and other public ministers. This, though it has been a rich theme of declamation, is more a matter of dignity than of authority. It is a circumstance which will be without consequence in the administration of the government; and it was far more convenient that it should be arranged in this manner, than that there should be a necessity of convening the legislature, or one of its branches, upon every arrival of a foreign minister, though it were merely to take the place of a departed predecessor.

The President is to nominate, and, *with the advice and consent of the Senate*, to appoint ambassadors and other public ministers, judges of the Supreme Court, and in general all officers of the United States established by law, and whose appointments are not otherwise provided for by the Constitution. The king of Great Britain is emphatically and truly styled the fountain of honor. He not only appoints to all offices, but can create offices. He can confer titles of nobility at pleasure; and has the disposal of an immense number of church preferments. There is evidently a great inferiority in the power of the President, in this particular, to that of the British king; nor is it equal to that of the governor of New York, if we are to interpret the meaning of the constitution of the State by the practice which has obtained under it. The power of appointment is with us lodged in a council, composed of the governor and four members of the Senate, chosen by the Assembly. The governor *claims*, and has frequently *exercised*, the right of nomination, and is *entitled* to a casting vote in the appointment. If he really has the right of nominating, his authority is in this respect equal to that of the President, and exceeds it in the article of the casting vote. In the national government, if the Senate should be divided, no appointment could be made; in the government of New York, if the council should be divided, the governor can turn the scale, and confirm his own nomination. If we compare the publicity which must necessarily attend the mode of appointment by the President and an entire branch of the national legislature, with the privacy in the mode of appointment by the governor of New York, closeted in a secret apartment with at most four, and frequently with only two persons; and if we at the same time consider how much more easy it must be to influence the small number of which a council of appointment consists, than the considerable number of which the national Senate would consist, we cannot hesitate to pronounce that the power of the chief magistrate of this State, in the disposition of offices, must, in practice, be greatly superior to that of the Chief Magistrate of the Union.

Hence it appears that, except as to the concurrent authority of the President in the article of treaties, it would be difficult to determine whether that magistrate would in the aggregate, possess more or less power than the governor of New York. And it appears yet more unequivocally, that there is no pretense for the parallel which has been attempted between him and the king of Great Britain. But to render the contrast in this respect still more striking, it may be of use to throw the principal circumstances of dissimilitude into a closer group.

The President of the United States would be an officer elected by the people for *four* years; the king of Great Britain is a perpetual and *hereditary* prince. The one would be amenable to personal punishment and disgrace; the person of the other is sacred and inviolable. The one would have a *qualified* negative upon the acts of the legislative body; the other has an *absolute* negative. The one would have a right to command the military and naval forces of the nation; the other, in addition to this right, possesses that of *declaring* war, and of *raising* and *regulating* fleets and armies by his own authority. The one would have a concurrent power with a branch of the legislature in the formation of treaties; the other is the *sole possessor* of the power of making treaties. The one would have a like concurrent authority in appointing to offices; the other is the sole author of all appointments. The one can confer no privileges whatever: the other can make denizens of aliens, noblemen of commoners: can erect corporations with all the rights incident to corporate bodies. The one can prescribe no rules concerning the commerce or currency of the nation; the other is in several respects the arbiter of commerce, and in this capacity can establish markets and fairs, can regulate weights and measures, can lay embargoes for a limited time, can coin money, can authorize or prohibit the circulation of foreign coin. The one has no particle of spiritual jurisdiction; the other is the supreme head and governor of the national church! What answer shall we give to those who would persuade us that things so unlike resemble each other? The same that ought to be given to those who tell us that a government, the whole power of which would be in the hands of the elective and periodical servants of the people, is an aristocracy, a monarchy, and a despotism.

☆

ALEXANDER HAMILTON: *The Federalist, No. 70*

To the People of the State of New York:
There is an idea, which is not without its advocates, that a vigorous
Executive is inconsistent with the genius of republican government.
The enlightened well-wishers to this species of government must
at least hope that the supposition is destitute of foundation; since
they can never admit its truth, without at the same time admitting
the condemnation of their own principles. Energy in the Executive
is a leading character in the definition of good government. It is
essential to the protection of the community against foreign attacks;
it is not less essential to the steady administration of the laws; to
the protection of property against those irregular and high-handed
combinations which sometimes interrupt the ordinary course of justice; to the security of liberty against the enterprises and assaults
of ambition, of faction, and of anarchy. Every man the least con-
versant in Roman story, knows how often that republic was obliged
to take refuge in the absolute power of a single man, under the
formidable title of Dictator, as well against the intrigues of ambitious individuals who aspired to the tyranny, and the seditions of
whole classes of the community whose conduct threatened the
existence of all government, as against the invasions of external
enemies who menaced the conquest and destruction of Rome.

There can be no need, however, to multiply arguments or examples on this head. A feeble Executive implies a feeble execution
of the government. A feeble execution is but another phrase for a
bad execution; and a government ill executed, whatever it may be
in theory, must be, in practice, a bad government.

This essay by "Publius" was originally published in the *New York Packet*,
March 18, 1788.

Taking it for granted, therefore, that all men of sense will agree in the necessity of an energetic Executive, it will only remain to inquire, what are the ingredients which constitute this energy? How far can they be combined with those other ingredients which constitute safety in the republican sense? And how far does this combination characterize the plan which has been reported by the convention?

The ingredients which constitute energy in the Executive are, first, unity; secondly, duration; thirdly, an adequate provision for its support; fourthly, competent powers.

The ingredients which constitute safety in the republican sense are, first, a due dependence on the people; secondly, a due responsibility.

Those politicians and statesmen who have been the most celebrated for the soundness of their principles and for the justice of their views, have declared in favor of a single Executive and a numerous legislature. They have, with great propriety, considered energy as the most necessary qualification of the former, and have regarded this as most applicable to power in a single hand; while they have, with equal propriety, considered the latter as best adapted to deliberation and wisdom, and best calculated to conciliate the confidence of the people and to secure their privileges and interests.

That unity is conducive to energy will not be disputed. Decision, activity, secrecy, and despatch will generally characterize the proceedings of one man in a much more eminent degree than the proceedings of any greater number; and in proportion as the number is increased, these qualities will be diminished.

This unity may be destroyed in two ways: either by vesting the power in two or more magistrates of equal dignity and authority; or by vesting it ostensibly in one man, subject, in whole or in part, to the control and cooperation of others, in the capacity of counsellors to him. . . .

Wherever two or more persons are engaged in any common enterprise or pursuit, there is always danger of difference of opinion. If it be a public trust or office, in which they are clothed with equal dignity and authority, there is peculiar danger of personal emulation and even animosity. From either, and especially from all these causes, the most bitter dissensions are apt to spring. Whenever these happen, they lessen the respectability, weaken the authority, and distract the plans and operations of those whom they divide. If they should unfortunately assail the supreme executive magistracy of a country, consisting of a plurality of persons, they might impede or frustrate the most important measures of the government, in the most critical emergencies of the state. And what is still worse, they might split the community into the most violent and irreconcilable factions, adhering differently to the different individuals who composed the magistracy.

Men often oppose a thing, merely because they have had no agency in planning it, or because it may have been planned by those whom they dislike. But if they have been consulted, and have happened to disapprove, opposition then becomes, in their estimation, an indispensable duty of self-love. They seem to think themselves bound in honor, and by all the motives of personal infallibility, to defeat the success of what has been resolved upon contrary to their sentiments. Men of upright, benevolent tempers have too many opportunities of remarking, with horror, to what desperate lengths this disposition is sometimes carried, and how often the great interests of society are sacrificed to the vanity, to the conceit, and to the obstinacy of individuals, who have credit enough to make their passions and their caprices interesting to mankind. Perhaps the question now before the public may, in its consequences, afford melancholy proofs of the effects of this despicable frailty, or rather detestable vice, in the human character.

Upon the principles of a free government, inconveniences from the source just mentioned must necessarily be submitted to in the formation of the legislature; but it is unnecessary, and therefore unwise, to introduce them into the constitution of the Executive. It is here too that they may be most pernicious. In the legislature, promptitude of decision is oftener an evil than a benefit. The differences of opinion, and the jarrings of parties in that department of the government, though they may sometimes obstruct salutary plans, yet often promote deliberation and circumspection, and serve to check excesses in the majority. When a resolution too is once taken, the opposition must be at an end. That resolution is a law, and resistance to it punishable. But no favorable circumstances palliate or atone for the disadvantages of dissension in the executive department. Here, they are pure and unmixed. There is no point at which they cease to operate. They serve to embarrass and weaken the execution of the plan or measure to which they relate, from the first step to the final conclusion of it. They constantly counteract those qualities in the Executive which are the most necessary ingredients in its composition—vigor and expedition, and this without any counterbalancing good. In the conduct of war, in which the energy of the Executive is the bulwark of the national security, every thing would be to be apprehended from its plurality.

It must be confessed that these observations apply with principal weight to the first case supposed—that is, to a plurality of magistrates of equal dignity and authority, a scheme, the advocates for which are not likely to form a numerous sect; but they apply, though not with equal, yet with considerable weight to the project of a council, whose concurrence is made constitutionally necessary to the operations of the ostensible Executive. An artful cabal in that council would be able to distract and to enervate the whole system of administration. If no such cabal should exist, the mere diversity of views and opinions would alone be sufficient to tincture the exercise of the executive authority with a spirit of habitual feebleness and dilatoriness.

But one of the weightiest objections to a plurality in the Executive, and which lies as much against the last as the first plan, is, that it tends to conceal faults and destroy responsibility. Responsibility is of two kinds—to censure and to punishment. The first is the more important of the two, especially in an elective office. Man, in public trust, will much oftener act in such a manner as to render him unworthy of being any longer trusted, than in such a manner as to make him obnoxious to legal punishment. But the multiplication of the Executive adds to the difficulty of detection in either case. It often becomes impossible, amidst mutual accusations, to determine on whom the blame or the punishment of a pernicious measure, or series of pernicious measures, ought really to fall. It is shifted from one to another with so much dexterity, and under such plausible appearances, that the public opinion is left in suspense about the real author. The circumstances which may have led to any national miscarriage of misfortune are sometimes so complicated that, where there are a number of actors who may have had different degrees and kinds of agency, though we may clearly see upon the whole that there has been mismanagement, yet it may be impracticable to pronounce to whose account the evil which may have been incurred is truly chargeable.

"I was overruled by my council. The council were so divided in their opinions that it was impossible to obtain any better resolution on the point." These and similar pretexts are constantly at hand, whether true or false. And who is there that will either take the trouble or incur the odium of a strict scrutiny into the secret springs of the transaction? Should there be found a citizen zealous enough to undertake the unpromising task, if there happen to be collusion between the parties concerned, how easy it is to clothe the circumstances with so much ambiguity, as to render it uncertain what was the precise conduct of any of those parties?

In the single instance in which the governor of this State is coupled with a council—that is, in the appointment to offices, we have seen the mischiefs of it in the view now under consideration. Scandalous appointments to important offices have been made. Some cases, indeed, have been so flagrant that ALL PARTIES have agreed in the impropriety of the thing. When inquiry has been made, the blame has been laid by the governor on the members of the council, who, on their part, have charged it upon his nomination; while the people remain altogether at a loss to determine, by whose influence their interests have been committed to hands so unqualified and so manifestly improper. In tenderness to individuals, I forbear to descend to particulars.

It is evident from these considerations, that the plurality of the Executive tends to deprive the people of the two greatest securities they can have for the faithful exercise of any delegated power, *first*, the restraints of public opinion, which lose their efficacy, as well on account of the division of the censure attendant on bad measures among a number, as on account of the uncertainty on whom it ought to fall; and, *secondly*, the opportunity of discovering with facility and clearness the misconduct of the persons they trust, in order either to their removal from office, or to their actual punishment in cases which admit of it.

In England, the king is a perpetual magistrate; and it is a maxim which has obtained for the sake of the public peace, that he is unaccountable for his administration, and his person sacred. Nothing, therefore, can be wiser in that kingdom, than to annex to the king a constitutional council, who may be responsible to the nation for the advice they give. Without this, there would be no responsibility whatever in the executive department—an idea inadmissible in a free government. But even there the king is not bound by the resolutions of his council, though they are answerable for the advice they give. He is the absolute master of his own conduct in the exercise of his office, and may observe or disregard the counsel given to him at his sole discretion.

But in a republic, where every magistrate ought to be personally responsible for his behavior in office, the reason which in the British Constitution dictates the propriety of a council, not only ceases to apply, but turns against the institution. In the monarchy of Great Britain, it furnishes a substitute for the prohibited responsibility of the chief magistrate, which serves in some degree as a hostage to the national justice for his good behavior. In the American republic, it would serve to destroy, or would greatly diminish, the intended and necessary responsibility of the Chief Magistrate himself.

The idea of a council to the Executive, which has so generally obtained in the State constitutions, has been derived from that maxim of republican jealousy which considers power as safer in the hands of a number of men than of a single man. If the maxim should be admitted to be applicable to the case, I should contend that the advantage on that side would not counterbalance the numerous disadvantages on the opposite side. But I do not think the rule at all applicable to the executive power. I clearly concur in opinion, in this particular, with a writer whom the celebrated Junius pronounces to be "deep, solid, and ingenious," that "the executive power is more easily confined when it is ONE"; that it is far more safe there should be a single object for the jealousy and watchfulness of the people; and, in a word, that all multiplication of the Executive is rather dangerous than friendly to liberty.

II

PRESIDENTIAL VIEWS

BECAUSE THE POWER of the Presidency is to a large extent what the President says it is, the most important views of presidential power are those expressed by Presidents themselves. Clear and systematic exposition of such views is rare, but the speeches, messages, letters, memoirs, and other documentary materials of Presidents—before, during, and after their tenure of office—reveal their perceptions of executive authority and constitute the most meaningful definitions of its scope and limits.

Reflecting the different political orientations and personalities of the Presidents, as well as the different problems with which they had to deal, these presidential conceptions of presidential power vary widely. Those that are historically as well as conceptually the most significant are presented here, beginning with the first President's assertion of his independent authority to chart the nation's course in foreign affairs, and ending with the strikingly similar position assumed by his latest successor.

The selections are grouped in four sets, each of which marks an important turning point in the interpretation and development of presidential power. The first group of readings deals with the establishment of the Presidency as an office of independent authority and focuses on the controversy surrounding George Washington's proclamation of neutrality in 1793. Based on a claim to executive prerogative in determining American foreign policy, this action outraged not only democrats sympathetic to the French Revolution but also unreconstructed antifederalists (now called republicans) who had all along distrusted the central government and its "elected monarch." Ultimately the argument involved interpretation of the President's constitutional powers, and in a series of essays James

Madison—at the instigation of Secretary of State Thomas Jefferson and writing under the pseudonym Helvidius—attacked Washington's "usurpation" of congressional authority to decide the issue of war or peace. The Administration was defended by Alexander Hamilton who, using the pen-name Pacificus, contended that under his "executive power" the President could establish the nation's foreign policy, although the consequences of his actions might "affect" the legislature's exclusive power to declare war.

Thus the crucial issue of executive authority to determine America's position in world affairs—an issue of the most far-reaching importance for our own time—was raised at the inception of the Presidency. It was then resolved in favor of the Washington-Hamilton concept attributing broad and independent power to the President as the nation's "sole organ of foreign relations." But the controversy has continued and the arguments of Hamilton and Madison were heard again in 1967 when President Johnson's Undersecretary of State and Senator J. William Fulbright clashed at the Foreign Relations Committee's hearings on the Gulf of Tonkin Resolution and the President's authority to conduct the war in Vietnam.

The second set of selections deals with the greatest test of presidential power in American history—the crisis of secession and civil war—and includes the response to that crisis of three Presidents: Jackson, Buchanan, and Lincoln. The issue of presidential power as a means to prevent the Union's dissolution first arose in 1832, when South Carolina adopted an ordinance nullifying congressional tariff acts, denying the federal government's authority to enforce them, and threatening to secede if enforcement was attempted. Although incensed by the action of his native state, Andrew Jackson responded calmly and effectively. Strengthening the government's military position in South Carolina and preparing a political compromise, he also issued a proclamation firmly rejecting the doctrine of nullification and clearly asserting his intention to preserve the Union. The combination of forcefulness and conciliation worked, and the bloody showdown was postponed for a generation.

The decisive confrontation finally came in 1860. With Abraham Lincoln's election the movement toward Southern withdrawal began, and only a strong stand by the President might have averted civil war. But James Buchanan did not have a Jacksonian conception of the Presidency's power. Faced with the most agonizing decision any President before the nuclear age has had to make, Buchanan considered issuing a proclamation condemning secession but ended with a message to Congress adopting the equivocal position that while no state had a right to secede the President was powerless to prevent such action. Abdicating responsibility to a paralyzed legislature, he then withdrew from the political arena.

His successor had a radically different view of executive authority in time of crisis, and though initially he sought reconciliation, ultimately he was prepared to act. In his first address to the nation, Lincoln made it clear that he regarded secession as rebellion, and that as Chief Executive and Commander in Chief he had both the duty and the authority to use whatever means were necessary to preserve the Union. That he was resolute in his purpose became even clearer in the critical period that followed, and particularly during the eleven weeks after Fort Sumter's fall when he alone constituted the government of the United States. Lincoln's conception of executive power went beyond that of any President before or since. As expressed in his message to the special session of Congress in 1861 and in an 1864 campaign document, his view included the arrogation to himself of the "war power of the government," unlimited inherent authority to meet the crisis, and a popular mandate to transcend the bounds of constitutionality in defense of the nation. Responding to the emergency and prosecuting the war on his own initiative, without any reference to Congress at its inception and with as little as possible throughout its duration, Lincoln's Civil War regime was a "presidential dictatorship." Such a spectacular administration has not reappeared on the American scene, but the Lincolnian conception of presidential power became the model for all of his strong successors, and its basic principles have been adopted by all subsequent crisis Presidents.

The third set of readings reflects the long period of transition from the post-Civil War Presidency to the modern office. As with all institutional transformations, this development of the Presidency was directly related to fundamental economic, social, and political changes, and consequently was slow, uneven, and bitterly resisted. The selections reveal the basic conflict going on in American society at the time and take the form of a disputation involving three successive Presidents—Theodore Roosevelt, William Howard Taft, and Woodrow Wilson—each of whom contributed to the debate a classic conceptualization of the executive's position and power as the nation entered a new era.

Characterized by a laissez-faire economy, an isolationist foreign policy, and congressionally-dominated government, the period after the Civil War witnessed a sharp decline in executive authority. But as demands for economic reform and world involvement grew, there was a concomitant revival of interest in the strong Presidency. Indeed, by the turn of the century the issue of presidential power had again become controversial as a result of Theodore Roosevelt's accidental succession to the office. For TR's energetic tenure broke the pattern of executive subservience to Congress, and his "stewardship theory" of the Presidency expressed the new, activist conception of its authority. Roosevelt saw the President as the representative and protector of the "plain people" in a system controlled by special interests, and he acknowledged no restrictions on his power to further the "general welfare" except those specifically imposed by the Constitution or the laws.

This assertive view of the executive was anathema to Roosevelt's hand-picked successor, William Howard Taft, whose counterargument reflected the basic philosophic differences as well as the personal antagonism between the two men. Taft's denial of inherent executive power to act in the public interest, as set forth in *Our Chief Magistrate and His Powers*, is the most explicit statement of the literalist-limitationist concept ever formulated by a President. But if this view was still dominant at the beginning of the century, Theodore Roosevelt's ideas pointed toward the future. Indeed it was in the next President, Woodrow Wilson, that TR found his intellectual successor and the powerful Presidency its most eloquent advocate. Wilson's conception of the office was drawn from many sources, both British and American, and it was infused with the democratic spirit of his two idols, Jefferson and Lincoln. Systematically developed in a series of 1908 lectures and applied in practice during his administration, the Wilsonian view of the executive as "the representative of no constituency but of the whole people" and as the "vital place of action" in American government heralded the modern Presidency.

Wilson's World War I regime provided a full-dress preview of that office, but it was not until the current era of continuing crisis that the powerful Presidency concept became institutionalized. The final set of selections deals with this period and includes the views of all the modern Presidents, beginning with the dominant figure in the establishment of the contemporary office—Franklin Roosevelt—and ending with his direct political descendant, Lyndon Johnson. A pragmatist of the first order, FDR never theorized about presidential power. But his performance in meeting the economic catastrophe of the 1930s and the war emergency of the 1940s gives ample evidence that no President since Lincoln has had a broader conception of that power. Encompassing the Lincolnian view of independent authority and the Wilsonian of legislative direction, Roosevelt's was the consummate crisis Presidency. Its keynotes were leadership and action. Sounded in every major public statement from his stirring Inaugural Address through the war years, these were the themes by which he captured the popular imagination and dominated the political scene more completely and for a longer time than any other President. Over the course of thirteen critical years, he created an office whose power was commensurate with its national and world responsibilities.

Harry Truman inherited those responsibilities as well as the Rooseveltian conception of power in meeting them. Domestic politics and the conditions of cold war made Truman's application of that concept difficult, but in formulating a policy which continues to govern American foreign affairs, and in acting independently to halt Communist aggression in Korea, he projected the crisis Presidency into the nuclear age. To Truman the Presidency was "the greatest office in the history of the world," and he guarded its prerogatives jealously. Despite the absence of charisma, he secured his place in the ranks of strong Presidents and passed the office undiminished in its authority to his successor.

Dwight Eisenhower had a more limited idea of the Presidency's power and functions, however, and a less assertive view of his own role as President. His emphasis on "organization" and "teamwork," his rejection of a "personality cult," and his fear of executive "autocracy" betrayed an emotional attachment to the Taftian school of thought, and his tenure made it clear that despite the institutionalization of its power the Presidency remains a highly personal position. But the Eisenhower years were more significant in demonstrating rather than disproving the contemporary need for and acceptance of a strong Presidency. For if his administration lacked the vigor of the Lincoln-Wilson-Roosevelt regimes, nonetheless Eisenhower's actual conduct of the office and his uses of its authority were more closely related to those power-oriented Presidencies than to the administrations of his limitationist predecessors. For all his failure to provide leadership and to act decisively, Eisenhower was neither a Buchanan nor a Hoover, and the powerful Presidency was maintained (or survived) during his incumbency.

More important, the end of the Eisenhower interlude saw an immediate return to the strong Presidency in both conception and practice. John Kennedy was the first presidential candidate since Woodrow Wilson to make his view of executive authority a major campaign issue, and like Wilson he sounded the call for "a Chief Executive who is the vital center of action in our whole scheme of government." Concept came into conflict with reality, as Kennedy himself admitted at mid-term, but his independent (indeed secret) handling of the Cuban Missile Crisis in 1962 gave Americans their first frightening glimpse of the Presidency's power—and limits—in the nuclear era.

Kennedy's view of that power, as expressed in a 1960 campaign statement and consistently during his brief tenure, was in the strong Presidency tradition. And so too was Lyndon Johnson's. Although he came to office with greater governmental experience than any of his predecessors, Johnson never conceptualized his authority. From the start of his public career, however, he was committed by political inheritance and basic personality to the Presidency of leadership and action. Reflected in his conduct of the Vietnam war, as well as in his initial efforts to achieve the "Great Society" program, his conception of the office was deeply rooted in Rooseveltian principles and practices.

But if Johnson was a strong President, his war policy also generated renewed concern about the strong Presidency—concern that did not die with Johnson's political demise. On the contrary, the issue of presidential power became the focus of national controversy under Richard Nixon. For despite Nixon's efforts to "wind down" American involvement in Southeast Asia, his attempts to exercise exclusive control over all aspects of Indochina policy kept the issue very much alive.

During his campaign for the Presidency, Mr. Nixon projected an "activist" conception of the office, and though the tone of his administration was more reminiscent of Eisenhower than of Roosevelt, in foreign affairs and especially with regard to Vietnam, his assertion of authority to determine the nation's course once again compelled the American people to ponder the problem of presidential power.

THE INITIAL EXPANSION OF PRESIDENTIAL POWER

☆

ON GEORGE WASHINGTON'S PROCLAMATION OF
NEUTRALITY: *The First Letter of "Pacificus"*
by Alexander Hamilton

As attempts are making, very dangerous to the peace, and, it is to
be feared, not very friendly to the Constitution, of the United
States, it becomes the duty of those who wish well to both, to endeavor to prevent their success. . . .

The objections which have been raised against the proclamation
of neutrality, lately issued by the President, have been urged in a
spirit of acrimony and invective, which demonstrates that more was
in view than merely a free discussion of an important public measure.
They exhibit evident indications of a design to weaken. the confidence of the people in the author of the measure, in order to remove or lessen a powerful obstacle to the success of an opposition
to the government, which, however it may change its form according to circumstances, seems still to be persisted in with unremitting
industry. . . .

It will not be disputed, that the management of the affairs of
this country with foreign nations, is confided to the government of
the United States.

It can as little be disputed, that a proclamation of neutrality,
when a nation is at liberty to decline or avoid a war in which other
nations are engaged, and means to do so, is a *usual* and a *proper*
measure. Its main object is to prevent the nation's being responsible

Alexander Hamilton served as Secretary of the Treasury under Washington
(1789–1795). This essay was originally published in *The Gazette of the United
States*, Philadelphia, June 29, 1793.

for acts done by its citizens, without the privity or connivance of the government, in contravention of the principles of neutrality; an object of the greatest moment to a country, whose true interest lies in the preservation of peace.

The inquiry then is, what department of our government is the proper one to make a declaration of neutrality, when the engagements of the nation permit, and its interests require that it should be done?

A correct mind will discern at once, that it can belong neither to the legislative nor judicial department; of course it must belong to the executive.

The legislative department is not the organ of intercourse between the United States and foreign nations. It is charged neither with making nor interpreting treaties. It is therefore not naturally that member of the government, which is to pronounce the existing condition of the nation, with regard to foreign powers, or to admonish the citizens of their obligations and duties in consequence; still less is it charged with enforcing the observance of those obligations and duties.

It is equally obvious, that the act in question is foreign to the judiciary department. The province of that department is to decide litigations in particular cases. It is indeed charged with the interpretation of treaties, but it exercises this function only where contending parties bring before it a specific controversy. It has no concern with pronouncing upon the external political relations of treaties between government and government. This position is too plain to need being insisted upon.

It must then of necessity belong to the executive department to exercise the function in question, when a proper case for it occurs.

It appears to be connected with that department in various capacities: As the *organ* of intercourse between the nation and foreign nations; as the *interpreter* of the national treaties, in those cases in which the judiciary is not competent, that is, between government and government; as the *power*, which is charged with the execution of the laws, of which treaties form a part: as that which is charged with the command and disposition of the public force.

This view of the subject is so natural and obvious, so analogous to general theory and practice, that no doubt can be entertained of its justness, unless to be deduced from particular provisions of the Constitution of the United States.

Let us see, then, if cause for such doubt is to be found there.

The second article of the Constitution of the United States, section first, establishes this general proposition, that "the EXECUTIVE

POWER shall be vested in a President of the United States of America."

The same article, in a succeeding section, proceeds to delineate particular cases of executive power. It declares, among other things, that the President shall be Commander in Chief of the army and navy of the United States, and of the militia of the several states, when called into the actual service of the United States; that he shall have power, by and with the advice and consent of the Senate, to make treaties; that it shall be his duty to receive ambassadors and other public ministers, and to take care that the laws be faithfully executed.

It would not consist with the rules of sound construction to consider this enumeration of particular authorities as derogating from the more comprehensive grant in the general clause, further than as it may be coupled with express restrictions of limitations; as in regard to the cooperation of the Senate in the appointment of officers, and the making of treaties; which are plainly qualifications of the general executive powers of appointing officers and making treaties. The difficulty of a complete enumeration of all the cases of executive authority, would naturally dictate the use of general terms, and would render it improbable, that a specification of certain particulars was designed as a substitute for those terms, when antecedently used. The different mode of expression employed in the Constitution, in regard to the two powers, the legislative and the executive, serves to confirm this inference. In the article which gives the legislative powers of the government, the expressions are, "All legislative powers herein granted shall be vested in a Congress of the United States." In that which grants the executive power, the expressions are, "*The executive power* shall be vested in a President of the United States."

The enumeration ought therefore to be considered, as intended merely to specify the principal articles implied in the definition of executive power; leaving the rest to flow from the general grant of that power, interpreted in conformity with other parts of the Constitution, and with the principles of free government.

The general doctrine of our Constitution then is, that the *executive power* of the nation is vested in the President; subject only to the *exceptions* and *qualifications*, which are expressed in the instrument.

Two of these have been already noticed; the participation of the Senate in the appointment of officers, and in the making of treaties. A third remains to be mentioned; the right of the legislature "to declare war, and grant letters of marque and reprisal."

With these exceptions, the executive power of the United States is completely lodged in the President. This mode of construing the Constitution has indeed been recognized by Congress in formal acts, upon full consideration and debate; of which the power of removal from office is an important instance. It will follow, that if a proclamation of neutrality is merely an executive act, as, it is believed, has been shown, the step which has been taken by the President is liable to no just exception on the score of authority.

It may be said, that this inference would be just, if the power of declaring war had not been vested in the legislature; but that this power naturally includes the right of judging, whether the nation is or is not under obligations to make war.

The answer is, that however true this position may be, it will not follow, that the executive is in any case excluded from a similar right of judgment, in the execution of its own functions.

If, on the one hand, the legislature have a right to declare war, it is, on the other, the duty of the executive to preserve peace, till the declaration is made; and in fulfilling this duty, it must necessarily possess a right of judging what is the nature of the obligations which the treaties of the country impose on the government: and when it has concluded that there is nothing in them inconsistent with neutrality, it becomes both its province and its duty to enforce the laws incident to that state of the nation. The executive is charged with the execution of all laws, the law of nations, as well as the municipal law, by which the former are recognized and adopted. It is consequently bound, by executing faithfully the laws of neutrality when the country is in a neutral position, to avoid giving cause of war to foreign powers.

This is the direct end of the proclamation of neutrality. It declares to the United States their situation with regard to the contending parties, and makes known to the community, that the laws incident to that state will be enforced. In doing this, it conforms to an established usage of nations, the operation of which, as before remarked, is to obviate a responsibility on the part of the whole society, for secret and unknown violations of the rights of any of the warring powers by its citizens.

Those who object to the proclamation will readily admit, that it is the right and duty of the executive to interpret those articles of our treaties which give to France particular privileges, in order to the enforcement of them: but the necessary consequence of this is, that the executive must judge what are their proper limits; what rights are given to other nations, by our contracts with them; what rights the law of nature and nations gives, and our treaties permit, in respect to those countries with which we have none; in fine, what are the reciprocal rights and obligations of the United States, and of all and each of the powers at war?

The right of the executive to receive ambassadors and other public ministers, may serve to illustrate the relative duties of the executive and legislative departments. This right includes that of judging, in the case of a revolution of government in a foreign country, whether the new rulers are competent organs of the national will, and ought to be recognized, or not; which, where a treaty antecedently exists between the United States and such nation, involves the power of continuing or suspending its operation. For until the new government is acknowledged, the treaties between the nations, so far at least as regards public rights, are of course suspended.

This power of determining virtually upon the operation of national treaties, as a consequence of the power to receive public ministers, is an important instance of the right of the executive, to decide upon the obligations of the country with regard to foreign nations. To apply it to the case of France, if there had been a treaty of alliance, *offensive* and defensive, between the United States and that country, the unqualified acknowledgment of the new government would have put the United States in a condition to become an associate in the war with France, and would have laid the legislature under an obligation, if required, and there was otherwise no valid excuse, of exercising its power of declaring war.

This serves as an example of the right of the executive, in certain cases, to determine the condition of the nation, though it may, in its consequences, affect the exercise of the power of the legislature to declare war. Nevertheless, the executive cannot thereby control the exercise of that power. The legislature is still free to perform its duties, according to its own sense of them; though the executive, in the exercise of its constitutional powers, may establish an antecedent state of things, which ought to weigh in the legislative decisions.

The division of the executive power in the Constitution, creates a *concurrent* authority in the cases to which it relates.

Hence, in the instance stated, treaties can only be made by the President and Senate jointly; but their activity may be continued or suspended by the President alone.

No objection has been made to the President's having acknowledged the republic of France, by the reception of its minister, without having consulted the Senate; though that body is connected with him in the making of treaties, and though the consequence of his act of reception is, to give operation to those heretofore made with that country. But he is censured for having declared the United States to be in a state of peace and neutrality, with regard to the powers at war; because the right of changing that state, and declaring war, belongs to the legislature.

It deserves to be remarked, that as the participation of the Senate in the making of treaties, and the power of the legislature to declare war, are exceptions out of the general "executive power" vested in the President; they are to be construed strictly, and ought to be extended no further than is essential to their execution.

While, therefore, the legislature can alone declare war, can alone actually transfer the nation from a state of peace to a state of hostility, it belongs to the "executive power" to do whatever else the law of nations, cooperating with the treaties of the country, enjoin in the intercourse of the United States with foreign powers.

In this distribution of authority, the wisdom of our Constitution is manifested. It is the province and duty of the executive to preserve to the nation the blessings of peace. The legislature alone can interrupt them by placing the nation in a state of war.

But though it has been thought advisable to vindicate the authority of the executive on this broad and comprehensive ground, it was not absolutely necessary to do so. That clause of the Constitution which makes it his duty to "take care that the laws be faithfully executed," might alone have been relied upon, and this simple process of argument pursued.

The President is the constitutional EXECUTOR of the laws. Our treaties, and the laws of nations, form a part of the law of the land. He, who is to execute the laws, must first judge for himself of their meaning. In order to the observance of that conduct which the laws of nations, combined with our treaties, prescribed to this country, in reference to the present war in Europe, it was necessary for the President to judge for himself, whether there was anything in our treaties, incompatible with an adherence to neutrality. Having decided that there was not, he had a right, and if in his opinion the interest of the nation required it, it was his duty, as executor of the laws, to proclaim the neutrality of the nation, to exhort all persons to observe it, and to warn them of the penalties which would attend its nonobservance.

The proclamation has been represented as enacting some new law. This is a view of it entirely erroneous. It only proclaims a fact, with regard to the existing state of the nation: informs the citizens of what the laws previously established require of them in that state, and notifies them that these laws will be put in execution against the infractors of them.

☆

ON WASHINGTON'S PROCLAMATION OF NEUTRALITY:

The First Letter of "Helvidius"
by James Madison

Several pieces with the signature of PACIFICUS were lately published, which have been read with singular pleasure and applause, by the foreigners and degenerate citizens among us, who hate our republican government, and the French revolution; whilst the publication seems to have been too little regarded, or too much despised by the steady friends to both. . . .

Had the doctrines inculcated by the writer, with the natural consequences from them, been nakedly presented to the public, this treatment might have been proper. Their true character would then have struck every eye, and been rejected by the feelings of every heart. But they offer themselves to the reader in the dress of an elaborate dissertation; they are mingled with a few truths that may serve them as a passport to credulity; and they are introduced with professions of anxiety for the preservation of peace, for the welfare of the government, and for the respect due to the present head of the executive, that may prove a snare to patriotism.

In these disguises they have appeared to claim the attention I propose to bestow on them; with a view to show, from the publication itself, that under color of vindicating an important public act, of a chief magistrate who enjoys the confidence and love of his country, principles are advanced which strike at the vitals of its Constitution, as well as to its honor and true interest.

As it is not improbable that attempts may be made to apply in-

James Madison, one of the Framers of the Constitution, was the 4th President of the United States (1809–1817). This essay was originally published in *The Gazette of the United States*, Philadelphia, August 24, 1793.

sinuations which are seldom spared when particular purposes are to be answered, to the author of the ensuing observations, it may not be improper to premise, that he is a friend to the Constitution, that he wishes for the preservation of peace, and that the present chief magistrate has not a fellow-citizen, who is penetrated with deeper respect for his merits, or feels a purer solicitude for his glory.

This declaration is made with no view of courting a more favorable ear to what may be said than it deserves. The sole purpose of it is, to obviate imputations which might weaken the impressions of truth; and which are the more likely to be resorted to, in proportion as solid and fair arguments may be wanting.

The substance of the first piece, sifted from its inconsistencies and its vague expressions, may be thrown into the following propositions:

That the powers of declaring war and making treaties are, in their nature, executive powers.

That being particularly vested by the Constitution in other departments, they are to be considered as exceptions out of the general grant to the executive department:

That being, as exceptions, to be construed strictly, the powers not strictly within them, remain with the executive:

That the executive consequently, as the organ of intercourse with foreign nations, and the interpreter and executor of treaties, and the law of nations, is authorized to expound all articles of treaties, those involving questions of war and peace, as well as others; to judge of the obligations of the United States to make war or not, under any *casus fœderis* or eventual operation of the contract, relating to war; and to pronounce the state of things resulting from the obligations of the United States, as understood by the executive:

That in particular the executive had authority to judge, whether in the case of the mutual guaranty between the United States and France, the former were bound by it to engage in the war:

That the executive has, in pursuance of that authority, decided that the United States are not bound: And

That its proclamation of the 22nd of April last, is to be taken as the effect and expression of that decision.

The basis of the reasoning is, we perceive, the extraordinary doctrine, that the powers of making war, and treaties, are in their nature executive; and therefore comprehended in the general grant of executive power, where not especially and strictly excepted out of the grant. . . .

If we consult for a moment, the nature and operation of the two powers to declare war and to make treaties, it will be impossible not to see, that they can never fall within a proper definition of executive powers. The natural province of the executive magistrate is to execute laws, as that of the legislature is to make laws. All his acts, therefore, properly executive, must presuppose the existence of the laws to be executed. A treaty is not an execution of laws: it does not presuppose the existence of laws. It is, on the contrary, to have itself the force of a law, and to be carried into execution, like all other laws by the executive magistrate. To say then that the power of making treaties, which are confessedly laws, belongs naturally to the department which is to execute laws, is to say, that the executive department naturally includes a legislative power. In theory this is an absurdity—in practice a tyranny.

The power to declare war is subject to similar reasoning. A declaration that there shall be war, is not an execution of laws: it does not suppose pre-existing laws to be executed: it is not, in any respect, an act merely executive. It is, on the contrary, one of the most deliberative acts that can be performed; and when performed, has the effect of repealing all the laws operating in a state of peace, so far as they are inconsistent with a state of war; and of enacting, as a rule for the executive, a new code adapted to the relation between the society and its foreign enemy. In like manner, a conclusion of peace annuls all the laws peculiar to a state of war, and revives the general laws incident to a state of peace.

These remarks will be strengthened by adding that treaties, particularly treaties of peace, sometimes have the effect of changing not only the external laws of the society but also the internal code, which is purely municipal, and to which the legislative authority of the country is of itself competent and complete.

From this view of the subject it must be evident, that although the executive may be a convenient organ of preliminary communications with foreign governments, on the subjects of treaty or war; and the proper agent for carrying into execution the final determinations of the competent authority; yet it can have no pretensions, from the nature of the powers in question compared with the nature of the executive trust, to that essential agency which gives validity to such determinations. It must be further evident, that if these powers be not in their nature purely legislative, they partake so much more of that, than of any other quality, that under a Constitution leaving them to result to their most natural department, the legislature would be without a rival in its claim.

Another important inference to be noted is, that the powers of making war and treaty being substantially of a legislative, not an executive nature, the rule of interpreting exceptions strictly must narrow, instead of enlarging, executive pretensions on those subjects.

It remains to be inquired, whether there be anything in the Constitution itself, which shows, that the powers of making war and peace are considered as of an executive nature, and as comprehended within a general grant of executive power.

It will not be pretended, that this appears from any *direct* position to be found in the instrument.

If it were *deducible* from any particular expressions, it may be presumed, that the publication would have saved us the trouble of the research.

Does the doctrine, then, result from the actual distribution of powers among the several branches of the government? or from any fair analogy between the powers of war and treaty, and the enumerated powers vested in the executive alone?

Let us examine:

In the general distribution of powers we find that of declaring war expressly vested in the Congress, where every other legislative power is declared to be vested; and without any other qualification than what is common to every other legislative act. The constitutional idea of this power would seem then clearly to be, that it is of a legislative, and not an executive nature.

This conclusion becomes irresistible, when it is recollected, that the Constitution cannot be supposed to have placed either any power legislative in its nature, entirely among executive powers, or any power executive in its nature, entirely among legislative powers, without charging the Constitution, with that kind of intermixture and consolidation of different powers, which would violate a fundamental principle in the organization of free governments. If it were not unnecessary to enlarge on this topic here, it could be shown, that the Constitution was originally vindicated, and has been constantly expounded, with a disavowal of any such intermixture.

The power of treaties is vested jointly in the President and in the Senate, which is a branch of the legislature. From this arrangement merely, there can be no inference that would necessarily exclude the power from the executive class: since the Senate is joined with the President in another power, that of appointing to offices, which, as far as relate to executive offices at least, is considered as of an executive nature. Yet on the other hand, there are sufficient indications that the power of treaties is regarded by the Constitution as materially different from mere executive power, and as having more affinity to the legislative than to the executive character.

One circumstance indicating this, is the constitutional regulation under which the Senate give their consent in the case of treaties. In all other cases, the consent of the body is expressed by a majority of voices. In this particular case, a concurrence of two thirds at least is made necessary, as a substitute or compensation for the other branch of the legislature, which, on certain occasions, could not be conveniently a party to the transaction.

But the conclusive circumstance is, that treaties, when formed according to the constitutional mode, are confessedly to have the force and operation of laws, and are to be a rule for the courts in controversies between man and man, as much as any other laws. They are even emphatically declared by the Constitution to be "the supreme law of the land."

So far the argument from the Constitution is precisely in opposition to the doctrine. As little will be gained in its favor from a comparison of the two powers, with those particularly vested in the President alone.

As there are but few, it will be most satisfactory to review them one by one.

"The President shall be Commander in Chief of the army and navy of the United States, and of the militia when called into the actual service of the United States."

There can be no relation worth examining between this power and the general power of making treaties. And instead of being analogous to the power of declaring war, it affords a striking illustration of the incompatibility of the two powers in the same hands. Those who are to conduct a war cannot in the nature of things, be proper or safe judges, whether a war ought to be commenced, continued, or concluded. They are barred from the latter functions by a great principle in free government, analogous to that which separates the sword from the purse, or the power of executing from the power of enacting laws.

"He may require the opinion in writing of the principal officers in each of the executive departments upon any subject relating to the duties of their respective offices; and he shall have power to grant reprieves and pardons for offences against the United States, except in case of impeachment." These powers can have nothing to do with the subject.

"The President shall have power to fill up vacancies that may happen during the recess of the Senate, by granting commissions which shall expire at the end of the next session." The same remark is applicable to this power, as also to that of "receiving ambassadors, other public ministers, and consuls." The particular use attempted to be made of this last power will be considered in another place.

"He shall take care that the laws shall be faithfully executed, and shall commission all officers of the United States." To see the laws faithfully executed constitutes the essence of the executive authority. But what relation has it to the power of making treaties and war, that is, of determining what the laws shall be with regard to other nations? No other certainly than what subsists between the powers of executing and enacting laws; no other, consequently, than what forbids a coalition of the powers in the same department.

I pass over the few other specified functions assigned to the President, such as that of convening the legislature, etc., etc., which cannot be drawn into the present question.

It may be proper however, to take notice of the power of removal from office, which appears to have been adjudged to the President by the laws establishing the executive departments; and which the writer has endeavored to press into his service. To justify any favorable inference from this case it must be shown that the powers of war and treaties are of a kindred nature to the power of removal, or at least are equally within a grant of executive power. Nothing of this sort has been attempted, nor probably will be attempted. Nothing can in truth be clearer, than that no analogy, or shade of analogy, can be traced between a power in the supreme officer responsible for the faithful execution of the laws, to displace a subaltern officer employed in the execution of the laws; and a power to make treaties, and to declare war, such as these have been found to be in their nature, their operation, and their consequences.

Thus it appears that by whatever standard we try this doctrine, it must be condemned as no less vicious in theory than it would be dangerous in practice. It is countenanced neither by the writers on law; nor by the nature of the powers themselves; nor by any general arrangements, or particular expressions, or plausible analogies, to be found in the Constitution.

Whence then can the writer have borrowed it?

There is but one answer to this question.

The power of making treaties and the power of declaring war, are *royal prerogatives* in the *British government,* and are accordingly treated as executive prerogatives by British commentators.

We shall be the more confirmed in the necessity of this solution to the problem, by looking back to the era of the Constitution, and satisfying ourselves that the writer could not have been misled by the doctrines maintained by our own commentators on our own government. That I may not ramble beyond prescribed limits, I shall content myself with an extract from a work which entered into a systematic explanation and defense of the Constitution; and to which there has frequently been ascribed some influence in conciliating the public assent to the government in the form proposed. Three circumstances conspire in giving weight to this contemporary exposition. It was made at a time when no application to persons or measures could bias: the opinion given was not transiently mentioned, but formally and critically elucidated: it related to a point in the Constitution which must consequently have been viewed as of importance in the public mind. The passage relates to the power of making treaties; that of declaring war, being arranged with such obvious propriety among the legislative powers, as to be passed over without particular discussion.

Though several writers on the subject of government place that power [of making treaties] in the class of *executive authorities*, yet this is evidently an arbitrary disposition. For if we attend carefully to its operation, it will be found to partake more of the legislative than of the executive character, though it does not seem strictly to fall within the definition of either of them. The essence of the legislative authority, is to enact laws; or in other words, to prescribe rules for the regulation of the society: while the execution of the laws and the employment of the common strength, either for this purpose, or for the common defense, seem to comprise all the functions of the executive magistrate. The power of making treaties is plainly neither the one nor the other. It relates neither to the execution of the subsisting laws, nor to the enaction of new ones, and still less to an exertion of the common strength. Its objects are contracts with foreign nations, which have the force of law, but derive it from the obligations of good faith. They are not rules prescribed by the sovereign to the subject, but agreements between sovereign and sovereign. The power in question seems therefore to form a distinct department, and to belong properly neither to the legislative nor to the executive. The qualities elsewhere detailed as indispensable in the management of foreign negotiations, point out the executive as the most fit agent in those transactions: whilst the vast importance of the trust, and the operation of treaties as laws plead strongly for the participation of the whole or a part of the legislative body, in the office of making them [Federalist, 75, written by Hamilton].

It will not fail to be remarked on this commentary, that whatever doubts may be stated as to the correctness of its reasoning against the legislative nature of the power to make treaties; it is clear, consistent, and confident, in deciding that the power is plainly and evidently not an *executive power*.

PRESIDENTIAL POWER AND
THE GREAT CRISIS

☆

ANDREW JACKSON: *Proclamation on Nullification*

To preserve [the] bond of our political existence from destruction, to maintain inviolate [the] state of national honor and prosperity, and to justify the confidence my fellow-citizens have reposed in me, I, Andrew Jackson, President of the United States, have thought proper to issue this my proclamation, stating my views of the Constitution and laws applicable to the measures adopted by the convention of South Carolina and to the reasons they have put forth to sustain them, declaring the course which duty will require me to pursue, and, appealing to the understanding and patriotism of the people, warn them of the consequences that must inevitably result from an observance of the dictates of the convention.

Strict duty would require of me nothing more than the exercise of those powers with which I am now or may hereafter be invested for preserving the peace of the Union and for the execution of the laws; but the imposing aspect which opposition has assumed in this case, by clothing itself with State authority, and the deep interest which the people of the United States must all feel in preventing a resort to stronger measures while there is a hope that anything will be yielded to reasoning and remonstrance, perhaps demand, and will certainly justify, a full exposition to South Carolina and the nation of the views I entertain of this important question, as well as a distinct enunciation of the course which my sense of duty will require me to pursue. . . .

I consider . . . the power to annul a law of the United States, assumed by one State, *incompatible with the existence of the Union,*

Andrew Jackson was the 7th President of the United States (1829–1837). This selection is from his *Proclamation to the People of South Carolina*, December 10, 1832.

contradicted expressly by the letter of the Constitution, unauthorized by its spirit, inconsistent with every principle on which it was founded, and destructive of the great object for which it was formed. . . .

This, then, is the position in which we stand: A small majority of the citizens of one State in the Union have elected delegates to a State convention; that convention has ordained that all the revenue laws of the United States must be repealed, or that they are no longer a member of the Union. The governor of that State has recommended to the legislature the raising of an army to carry the secession into effect, and that he may be empowered to give clearances to vessels in the name of the State. No act of violent opposition to the laws has yet been committed, but such a state of things is hourly apprehended. And it is the intent of this instrument to *proclaim*, not only that the duty imposed on me by the Constitution "to take care that the laws be faithfully executed" shall be performed to the extent of the powers already vested in me by law, or of such others as the wisdom of Congress shall devise and intrust to me for that purpose, but to warn the citizens of South Carolina who have been deluded into an opposition to the laws of the danger they will incur by obedience to the illegal and disorganizing ordinance of the convention; to exhort those who have refused to support it to persevere in their determination to uphold the Constitution and laws of their country; and to point out to all the perilous situation into which the good people of that State have been led, and that the course they are urged to pursue is one of ruin and disgrace to the very State whose rights they affect to support.

Fellow-citizens of my native State, let me not only admonish you, as the First Magistrate of our common country, not to incur the penalty of its laws, but use the influence that a father would over his children whom he saw rushing to certain ruin.

[The] dictates of a high duty oblige me solemnly to announce that you can not succeed. The laws of the United States must be executed. I have no discretionary power on the subject; my duty is emphatically pronounced in the Constitution. Those who told you that you might peaceably prevent their execution deceived you; they could not have been deceived themselves. They know that a forcible opposition could alone prevent the execution of the laws, and they know that such opposition must be repelled. Their object is disunion. But be not deceived by names. Disunion by armed forces is *treason*. Are you really ready to incur its guilt? If you are, on the heads of the instigators of the act be the dreadful consequences; on their heads be the dishonor, but on yours may fall the punishment. On your unhappy State will inevitably fall all the evils of the conflict you force upon the Government of your country. It can not accede to the mad project of disunion, of which you would be the first victims. Its First

Magistrate can not, if he would, avoid the performance of his duty.
. . .

Fellow-citizens of the United States, the threat of unhallowed disunion, the names of those once respected by whom it is uttered, the
array of military force to support it, denote the approach of a crisis in
our affairs on which the continuance of our unexampled prosperity,
our political existence, and perhaps that of all free governments may
depend. The conjuncture demanded a free, a full, and explicit enunciation, not only of my intentions, but of my principles of action; and
as the claim was asserted of a right by a State to annul the laws of
the Union, and even to secede from it at pleasure, a frank exposition
of my opinions in relation to the origin and form of our Government
and the construction I give to the instrument by which it was created
seemed to be proper. Having the fullest confidence in the justness of
the legal and constitutional opinion of my duties which has been expressed, I rely with equal confidence on your undivided support in
my determination to execute the laws, to preserve the Union by all
constitutional means, to arrest, if possible, by moderate and firm
measures the necessity of a recourse to force; and if it be the will of
Heaven that the recurrence of its primeval curse on man for the
shedding of a brother's blood should fall upon our land, that it be
not called down by any offensive act on the part of the United States.

Fellow-citizens, the momentous case is before you. On your undivided support of your Government depends the decision of the
great question it involves—whether your sacred Union will be preserved and the blessing it secures to us as one people shall be perpetuated. No one can doubt that the unanimity with which that
decision will be expressed will be such as to inspire new confidence in
republican institutions, and that the prudence, the wisdom, and the
courage which it will bring to their defense will transmit them unimpaired and invigorated to our children.

May the Great Ruler of Nations grant that the signal blessings
with which He has favored ours may not, by the madness of party or
personal ambition, be disregarded and lost; and may His wise providence bring those who have produced this crisis to see the folly before
they feel the misery of civil strife, and inspire a returning veneration
for that Union which, if we may dare to penetrate His designs, He
has chosen as the only means of attaining the high destinies to which
we may reasonably aspire.

☆

JAMES BUCHANAN: *Message to Congress*

Fellow-Citizens of the Senate and House of Representatives:
Throughout the year since our last meeting the country has been
eminently prosperous in all its material interests. The general health
has been excellent, our harvests have been abundant, and plenty
smiles throughout the land. Our commerce and manufactures have
been prosecuted with energy and industry, and have yielded fair and
ample returns. In short, no nation in the tide of time has ever presented a spectacle of greater material prosperity than we have done
until within a very recent period.

Why is it, then, that discontent now so extensively prevails, and
the Union of the States, which is the source of all these blessings, is
threatened with destruction?

The long-continued and intemperate interference of the Northern
people with the question of slavery in the Southern States has at
length produced its natural effects. The different sections of the
Union are now arrayed against each other, and the time has arrived,
so much dreaded by the Father of his Country, when hostile geographical parties have been formed.

I have long foreseen and often forewarned my countrymen of the
now impending danger. This does not proceed solely from the claim
on the part of Congress or the Territorial legislatures to exclude
slavery from the Territories, nor from the efforts of different States
to defeat the execution of the fugitive-slave law. All or any of these
evils might have been endured by the South without danger to the
Union (as others have been) in the hope that time and reflection

James Buchanan was the 15th President of the United States (1857–1861).
The selection is from his *Fourth Annual Message to the Congress*, December 3,
1860.

might apply the remedy. The immediate peril arises not so much from these causes as from the fact that the incessant and violent agitation of the slavery question throughout the North for the last quarter of a century has at length produced its malign influence on the slaves and inspired them with vague notions of freedom. Hence a sense of security no longer exists around the family altar. This feeling of peace at home has given place to apprehensions of servile insurrections. Many a matron throughout the South retires at night in dread of what may befall herself and children before the morning. Should this apprehension of domestic danger, whether real or imaginary, extend and intensify itself until it shall pervade the masses of the Southern people, then disunion will become inevitable. Self-preservation is the first law of nature, and has been implanted in the heart of man by his Creator for the wisest purpose; and no political union, however fraught with blessings and benefits in all other respects, can long continue if the necessary consequence be to render the homes and the firesides of nearly half the parties to it habitually and hopelessly insecure. Sooner or later the bonds of such a union must be severed. It is my conviction that this fatal period has not yet arrived, and my prayer to God is that He would preserve the Constitution and the Union throughout all generations. . . .

How easy would it be for the American people to settle the slavery question forever and to restore peace and harmony to this distracted country! They, and they alone, can do it. All that is necessary to accomplish the object, and all for which the slave States have ever contended, is to be let alone and permitted to manage their domestic institutions in their own way. As sovereign States, they, and they alone, are responsible before God and the world for the slavery existing among them. For this the people of the North are not more responsible and have no more right to interfere than with similar institutions in Russia or in Brazil.

Upon their good sense and patriotic forbearance I confess I still greatly rely. Without their aid it is beyond the power of any President, no matter what may be his own political proclivities, to restore peace and harmony among the States. Wisely limited and restrained as is his power under our Constitution and laws, he alone can accomplish but little for good or for evil on such a momentous question. . . .

The most palpable violations of constitutional duty which have yet been committed consist in the acts of different State legislatures to defeat the execution of the fugitive-slave law. It ought to be remembered, however, that for these acts neither Congress nor any President can justly be held responsible. Having been passed in violation of the Federal Constitution, they are therefore null and void,

All the courts, both State and national, before whom the question has arisen have from the beginning declared the fugitive-slave law to be constitutional. The single exception is that of a State court in Wisconsin, and this has not only been reversed by the proper appellate tribunal, but has met with such universal reprobation that there can be no danger from it as a precedent. The validity of this law has been established over and over again by the Supreme Court of the United States with perfect unanimity. It is founded upon an express provision of the Constitution, requiring that fugitive slaves who escape from service in one State to another shall be "delivered up" to their masters. Without this provision it is a well-known historical fact that the Constitution itself could never have been adopted by the Convention. In one form or other, under the acts of 1793 and 1850, both being substantially the same, the fugitive-slave law has been the law of the land from the days of Washington until the present moment. Here, then, a clear case is presented in which it will be the duty of the next President, as it has been my own, to act with vigor in executing this supreme law against the conflicting enactments of State legislatures. Should he fail in the performance of this high duty, he will then have manifested a disregard of the Constitution and laws, to the great injury of the people of nearly one-half of the States of the Union. But are we to presume in advance that he will thus violate his duty? This would be at war with every principle of justice and of Christian charity. Let us wait for the overt act. The fugitive-slave law has been carried into execution in every contested case since the commencement of the present Administration, though often, it is to be regretted, with great loss and inconvenience to the master and with considerable expense to the government. Let us trust that the State legislatures will repeal their unconstitutional and obnoxious enactments. Unless this shall be done without unnecessary delay, it is impossible for any human power to save the Union. . . .

What, in the mean time, is the responsibility and true position of the Executive? He is bound by solemn oath, before God and the country, "to take care that the laws be faithfully executed," and from this obligation he can not be absolved by any human power. But what if the performance of this duty, in whole or in part, has been rendered impracticable by events over which he could have exercised no control? Such at the present moment is the case throughout the State of South Carolina so far as the laws of the United States to secure the administration of justice by means of the federal judiciary are concerned. All the federal officers within its limits through whose agency alone these laws can be carried into execution have already resigned. We no longer have a district judge, a district attorney, or a marshal in South Carolina. In fact, the whole machinery of the federal government necessary for the distribution of remedial justice among the people has been demolished, and it would be difficult, if not impossible, to replace it. . . .

Apart from the execution of the laws, so far as this may be practicable, the Executive has no authority to decide what shall be the relations between the federal government and South Carolina. He has been invested with no such discretion. He possesses no power to change the relations heretofore existing between them, much less to acknowledge the independence of that State. This would be to invest a mere executive officer with the power of recognizing the dissolution of the confederacy among our thirty-three sovereign States. It bears no resemblance to the recognition of a foreign *de facto* government, involving no such responsibility. Any attempt to do this would, on his part, be a naked act of usurpation. It is therefore my duty to submit to Congress the whole question in all its bearings. The course of events is so rapidly hastening forward that the emergency may soon arise when you may be called upon to decide the momentous question whether you possess the power by force of arms to compel a State to remain in the Union. I should feel myself recreant to my duty were I not to express an opinion on this important subject.

The question fairly stated is: Has the Constitution delegated to Congress the power to coerce a State into submission which is attempting to withdraw or has actually withdrawn from the Confederacy? If answered in the affirmative, it must be on the principle that the power has been conferred upon Congress to declare and to make war against a State. After much serious reflection I have arrived at the conclusion that no such power has been delegated to Congress or to any other department of the federal government. . . .

The fact is that our Union rests upon public opinion, and can never be cemented by the blood of its citizens shed in civil war. If it can not live in the affections of the people, it must one day perish. Congress possesses many means of preserving it by conciliation, but the sword was not placed in their hand to preserve it by force. . . .

The slavery question, like everything human, will have its day. I firmly believe that it has reached and passed the culminating point. But if in the midst of the existing excitement the Union shall perish, the evil may then become irreparable.

Congress can contribute much to avert it by proposing and recommending to the legislatures of the several States the remedy for existing evils which the Constitution has itself provided for its own preservation. . . .

This is the very course which I earnestly recommend in order to obtain an "explanatory amendment" of the Constitution on the subject of slavery. This might originate with Congress or the State legislatures, as may be deemed most advisable to attain the object. The explanatory amendment might be confined to the final settlement of the true construction of the Constitution on three special points:

1. An express recognition of the right of property in slaves in the States where it now exists or may hereafter exist.

2. The duty of protecting this right in all the common Territories throughout their Territorial existence, and until they shall be admitted as States into the Union, with or without slavery, as their constitutions may prescribe.

3. A like recognition of the right of the master to have his slave who has escaped from one State to another restored and "delivered up" to him, and of the validity of the fugitive-slave law enacted for this purpose, together with a declaration that all State laws impairing or defeating this right are violations of the Constitution, and are consequently null and void. It may be objected that this construction of the Constitution has already been settled by the Supreme Court of the United States, and what more ought to be required? The answer is that a very large proportion of the people of the United States still contest the correctness of this decision, and never will cease from agitation and admit its binding force until clearly established by the people of the several States in their sovereign character. Such an explanatory amendment would, it is believed, forever terminate the existing dissensions, and restore peace and harmony among the States. . . .

It ought not to be doubted that such an appeal to the arbitrament established by the Constitution itself would be received with favor by all the States of the Confederacy. In any event, it ought to be tried in a spirit of conciliation before any of these States shall separate themselves from the Union. . . .

☆

ABRAHAM LINCOLN: *First Inaugural Address*

Fellow-Citizens of the United States:

In compliance with a custom as old as the Government itself, I appear before you to address you briefly and to take in your presence the oath prescribed by the Constitution of the United States to be taken by the President "before he enters on the execution of his office."

I do not consider it necessary at present for me to discuss those matters of administration about which there is no special anxiety or excitement.

Apprehension seems to exist among the people of the Southern States that by the accession of a Republican Administration their property and their peace and personal security are to be endangered. There has never been any reasonable cause for such apprehension. Indeed, the most ample evidence to the contrary has all the while existed and been open to their inspection. It is found in nearly all the published speeches of him who now addresses you. I do but quote from one of those speeches when I declare that "I have no purpose, directly or indirectly, to interfere with the institution of slavery in the States where it exists. I believe I have no lawful right to do so, and I have no inclination to do so."

Those who nominated and elected me did so with full knowledge that I had made this and many similar declarations and had never recanted them; and more than this, they placed in the platform for my acceptance, and as a law to themselves and to me, the clear and emphatic resolution which I now read:

Abraham Lincoln, 16th President of the United States (1861–1865), delivered his *First Inaugural Address* on March 4th, 1861.

Resolved, That the maintenance inviolate of the rights of the States, and especially the right of each State to order and control its own domestic institutions according to its own judgment exclusively, is essential to that balance of power on which the perfection and endurance of our political fabric depend; and we denounce the lawless invasion by armed force of the soil of any State or Territory, no matter under what pretext, as among the gravest of crimes.

I now reiterate these sentiments, and in doing so I only press upon the public attention the most conclusive evidence of which the case is susceptible that the property, peace, and security of no section are to be in any wise endangered by the now incoming Administration. I add, too, that all the protection which, consistently with the Constitution and the laws, can be given will be cheerfully given to all the States when lawfully demanded, for whatever cause—as cheerfully to one section as to another. . . .

I take the official oath today with no mental reservations and with no purpose to construe the Constitution or laws by any hypercritical rules; and while I do not choose now to specify particular acts of Congress as proper to be enforced, I do suggest that it will be much safer for all, both in official and private stations, to conform to and abide by all those acts which stand unrepealed than to violate any of them trusting to find impunity in having them held to be unconstitutional.

It is seventy-two years since the first inauguration of a President under our National Constitution. During that period fifteen different and greatly distinguished citizens have in succession administered the executive branch of the Government. They have conducted it through many perils, and generally with great success. Yet, with all this scope of precedent, I now enter upon the same task for the brief constitutional term of four years under great and peculiar difficulty. A disruption of the Federal Union, heretofore only menaced, is now formidably attempted.

I hold that in contemplation of universal law and of the Constitution the Union of these States is perpetual. Perpetuity is implied, if not expressed, in the fundamental law of all national governments. It is safe to assert that no government proper ever had a provision in its organic law for its own termination. Continue to execute all the express provisions of our National Constitution, and the Union will endure forever it being impossible to destroy it except by some action not provided for in the instrument itself. . . .

It follows from these views that no State upon its own mere motion can lawfully get out of the Union; that *resolves* and *ordinances* to that effect are legally void, and that acts of violence within any State or States against the authority of the United States are insurrectionary or revolutionary, according to circumstances.

I therefore consider that in view of the Constitution and the laws the Union is unbroken, and to the extent of my ability I shall take care, as the Constitution itself expressly enjoins upon me, that the laws of the Union be faithfully executed in all the States. Doing this I deem to be only a simple duty on my part, and I shall perform it so far as practicable unless my rightful masters, the American people, shall withhold the requisite means or in some authoritative manner direct the contrary. I trust this will not be regarded as a menace, but only as the declared purpose of the Union that it *will* constitutionally defend and maintain itself.

In doing this there needs to be no bloodshed or violence, and there shall be none unless it be forced upon the national authority. The power confided to me will be used to hold, occupy, and possess the property and places belonging to the government and to collect the duties and imposts; but beyond what may be necessary for these objects, there will be no invasion, no using of force against or among the people anywhere. Where hostility to the United States in any interior locality shall be so great and universal as to prevent competent resident citizens from holding the federal offices, there will be no attempt to force obnoxious strangers among the people for that object. While the strict legal right may exist in the government to enforce the exercise of these offices, the attempt to do so would be so irritating and so nearly impracticable withal that I deem it better to forego for the time the uses of such offices. . . .

Plainly the central idea of secession is the essence of anarchy. A majority held in restraint by constitutional checks and limitations, and always changing easily with deliberate changes of popular opinions and sentiments, is the only true sovereign of a free people. Whoever rejects it does of necessity fly to anarchy or to despotism. Unanimity is impossible. The rule of a minority, as a permanent arrangement, is wholly inadmissible; so that, rejecting the majority principle, anarchy or despotism in some form is all that is left.

I do not forget the position assumed by some that constitutional questions are to be decided by the Supreme Court, nor do I deny that such decisions must be binding in any case upon the parties to a suit as to the object of that suit, while they are also entitled to very high respect and consideration in all parallel cases by all other departments of the government. And while it is obviously possible that such decision may be erroneous in any given case, still the evil effect following it, being limited to that particular case, with the chance that it may be overruled and never become a precedent for other cases, can better be borne than could the evils of a different practice. At the same time, the candid citizen must confess that if the policy of the government upon vital questions affecting the whole people is to be irrevocably fixed by decisions of the Supreme Court, the instant they are made in ordinary litigation between parties in personal actions the people will have ceased to be their own rulers, having to that extent practically resigned their government into the hands of that eminent tribunal. Nor is there in this view any assault upon the court or the judges. It is a duty from which they may not shrink to decide cases properly brought before them, and it is no fault of theirs if others seek to turn their decisions to political purposes.

One section of our country believes slavery is *right* and ought to be extended, while the other believes it is *wrong* and ought not to be extended. This is the only substantial dispute. The fugitive-slave clause of the Constitution and the law for the suppression of the foreign slave trade are each as well enforced, perhaps, as any law can ever be in a community where the moral sense of the people imperfectly supports the law itself. The great body of the people abide by the dry legal obligation in both cases, and a few break over in each. This, I think, can not be perfectly cured, and it would be worse in both cases *after* the separation of the sections than before. The foreign slave trade, now imperfectly suppressed, would be ultimately revived without restriction in one section, while fugitive slaves, now only partially surrendered, would not be surrendered at all by the other.

Physically speaking, we can not separate. We can not remove our respective sections from each other nor build an impassable wall between them. A husband and wife may be divorced and go out of the presence and beyond the reach of each other, but the different parts of our country can not do this. They can not but remain face to face, and intercourse, either amicable or hostile, must continue between them. Is it possible, then, to make that intercourse more advantageous or more satisfactory *after* separation than *before*? Can aliens make treaties easier than friends can make laws? Can treaties be more faithfully enforced between aliens than laws can among friends? Suppose you go to war, you can not fight always; and when, after much loss on both sides and no gain on either, you cease fighting, the identical old questions, as to terms of intercourse, are again upon you.

This country, with its institutions, belongs to the people who inhabit it. Whenever they shall grow weary of the existing government, they can exercise their *constitutional* right of amending it or their *revolutionary* right to dismember or overthrow it. I can not be ignorant of the fact that many worthy and patriotic citizens are desirous of having the National Constitution amended. While I make no recommendation of amendments, I fully recognize the rightful authority of the people over the whole subject, to be exercised in either of the modes prescribed in the instrument itself; and I should, under existing circumstances, favor rather than oppose a fair opportunity being afforded the people to act upon it. I will venture to add that to me the convention mode seems preferable, in that it allows amendments to originate with the people themselves, instead of only permitting them to take or reject propositions originated by others, not especially chosen for the purpose, and which might not be precisely such as they would wish to either accept or refuse. I understand a proposed amendment to the Constitution—which amendment, however, I have not seen—has passed Congress, to the effect that the federal government shall never interfere with the domestic institutions of the States, including that of persons held to service. To avoid misconstruction of what I have said, I depart from my purpose not to speak of particular amendments so far as to say that, holding such a provision to now be implied constitutional law, I have no objection to its being made express and irrevocable.

The Chief Magistrate derives all his authority from the people, and they have conferred none upon him to fix terms for the separation of the States. The people themselves can do this also if they choose, but the Executive as such has nothing to do with it. His duty is to administer the present government as it came to his hands and to transmit it unimpaired by him to his successor.

Why should there not be a patient confidence in the ultimate justice of the people? Is there any better or equal hope in the world? In our present differences, is either party without faith of being in the right? If the Almighty Ruler of Nations, with His eternal truth and justice, be on your side of the North, or on yours of the South, that truth and that justice will surely prevail by the judgment of this great tribunal of the American people.

By the frame of the government under which we live this same people have wisely given their public servants but little power for mischief, and have with equal wisdom provided for the return of that little to their own hands at very short intervals. While the people retain their virtue and vigilance no Administration by any extreme of wickedness or folly can very seriously injure the Government in the short space of four years.

My countrymen, one and all, think calmly and *well* upon this whole subject. Nothing valuable can be lost by taking time. If there be an object to *hurry* any of you in hot haste to a step which you would never take *deliberately*, that object will be frustrated by taking time; but no good object can be frustrated by it. Such of you as are now dissatisfied still have the old Constitution unimpaired, and, on the sensitive point, the laws of your own framing under it; while the new Administration will have no immediate power, if it would, to change either. If it were admitted that you who are dissatisfied hold the right side in the dispute, there still is no single good reason for precipitate action. Intelligence, patriotism, Christianity, and a firm reliance on Him who has never yet forsaken this favored land are still competent to adjust in the best way all our present difficulty.

In *your* hands, my dissatisfied fellow-countrymen, and not in *mine*, is the momentous issue of civil war. The government will not assail *you*. You can have no conflict without being yourselves the aggressors. *You* have no oath registered in heaven to destroy the government, while *I* shall have the most solemn one to "preserve, protect, and defend it."

I am loath to close. We are not enemies, but friends. We must not be enemies. Though passion may have strained it must not break our bonds of affection. The mystic chords of memory, stretching from every battlefield and patriot grave to every living heart and hearthstone all over this broad land, will yet swell the chorus of the Union, when again touched, as surely they will be, by the better angels of our nature.

☆

ABRAHAM LINCOLN: *Message to Congress in Special Session*

Fellow-Citizens of the Senate and House of Representatives:
Having been convened on an extraordinary occasion, as authorized by the Constitution, your attention is not called to any ordinary subject of legislation. . . .

[The] issue embraces more than the fate of these United States. It presents to the whole family of man the question whether a constitutional republic or democracy—a government of the people by the same people—can or cannot maintain its territorial integrity against its own domestic foes. It presents the question whether discontented individuals, too few in numbers to control administration according to organic law in any case, can always, upon the pretenses made in this case, or on any other pretenses, or arbitrarily without any pretense, break up their government, and thus practically put an end to free government upon the earth. It forces us to ask: "Is there, in all republics, this inherent and fatal weakness?" "Must a government, of necessity, be too strong for the liberties of its own people, or too weak to maintain its own existence?"

So viewing the issue, no choice was left but to call out the war power of the government; and so to resist force employed for its destruction, by force for its preservation. . . .

Our popular government has often been called an experiment. Two points in it our people have already settled—the successful establishing and the successful administering of it. One still remains —its successful maintenance against a formidable internal attempt

President Lincoln sent this Message to Congress on July 4, 1861.

76

to overthrow it. It is now for them to demonstrate to the world that those who can fairly carry an election can also suppress a rebellion; that ballots are the rightful and peaceful successors of bullets; and that when ballots have fairly and constitutionally decided, there can be no successful appeal back to bullets; that there can be no successful appeal, except to ballots themselves, at succeeding elections. Such will be a great lesson of peace: teaching men that what they cannot take by an election, neither can they take it by a war; teaching all the folly of being the beginners of a war.

Lest there be some uneasiness in the minds of candid men as to what is to be the course of the government toward the Southern States after the rebellion shall have been suppressed, the executive deems it proper to say it will be his purpose then, as ever, to be guided by the Constitution and the laws; and that he probably will have no different understanding of the powers and duties of the federal government relatively to the rights of the States and the people, under the Constitution, than that expressed in the inaugural address.

He desires to preserve the government, that it may be administered for all as it was administered by the men who made it. Loyal citizens everywhere have the right to claim this of their government, and the government has no right to withhold or neglect it. It is not perceived that in giving it there is any coercion, any conquest, or any subjugation, in any just sense of those terms.

The Constitution provides, and all the States have accepted the provision, that "the United States shall guarantee to every State in this Union a republican form of government." But if a State may lawfully go out of the Union, having done so, it may also discard the republican form of government; so that to prevent its going out is an indispensable means to the end of maintaining the guarantee mentioned; and when an end is lawful and obligatory, the indispensable means to it are also lawful and obligatory.

It was with the deepest regret that the executive found the duty of employing the war power in defense of the government forced upon him. He could but perform this duty or surrender the existence of the government. No compromise by public servants could, in this case, be a cure; not that compromises are not often proper, but that no popular government can long survive a marked precedent that those who carry an election can only save the government from immediate destruction by giving up the main point upon which the people gave the election. The people themselves, and not their servants, can safely reverse their own deliberate decisions.

As a private citizen the executive could not have consented that these institutions shall perish; much less could he, in betrayal of so vast and so sacred a trust as the free people have confided to him. He felt that he had no moral right to shrink, nor even to count the chances of his own life in what might follow. In full view of his great responsibility he has, so far, done what he has deemed his duty. You will now, according to your own judgment, perform yours.

He sincerely hopes that your views and your actions may so accord with his, as to assure all faithful citizens who have been disturbed in their rights of a certain and speedy restoration to them, under the Constitution and the laws.

And having thus chosen our course, without guile and with pure purpose, let us renew our trust in God, and go forward without fear and with manly hearts.

☆

ABRAHAM LINCOLN: *Letter to A. G. Hodges*

My dear Sir:

You ask me to put in writing the substance of what I verbally said the other day, in your presence, to Governor Bramlette and Senator Dixon. It was about as follows:

I am naturally anti-slavery. If slavery is not wrong, nothing is wrong. I can not remember when I did not so think, and feel. And yet I have never understood that the Presidency conferred upon me an unrestricted right to act officially upon this judgment and feeling. It was in the oath I took that I would, to the best of my ability, preserve, protect, and defend the Constitution of the United States. I could not take the office without taking the oath. Nor was it my view that I might take an oath to get power, and break the oath in using the power. I understood, too, that in ordinary civil administration this oath even forbade me to practically indulge my primary abstract judgment on the moral question of slavery. I had publicly declared this many times, and in many ways. And I aver that, to this day, I have done no official act in mere deference to my abstract judgment and feeling on slavery.

I did understand, however, that my oath to preserve the Constitution to the best of my ability, imposed upon me the duty of preserving, by every indispensable means, that government—that nation—of which that Constitution was the organic law. Was it possible to lose the nation, and yet preserve the Constitution? By general law life *and* limb must be protected; yet often a limb must be

This letter to Albert G. Hodges, editor of the Frankfort, Kentucky, *Commonwealth*, was used as a campaign document in the election of 1864. From *The Complete Works of Abraham Lincoln*, John Nicolay and John Hay, eds. (New York: Francis D. Tandy Co., 1894), Vol. X, pp. 65–68.

amputated to save a life; but a life is never wisely given to save a limb. I felt that measures, otherwise unconstitutional, might become lawful, by becoming indispensable to the preservation of the Constitution, through the preservation of the nation. Right or wrong, I assumed this ground, and now avow it. I could not feel that, to the best of my ability, I had even tried to preserve the Constitution, if, to save slavery, or any minor matter, I should permit the wreck of government, country, and Constitution all together.

When, early in the war, Gen. Fremont attempted military emancipation, I forbade it, because I did not then think it an indispensable necessity. When a little later, Gen. Cameron, then Secretary of War, suggested the arming of the blacks, I objected, because I did not yet think it an indispensable necessity. When, still later, Gen. Hunter attempted military emancipation, I again forbade it, because I did not yet think the indispensable necessity had come. When, in March, and May, and July 1862 I made earnest, and successive appeals to the border states to favor compensated emancipation, I believed the indispensable necessity for military emancipation, and arming the blacks would come, unless averted by that measure. They declined the proposition; and I was, in my best judgment, driven to the alternative of either surrendering the Union, and with it, the Constitution, or of laying strong hand upon the colored element. I chose the latter. In choosing it, I hoped for greater gain than loss; but of this, I was not entirely confident. More than a year of trial now shows no loss by it in our foreign relations, none in our home popular sentiment, none in our white military force—no loss by it any how or any where. On the contrary, it shows a gain of quite a hundred and thirty thousand soldiers, seamen, and laborers. These are palpable facts, about which, as facts, there can be no cavilling. We have the men; and we could not have had them without the measure.

And now let any Union man who complains of the measure, test himself by writing down in one line that he is for subduing the rebellion by force of arms; and in the next, that he is for taking these hundred and thirty thousand men from the Union side, and placing them where they would be but for the measure he condemns. If he can not face his case so stated, it is only because he can not face the truth.

I add a word which was not in the verbal conversation. In telling this tale I attempt no compliment to my own sagacity. I claim not to have controlled events, but confess plainly that events have controlled me. Now, at the end of three years struggle the nation's condition is not what either party, or any man devised, or expected.

God alone can claim it. Whither it is tending seems plain. If God now wills the removal of a great wrong, and wills also that we of the North as well as you of the South, shall pay fairly for our complicity in that wrong, impartial history will find therein new cause to attest and revere the justice and goodness of God.

THE EMERGENCE OF THE
MODERN PRESIDENCY

☆

THEODORE ROOSEVELT: *The "Stewardship Theory"*

The most important factor in getting the right spirit in my Administration, next to the insistence upon courage, honesty, and a genuine democracy of desire to serve the plain people, was my insistence
upon the theory that the executive power was limited only by specific restrictions and prohibitions appearing in the Constitution or
imposed by the Congress under its constitutional powers.

My view was that every executive officer, and above all every
executive officer in high position, was a steward of the people bound
actively and affirmatively to do all he could for the people, and not
to content himself with the negative merit of keeping his talents
undamaged in a napkin. I declined to adopt the view that what
was imperatively necessary for the nation could not be done by the
President unless he could find some specific authorization to do it.
My belief was that it was not only his right but his duty to do anything that the needs of the nation demanded, unless such action
was forbidden by the Constitution or by the laws. Under this interpretation of executive power I did and caused to be done many
things not previously done by the President and the heads of the
departments. I did not usurp power, but I did greatly broaden the
use of executive power. In other words, I acted for the public welfare, I acted for the common well-being of all our people, whenever and in whatever manner was necessary, unless prevented by
direct constitutional or legislative prohibition. . . .

Theodore Roosevelt was the 26th President of the United States (1901–
1909). This selection is from *The Autobiography of Theodore Roosevelt*, edited
by Wayne Andrews (New York: Scribner's, 1958), pp. 197–200. Copyright ©
1958 Charles Scribner's Sons. Reprinted by permission.

The course I followed, of regarding the Executive as subject only to the people, and, under the Constitution, bound to serve the people affirmatively in cases where the Constitution does not explicitly forbid him to render the service, was substantially the course followed by both Andrew Jackson and Abraham Lincoln. Other honorable and well-meaning Presidents, such as James Buchanan, took the opposite and, as it seems to me, narrowly legalistic view that the President is the servant of Congress rather than of the people, and can do nothing, no matter how necessary it be to act, unless the Constitution explicitly commands the action. Most able lawyers who are past middle age take this view, and so do large numbers of well-meaning, respectable citizens. My successor in office took this, the Buchanan, view of the President's powers and duties.

For example, under my administration we found that one of the favorite methods adopted by the men desirous of stealing the public domain was to carry the decision of the secretary of the interior into court. By vigorously opposing such action, and only by so doing, we were able to carry out the policy of properly protecting the public domain. My successor not only took the opposite view, but recommended to Congress the passage of a bill which would have given the courts direct appellate power over the secretary of the interior in these land matters. . . . Fortunately, Congress declined to pass the bill. Its passage would have been a veritable calamity.

I acted on the theory that the President could at any time in his discretion withdraw from entry any of the public lands of the United States and reserve the same for forestry, for water-power sites, for irrigation, and other public purposes. Without such action it would have been impossible to stop the activity of the land-thieves. No one ventured to test its legality by lawsuit. My successor, however, himself questioned it, and referred the matter to Congress. Again Congress showed its wisdom by passing a law which gave the President the power which he had long exercised, and of which my successor had shorn himself.

Perhaps the sharp difference between what may be called the Lincoln-Jackson and the Buchanan-Taft schools, in their views of the power and duties of the President, may be best illustrated by comparing the attitude of my successor toward his Secretary of the Interior, Mr. Ballinger, when the latter was accused of gross misconduct in office, with my attitude toward my chiefs of department and other subordinate officers. More than once while I was President my officials were attacked by Congress, generally because these officials did their duty well and fearlessly. In every such case I stood by the official and refused to recognize the right of Congress to interfere with me excepting by impeachment or in other constitutional manner. On the other hand, wherever I found the officer unfit for his position, I promptly removed him, even although the most influential men in Congress fought for his retention.

The Jackson-Lincoln view is that a President who is fit to do good work should be able to form his own judgment as to his own subordinates, and, above all, of the subordinates standing highest and in closest and most intimate touch with him. My secretaries and their subordinates were responsible to me, and I accepted the responsibility for all their deeds. As long as they were satisfactory to me I stood by them against every critic or assailant, within or without Congress; and as for getting Congress to make up my mind for me about them, the thought would have been inconceivable to me. My successor took the opposite, or Buchanan, view when he permitted and requested Congress to pass judgment on the charges made against Mr. Ballinger as an executive officer. These charges were made to the President; the President had the facts before him and could get at them at any time, and he alone had power to act if the charges were true. However, he permitted and requested Congress to investigate Mr. Ballinger. The party minority of the committee that investigated him, and one member of the majority, declared that the charges were well-founded and that Mr. Ballinger should be removed. The other members of the majority declared the charges ill-founded. The President abode by the view of the majority. Of course believers in the Jackson-Lincoln theory of the Presidency would not be content with this town-meeting majority and minority method of determining by another branch of the government what it seems the especial duty of the President himself to determine for himself in dealing with his own subordinate in his own department. . . .

☆

WILLIAM HOWARD TAFT: *Our Chief Magistrate and His Powers*

The true view of the Executive functions is, as I conceive it, that the President can exercise no power which cannot be fairly and reasonably traced to some specific grant of power or justly implied and included within such express grant as proper and necessary to its exercise. Such specific grant must be either in the federal Constitution or in an act of Congress passed in pursuance thereof. There is no undefined residuum of power which he can exercise because it seems to him to be in the public interest, and there is nothing in the Neagle case and its definition of a law of the United States, or in other precedents, warranting such an inference. The grants of Executive power are necessarily in general terms in order not to embarrass the Executive within the field of action plainly marked for him, but his jurisdiction must be justified and vindicated by affirmative constitutional or statutory provision, or it does not exist.

There have not been wanting, however, eminent men in high public office holding a different view and who have insisted upon the necessity for an undefined residuum of Executive power in the public interest. They have not been confined to the present generation. We may learn this from the complaint of a Virginia statesman, Abel P. Upshur, a strict constructionist of the old school,

William Howard Taft was 27th President of the United States (1909–1913) and 10th Chief Justice of the United States (1921–1930). This selection is from *Our Chief Magistrate and His Powers* (New York: Columbia University Press, 1916), pp. 139–145, 156–157. Copyright 1916 by Columbia University Press. Reprinted by permission.

who succeeded Daniel Webster as Secretary of State under President Tyler. He was aroused by Story's commentaries on the Constitution to write a monograph answering and criticizing them, and in the course of this he comments as follows on the Executive power under the Constitution:

> The most defective part of the Constitution beyond all question, is that which related to the Executive Department. It is impossible to read that instrument, without being struck with the loose and unguarded terms in which the powers and duties of the President are pointed out. So far as the legislature is concerned, the limitations of the Constitution, are, perhaps, as precise and strict as they could safely have been made; but in regard to the Executive, the Convention appears to have studiously selected such loose and general expressions, as would enable the President, by implication and construction either to neglect his duties or to enlarge his powers. *We have heard it gravely asserted in Congress that whatever power is neither legislative nor judiciary, is of course executive, and, as such, belongs to the President under the Constitution.* How far a majority of that body would have sustained a doctrine so monstrous, and so utterly at war with the whole genius of our government, it is impossible to say, but this, at least, we know, that it met with no rebuke from those who supported the particular act of Executive power, in defense of which it was urged. Be this as it may, it is a reproach to the Constitution that the Executive trust is so ill-defined, as to leave any plausible pretense even to the insane zeal of party devotion, for attributing to the President of the United States the powers of a despot; powers which are wholly unknown in any limited monarchy in the world.

The view that he takes as a result of the loose language defining the Executive powers seems exaggerated. But one must agree with him in his condemnation of the view of the Executive power which he says was advanced in Congress. In recent years there has been put forward a similar view by executive officials and to some extent acted on. Men who are not such strict constructionists of the Constitution as Mr. Upshur may well feel real concern if such views are to receive the general acquiescence. . . .

. . . Mr. Roosevelt, by way of illustrating his meaning as to the differing usefulness of Presidents, divides the Presidents into two classes, and designates them as "Lincoln Presidents" and "Buchanan Presidents." In order more fully to illustrate his division of Presidents on their merits, he places himself in the Lincoln class of

Presidents, and me in the Buchanan class. The identification of Mr. Roosevelt with Mr. Lincoln might otherwise have escaped notice, because there are many differences between the two, presumably superficial, which would give the impartial student of history a different impression. It suggests a story which a friend of mine told of his little daughter Mary. As he came walking home after a business day, she ran out from the house to greet him, all aglow with the importance of what she wished to tell him. She said, "Papa, I am the best scholar in the class." The father's heart throbbed with pleasure as he inquired, "Why, Mary, you surprise me. When did the teacher tell you? This afternoon?" "Oh, no," Mary's reply was, "the teacher didn't tell me—I just noticed it myself."

My judgment is that the view of . . . Mr. Roosevelt, ascribing an undefined residuum of power to the President is an unsafe doctrine and that it might lead under emergencies to results of an arbitrary character, doing irremediable injustice to private right. The mainspring of such a view is that the Executive is charged with responsibility for the welfare of all the people in a general way, that he is to play the part of a Universal Providence and set all things right, and that anything that in his judgment will help the people he ought to do, unless he is expressly forbidden not to do it. The wide field of action that this would give to the Executive one can hardly limit. . . .

I have now concluded a review of the Executive power, and hope that I have shown that it is limited, so far as it is possible to limit such a power consistent with that discretion and promptness of action that are essential to preserve the interests of the public in times of emergency, or legislative neglect or inaction.

There is little danger to the public weal from the tyranny or reckless character of a President who is not sustained by the people. The absence of popular support will certainly in the course of two years withdraw from him the sympathetic action of at least one House of Congress, and by the control that that House has over appropriations, the Executive arm can be paralyzed, unless he resorts to a coup d'état, which means impeachment, conviction and deposition. The only danger in the action of the Executive under the present limitations and lack of limitation of his powers is when his popularity is such that he can be sure of the support of the electorate and therefore of Congress, and when the majority in the legislative halls respond with alacrity and sycophancy to his will. This condition cannot probably be long continued. We have had Presidents who felt the public pulse with accuracy, who played their parts upon the political stage with histrionic genius and commanded the people almost as if they were an army and the President their Commander in Chief. Yet in all these cases, the good sense of the people has ultimately prevailed and no danger has been done to our political structure and the reign of law has continued. In such times when the Executive power seems to be all prevailing, there have always been men in this free and intelligent people of ours, who apparently courting political humiliation and disaster have registered protest against this undue Executive domination and this use of the Executive power and popular support to perpetuate itself.

The cry of Executive domination is often entirely unjustified, as when the President's commanding influence only grows out of a proper cohesion of a party and its recognition of the necessity for political leadership; but the fact that Executive domination is regarded as a useful ground for attack upon a successful administration, even when there is no ground for it, is itself proof of the dependence we may properly place upon the sanity and clear perceptions of the people in avoiding its baneful effects when there is real danger. Even if a vicious precedent is set by the Executive, and injustice done, it does not have the same bad effect that an improper precedent of a court may have, for one President does not consider himself bound by the policies or constitutional views of his predecessors.

The Constitution does give the President wide discretion and great power, and it ought to do so. It calls from him activity and energy to see that within his proper sphere he does what his great responsibilities and opportunities require. He is no figurehead, and it is entirely proper that an energetic and active clear-sighted people, who, when they have work to do, wish it done well, should be willing to rely upon their judgment in selecting their Chief Agent, and having selected him, should entrust to him all the power needed to carry out their governmental purpose, great as it may be.

☆

WOODROW WILSON: *The President's Role in American Government*

The makers of the Constitution seem to have thought of the President as what the stricter Whig theorists wished the king to be: only the legal executive, the presiding and guiding authority in the application of law and the execution of policy. His veto upon legislation was only his "check" on Congress—was a power of restraint, not of guidance. He was empowered to prevent bad laws, but he was not to be given an opportunity to make good ones. As a matter of fact he has become very much more. He has become the leader of his party and the guide of the nation in political purpose, and therefore in legal action. The constitutional structure of the government has hampered and limited his action in these significant roles, but it has not prevented it. The influence of the President has varied with the men who have been Presidents and with the circumstances of their times, but the tendency has been unmistakably disclosed, and springs out of the very nature of government itself. It is merely the proof that our government is a living, organic thing, and must, like every other government, work out the close synthesis of active parts which can exist only when leadership is lodged in some one man or group of men. You cannot compound a successful government out of antagonisms. Greatly as the practice and influence

Woodrow Wilson was Professor of Political Science at Princeton University (1890–1902), President of Princeton (1902–1910), and Governor of New Jersey (1911–1912) before becoming the 28th President of the United States (1913–1921). This selection is from his chapter on "The President of the United States" in *Constitutional Government in the United States* (New York: Columbia University Press, 1908), pp. 54–81. Copyright © 1908 by Columbia University Press. Reprinted by permission.

of Presidents has varied, there can be no mistaking the fact that we have grown more and more inclined from generation to generation to look to the President as the unifying force in our complex system, the leader both of his party and of the nation. To do so is not inconsistent with the actual provisions of the Constitution; it is only inconsistent with a very mechanical theory of its meaning and intention. The Constitution contains no theories. It is as practical a document as Magna Carta. . . .

[The] office of President, as we have used and developed it, really does not demand actual experience in affairs so much as particular qualities of mind and character which we are at least as likely to find outside the ranks of our public men as within them. What is it that a nominating convention wants in the man it is to present to the country for its suffrages? A man who will be and who will seem to the country in some sort an embodiment of the character and purpose it wishes its government to have—a man who understands his own day and the needs of the country, and who has the personality and the initiative to enforce his views both upon the people and upon Congress. It may seem an odd way to get such a man. It is even possible that nominating conventions and those who guide them do not realize entirely what it is that they do. But in simple fact the convention picks out a party leader from the body of the nation. Not that it expects its nominee to direct the interior government of the party and to supplant its already accredited and experienced spokesmen in Congress and in its state and national committees; but it does of necessity expect him to represent it before public opinion and to stand before the country as its representative man, as a true type of what the country may expect of the party itself in purpose and principle. It cannot but be led by him in the campaign; if he be elected, it cannot but acquiesce in his leadership of the government itself. What the country will demand of the candidate will be, not that he be an astute politician, skilled and practiced in affairs, but that he be a man such as it can trust, in character, in intention, in knowledge of its needs, in perception of the best means by which those needs may be met, in capacity to prevail by reason of his own weight and integrity. Sometimes the country believes in a party, but more often it believes in a man; and conventions have often shown the instinct to perceive which it is that the country needs in a particular presidential year, a mere representative partisan, a military hero, or some one who will genuinely speak for the country itself, whatever be his training and antecedents. It is in this sense that the President has the role of party leader thrust upon him by the very method by which he is chosen.

As legal executive, his constitutional aspect, the President cannot be thought of alone. He cannot execute laws. Their actual daily execution must be taken care of by the several executive departments and by the now innumerable body of federal officials throughout the country. In respect of the strictly executive duties of his office the President may be said to administer the Presidency in conjunction with the members of his Cabinet, like the chairman of a commission. He is even of necessity much less active in the actual carrying out of the law than are his colleagues and advisers. It is therefore becoming more and more true, as the business of the government becomes more and more complex and extended, that the President is becoming more and more a political and less and less an executive officer. His executive powers are in commission, while his political powers more and more center and accumulate upon him and are in their very nature personal and inalienable.

Only the larger sort of executive questions are brought to him. Departments which run with easy routine and whose transactions bring few questions of general policy to the surface may proceed with their business for months and even years together without demanding his attention; and no department is in any sense under his direct charge. Cabinet meetings do not discuss detail: they are concerned only with the larger matters of policy or expediency which important business is constantly disclosing. There are no more hours in the President's day than in another man's. If he is indeed the executive, he must act almost entirely by delegation, and is in the hands of his colleagues. He is likely to be praised if things go well, and blamed if they go wrong; but his only real control is of the persons to whom he deputes the performance of executive duties. It is through no fault or neglect of his that the duties apparently assigned to him by the Constitution have come to be his less conspicuous, less important duties, and that duties apparently not assigned to him at all chiefly occupy his time and energy. The one set of duties it has proved practically impossible for him to perform; the other it has proved impossible for him to escape.

He cannot escape being the leader of his party except by incapacity and lack of personal force, because he is at once the choice of the party and of the nation. He is the party nominee, and the only party nominee for whom the whole nation votes. Members of the House and Senate are representatives of localities, are voted for only by sections of voters, or by local bodies of electors like the members of the state legislatures. There is no national party choice except that of President. No one else represents the people as a whole, exercising a national choice; and inasmuch as his strictly executive duties are in fact subordinated, so far at any rate as all detail is concerned, the President represents not so much the party's governing efficiency as its controlling ideals and principles. He is not so much part of its organization as its vital link of connection with the thinking nation. He can dominate his party by being spokesman for the real sentiment and purpose of the country, by giving direction to opinion, by giving the country at once the information and the statements of policy which will enable it to form its judgments alike of parties and of men.

For he is also the political leader of the nation, or has it in his choice to be. The nation as a whole has chosen him, and is conscious that it has no other political spokesman. His is the only national voice in affairs. Let him once win the admiration and confidence of the country, and no other single force can withstand him, no combination of forces will easily overpower him. His position takes the imagination of the country. He is the representative of no constituency, but of the whole people. When he speaks in his true character, he speaks for no special interest. If he rightly interpret the national thought and boldly insist upon it, he is irresistible; and the country never feels the zest of action so much as when its President is of such insight and calibre. Its instinct is for unified action, and it craves a single leader. It is for this reason that it will often prefer to choose a man rather than a party. A President whom it trusts can not only lead it, but form it to his own views.

It is the extraordinary isolation imposed upon the President by our system that makes the character and opportunity of his office so extraordinary. In him are centered both opinion and party. He may stand, if he will, a little outside party and insist as if it were upon the general opinion. It is with the instinctive feeling that it is upon occasion such a man that the country wants that nominating conventions will often nominate men who are not their acknowledged leaders, but only such men as the country would like to see lead both its parties. The President may also, if he will, stand within the party counsels and use the advantage of his power and personal force to control its actual programs. He may be both the leader of his party and the leader of the nation, or he may be one or the other. If he lead the nation, his party can hardly resist him. His office is anything he has the sagacity and force to make it.

That is the reason why it has been one thing at one time, another at another. The Presidents who have not made themselves leaders have lived no more truly on that account in the spirit of the Constitution than those whose force has told in the determination of law and policy. No doubt Andrew Jackson overstepped the bounds meant to be set to the authority of his office. It was certainly in direct contravention of the spirit of the Constitution that he should have refused to respect and execute decisions of the Supreme Court of the United States, and no serious student of our history can righteously condone what he did in such matters on the ground that his intentions were upright and his principles pure. But the Constitution of the United States is not a mere lawyers' document: it is a vehicle of life, and its spirit is always the spirit of the age. Its prescriptions are clear and we know what they are; a written document makes lawyers of us all, and our duty as citizens should make us conscientious lawyers, reading the text of the Constitution without subtlety or sophistication; but life is always your last and most authoritative critic.

Some of our Presidents have deliberately held themselves off from using the full power they might legitimately have used, because of conscientious scruples, because they were more theorists than statesmen. They have held the strict literary theory of the Constitution, the Whig theory, the Newtonian theory, and have acted as if they thought that Pennsylvania Avenue should have been even longer than it is; that there should be no intimate communication of any kind between the Capitol and the White House; that the President as a man was no more at liberty to lead the houses of Congress by persuasion than he was at liberty as President to dominate them by authority—supposing that he had, what he has not, authority enough to dominate them. But the makers of the Constitution were not enacting Whig theory, they were not making laws with the expectation that, not the laws themselves, but their opinions, known by future historians to lie back of them, should govern the constitutional action of the country. They were statesmen, not pedants, and their laws are sufficient to keep us to the paths they set us upon. The President is at liberty, both in law and conscience, to be as big a man as he can. His capacity will set the limit; and if Congress be overborne by him, it will be no fault of the makers of the Constitution—it will be from no lack of constitutional powers on its part, but only because the President has the nation behind him, and Congress has not. He has no means of compelling Congress except through public opinion.

That I say he has no means of compelling Congress will show what I mean, and that my meaning has no touch of radicalism or iconoclasm in it. There are illegitimate means by which the President may influence the action of Congress. He may bargain with members, not only with regard to appointments, but also with regard to legislative measures. He may use his local patronage to assist members to get or retain their seats. He may interpose his powerful influence, in one covert way or another, in contests for places in the Senate. He may also overbear Congress by arbitrary acts which ignore the laws or virtually override them. He may even substitute his own orders for acts of Congress which he wants but cannot get. Such things are not only deeply immoral, they are destructive of the fundamental understandings of constitutional government and, therefore, of constitutional government itself. They are sure, moreover, in a country of free public opinion, to bring their own punishment, to destroy both the fame and the power of the man who dares to practice them. No honorable man includes such agencies in a sober exposition of the Constitution or allows himself to think of them when he speaks of the influences of "life" which govern each generation's use and interpretation of that great instrument, our sovereign guide and the object of our deepest reverence. Nothing in a system like ours can be constitutional which is immoral or which touches the good faith of those who have sworn to obey the fundamental law. The reprobation of all good men will aways overwhelm such influences with shame and failure. But the personal force of the President is perfectly constitutional to any extent to which he chooses to exercise it, and it is by the clear logic of our constitutional practice that he has become alike the leader of his party and the leader of the nation.

The political powers of the President are not quite so obvious in their scope and character when we consider his relations with Congress as when we consider his relations to his party and to the nation. They need, therefore, a somewhat more critical examination. Leadership in government naturally belongs to its executive officers, who are daily in contact with practical conditions and exigencies and whose reputations alike for good judgment and for fidelity are at stake much more than are those of the members of the legislative body at every turn of the law's application. The law-making part of the government ought certainly to be very hospitable to the suggestions of the planning and acting part of it. Those Presidents who have felt themselves bound to adhere to the strict literary theory of the Constitution have scrupulously refrained from attempting to determine either the subjects or the character of legislation, except so far as they were obliged to decide for themselves, after Congress had acted, whether they should acquiesce in it or not. And yet the Constitution explicitly authorizes the President to recommend to Congress "such measures as he shall deem necessary and expedient," and it is not necessary to the integrity of even the literary theory of the Constitution to insist that such recommendations should be merely perfunctory. Certainly General Washington did not so regard them, and he stood much nearer the

Whig theory than we do. A President's messages to Congress have no more weight or authority than their intrinsic reasonableness and importance give them: but that is their only constitutional limitation. The Constitution certainly does not forbid the President to back them up, as General Washington did, with such personal force and influence as he may possess. Some of our Presidents have felt the need, which unquestionably exists in our system, for some spokesman of the nation as a whole, in matters of legislation no less than in other matters, and have tried to supply Congress with the leadership of suggestion, backed by argument and by iteration and by every legitimate appeal to public opinion. Cabinet officers are shut out from Congress; the President himself has, by custom, no access to its floor; many long-established barriers of precedent, though not of law, hinder him from exercising any direct influence upon its deliberations; and yet he is undoubtedly the only spokesman of the whole people. They have again and again, as often as they were afforded the opportunity, manifested their satisfaction when he has boldly accepted the role of leader, to which the peculiar origin and character of his authority entitle him. The Constitution bids him speak, and times of stress and change must more and more thrust upon him the attitude of originator of policies.

His is the vital place of action in the system, whether he accept it as such or not, and the office is the measure of the man—of his wisdom as well as of his force. His veto abundantly equips him to stay the hand of Congress when he will. It is seldom possible to pass a measure over his veto, and no President has hesitated to use the veto when his own judgment of the public good was seriously at issue with that of the houses. The veto has never been suffered to fall into even temporary disuse with us. In England it has ceased to exist, with the change in the character of the executive. There has been no veto since Anne's day, because ever since the reign of Anne the laws of England have been originated either by ministers who spoke the king's own will or by ministers whom the king did not dare gainsay; and in our own time the ministers who formulate the laws are themselves the executive of the nation; a veto would be a negative upon their own power. If bills pass of which they disapprove, they resign and give place to the leaders of those who approve them. The framers of the Constitution made in our President a more powerful, because a more isolated, king than the one they were imitating; and because the Constitution gave them their veto in such explicit terms, our Presidents have not hesitated to use it, even when it put their mere individual judgment against that of large majorities in both houses of Congress. And yet in the exercise of the power to suggest legislation, quite as explicitly conferred upon them by the Constitution, some of our Presidents have seemed to have a timid fear that they might offend some law of taste which had become a constitutional principle.

In one sense their messages to Congress have no more authority than the letters of any other citizen would have. Congress can heed or ignore them as it pleases; and there have been periods of our history when presidential messages were utterly without practical significance, perfunctory documents which few persons except the editors of newspapers took the trouble to read. But if the President has personal force and cares to exercise it, there is this tremendous difference between his messages and the views of any other citizen, either outside Congress or in it: that the whole country reads them and feels that the writer speaks with an authority and a responsibility which the people themselves have given him.

The history of our Cabinets affords a striking illustration of the progress of the idea that the President is not merely the legal head but also the political leader of the nation. In the earlier days of the government it was customary for the President to fill his Cabinet with the recognized leaders of his party. General Washington even tried the experiment which William of Orange tried at the very beginning of the era of cabinet government. He called to his aid the leaders of both political parties, associating Mr. Hamilton with Mr. Jefferson, on the theory that all views must be heard and considered in the conduct of the government. . . . But our later Presidents have apparently ceased to regard the Cabinet as a council of party leaders such as the party they represent would have chosen. They look upon it rather as a body of personal advisers whom the President chooses from the ranks of those whom he personally trusts and prefers to look to for advice. . . . Mr. Cleveland may be said to have been the first President to make this conception of the Cabinet prominent in his choices, and he did not do so until his second administration. Mr. Roosevelt has emphasized the idea.

Upon analysis it seems to mean this: the Cabinet is an executive, not a political body. The President cannot himself be the actual executive; he must therefore find, to act in his stead, men of the best legal and business gifts, and depend upon them for the actual administration of the government in all its daily activities. If he seeks political advice of his executive colleagues, he seeks it because he relies upon their natural good sense and experienced judgment, upon their knowledge of the country and its business and social conditions, upon their sagacity as representative citizens of more than usual observation and discretion; not because they are supposed to have had any very intimate contact with politics or to have made a profession of public affairs. He has chosen not representative politicians, but eminent representative citizens, selecting them rather for their special fitness for the great business posts to which he has assigned them than for their political experience, and looking to them for advice in the actual conduct of the government rather than in the shaping of political policy. They are, in his view, not necessarily political officers at all.

It may with a great deal of plausibility be argued that the Constitution looks upon the President himself in the same way. It does not seem to make him a prime minister or the leader of the nation's counsels. Some Presidents are, therefore, and some are not. It depends upon the man and his gifts. He may be like his Cabinet, or he may be more than his Cabinet. His office is a mere vantage ground from which he may be sure that effective words of advice and timely efforts at reform will gain telling momentum. He has the ear of the nation as of course, and a great person may use such an advantage greatly. If he use the opportunity, he may take his Cabinet into partnership or not, as he pleases; and so its character may vary with his. Self-reliant men will regard their Cabinets as executive councils; men less self-reliant or more prudent will regard them as also political councils, and will wish to call into them men who have earned the confidence of their party. The character of the Cabinet may be made a nice index of the theory of the presidential office, as well as of the President's theory of party government; but the one view is, so far as I can see, as constitutional as the other.

One of the greatest of the President's powers I have not yet spoken of at all: his control, which is very absolute, of the foreign relations of the nation. The initiative in foreign affairs, which the President possesses without any restriction whatever, is virtually the power to control them absolutely. The President cannot conclude a treaty with a foreign power without the consent of the Senate, but he may guide every step of diplomacy, and to guide diplomacy is to determine what treaties must be made, if the faith and prestige of the government are to be maintained. He need disclose no step of negotiation until it is complete, and when in any critical matter it is completed the government is virtually committed. Whatever its disinclination, the Senate may feel itself committed also.

I have not dwelt upon this power of the President, because it has been decisively influential in determining the character and influence of the office at only two periods in our history; at the very first, when the government was young and had so to use its incipient force as to win the respect of the nations into whose family it had thrust itself, and in our own day when the results of the Spanish War, the ownership of distant possessions, and many sharp struggles for foreign trade make it necessary that we should turn our best talents to the task of dealing firmly, wisely, and justly with political and commercial rivals. The President can never again be the mere domestic figure he has been throughout so large a part of our history. The nation has risen to the first rank in power and resources. The other nations of the world look askance upon her, half in envy, half in fear, and wonder with a deep anxiety what she will do with her vast strength. They receive the frank professions of men like Mr. John Hay, whom we wholly trusted, with a grain of salt, and doubt what we were sure of, their truthfulness and sincerity, suspecting a hidden design under every utterance he makes. Our President must always, henceforth, be one of the great powers of the world, whether he act greatly and wisely or not, and the best statesmen we can produce will be needed to fill the office of Secretary of State. We have but begun to see the presidential office in this light; but it is the light which will more and more beat upon it, and more and more determine its character and its effect upon the politics of the nation. We can never hide our President again as a mere domestic officer. We can never again see him the mere executive he was in the thirties and forties. He must stand always at the front of our affairs, and the office will be as big and as influential as the man who occupies it.

How is it possible to sum up the duties and influence of such an office in such a system in comprehensive terms which will cover all its changeful aspects? In the view of the makers of the Constitution the President was to be legal executive; perhaps the leader of the nation; certainly not the leader of the party, at any rate while in office. But by the operation of forces inherent in the very nature of government he has become all three, and by inevitable consequence the most heavily burdened officer in the world. No other man's day is so full as his, so full of the responsibilities which tax mind and conscience alike and demand an inexhaustible vitality. The mere task of making appointments to office, which the Constitution imposes upon the President, has come near to breaking some of our Presidents down, because it is a never-ending task in a civil service not yet put upon a professional footing, confused with short terms of office, always forming and dissolving. And in proportion as the President ventures to use his opportunity to lead opinion and act as spokesman of the people in affairs the people stand ready to overwhelm him by running to him with every question, great and small. They are as eager to have him settle a literary question as a political; hear him as acquiescently with regard to matters of special expert knowledge as with regard to public affairs, and call upon him to quiet all troubles by his personal intervention.

Men of ordinary physique and discretion cannot be Presidents and live, if the strain be not somehow relieved. We shall be obliged always to be picking our chief magistrates from among wise and prudent athletes—a small class.

The future development of the Presidency, therefore, must certainly, one would confidently predict, run along such lines as the President's later relations with his Cabinet suggest. General Washington, partly out of unaffected modesty, no doubt, but also out of the sure practical instinct which he possessed in so unusual a degree, set an example which few of his successors seem to have followed in any systematic manner. He made constant and intimate use of his colleagues in every matter that he handled, seeking their assistance and advice by letter when they were at a distance and he could not obtain it in person. It is well known to all close students of our history that his greater state papers, even those which seem in some peculiar and intimate sense his personal utterances, are full of the ideas and the very phrases of the men about him whom he most trusted. His rough drafts came back to him from Mr. Hamilton and Mr. Madison in great part rephrased and rewritten, in many passages reconceived and given a new color. He thought and acted always by the light of counsel, with a will and definite choice of his own, but through the instrumentality of other minds as well as his own. The duties and responsibilities laid upon the President by the Constitution can be changed only by constitutional amendment—a thing too difficult to attempt except upon some greater necessity than the relief of an overburdened office, even though that office be the greatest in the land; and it is to be doubted whether the deliberate opinion of the country would consent to make of the President a less powerful officer than he is. He can secure his own relief without shirking any real responsibility. Appointments, for example, he can, if he will, make more and more upon the advice and choice of his executive colleagues; every matter of detail not only, but also every minor matter of counsel or of general policy, he can more and more depend upon his chosen advisers to determine; he need reserve for himself only the larger matters of counsel and that general oversight of the business of the government and of the persons who conduct it which is not possible without intimate daily consultations, indeed, but which is possible without attempting the intolerable burden of direct control. This is, no doubt, the idea of their functions which most Presidents have entertained and which most Presidents suppose themselves to have acted on; but we have reason to believe that most of our Presidents have taken their duties too literally and have attempted the impossible. But we can safely predict that as the multitude of the President's duties increases, as it must with the growth and widening activities of the nation itself, the incumbents of the great office will more and more come to feel that they are administering it in its truest purpose and with greatest effect by regarding themselves as less and less executive officers and more and more directors of affairs and leaders of the nation—men of counsel and of the sort of action that makes for enlightenment.

THE CONTEMPORARY
PRESIDENCY

☆

ON FRANKLIN ROOSEVELT: *from* Roosevelt's View
of the Big Job *by Anne O'Hare McCormick*

[Roosevelt] is a potent name, easily the most potent influence in the
destiny of Franklin Roosevelt. Yet, though the Governor's versatile
interests and unconventional methods are Rooseveltian, they do
represent, nevertheless, his own conception of the personal and
human relationship that should exist between the Executive and
his State and by extension, between the Chief Executive and the
nation. He thinks that the President should personify government
to the citizen, should express the ideas germinating, ready for realization, in the popular mind.

"The Presidency," he says, "is not merely an administrative
office. That's the least of it. It is more than an engineering job,
efficient or inefficient. It is preeminently a place of moral leadership.
All of our great Presidents were leaders of thought at times when
certain historic ideas in the life of the nation had to be clarified.
Washington personified the idea of federal union. Jefferson practically originated the party system as we know it by opposing the
democratic theory to the republicanism of Hamilton. This theory was
reaffirmed by Jackson. Two great principles of our government were
forever put beyond question by Lincoln. Cleveland, coming into
office following an era of great political corruption, typified rugged

Franklin D. Roosevelt, the 32nd President of the United States, was elected
to the office four times and served from 1933 to 1945. This selection is from
"Roosevelt's View of the Big Job" by Anne O'Hare McCormick, who inter-
viewed Governor Roosevelt during his first campaign for the Presidency. *The
New York Times Magazine*, September 11, 1932, © 1932 by The New York
Times Company. Reprinted by permission.

honesty. T.R. and Wilson were both moral leaders, each in his own way and for his own time, who used the Presidency as a pulpit.

"Isn't that what the office is—a superb opportunity for reapplying, applying in new conditions, the simple rules of human conduct we always go back to? I stress the modern application, because we are always moving on; the technical and economic environment changes, and never so quickly as now. Without leadership alert and sensitive to change, we are bogged up or lose our way, as we have lost it in the past decade."

"And you?" I asked. "Is that the reason you want to be President? What particular affirmation or reaffirmation is required of the national leader of today?"

The Governor laughed. "Months before the nomination I told you I didn't know why any man should want to be President. I repeat that I didn't grow up burning to go to the White House, like the American boy of legend rather than of fact. I have read history and known Presidents; it's a terrible job. But somebody has to do it. I suppose I was picked out because the majority of the party thought I was the best vote-getter. Now that I am picked out, naturally I want to be President. I want to win." He laughed again, then went on gravely:

"The objective now, as I see it, is to put at the head of the nation someone whose interests are not special but general, someone who can understand and treat with the country as a whole. For as much as anything it needs to be reaffirmed at this juncture that the United States is one organic entity, that no interest, no class, no section, is either separate or supreme above the interests of all or divorced from the interests of all. We hear a good deal about the interdependence of the nations of the world. In the pit of universal calamity, with every country smothered by its own narrow policies and the narrow policies of other countries—and that goes for us, too—every one sees that connection. But there is a nearer truth, often forgotten or ignored, and that is the interdependence of every part of our own country.

"No valid economic sectionalism exists in these States. There are opposed economic interests within every section, town against country, suburb against city, but as a nation we are all mixed up, fluid. All the States are in some degree like New York, a blend of agriculture and industry. The rural South is changing, the Western prairies are planted with factory towns. East and West, as we use the terms, are mostly states of mind, not localized but everywhere. What we need is a common mind, and, even more, common sense to realize that if we are not acting for the interest of the whole country we are acting against the interests of every section."

Perhaps this is Governor Roosevelt's answer to the charge that he is trying to be all things to all sections, conservative in the East, radical in the West; he simply denies that there are sections in that sense. He classifies himself as a liberal. I asked what he meant by that elastic term, how he defined the difference between the outlooks vaguely called conservative and progressive, or between his program and that of the opposing party.

"Let's put it this way," he explained. "Every few years, say every half generation, the general problems of civilization change in such a way that new difficulties of adjustment are presented to government. The forms have to catch up with the facts. The radical, in order to meet these difficulties, jumps, jumps in groups, because he doesn't count unless he's part of a group. One group usually differs from another in its program, but they are all equally definite and dogmatic about it. They lay down categorical terms—'my plan or none.' Their characteristic is hard-and-fast processes, cut-and-dried methods, uncompromising formulas. The conservative says: 'No, we're not ready for change. It's dangerous. Let's wait and see what happens.' Half way in between is the liberal, who recognizes the need of new machinery for new needs but who works to control the processes of change, to the end that the break with the old pattern may not be too violent.

"Or say that civilization is a tree which, as it grows, continually produces rot and dead wood. The radical says: 'Cut it down.' The conservative says: 'Don't touch it.' The liberal compromises: 'Let's prune, so that we lose neither the old trunk nor the new branches.' This campaign is waged to teach the country to move upon its appointed course, the way of change, in an orderly march, avoiding alike the revolution of radicalism and the revolution of conservatism."

☆

FRANKLIN ROOSEVELT: *First Inaugural Address*

President Hoover, Mr. Chief Justice, my friends:
I am certain that my fellow Americans expect that on my induction into the Presidency I will address them with a candor and a decision which the present situation of our nation impels.

This is pre-eminently the time to speak the truth, the whole truth, frankly and boldly. Nor need we shrink from honestly facing conditions in our country today. This great nation will endure as it has endured, will revive and will prosper.

So first of all let me assert my firm belief that the only thing we have to fear is fear itself—nameless, unreasoning, unjustified terror which paralyzes needed efforts to convert retreat into advance.

In every dark hour of our national life a leadership of frankness and vigor has met with that understanding and support of the people themselves which is essential to victory. I am convinced that you will again give that support to leadership in these critical days.

In such a spirit on my part and on yours we face our common difficulties. They concern, thank God, only material things. Values have shrunken to fantastic levels; taxes have risen; our ability to pay has fallen, government of all kinds is faced by serious curtailment of income; the means of exchange are frozen in the currents of trade; the withered leaves of industrial enterprise lie on every side; farmers find no markets for their products; the savings of many years in thousands of families are gone.

More important, a host of unemployed citizens face the grim problem of existence, and an equally great number toil with little

President Roosevelt's *First Inaugural Address* was delivered on March 4, 1933.

return. Only a foolish optimist can deny the dark realities of the moment.

Yet our distress comes from no failure of substance. We are stricken by no plague of locusts. Compared with the perils which our forefathers conquered because they believed and were not afraid, we have still much to be thankful for. Nature still offers her bounty and human efforts have multiplied it. Plenty is at our doorstep, but a generous use of it languishes in the very sight of the supply.

Primarily, this is because the rulers of the exchange of mankind's goods have failed through their own stubbornness and their own incompetence, have admitted their failure and abdicated. Practices of the unscrupulous money changers stand indicted in the court of public opinion, rejected by the hearts and minds of men.

True, they have tried, but their efforts have been cast in the pattern of an outworn tradition. Faced by failure of credit, they have proposed only the lending of more money.

Stripped of the lure of profit by which to induce our people to follow their false leadership, they have resorted to exhortations, pleading tearfully for restored confidence. They know only the rules of a generation of self-seekers.

They have no vision, and when there is no vision the people perish.

The money changers have fled from their high seats in the temple of our civilization. We may now restore that temple to the ancient truths.

The measure of the restoration lies in the extent to which we apply social values more noble than mere monetary profit.

Happiness lies not in the mere possession of money; it lies in the joy of achievement, in the thrill of creative effort. The joy and moral stimulation of work no longer must be forgotten in the mad chase of evanescent profits. These dark days will be worth all they cost us if they teach us that our true destiny is not to be ministered unto but to minister to ourselves and to our fellow men.

Recognition of the falsity of material wealth as the standard of success goes hand in hand with the abandonment of the false belief that public office and high political position are to be valued only by the standards of pride of place and personal profit; and there must be an end to a conduct in banking and in business which too often has given to a sacred trust the likeness of callous and selfish wrongdoing.

Small wonder that confidence languishes, for it thrives only on honesty, on honor, on the sacredness of obligations, on faithful protection, on unselfish performance; without them it cannot live.

Restoration calls, however, not for changes in ethics alone. This nation asks for action, and action now.

Our greatest primary task is to put people to work. This is no un-solvable problem if we face it wisely and courageously. It can be ac-complished in part by direct recruiting by the government itself, treating the task as we would treat the emergency of a war, but at the same time, through this employment, accomplishing greatly needed projects to stimulate and reorganize the use of our natural resources.

Hand in hand with this we must frankly recognize the overbalance of population in our industrial centers and, by engaging on a national scale in a redistribution, endeavor to provide a better use of the land for those best fitted for the land.

The task can be helped by definite efforts to raise the values of ag-ricultural products and with this the power to purchase the output of our cities.

It can be helped by preventing realistically the tragedy of the growing loss, through foreclosure, of our small homes and our farms.

It can be helped by insistence that the federal, state and local gov-ernments act forthwith on the demand that their cost be drastically reduced.

It can be helped by the unifying of relief activities which today are often scattered, uneconomical and unequal. It can be helped by national planning for and supervision of all forms of transportation and of communications and other utilities which have a definitely public character.

There are many ways in which it can be helped, but it can never be helped merely by talking about it. We must act, and act quickly.

Finally, in our progress toward a resumption of work we require two safeguards against a return of the evils of the old order; there must be a strict supervision of all banking and credits and invest-ments; there must be an end to speculation with other people's money, and there must be provision for an adequate but sound cur-rency.

These are the lines of attack. I shall presently urge upon a new Congress, in special session, detailed measure for their fulfillment, and I shall seek the immediate assistance of the several States.

Through this program of action we address ourselves to putting our own national house in order and making income balance outgo. Our international trade relations, though vastly important, are in point of time and necessity secondary to the establishment of a sound national economy. I favor as a practical policy the putting of first things first. I shall spare no effort to restore world trade by interna-tional economic readjustment, but the emergency at home cannot wait on that accomplishment.

The basic thought that guides these specific means of national re-covery is not narrowly nationalistic.

It is the insistence, as a first consideration, upon the interdependence of the various elements in, and parts of, the United States—a recognition of the old and permanently important manifestation of the American spirit of the pioneer.

It is the way to recovery. It is the immediate way. It is the strongest assurance that the recovery will endure.

In the field of world policy I would dedicate this nation to the policy of the good neighbor—the neighbor who resolutely respects himself and, because he does so, respects the rights of others—the neighbor who respects his obligations and respects the sanctity of his agreements in and with a world of neighbors.

If I read the temper of our people correctly, we now realize as we have never realized before our interdependnce on each other; that we can not merely take but we must give as well; that if we are to go forward, we must move as a trained and loyal army willing to sacrifice for the good of a common discipline, because without such discipline no progress is made, no leadership becomes effective.

We are, I know, ready and willing to submit our lives and property to such discipline because it makes possible a leadership which aims at a larger good.

This I propose to offer, pledging that the larger purposes will bind upon us all as a sacred obligation with a unity of duty hitherto evoked only in time of armed strife.

With this pledge taken, I assume unhesitatingly the leadership of this great army of our people, dedicated to a disciplined attack upon our common problems.

Action in this image and to this end is feasible under the form of government which we have inherited from our ancestors.

Our Constitution is so simple and practical that it is possible always to meet extraordinary needs by changes in emphasis and arrangement without loss of essential form. That is why our constitutional system has proved itself the most superbly enduring political mechanism the modern world has produced. It has met every stress of vast expansion of territory, of foreign wars, of bitter internal strife, of world relations.

It is to be hoped that the normal balance of executive and legislative authority may be wholly adequate to meet the unprecedented task before us. But it may be that an unprecedented demand and need for undelayed action may call for temporary departure from that normal balance of public procedure.

I am prepared under my constitutional duty to recommend the measures that a stricken nation in the midst of a stricken world may require.

These measures, or such other measures as the Congress may build out of its experience and wisdom, I shall seek, within my constitutional authority, to bring to speedy adoption.

But in the event that the Congress shall fail to take one of these two courses, and in the event that the national emergency is still critical, I shall not evade the clear course of duty that will then confront me.

I shall ask the Congress for the one remaining instrument to meet the crisis—broad executive power to wage a war against the emergency as great as the power that would be given me if we were in fact invaded by a foreign foe.

For the trust reposed in me I will return the courage and the devotion that befit the time. I can do no less.

We face the arduous days that lie before us in the warm courage of national unity; with the clear consciousness of seeking old and precious moral values; with the clean satisfaction that comes from the stern performance of duty by old and young alike. We aim at the assurance of a rounded and permanent national life.

We do not distrust the future of essential democracy. The people of the United States have not failed. In their need they have registered a mandate that they want direct, vigorous action.

They have asked for discipline and direction under leadership. They have made me the present instrument of their wishes. In the spirit of the gift I take it.

In this dedication of a nation we humbly ask the blessing of God. May He protect each and every one of us! May He guide me in the days to come!

☆

FRANKLIN ROOSEVELT: *Message to Congress on Wartime Stabilization*

Four months ago, on April 27, 1942, I laid before the Congress a seven-point national economic policy designed to stabilize the domestic economy of the United States for the period of the war. The objective of that program was to prevent any substantial further rise in the cost of living.

It is not necessary for me to enumerate again the disastrous results of a runaway cost of living—disastrous to all of us, farmers, laborers, businessmen, the Nation itself. When the cost of living spirals upward, everybody becomes poorer, because the money he has and the money he earns buys so much less. At the same time the cost of the war, paid ultimately from taxes of the people, is needlessly increased by many billions of dollars. The national debt, at the end of the war, would become unnecessarily greater. Indeed, the prevention of a spiraling domestic economy is a vital part of the winning of the war itself.

I reiterate the 7-point program which I presented April 27, 1942:

1. To keep the cost of living from spiraling upward, we must tax heavily, and in that process keep personal and corporate profits at a reasonable rate, the word "reasonable" being defined at a low level.

2. To keep the cost of living from spiraling upward, we must fix ceilings on the prices which consumers, retailers, wholesalers, and manufacturers pay for the things they buy; and ceilings on rents for dwellings in all areas affected by war industries.

President Roosevelt sent this *Message to the Congress Asking for Quick Action to Stabilize the Economy* on September 7, 1942.

3. To keep the cost of living from spiraling upward, we must stabilize the remuneration received by individuals for their work.

4. To keep the cost of living from spiraling upward, we must stabilize the prices received by growers for the products of their lands.

5. To keep the cost of living from spiraling upward, we must encourage all citizens to contribute to the cost of winning this war by purchasing war bonds with their earnings instead of using those earnings to buy articles which are not essential.

6. To keep the cost of living from spiraling upward, we must ration all essential commodities of which there is a scarcity, so that they may be distributed fairly among consumers and not merely in accordance with financial ability to pay high prices for them.

7. To keep the cost of living from spiraling upward, we must discourage credit and installment buying, and encourage the paying off of debts, mortgages, and other obligations; for this promotes savings, retards excessive buying, and adds to the amount available to the creditors for the purchase of war bonds.

In my message of four months ago, I pointed out that in order to succeed in our objective of stabilization it was necessary to move on all seven fronts at the same time; but that two of them called for legislation by the Congress before action could be taken. It was obvious then, and it is obvious now, that unless those two are realized, the whole objective must fail. These are points numbered one and four: namely, an adequate tax program, and a law permitting the fixing of price ceilings on farm products at parity prices.

I regret to have to call to your attention the fact that neither of these two essential pieces of legislation has as yet been enacted into law. That delay has now reached the point of danger to our whole economy. . . .

Therefore, I ask the Congress to pass legislation under which the President would be specifically authorized to stabilize the cost of living, including the prices of all farm commodities. The purpose should be to hold farm prices at parity, or at levels of a recent date, whichever is higher.

I ask the Congress to take this action by the first of October. Inaction on your part by that date will leave me with an inescapable responsibility to the people of this country to see to it that the war effort is no longer imperiled by threat of economic chaos.

In the event that the Congress should fail to act, and act adequately, I shall accept the responsibility, and I will act.

At the same time that farm prices are stabilized, wages can and will be stabilized also. This I will do.

The President has the powers, under the Constitution and under

Congressional Acts, to take measures necessary to avert a disaster which would interfere with the winning of the war.

I have given the most thoughtful consideration to meeting this issue without further reference to the Congress. I have determined, however, on this vital matter to consult with the Congress.

There may be those who will say that, if the situation is as grave as I have stated it to be, I should use my powers and act now. I can only say that I have approached this problem from every angle, and that I have decided that the course of conduct which I am following in this case is consistent with my sense of responsibility as President in time of war, and with my deep and unalterable devotion to the processes of democracy.

The responsibilities of the President in wartime to protect the Nation are very grave. This total war, with our fighting fronts all over the world, makes the use of executive power far more essential than in any previous war.

If we were invaded, the people of this country would expect the President to use any and all means to repel the invader.

The Revolution and the War Between the States were fought on our own soil but today this war will be won or lost on other continents and remote seas.

I cannot tell what powers may have to be exercised in order to win this war.

The American people can be sure that I will use my powers with a full sense of my responsibility to the Constitution and to my country. The American people can also be sure that I shall not hesitate to use every power vested in me to accomplish the defeat of our enemies in any part of the world where our own safety demands such defeat.

When the war is won, the powers under which I act automatically revert to the people—to whom they belong. . . .

☆

HARRY TRUMAN: *Statement on the Situation in Korea*

In Korea the government forces, which were armed to prevent border raids and to preserve internal security, were attacked by invading forces from North Korea. The Security Council of the United Nations called upon the invading troops to cease hostilities and to withdraw to the 38th parallel. This they have not done, but on the contrary have pressed the attack. The Security Council called upon all members of the United Nations to render every assistance to the United Nations in the execution of this resolution. In these circumstances I have ordered United States air and sea forces to give the Korean government troops cover and support.

The attack upon Korea makes it plain beyond all doubt that communism has passed beyond the use of subversion to conquer independent nations and will now use armed invasion and war. It has defied the orders of the Security Council of the United Nations issued to preserve international peace and security. In these circumstances the occupation of Formosa by Communist forces would be a direct threat to the security of the Pacific area and to United States forces performing their lawful and necessary functions in that area.

Accordingly I have ordered the 7th Fleet to prevent any attack on Formosa. As a corollary of this action I am calling upon the Chinese government on Formosa to cease all air and sea operations against the mainland. The 7th Fleet will see that this is done. The determination of the future status of Formosa must await the restoration of security in the Pacific, a peace settlement with Japan, or consideration by the United Nations.

Harry S. Truman was the 33rd President of the United States (1945–1953). This *Statement* was issued on June 27, 1950.

I have also directed that United States forces in the Philippines be strengthened and that military assistance to the Philippine government be accelerated.

I have similarly directed acceleration in the furnishing of military assistance to the forces of France and the Associated States in Indochina and the dispatch of a military mission to provide close working relations with those forces.

I know that all members of the United Nations will consider carefully the consequences of this latest aggression in Korea in defiance of the Charter of the United Nations. A return to the rule of force in international affairs would have far-reaching effects. The United States will continue to uphold the rule of law.

I have instructed Ambassador Austin, as the representative of the United States to the Security Council, to report these steps to the Council.

☆

HARRY TRUMAN: *Speech on Presidential Power*

. . . There's never been an office—an executive office—in all the history of the world with the responsibility and the power of the Presidency of the United States. That is the reason in this day and age that it must be run and respected as at no other time in the history of the world because it can mean the welfare of the world or its destruction.

When the founding fathers outlined the Presidency in Article II of the Constitution, they left a great many details out and vague. I think they relied on the experience of the nation to fill in the outlines. The office of chief executive has grown with the progress of this great republic. It has responded to the many demands that our complex society has made upon the Government. It has given our nation a means of meeting our greatest emergencies. Today, it is one of the most important factors in our leadership of the free world.

Many diverse elements entered into the creation of the office, springing, as it did, from the parent idea of the separation of powers.

There was the firm conviction of such powerful and shrewd minds as that of John Adams that the greatest protection against unlimited power lay in an executive secured against the encroachment of the national assembly. Then there were the fears of those who suspected a plot to establish a monarchy on these shores. Others believed that the experience under the Confederation showed above all the need of stability through a strong central administration. Finally, there was the need for compromise among these and many other views.

President Truman delivered this speech at a Birthday Dinner in his honor on May 8, 1954. © 1954 by The New York Times Company. Reprinted by permission.

The result was a compromise—a compromise which that shrewd observer, Alexis de Tocqueville, over 120 years ago, believed would not work. He thought that the presidential office was too weak. The President, he thought, was at the mercy of Congress. The President could recommend, to be sure, he thought, but the President had no power and the Congress had the power. The Congress could disregard his recommendations, overrule his vetoes, reject his nominations. De Tocqueville thought that no man of parts, worthy of leadership, would accept such a feeble role.

This was not a foolish view and there was much in our early history which tended to bear it out. But there is a power in the course of events which plays its own part. In this case again, Justice Holmes' epigram proved true. He said a page of history is worth a whole volume of logic. And as the pages of history were written they unfolded powers in the Presidency not explicitly found in Article II of the Constitution.

In the first place, the President became the leader of a political party. The party under his leadership had to be dominant enough to put him in office. This political party leadership was the last thing the Constitution contemplated. The President's election was not intended to be mixed up in the hurly-burly of partisan politics.

I wish some of those old gentlemen could come back and see how it worked. The people were to choose wise and respected men who would meet in calm seclusion and choose a President and the runner-up would be Vice President.

All of this went by the board—though most of the original language remains in the Constitution. Out of the struggle and tumult of the political arena a new and different President emerged—the man who led a political party to victory and retained in his hands the power of party leadership. That is, he retained it, like the sword Excalibur, if he could wrest it from the scabbard and wield it.

Another development was connected with the first. As the President came to be elected by the whole people, he became responsible to the whole people. I used to say the only lobbyist the whole people had in Washington was the President of the United States. Our whole people looked to him for leadership, and not confined within the limits of a written document. Every hope and every fear of his fellow citizens, almost every aspect of their welfare and activity, falls within the scope of his concern—indeed, it falls within the scope of his duty. Only one who has held that office can really appreciate that. It is the President's responsibility to look at all questions from the point of view of the whole people. His written and spoken word commands national and often international attention.

These powers which are not explicitly written into the Constitution are the powers which no President can pass on to his successor. They go only to him who can take and use them. However, it is these powers, quite as much as those enumerated in Article II of the Constitution, which make the presidential system unique and which give the papers of Presidents their peculiarly revealing importance.

For it is through the use of these great powers that leadership arises, events are molded, and administrations take on their character. Their use can make a Jefferson or a Lincoln Administration; their non-use can make a Buchanan or a Grant Administration.

Moreover, a study of these aspects of our governmental and political history will save us from self-righteousness—from taking a holier-than-thou attitude toward other nations. For, brilliant and enduring as were the minds of the architects of our Constitution, they did not devise a foolproof system to protect us against the disaster of a weak government—that is, a government unable to face and resolve—one way or another—pressing national problems. Indeed, in some respects, the separation of powers requires stronger executive leadership than does the parliamentary and cabinet system.

As Justice Brandeis used to say, the separation of powers was not devised to promote efficiency in government. In fact, it was devised to prevent one form of deficiency—absolutism or dictatorship. By making the Congress separate and independent in the exercise of its powers, a certain amount of political conflict was built into the Constitution. For the price of independence is eternal vigilance and a good deal of struggle. And this is not a bad thing—on the contrary, it is a good thing for the preservation of the liberty of the people— if it does not become conflict just for its own sake.

I've always said that the President who didn't have a fight with the Congress wasn't any good anyhow. And that's no reflection on the Congress. They are always looking after their rights. You needn't doubt that.

Having been in these two branches of government, legislative and executive, I think I am expressing a considered and impartial opinion in saying that the powers of the President are much more difficult to exercise and to preserve from encroachment than those of the Congress. In part, this comes from the difficulty of the problems of our time, and from the fact that upon the President falls the responsibility of obtaining action, timely and adequate, to meet the nation's needs. Whatever the Constitution says, he is held responsible for any disaster which may come.

And so a successful administration is one of strong presidential leadership. Weak leadership—or no leadership—produces failure and often disaster.

This does not come from the inherent incapacity of the people of the nation. It is inherent in the legislative government where there is no executive strong and stable enough to rally the people to a sustained effort of will and prepared to use its power of party control to the fullest extent.

Today, also, one of the great responsibilities and opportunities of the President is to lead and inspire public opinion. The words of a President carry great weight. His acts carry even more weight.

All of us remember the words of Franklin D. Roosevelt in his first inaugural address which did so much to rally the spirit of the nation struggling through the depths of a depression. He said "the only thing we have to fear is fear itself." Those words, however, would have had little effect if President Roosevelt had not backed them up by action. Following that speech, President Roosevelt plunged into a vigorous course, striking at the depression on all fronts. He backed his words by his action, and words and action restored the faith of the nation in its government and in its form of government, too.

. . . Today the tasks of leadership falling upon the President spring not only from our national problems but from those of the whole world. Today that leadership will determine whether our Government will function effectively, and upon its functioning depends the survival of each of us and also on that depends the survival of the free world. . . .

☆

DWIGHT D. EISENHOWER: *Some Thoughts on the Presidency*

In the late afternoon of January 22, 1953—my first full day at the President's desk—my old friend Gen. Omar Bradley, then chairman of the Joint Chiefs of Staff, phoned me. For years we had been "Ike" and "Brad" to each other. But now, in the course of our conversation, he addressed me as "Mr. President."

Somehow this little incident rocked me back on my heels. Naturally, I knew all about Presidential protocol, but I suppose I had never quite realized the isolation that the job forces upon a man.

I couple this with another seemingly small circumstance that also put me on notice at once that the Presidency is something apart. During my first few hours in the Oval Room, a White House aide showed me a large push button concealed in the kneehole of my desk. If I were to touch the button with my knee, Secret Service guards would appear instantly.

Doubtless every new President has experiences which quickly teach him that he has undertaken a lonely job. After these two episodes, I understood with deep impact that now, except for my immediate family, I would in a sense be alone—far more so than when I commanded the Allied forces in Europe. I have always liked people, and it was hard to surrender the easy camaraderie of the old days. Nor was it easy to accept the fact that I would always be under

Dwight D. Eisenhower, Supreme Commander of the Allied Forces in Europe in World War II, was the 34th President of the United States (1953–1961). This selection is from "Some Thoughts on the Presidency" in the *Reader's Digest*, November, 1968. © 1968 by Dwight D. Eisenhower. Reprinted by permission of the *Reader's Digest* and Doubleday and Company.

guard, that all movements must be planned, that I could never go anywhere unattended.

But these, after all, are minor frustrations, to which one grows accustomed. The American people respect the Presidency, and want the office to be conducted with dignity and with as much personal safety for the incumbent as can be devised—and it is right that they should.

Far more important than protocol or any other outward trappings of the office are certain inner qualities that any President must have to be effective. On several occasions I have said publicly that there are four prime requisites of the Presidency: Character, Ability, Responsibility, Experience. These need no explanation. But, on a more specific level, there are also many identifiable qualities, moods, characteristics and attitudes that contribute to the success or defeat of a President. It is some of these human characteristics that I wish to discuss.

To See Beyond Today. One of the most important necessities of the Presidency is vision—the ability to look far into the future and see. the needs of the nation. Coupled with this is the courage to implement this vision with the necessary hard decisions, despite almost sure criticism—often actual vilification—from the press, the opposition party, and even from within the incumbent's own party.

Thomas Jefferson certainly displayed the kind of vision I am talking about when he made the Louisiana Purchase from France in 1803. Jefferson's political enemies and some segments of the press scoffed at his determination to acquire this territory—a desert wilderness of a million square miles, inhabited chiefly by Indians and buffalo, largely unfit for human use. But he and his Cabinet ministers ignored the criticism and went ahead with the deal, at a cost of about four cents an acre. Today this area is occupied by all or parts of 13 states, and is perhaps the greatest food-producing region in the world.

Frequently throughout our history, a President has displayed magnificent vision in the enunciation of a great principle. Such, surely, was James Monroe's courageous promulgation of the Monroe Doctrine, which warned the acquisitive nations of Europe to keep their hands off the Western Hemisphere.

Such, also, was Andrew Jackson's tough refusal to permit the nullification of federal law by a state. The confrontation came in 1832, when South Carolina attempted to prevent the collection of import duties at the port of Charleston. It was an early historic test of the states' rights doctrine in defiance of federal supremacy. Old Hickory, himself a Southerner, issued a call for federal troops to put down the insurrection. South Carolina grumbled that it would secede, but backed down before there was a clash of arms.

History gives Lincoln the credit for saving the Union, but if Jackson had not acted wisely and firmly in 1832, the nation might well have fallen apart before Abe ever appeared on the scene.

It was left to Abraham Lincoln, of course, to preserve the Union in the supreme test, the agony of bloodshed. His vision, his rock-like determination, his compassion, his aloneness in the midst of the worst public abuse any President has ever suffered, are a familiar story. But consider for a moment the superb selflessness of the man. Some months before the national election of 1864, prestigious leaders of his own party came to Lincoln and begged him to end the war through any kind of compromise he could arrange with the Confederacy. Otherwise, they predicted, he would go down to defeat at the polls. Abe's answer was a firm, historic No. He added that his own political future was unimportant—that the preservation of the Union was all that mattered. Fortunately, the tide of battle turned in time, he was re-elected, and the Union forces went on to complete victory a few months later.

Incidentally, the rebellious spirit of nullification still crops up occasionally even today. It was in September of 1957 that Gov. Orval Faubus, of Arkansas, attempted to thwart federal court orders to integrate a Little Rock high school. He called up the Arkansas National Guard to enforce his outrageous defiance of the federal government. After a fruitless conference with the governor, I sent U.S. paratroopers into Little Rock—and then braced myself for the inevitable storm of criticism. For a time, the South was outraged at my "high-handed tactics." But order was peacefully restored and eventually integration was effected. Once more the principle of federal supremacy had been upheld.

Andrew Johnson, who succeeded to the Presidency upon Lincoln's assassination, is usually catalogued as a "weak" President. It is true that his personal habits and comportment were anything but exemplary, and in many ways he was ineffectual. Yet he did two farseeing things: he "squandered" $7,200,000 to buy Alaska from Russia; he saved the office of the Presidency from destruction by Congress. Both of these acts took courage—and he was castigated unmercifully for them.

Johnson had been quarreling with Secretary of War Edwin M. Stanton, and wanted to remove him. To thwart Johnson, Congress had passed an obviously unconstitutional measure called the Tenure of Office Act, which forbade the President to dismiss Cabinet members or other appointive officials without the consent of the Senate. Despite the Act, Johnson fired Stanton. The House angrily impeached him. But in the Senate the President won his fight against conviction by one vote. It was enough. The right of a President to run the executive department was upheld.

Humility, Humor, Optimism. There are certain deeply personal characteristics that any President needs to cope with the pressures and the buffeting of the job. One of these is a working balance between humility and vanity. I have been amused to read occasionally that I was a "humble President," while just as often I have been called an autocrat or a martinet. Every human being, and certainly a President, needs a certain amount of personal pride, but he shouldn't be so proud that he cannot change his mind or admit his mistakes. Nor can any President achieve his objectives if he permits others to walk roughshod over him.

Lincoln's humility was one of his storied qualities, but he also demonstrated over and over that he had iron in his soul. On the other hand, although Woodrow Wilson was surely a great President, I have always felt that his unbending pride kept him from being even greater. George Washington was, I think, the ideal in this respect. He possessed pride and dignity, but he was also considerate of others, consulted constantly with his subordinates, unfailingly weighed their advice.

As part of this working balance in a man's nature, a sense of humor can be a great help—particularly a sense of humor about himself. William Howard Taft joked about his own corpulence, and people loved it; it took nothing from his inherent dignity. Lincoln eased tense moments with bawdy stories, and often poked fun at himself—and history honors him for this human quality. A sense of humor is part of the art of leadership, of getting along with people, of getting things done.

On the other hand, I found that getting things done sometimes required other weapons from the Presidential arsenal—persuasion, cajolery, even a little head-thumping here and there—to say nothing of a personal streak of obstinacy which on occasion fires my boilers.

It is an essential quality of leadership to be able to inspire people. I have often thought how fortunate it was that the two great Allies of World War II were led by two men, Winston Churchill and Franklin D. Roosevelt, who had that ability and used it masterfully.

Although I have always disagreed with some of Roosevelt's domestic policies—notably the trend toward highly centralized government that he set in motion—I admired him greatly as a war leader. The man exuded an infectious optimism. Even during the dark days of our early reverses in the Pacific, he was somehow able to convey his own exuberant confidence to the American people. As a result, despite often justified political opposition on domestic measures,

F.D.R. had the nation almost solidly behind him in his conduct of the war.

The Power of Organization. Executive ability, whose cornerstone is a talent for good organization and skill in selecting and using subordinates, certainly is a vital attribute of the Presidency. Any Chief Executive who tries to do everything himself, as some Presidents have, is in trouble. He will work himself into a state of exhaustion and frustration, and drive everyone around him half crazy. Franklin Pierce, for example, was so preoccupied with patronage decisions and other petty matters that he never was able really to be President.

George Washington's skill in organizing was superb. When he became our first President, he had a Congress and a fragmentary judicial system, but only small bits and pieces of an executive establishment. There were no precedents, and his only instruction guide was our new Constitution, a great document which nevertheless told him only in the broadest terms what he could and could not do. Upon this he had to build the structure of government.

Washington did it. He had the good sense to surround himself with men of stature, and he got the most out of them. History offers few examples of organizational achievement to compare with the eight years of his administration.

To accomplish this gigantic task, Washington had to invest the office of President with powers that the Constitution only hinted at or said nothing at all about. Predictably, he incurred an avalanche of savage abuse from a populace still sensitive to the excesses of monarchy. When he assumed office, his popularity was almost boundless, but by the time he retired he was being jeeringly referred to as a "tyrant" and "King George." But he had made the Presidency meaningful, with the power that any effective executive must have. Had he not done so, the Presidency might easily have deteriorated into a largely ceremonial office.

The Final Decision. In my own administration, we developed a fine working team of highly competent people. We had efficient organization and good staff work. Some writers have said that I conducted the Presidency largely through staff decisions. This, of course, is nonsense. Naturally, I consulted constantly with my staff, and I valued their opinions. But staff work doesn't mean that you take a vote of your subordinates and then abide by the majority opinion. On important matters, in the end, you alone must decide. As a military leader I had learned this hard lesson. Many times, during my two terms, my decisions ran contrary to the majority opinion of my advisers.

As an example of how decisions are hammered out, I shall mention just one knotty domestic problem that confronted us early in my first term. Even before I assumed the Presidency, I had become convinced that for the economy to forge ahead, government controls of prices and wages must be banished. The political opposition predicted that this would throw the nation into a new spiral of inflation. Some of my own close advisers were opposed; others were divided on how it should be done and when—gradually over a considerable period, or immediately. The decision was mine, and I concluded that we should do it quickly, but step by step.

That's what we did, and in a matter of weeks most controls were dropped. Happily for the country, it worked, and it continued to work. There was very little inflation during my administration, which was an era of remarkable prosperity.

Of all the men in my Cabinet there was no one whom I respected more than Secretary of State John Foster Dulles. I depended greatly on his wisdom. Yet Foster made no important move without consulting the President. I reviewed in advance all his major pronouncements and speeches, and when he was abroad he was constantly in touch by cable and telephone. If we did not see eye to eye—and these instances were rare—it was, of course, my opinion that prevailed; this is the way it has to be. The persistent statement that I turned foreign policy over to Dulles is—to use a more civilized word than it deserves—incorrect.

There is a strange theory among some pundits that smooth organization in the White House indicates that nothing is happening, whereas ferment and disorder are proof of progress. I recall that we had plenty of crises during my administration, but we were able to handle them without turning double handsprings—and usually without unnecessary public flap. In my opinion, a table-pounding executive is ridiculous.

With good executive organization in the White House and the departments, I do not think the heavy burdens of the Presidency need become intolerable. Nor do I believe that a plural Presidency, which has sometimes been suggested, is necessary or would work. In our kind of government, divided authority surely would result only in confusion and frustration.

Finally, I believe deeply that every occupant of the White House, whether he be conservative, liberal or middle-of-the-road, has one profound duty to the nation: to exert moral leadership. The President of the United States should stand, visible and uncompromising, for what is right and decent—in government, in the business community, in the private lives of the citizens. For decency is one of the main pillars of a sound civilization. An immoral nation invites its own ruin

☆

ON DWIGHT EISENHOWER: *from* The Ordeal of Power *by Emmet John Hughes*

The Eisenhower who rose to fame in the 1940s, under the wartime Presidency of Franklin Roosevelt, brought to the White House of the 1950s a view of the Presidency so definite and so durable as to seem almost a studied retort and rebuke to a Roosevelt. Where Roosevelt had sought and coveted power, Eisenhower distrusted and discounted it: one man's appetite was the other man's distaste. Where Roosevelt had avidly grasped and adroitly manipulated the abundant authorities of the office, Eisenhower fingered them almost hesitantly and always respectfully—or generously dispersed them. Where Roosevelt had challenged Congress, Eisenhower courted it. Where Roosevelt had been an extravagant partisan, Eisenhower was a tepid partisan. Where Roosevelt had trusted no one and nothing so confidently as his own judgment and his own instinct, Eisenhower trusted and required a consensus of Cabinet or staff to shape the supreme judgments and determinations. Where Roosevelt had sought to goad and taunt and prod the processes of government toward the new and the untried, Eisenhower sought to be both guardian of old values and healer of old wounds.

The contrast was quite as blunt in the case of an earlier—and a Republican—Roosevelt. For the Eisenhower who so deeply disliked all struttings of power, all histrionics of politics, would have found

Emmet John Hughes, a former Eisenhower adviser, is a columnist and editorial consultant for *Newsweek* magazine. The selection is from his *The Ordeal of Power* (New York: Atheneum, 1963), pp. 347–350. Copyright © 1962, 1963 by Emmet John Hughes. Reprinted by permission of Atheneum Publishers and the author.

the person and the Presidency of Theodore Roosevelt almost intolerable. He would have applied to this Roosevelt, too, the homely phrase of derision that he reserved for politicians of such verve and vehemence: they were "the desk-pounders." Echoing back across the decades would have come the lusty answer of T.R.—exulting in the Presidency as the "bully pulpit." And it is hard to imagine a concept of the Presidency more alien to Eisenhower: to preach and to yell.

A yet more exact and intimate insight into the Eisenhower Presidency was revealed by his particular tribute to the Abraham Lincoln of his admiration. He was asked, on one occasion, to describe this Lincoln. And he chose these adjectives: "dedicated, selfless, so modest and humble." He made no mention or suggestion of such possible attributes as: imagination, tenacity, single-mindedness, vision. Pressed gently by his interrogator as to whether Lincoln were not something of a "desk-pounder," Eisenhower denied such a notion and spontaneously related the one episode of Lincoln's life that surged to the surface of memory . . .

> Oh no. Lincoln was noted both for his modesty and his humility. For example, one night he wanted to see General McClellan. He walked over to General McClellan's house . . . but General McClellan was out. He . . . waited way late in the evening. But when the general came in, he told an aide . . . he was tired and he was going to bed, and he would see the President the next day. And when criticized later . . . someone told Mr. Lincoln he ought to have been more arbitrary about this. He said: "I would hold General McClellan's horse if he would just win the Union a victory."

The Eisenhower appreciation of Lincoln, in short, reflected one sovereign attitude: all esteemed qualities of the founder of Republicanism were personal and individual, and not one was political or historical. And if the logic of such an estimate were carried coldly to its extreme, it would end in the unspoken implication that the highest national office should be sought and occupied less as an exercise of political power than as a test of personal virtue. To excel in this test, the man would live not *with* the office but *within* it—intact and independent, proudly uncontaminated by power, essentially uninvolved with it. Rather than a political life, this would be a life in politics. Its supreme symbol would be not the sword of authority but the shield of rectitude.

While this self-conscious kind of idealism sprang from deep within the man who was Eisenhower, it found reinforcement—and rationalization—in his explicit theory of political leadership. This

theory was profoundly felt and emphatically argued. It claimed even
to bespeak a sense of responsibility more serious than the conventional shows of leadership.. And no words of Eisenhower stated this
theory more succinctly than these:

> I am not a . . . leader. I don't want you to follow me or any-
> thing else. If you are looking for a Moses to lead you out of the
> . . . wilderness, you will stay right where you are. I would not
> lead you into this promised land if I could, because if I could lead
> in, someone else could lead you out.

These words might have been spoken by Dwight David Eisenhower—at almost any moment in the years from 1952 to 1960—to
the Republican party or, indeed, to the American people at large.
They were actually spoken, however, by one of the great leaders of
American labor, Eugene V. Debs, more than half a century earlier.
And they are worthy of note here as simple evidence that, quite apart
from all impulses of personal character, the political posture assumed
by Eisenhower toward the challenge of national leadership could
not, in fact, be curtly described as negligent, eccentric, or even entirely original.

This posture *was* Eisenhower—remarkably and unshakably—because it was prescribed for him by *both* the temper of the man and
the tenets of his politics. In any President, or in any political leader,
these two need not necessarily coincide: they may fiercely clash. A
man of vigorous and aggressive spirit, restless with the urge for action
and accomplishment, may fight frantically against the limits of a
political role calling for calm, composure, and self-effacement. Or a
man of easy and acquiescent temper, content to perform the minimal duties of his office, may strain pathetically and vainly to fill the
vastness of a political role demanding force, boldness, and self-assur-
ance. Eisenhower suffered neither kind of conflict. The definition of
the office perfectly suited and matched the nature of the man. And
neither critical argument nor anxious appeal could persuade him to
question, much less to shed, an attire of leadership so appropriate, so
form-fitting, so comfortable.

The want and the weakness in all this was not a mere matter of
indecision. The man—and the President—was never more decisive
than when he held to a steely resolve *not* to do something that he
sincerely believed wrong in itself or alien to his office. The essential
flaw, rather, was one that had been suggested a full half-century ago
—when the outrageously assertive Theodore Roosevelt had occupied
the White House—and Woodrow Wilson had then prophesied that
"more and more" the Presidency would demand "*the sort of action*

that makes for enlightenment." The requisite for such action, however, is not merely a stout sense of responsibility, but an acute sense of history—a discerning, even intuitive, appreciation of the elusive and cumulative force of every presidential word and act, shaped and aimed to reach final goals, unglimpsed by all but a few. And as no such vision ever deeply inspired the Eisenhower Presidency, there could be no true "enlightenment" to shine forth from its somber acts of prudence or of pride.

This is not to say that the record of the Administration wholly lacked zeal—of a kind. It is doubtful if the leadership of any great nation can endure for nearly a decade without at least the flickering of some such flame of commitment. The man who came closest to a display of such fervor in these years, however, was not the President but his Secretary of State. This man possessed at least his own understanding of what Theodore Roosevelt meant when he spoke of a "pulpit." And yet, this particular ardor of John Foster Dulles could not be enough. For this kind of zeal was neither creative nor impassioned. It was austere, constrained, and cerebral. And in lieu of fire, it offered ice.

Ultimately, all that Eisenhower did, and refused to do, as a democratic leader was rigorously faithful to his understanding of democracy itself. When the record of his Presidency was written and done, he could look back upon it and soberly reflect: "One definition of democracy that I like is merely the opportunity for self-discipline." He lived by this definition. And by all acts of eight years of his Presidency, he urged its acceptance by the people of his nation.

The implications of this simple political credo could not instantly be dismissed as shallow. Forbearance and constraint, patience and discipline—those are not virtues for a democracy to deride. They can be fatefully relevant to the ways of free men.

And yet, by the year 1960, they did not seem to serve or to suffice, as full statement of either the nation's purpose or a President's policy.

☆

JOHN KENNEDY: *Campaign Speech*
on the Presidency

The modern presidential campaign covers every issue in and out of
the platform from cranberries to creation. But the public is rarely
alerted to a candidate's views about the central issue on which all the
rest turn. That central issue—and the point of my comments this
noon—is not the farm problem or defense or India. It is the Presidency itself. Of course a candidate's views on specific policies are
important—but Theodore Roosevelt and William Howard Taft
shared policy views with entirely different results in the White
House. Of course it is important to elect a good man with good intentions—but Woodrow Wilson and Warren G. Harding were both
good men of good intentions—so were Lincoln and Buchanan—but
there is a Lincoln Room in the White House, and no Buchanan
Room.

The history of this nation—its brightest and its bleakest pages—
has been written largely in terms of the different views our Presidents
have had of the Presidency itself. This history ought to tell us that
the American people in 1960 have an imperative right to know what
any man bidding for the Presidency thinks about the place he is bidding for—whether he is aware of and willing to use the powerful
resources of that office—whether his model will be Taft or Roosevelt—Wilson or Harding.

Not since the days of Woodrow Wilson has any candidate spoken

John Fitzgerald Kennedy, a Pulitzer Prize winner for his *Profiles in Courage*,
was 35th President of the United States (1961–1963). This speech was delivered
to the National Press Club on January 14, 1960. © 1960 by The New York
Times Company. Reprinted by permission.

on the Presidency itself before the votes have been irrevocably cast. Let us hope that the 1960 campaign, in addition to discussing the familiar issues where our positions too often blur, will also talk about the Presidency itself—as an instrument for dealing with those issues —as an office with varying roles, powers, and limitations.

During the past eight years, we have seen one concept of the Presidency at work. Our needs and hopes have been eloquently stated—but the initiative and follow-through have too often been left to others. And too often his own objectives have been lost by the President's failure to override objections from within his own party, in the Congress or even in his Cabinet.

The American people in 1952 and 1956 may well have preferred this detached, limited concept of the Presidency after twenty years of fast-moving, creative presidential rule. Perhaps historians will regard this as necessarily one of those frequent periods of consolidation, a time to draw breath, to recoup our national energy. To quote the State of the Union Message: "No Congress . . . on surveying the state of the nation, has met with a more pleasing prospect than that which appears at the present time." Unfortunately this is not Mr. Eisenhower's last message to the Congress, but Calvin Coolidge's. He followed to the White House Mr. Harding, whose "sponsor" declared very frankly that the times did not demand a first-rate President. If true, the times and the man met.

But the question is what do the times—and the people—demand for the next four years in the White House?

They demand a vigorous proponent of the national interest— not a passive broker for conflicting private interests. They demand a man capable of acting as the commander in chief of the grand alliance, not merely a bookkeeper who feels that his work is done when the numbers on the balance sheet come out even. They demand that he be the head of a responsible party, not rise so far above politics as to be invisible—a man who will formulate and fight for legislative policies, not be a casual bystander to the legislative process.

Today a restricted concept of the Presidency is not enough. For beneath today's surface gloss of peace and prosperity are increasingly dangerous, unsolved, long-postponed problems—problems that will inevitably explode to the surface during the next four years of the next Administration—the growing missile gap, the rise of Communist China, the despair of the underdeveloped nations, the explosive situations in Berlin and in the Formosa Straits, the deterioration of NATO, the lack of an arms control agreement, and all the domestic problems of our farms, cities, and schools.

This Administration has not faced up to these and other problems. Much has been said—but I am reminded of the old Chinese proverb: "There is a great deal of noise on the stairs but nobody comes into the room." The President's State of the Union Message reminded me of the exhortation from "King Lear" that goes: "I will do such things—what they are I know not . . . but they shall be the wonders of the earth."

In the decade that lies ahead—in the challenging, revolutionary Sixties—the American Presidency will demand more than ringing manifestoes issued from the rear of the battle. It will demand that the President place himself in the very thick of the fight, that he care passionately about the fate of the people he leads, that he be willing to serve them at the risk of incurring their momentary displeasure.

Whatever the political affiliation of our next President, whatever his views may be on all the issues and problems that rush in upon us, he must above all be the Chief Executive in every sense of the word. He must be prepared to exercise the fullest powers of his office—all that are specified and some that are not. He must master complex problems as well as receive one-page memoranda. He must originate action as well as study groups. He must reopen the channels of communication between the world of thought and the seat of power.

Ulysses Grant considered the President "a purely administrative officer." If he administered the government departments efficiently, delegated his functions smoothly, and performed his ceremonies of state with decorum and grace, no more was to be expected of him. But that is not the place the Presidency was meant to have in American life. The President is alone, at the top—the loneliest job there is, as Harry Truman has said. If there is destructive dissension among the services, he alone can step in and straighten it out—instead of waiting for unanimity. If administrative agencies are not carrying out their mandate—if a brushfire threatens some part of the globe— he alone can act, without waiting for the Congress. If his farm program fails, he alone deserves the blame, not his Secretary of Agriculture.

"The President is at liberty, both in law and conscience, to be as big a man as he can." So wrote Professor Woodrow Wilson. But President Woodrow Wilson discovered that to be a big man in the White House inevitably brings cries of dictatorship. So did Lincoln and Jackson and the two Roosevelts. And so may the next occupant of that office, if he is the man the times demand. But how much better it would be, in the turbulent Sixties, to have a Roosevelt or a Wilson than to have another James Buchanan, cringing in the White House, afraid to move.

Nor can we afford a Chief Executive who is praised primarily for what he did not do, the disasters he prevented, the bills he vetoed—a President wishing his subordinates would produce more missiles or build more schools. We will need instead what the Constitution envisioned: a Chief Executive who is the vital center of action in our whole scheme of government.

This includes the legislative process as well. The President cannot afford—for the sake of the office as well as the nation—to be another Warren G. Harding, described by one backer as a man who "would, when elected, sign whatever bill the Senate sent him—and not send bills for the Senate to pass." Rather he must know when to lead the Congress, when to consult it and when he should act alone. Having served fourteen years in the Legislative Branch, I would not look with favor upon its domination by the Executive. Under our government of "power as the rival of power," to use Hamilton's phrase, Congress must not surrender its responsibilities. But neither should it dominate. However large its share in the formulation of domestic programs, it is the President alone who must make the major decisions of our foreign policy.

That is what the Constitution wisely commands. And even domestically, the President must initiate policies and devise laws to meet the needs of the nation. And he must be prepared to use all the resources of his office to insure the enactment of that legisla tion—even when conflict is the result. By the end of his term Theo dore Roosevelt was not popular in the Congress—particularly wher he criticized an amendment to the Treasury appropriation which forbade the use of Secret Service men to investigate congressmen! And the feeling was mutual, Roosevelt saying: "I do not much admire the Senate, because it is such a helpless body when efficient work is to be done." And Woodrow Wilson was even more bitter after his frustrating quarrels—asked if he might run for the Senate in 1920, he replied: "Outside of the United States, the Senate does not amount to a damn. And inside the United States, the Senate is mostly despised. They haven't had a thought down there in fifty years."

But, however bitter their farewells, the facts of the matter are that Roosevelt and Wilson did get things done—not only through their Executive powers but through the Congress as well. Calvin Coolidge, on the other hand, departed from Washington with cheers of Congress still ringing in his ears. But when his World

Court bill was under fire on Capitol Hill he sent no messages, gave no encouragement to the bill's leaders and paid little or no attention to the whole proceeding—and the cause of world justice was set back. To be sure, Coolidge had held the usual White House breakfasts with congressional leaders—but they were aimed, as he himself said, at "good fellowship," not a discussion of "public business." And at his press conferences, according to press historians, where he preferred to talk about the local flower show and its exhibits, reporters who finally extracted from him a single sentence —"I am against that bill"—would rush to file tongue-in-cheek dispatches, proclaiming that: "President Coolidge, in a fighting mood, today served notice on Congress that he intended to combat, with all the resources at his command, the pending bill. . . ."

But in the coming years, we will need a real fighting mood in the White House—a man who will not retreat in the face of pressure from his congressional leaders—who will not let down those supporting his views on the floor. Divided government over the past six years has only been further confused by this lack of legislative leadership. To restore it next year will help restore purpose to both the Presidency and the Congress.

The facts of the matter are that legislative leadership is not possible without party leadership, in the most political sense—and Mr. Eisenhower prefers to stay above politics (although a weekly news magazine last fall reported the startling news that "President Eisenhower is emerging as a major political figure"). When asked, early in his first term, how he liked the "game of politics," he replied with a frown that his questioner was using a derogatory phrase. "Being President," he said, "is a very great experience . . . but the word 'politics' . . . I have no great liking for that." But no President, it seems to me, can escape politics. He has not only been chosen by the nation—he has been chosen by his party. And if he insists that he is "President of all the people" and should, therefore, offend none of them—if he blurs the issues and differences between the parties—if he neglects the party machinery and avoids his party's leadership—then he has not only weakened the political party as an instrument of the democratic process—he has dealt a blow to the democratic process itself. I prefer the example of Abe Lincoln, who loved politics with the passion of a born practitioner. For example, he waited up all night in 1863 to get the crucial returns on the Ohio governorship. When the Unionist candidate was elected, Lincoln wired: "Glory to God in the highest! Ohio has saved the nation!"

But the White House is not only the center of political leadership. It must be the center of moral leadership—a "bully pulpit," as Theodore Roosevelt described it. For only the President represents the national interest. And upon him alone converge all the needs and aspirations of all parts of the country, all departments of the government, all nations of the world. It is not enough merely to represent prevailing sentiment—to follow McKinley's practice, as described by Joe Cannon, of "keeping his ear so close to the ground he got it full of grasshoppers." We will need in the Sixties a President who is willing and able to summon his national constituency to its finest hour—to alert the people to our dangers and our opportunities—to demand of them the sacrifices that will be necessary. Despite the increasing evidence of a lost national purpose and a soft national will, F.D.R.'s words in his first inaugural still ring true: "In every dark hour of our national life, a leadership of frankness and vigor has met with that understanding and support of the people themselves which is essential to victory."

Roosevelt fulfilled the role of moral leadership. So did Wilson and Lincoln, Truman and Jackson and Teddy Roosevelt. They led the people as well as the government—they fought for great ideals as well as bills. And the time has come to demand that kind of leadership again. And so, as this vital campaign begins, let us discuss the issues the next President will face—but let us also discuss the powers and tools with which he must face them. For he must endow that office with extraordinary strength and vision. He must act in the image of Abraham Lincoln summoning his wartime Cabinet to a meeting on the Emancipation Proclamation. That Cabinet had been carefully chosen to please and reflect many elements in the country. But "I have gathered you together," Lincoln said, "to hear what I have written down. I do not wish your advice about the main matter—that I have determined for myself." And later when he went to sign it after several hours of exhausting handshaking that had left his arm weak, he said to those present: "If my name goes down in history, it will be for this act. My whole soul is in it. If my hand trembles when I sign this proclamation, all who examine the document hereafter will say: 'He hesitated.'" But Lincoln's hand did not tremble. He did not hesitate. He did not equivocate. For he was the President of the United States. It is in this spirit that we must go forth in the coming months and years.

☆

JOHN KENNEDY: *Mid-Term Television Conversation on the Presidency*

WILLIAM H. LAWRENCE, American Broadcasting Company. As you look back upon your first two years in office, sir, has your experience in the office matched your expectations? You had studied a good deal the power of the Presidency, the methods of its operations. How has this worked out as you saw it in advance?

THE PRESIDENT. Well, I think in the first place the problems are more difficult than I had imagined they were. Secondly, there is a limitation upon the ability of the United States to solve these problems. We are involved now in the Congo in a very difficult situation. We have been unable to secure an implementation of the policy which we have supported. We are involved in a good many other areas. We are trying to see if a solution can be found to the struggle between Pakistan and India, with whom we want to maintain friendly relations. Yet they are unable to come to an agreement. There is a limitation, in other words, upon the power of the United States to bring about solutions.

I think our people get awfully impatient and maybe fatigued and tired, and saying "We have been carrying this burden for seventeen years; can we lay it down?" We can't lay it down, and I don't see how we are going to lay it down in this century.

So that I would say that the problems are more difficult than I had imagined them to be. The responsibilities placed on the United States are greater than I imagined them to be, and there are greater limitations upon our ability to bring about a favorable

This "Conversation with President Kennedy" was broadcast on December 17, 1962.

134

result than I had imagined them to be. And I think that is probably true of anyone who becomes President, because there is such a
difference between those who advise or speak or legislate, and between the man who must select from the various alternatives proposed and say that this shall be the policy of the United States. It
is much easier to make the speeches than it is to finally make the
judgments, because unfortunately your advisers are frequently divided. If you take the wrong course, and on occasion I have, the
President bears the burden of the responsibility quite rightly. The
advisers may move on to new advice.

MR. LAWRENCE: Well, Mr. President, that brings up a point that
has always interested me. How does a President go about making
a decision, like Cuba, for example?

THE PRESIDENT. The most recent one was hammered out really
on policy and decision over a period of five or six days. During that
period, the fifteen people more or less who were directly consulted
frequently changed their view, because whatever action we took had
so many disadvantages to it, and each action that we took raised
the prospect that it might escalate with the Soviet Union into a
nuclear war. Finally, however, I think a general consensus developed,
and certainly seemed after all alternatives were examined, that the
course of action that we finally adopted was the right one.

Now, when I talked to members of the Congress, several of
them suggested a different alternative, when we confronted them
on that Monday with the evidence. My feeling is that if they had
gone through the five-day period we had gone through in looking at
the various alternatives, the advantages and disadvantages of action,
they probably would have come out the same way that we did. I
think that we took the right one. If we had had to act on Wednes-
day in the first twenty-four hours, I don't think probably we would
have chosen as prudently as we finally did, a quarantine against the
use of offensive weapons.

In addition, that had much more power than we first thought it
did, because I think the Soviet Union was very reluctant to have
us stop ships which carried with them a good deal of their highly
secret and sensitive material. One of the reasons I think that the
Soviet Union withdrew the IL-28's was because we were carrying on
very intensive low-level photography. Now, no one would have
guessed, probably, that that would have been such a harassment.
Mr. Castro could not permit us to indefinitely continue widespread
flights over his island at 200 feet every day, and yet he knew if he
shot down one of our planes, that then it would bring back a much
more serious reprisal on him. So it is very difficult to always make
judgments here about what the effect will be of our decisions on

other countries. In this case, it seems to me that we did pick the right one; in Cuba of 1961 we picked the wrong one.

GEORGE E. HERMAN, Columbia Broadcasting System: I would like to go back to the question of the consensus and your relationship to the consensus. You have said and the Constitution says that the decision can be made only by the President.

THE PRESIDENT. Well, you know that old story about Abraham Lincoln and the Cabinet. He says, "All in favor, say 'aye,'" and the whole Cabinet voted "aye," and then, "All opposed, 'no,'" and Lincoln voted "no," and he said, "The vote is no." So that naturally the Constitution places the responsibility on the President. There was some disagreement with the course we finally adopted, but the course we finally adopted had the advantage of permitting other steps if this one was unsuccessful. In other words, we were starting in a sense at a minimum place. Then if that were unsuccessful, we could have gradually stepped it up until we had gone into a much more massive action, which might have become necessary if the first step had been unsuccessful. I would think that the majority finally came to accept that, though at the beginning there was a much sharper division. And after all, this was very valuable, because the people who were involved had particular responsibilities of their own; Mr. McNamara, Secretary of Defense, who therefore had to advise me on the military capacity of the United States in that area, the Secretary of State, who had to advise on the attitude of the OAS and NATO. So that in my opinion the majority came to accept the course we finally took. It made it much easier. In the Cuba of 1961 the advice of those who were brought in on the executive branch was also unanimous, and the advice was wrong. And I was responsible. So that finally it comes down that no matter how many advisers you have, frequently they are divided, and the President must finally choose.

The other point is something that President Eisenhower said to me on January 19th. He said "There are no easy matters that will ever come to you as President. If they are easy, they will be settled at a lower level." So that the matters that come to you as President are always the difficult matters, and matters that carry with them large implications. So this contributes to some of the burdens of the office of the Presidency, which other Presidents have commented on.

SANDER VANOCUR, National Broadcasting Company: Mr. President, during the Cuban crisis, there was some problem that you are apparently familiar with and bored with by now, about the possibility of a President talking in very private and secret conversations with his advisers, and that somehow leaking out. Do you think that this is going to inhibit the free, frank flow of advice that every President has to have?

THE PRESIDENT. No, I think it is unfortunate there are that sort of conversations, but there are what—1300 reporters accredited to the White House alone? There are I suppose 100 or 150 people who are familiar with what goes on in the Security Council meetings in one way or another. You have the people who are actually there. Then you have got the others who are given instructions as a result of the decisions there, and I suppose people do talk. And then as I said at the time of the Cuban disaster in April of 1961 that success has a hundred fathers and defeat is an orphan. I suppose when something goes well, there is more tendency to talk at all levels, and frequently the reports are inaccurate. I would say the security is pretty good at the National Security Council. It is unfortunate when it is breached.

MR. VANOCUR: Is it true that during your first year, sir, you would get on the phone personally to the State Department and try to get a response to some inquiry that had been made?

THE PRESIDENT. Yes, I still do that when I can, because I think there is a great tendency in government to have papers stay on desks too long, and it seems to me that is really one function. After all, the President can't administer a department, but at least he can be a stimulant.

MR. VANOCUR: Do you recall any response that you received from somebody who was not suspecting a phone call in the State Department, any specific response somebody made to you?

THE PRESIDENT. No, they always respond. They always say "yes." It takes a little while to get it. You know, after I met Mr. Khrushchev in Vienna and they gave us an aide memoire, it took me many weeks to get our answer out through the State Department coordinated with the British, the French, and the Germans. It took much too long. Now, it seems to me we have been able to speed it up, but this is a constant problem in various departments. There are so many interests that are involved in any decision. No matter whether the decision is about Africa or Asia, it involves the Europe desk, it involves the desk of the place, it involves the Defense Department, it might involve the CIA, it frequently involves the Treasury, it might involve the World Bank, it involves the United Nations delegation. So it seems to me that one of the functions of the President is to try to have it move with more speed. Otherwise you can wait while the world collapses.

MR. VANOCUR: You once said that you were reading more and

enjoying it less. Are you still as avid a newspaper reader, magazine—
I remember those of us who traveled with you on the campaign, a
magazine wasn't safe around you.

THE PRESIDENT. Oh, yes. No, no, I think it is invaluable, even
though it may cause you—it is never pleasant to be reading things
that are not agreeable news, but I would say that it is an invaluable
arm of the Presidency, as a check really on what is going on in the
administration, and more things come to my attention that cause
me concern or give me information. So I would think that Mr.
Khrushchev operating a totalitarian system which has many advantages as far as being able to move in secret, and all the rest—there
is a terrific disadvantage not having the abrasive quality of the press
applied to you daily, to an administration, even though we never
like it, and even though we wish they didn't write it, and even
though we disapprove, there isn't any doubt that we could not do
the job at all in a free society without a very very active press.

Now, on the other hand, the press has the responsibility not to
distort things for political purposes, not to just take some news in
order to prove a political point. It seems to me their obligation is
to be as tough as they can on the administration but do it in a way
which is directed towards getting as close to the truth as they can
get and not merely because of some political motivation.

MR. LAWRENCE: Mr. President, in the light of the election returns, which at the congressional level at least were certainly a defeat for the Republican hopes, how do you measure your chances
for significant success domestically in the Congress just ahead?

THE PRESIDENT. Well, I think we will be about in the same position as the last two years. As I say, what we have that is controversial will be very closely contested.

MR. LAWRENCE: Did the complexion of the House change a little
bit by these shifts?

THE PRESIDENT. I would say slightly against us more than it was.
We are not in quite as good shape as we were for the last two years,
but we are about where we were the last two years, which means
that every vote will be three or four votes either way, winning or
losing.

MR. LAWRENCE: Do you have a very crucial vote at the outset on
this Rules Committee fight again, do you think?

THE PRESIDENT. I hope that the Rules Committee is kept to its
present number, because we can't function if it isn't. We are through
if we lose—if they try to change the rules. Nothing controversial
in that case would come to the floor of the Congress. Our whole
program in my opinion would be emasculated.

MR. LAWRENCE: As a young Congressman, sir, you voted to impose a two-term limitation on Presidents. Now that you have held the office for a while, and also observed its effect on President Eisenhower's second term, would you repeat that vote, even if the amendment did not apply to yourself?

THE PRESIDENT. Yes, I would. I would. I know the conditions were special in '47, but I think eight years is enough, and I am not sure that a President, in my case if I were re-elected, that you are at such a disadvantage. There are not many jobs. That is not the power of the Presidency—patronage—at all. They are filled in the first months. Most of those jobs belong to the members of the Congress, anyway. So patronage is not a factor. I think there are many other powers of the Presidency that run in the second term as well as the first. . . . The fact is, President Eisenhower has great influence today in the Republican Party, and therefore in the country, and has great influence in foreign policy, and he does not even hold office. In some ways his influence is greater to some degree. So that the same is really also true of President Truman and President Hoover. I don't think that it depends—the influence of a President is still substantial in his second term, though I haven't had a second term—I think it is.

MR. VANOCUR: Mr. President, on that point, much of your program still remains to be passed by the Congress. There are some people who say that you either do it in the next two years, or it won't be done, should you be elected to a second term. Do you share that point of view?

THE PRESIDENT. No. In the first place, I think we have got a lot by. I was looking at what we set out to do in January of '61 the other day, and on taxes, and on social security, welfare changes, area redevelopment, minimum wage, Peace Corps, the Alliance for Progress, the Disarmament Agency, and strengthening the defenses and strengthening our space program—we did all those things, the trade bill, not perhaps to the extent in every case of our original proposal, but substantial progress. I think we can do some more the next two years. I would think there are going to be new problems if I were re-elected in 1965, and I don't think—I don't look at the second term as necessarily a decline. I don't think that at all. In fact, I think you know much more about the position.

It is a tremendous change to go from being a Senator to being President. In the first months, it is very difficult. But I have no reason to believe that a President with the powers of this office and the responsibilities placed on it, if he has a judgment that some things need to be done, I think he can do it just as well the second time as the first, depending of course on the makeup of the Congress. The fact is I think the Congress looks more powerful sitting

here than it did when I was there in the Congress. But that is because when you are in Congress you are one of a hundred in the
Senate or one of 435 in the House, so that the power is so divided.
But from here I look at a Congress, and I look at the collective
power of the Congress, particularly the bloc action, and it is a substantial power. . . .

MR. LAWRENCE: Mr. President, is your problem of getting an
education bill through this year made more difficult by the events
at Oxford, Mississippi, and the use of federal troops there?

THE PRESIDENT. Yes, I think so . . . this is a case of where we
have come very close, and President Eisenhower came close, and we
came close once, we got a bill through the House—through the
Senate, almost through the House—and we didn't get it. Then another try for higher education through the Senate and the House,
and then it failed—the conference failed. Now, Oxford, Mississippi,
which has made this whole question of the federal government and
education more sensitive, in some parts of the country I suppose
that is going to be a factor against us. I don't really know what
other role they would expect the President of the United States to
play. The court made up of Southern judges determined it was according to the Constitution that Mr. Meredith go to the University
of Mississippi. The Governor of Mississippi opposed it, and there
was rioting against Mr. Meredith, which endangered his life. We
sent in marshals, and after all, 150 or 160 marshals were wounded
in one way or another out of four or five hundred, and at least
three-fourths of the marshals were from the South themselves. Then
we sent in troops when it appeared that the marshals were going
to be overrun. I don't think that anybody who looks at the situation can think we could possibly do anything else. We couldn't
possibly do anything else. But on the other hand, I recognize that
it has caused a lot of bitterness against me and against the national
government in Mississippi and other parts, and though they expect
me to carry out my oath under the Constitution and that is what
we are going to do. But it does make it more difficult to pass an
education bill. . . .

MR. VANOCUR: Do you think we could turn for a moment to this
subject of the President's responsibility in foreign affairs? Now, when
some congressmen disagreed with your course of action over Cuba
on that Monday, the responsibility you have by the Constitution
in this is very clear, but in domestic matters the responsibility is
divided. How do you use the Presidency, in Theodore Roosevelt's
phrase "the bully pulpit," to move these men who really are kind
of barons and sovereigns in their own right up there on the Hill?

Have you any way to move them toward a course of action which you think is imperative?

THE PRESIDENT. Well, the Constitution and the development of the Congress all give advantage to delay. It is very easy to defeat a bill in the Congress. It is much more difficult to pass one. To go through a committee, say the Ways and Means Committee of the House subcommittee and get a majority vote, the full committee and get a majority vote, go to the Rules Committee and get a rule, go to the Floor of the House and get a majority, start over again in the Senate, subcommittee and full committee, and in the Senate there is unlimited debate, so you can never bring a matter to a vote if there is enough determination on the part of the opponents, even if they are a minority, to go through the Senate with the bill. And then unanimously get a conference between the House and Senate to adjust the bill, or if one member objects, to have it go back through the Rules Committee, back through the Congress, and have this done on a controversial piece of legislation where powerful groups are opposing it, that is an extremely difficult task. So that the struggle of a President who has a program to move it through the Congress, particularly when the seniority system may place particular individuals in key positions who may be wholly unsympathetic to your program, and may be, even though they are members of your own party, in political opposition to the President—this is a struggle which every President who has tried to get a program through has had to deal with. After all, Franklin Roosevelt was elected by the largest majority in history in 1936, and he got his worst defeat a few months afterwards in the Supreme Court bill.

So that they are two separate offices and two separate powers, the Congress and the Presidency. There is bound to be conflict, but they must cooperate to the degree that is possible. But that is why no President's program is ever put in. The only time a President's program is put in quickly and easily is when the program is insignificant. But if it is significant and affects important interest and is controversial, therefore, then there is a fight, and the President is never wholly successful.

MR. VANOCUR: Mr. President, which is the better part of wisdom, to take a bill which is completely emasculated, that you had great interest in and accept it, or accept its defeat in the hope of building up public support for it at a later time?

THE PRESIDENT. Well, I would say given the conditions you described, I think it would be better to accept the defeat, but usually what has happened, and what has happened to us in the last two years, a good many of our bills passed in reasonable position, not the way we sent them up, but after all, the Congress has its own will and its own feelings and its own judgment, and they are close to the people. The whole House of Representatives has just been elected. So that it is quite natural that they will have a different perspective than I may have. So I would say that what we ought to do is to do the best we can. But if it is completely emasculated, then there is no sense in having a shadow of success and not the substance.

MR. LAWRENCE: Mr. President, in the exercise of presidential power, and I think perhaps the best-known case and the most widely talked about was your rollback of steel prices after they had been announced by the steel companies, some people have suggested that in retrospect that perhaps you would not have acted so vigorously. Is there any truth in this suggestion?

THE PRESIDENT. I must say it would have been a very serious situation though I don't like to rake over old fires, I think it would have been a serious situation if I had not attempted with all my influence to try to get a rollback, because there was an issue of good faith involved. The steel union had accepted the most limited settlement that they had had since the end of the second war, they had accepted it three or four months ahead, they did it in part, I think, because I said that we could not afford another inflationary spiral, that it would affect our competitive position abroad, so they signed up. Then when their last contract was signed, which was the Friday or Saturday before, then steel put its prices up immediately. It seemed to me that the question of good faith was involved, and that if I had not attempted, after asking the unions to accept the noninflationary settlement, if I had not attempted to use my influence to have the companies hold their prices stable, I think the union could have rightfully felt that they had been misled. In my opinion it would have endangered the whole bargaining between labor and management, would have made it impossible for us to exert any influence from the public point of view in the future on these great labor-management disputes which do affect the public interest. So I have no regrets. The fact is, we were successful.

Now, supposing we had tried and made a speech about it, and then failed. I would have thought that would have been an awful setback to the office of the Presidency. Now, I just think, looking back on it, that I would not change it at all. There is no sense in raising hell, and then not being successful. There is no sense in putting the office of the Presidency on the line on an issue, and then being defeated. Now, an unfortunate repercussion of that was the strong feeling that the government might interfere in a good many labor-management matters, or that it might interfere in the whole question of the free enterprise system. It was regrettable that that general conclusion was drawn in this particular incident. Given the problem that I had on that Tuesday night, I must say I think we had to do everything we could to get it reversed. . . .

MR. VANOCUR: Mr. President, have you noted since you have been in office that this terrible responsibility for the fate of mankind has—notwithstanding the differences that divide you—drawn you and Mr. Khrushchev somewhat closer in this joint sense of responsibility? He seems to betray it, especially in his speech to the Supreme Soviet earlier.

THE PRESIDENT. I think in that speech this week he showed his awareness of the nuclear age. But of course, the Cuban effort has made it more difficult for us to carry out any successful negotiations, because this was an effort to materially change the balance of power, it was done in secret, steps were taken really to deceive us by every means they could, and they were planning in November to open to the world the fact that they had these missiles so close to the United States; not that they were intending to fire them, because if they were going to get into a nuclear struggle, they have their own missiles in the Soviet Union. But it would have politically changed the balance of power. It would have appeared to, and appearances contribute to reality. So it is going to be some time before it is possible for us to come to any real understandings with Mr. Khrushchev. But I do think his speech shows that he realizes how dangerous a world we live in.

The real problem is the Soviet desire to expand their power and influence. If Mr. Khrushchev would concern himself with the real interests of the people of the Soviet Union, that they have a higher standard of living, to protect his own security, there is no real reason why the United States and the Soviet Union, separated by so many thousands of miles of land and water, both rich countries, both with very energetic people, should not be able to live in peace. But it is this constant determination which the Chinese show in the most militant form, and which the Soviets also have shown, that they will not settle for that kind of a peaceful world, but must settle for a Communist world. That is what makes the real danger, the combination of these two systems in conflict around the world in a nuclear age is what makes the sixties so dangerous.

MR. VANOCUR: Ambassador Kennan, who has some knowledge of the Soviet Union, wrote in one of his recent books that what you are dealing with here is a conditioned state of mind, that there is no misunderstanding here, that the only thing the Soviets really understand is when you present them with a set of facts and say to them, "This is what we are going to do." This they understand. Have you found that there is any way to break through to Mr. Khrushchev, to make him really aware that you are quite sincere and determined about what you say, sir, or is this a total——

THE PRESIDENT. Well, it is difficult. I think, looking back on Cuba, what is of concern is the fact that both governments were so far out of contact, really. I don't think that we expected that he would put the missiles in Cuba, because it would have seemed such an imprudent action for him to take, as it was later proved. Now, he obviously must have thought that he could do it in secret and that the United States would accept it. So that he did not judge our intentions accurately.

Well, now, if you look at the history of this century, where World War I really came through a series of misjudgments of the intentions of others, certainly World War II, where Hitler thought that he could seize Poland, that the British might not fight, and if they fought, after the defeat of Poland they might not continue to fight, Korea, where obviously the North Koreans did not think we were going to come in, and Korea, when we did not think the Chinese were going to come in, when you look at all those misjudgments which brought on war, and then you see the Soviet Union and the United States so far separated in their beliefs, we believing in a world of independent sovereign and different diverse nations, they believing in a monolithic Communist world, and you put the nuclear equation into that struggle, that is what makes this, as I said before, such a dangerous time, and that we must proceed with firmness and also with the best information we can get, and also with care. There is nothing—one mistake can make this whole thing blow up. So that—one major mistake either by Mr. Khrushchev or by us here—so that is why it is much easier to make speeches about some of the things which we ought to be doing, but I think that anybody who looks at the fatality lists on atomic weapons, and realizes that the Communists have a completely twisted view of the United States, and that we don't comprehend them, that is what makes life in the sixties hazardous. . . .

MR. HERMAN: Would you explain, sir, why you said in your toast to Chancellor Adenauer that [Cuba] was a turning point, a new era in history?

THE PRESIDENT. I think it is a climactic period. We have had a number of them. It is not *the*, but it is—after all, Cuba was the first time that the Soviet Union and the United States directly faced each other with the prospect of the use of military forces being used by the United States and the Soviet Union, which could possibly have escalated into a nuclear struggle. That is an important fact. Secondly, the Chinese-Indian struggle, between these two enormous countries, the two largest countries in the world, when the Soviet has devoted so many years to building its policy of friendship with India, the fact that China then attacked them. And third, the relation between the Soviet Union and China, as a result of the Sino-Indian dispute, as a result of the United States dispute with the Soviet Union over Cuba, I would say that that makes this a very important period.

MR. VANOCUR: Sir, how do you as the leader of the Western alliance, of the strongest member nation, how do you get the European countries, which are becoming increasingly more independent, increasingly more prosperous, which is what you said you hoped they would become, how do you get them to follow your lead? Apparently Secretaries McNamara and Rusk have not come back with an altogether satisfactory report from the NATO meeting, the Europeans seem unwilling to build conventional forces. Do you have any great power to determine——

THE PRESIDENT. No, in the first place you can do your part. We are doing our part. We have—our troops in Western Europe are the best equipped, we have six divisions, which is about a fourth of all of the divisions on the Western front. They are the best equipped. They can fight tomorrow, which is not true of most of the other units. So we are doing our part there, and we are also providing the largest naval force in the world. We are also providing the nuclear force in the world, and we are also carrying out the major space program for the free world, as well as carrying the whole burden in South Vietnam. So the United States is more than doing its part. We hope Western Europe will make a greater effort on its own, both in developing conventional forces, and in assistance to the underdeveloped world.

Now, we can't force them to do it. We can't say, "Well, if you won't do it, we are going to withdraw our forces and leave Europe naked." But I think the United States has done pretty well in carrying its burdens, and we hope that Western Europe, now that it is prosperous, will do its part. . . .

MR. VANOCUR: Mr. President, back before you were elected, your father used to have a favorite story he told reporters. He asked you once why do you want the job, and he cited the reasons why you shouldn't want it, and you apparently gave him an answer—I don't know whether it satisfied him, but apparently you satisfied yourself. Would you give him the same answer today after serving in this office for two years?

THE PRESIDENT. Oh, you mean that somebody is going to do it?

MR. VANOCUR: Yes, sir.

THE PRESIDENT. Yes. I think that there are a lot of satisfactions to the Presidency, particularly, as I say, we are all concerned as citizens and as parents and all the rest, with all the problems we have been talking about tonight. They are all the problems which if I was not the President, I would be concerned about as a father or as a citizen. So at least you have an opportunity to do something about them. And if what you do is useful and successful, then of course that is a great satisfaction. When as a result of a decision of yours, failure comes or you are unsuccessful, then of course that is a great setback. But I must say after being here for two years, and having the experience of the Presidency, and there is no experience you can get that can possibly prepare you adequately for the Presidency, I must say that I have a good deal of hope for the United States. Just because I think that this country, which as I say criticizes itself and is criticized around the world, 180 million people, for seventeen years, really for more than that, for almost twenty years, have been the great means of defending first the world against the Nazi threat, and since then against the Communist threat, and if it were not for us, the Communists would be dominant in the world today, and because of us, we are in a strong position. Now, I think that is a pretty good record for a country with 6 per cent of the world's population, which is very reluctant to take on these burdens. I think we ought to be rather pleased with ourselves this Christmas.

☆

LYNDON JOHNSON: *Comments on the Presidency*

[The Presidency] is a much tougher job from the inside than I thought it was from the outside.

I have watched it since Mr. Hoover's days, and I realized the responsibilities it carried, and the obligations of leadership that were there, and the decisions that had to be made, and the awesome responsibilities of the office.

But I must say that, when I started having to make those decisions and started hearing from the Congress, the Presidency looked a little different when you are in the Presidency than it did when you are in the Congress, and vice versa. . . .

Thomas Jefferson said the second office of the land was an honorable and easy one. The Presidency was a splendid misery. But I found great interest in serving in both offices, and it carries terrific and tremendous and awesome responsibilities, but I am proud of this nation and I am so grateful that I could have an opportunity that I have had in America that I want to give my life seeing that the opportunity is perpetuated for others.

I am so proud of our system of government, of our free enterprise, where our incentive system and our men who head our big industries are willing to get up at daylight and get to bed at midnight to offer employment and create new jobs for people, where our men working there will try to get decent wages but will sit across the table and not act like cannibals, but will negotiate and reason things out together.

Lyndon B. Johnson, the 36th President of the United States (1963–1969), made these comments during a television interview on March 15, 1964; at a reception for members of the American Society of Newspaper Editors on April 17, 1964; at a campaign rally in Wilkes-Barre, Pennsylvania on October 14, 1964; and at a meeting of the National Association of Broadcasters on April 1, 1968.

I am so happy to be a part of a system where the average per capita income is in excess of $200 per month, when there are only six nations in the entire world that have as much as $80 per month, and while the Soviet Union has three times as many tillable acres of land as we have and a population that's in excess of ours and a great many resources that we don't have, that if properly developed would exceed our potential in water and oil and so forth, nevertheless we have one thing they don't have and that is our system of private enterprise, free enterprise, where the employer, hoping to make a little profit, the laborer, hoping to justify his wages, can get together and make a better mousetrap.

They have developed this into the most powerful and leading nation in the world, and I want to see it preserved. And I have an opportunity to do something about it as President.

And I may not be a great President, but as long as I am here, I am going to try to be a good President and do my dead-level best to see this system preserved, because when the final chips are down it is not going to be the number of people we have or the number of acres or the number of resources that win; the thing that is going to make us win is our system of government.

☆

. . . One of the hardest tasks that a President faces is to keep the time scale of his decisions always in mind and to try to be the President of all the people.

He is not simply responsible to an immediate electorate, either. He knows over the long stretch of time how great can be the repercussions of all that he does or that he fails to do, and over that span of time the President always has to think of America as a continuing community.

He has to try to see how his decisions will affect not only today's citizens, but their children and their children's children unto the third and the fourth generation. He has to try to peer into the future, and he has to prepare for that future.

If the policies he advocates lack this dimension of depth and this dimension of staying power, he may gain this or that advantage in the short term, but he can set the country on a false course and profit today at the expense of all the world tomorrow. So it is this solemn and this most difficult responsibility, and it is always hard to interpret confidently the future patterns of the world.

There are always critics around imploring the President to stick to the facts and not to go crystal-gazing. Some of them tell me to try to keep my feet on the ground, if not my head in the sand.

But this is the point: The facts include today, the overwhelming, built-in, irresistible forces of change that have been unleashed by modern science and technology. And the very facts dissolve and re-group as we look into them.

To make no predictions is to be sure to be wrong. Whatever else is or is not that certain in our dynamic world, there is one thing that is very sure: Tomorrow will be drastically different from today. Yet it is in all of these tomorrows that we and our children and our children's children are going to be forced to live. We have to try to see that pattern and we have to try to prepare for it.

The President of this country, more than any other single man in the world, must grapple with the course of events and the directions of history. What he must try to do, try to do always, is to build for tomorrow in the immediacy of today.

For if we can, the President, and the Congress, and you leaders of the communities throughout the Nation, will have made their mark in history. Somehow we must ignite a fire in the breast of this land, a flaming spirit of adventure that soars beyond the ordinary and the contented, and really demands greatness from our society, and demands achievement from our government. . . .

The world is no longer the world that your fathers and mine once knew. Once it was dominated by the balance of power. Today, it is diffused and emergent. But though most of the world struggles fit-fully to assert its own initiative, the people of the world look to this land for inspiration. Two-thirds of the teeming masses of humanity, most of them in their tender years under forty, are decreeing that they are not going to take it without food to sustain their body and a roof over their head.

And from our science and our technology, from our compassion and from our tolerance, from our unity and from our heritage, we stand uniquely on the threshold of a high adventure of leadership by example and by precept. "Not by might, nor by power, but by my spirit, saith the Lord." From our Jewish and Christian heritage, we draw the image of the God of all mankind, who will judge his children not by their prayers and by their pretensions, but by their mercy to the poor and their understanding of the weak.

We cannot cancel that strain and then claim to speak as a Christian society. To visit the widow and the fatherless in their affliction is still pure religion and undefiled. I tremble for this Nation. I tremble for our people if at the time of our greatest prosperity we turn our back on the moral obligations of our deepest faith. If the face we turn to this aspiring, laboring world is a face of indifference and contempt, it will rightly rise up and strike us down.

Believe me, God is not mocked. We reap as we sow. Our God is still a jealous God, jealous of his righteousness, jealous of his mercy, jealous for the last of the little ones who went unfed while the rich sat down to eat and rose up to play. And unless my administration profits the present and provides the foundation for a better life for all humanity, not just now but for generations to come, I shall have failed. . . .

☆

. . . I think I know some of the things that Americans want. They want their President to be a source of leadership and responsibility. They know that a President who strides forward to do the people's business is a bulwark against the decline and chaos in this country. They know that a President who is willing to move ahead, whose means are just, whose ends are democratic, can be the difference between national stagnation and national progress.

And the people want progress. They want to keep moving.

Americans know that the Presidency belongs to all the people. And they want the President to act and be President of all the people.

Something else is very clear. The source of the President's authority is the people. A President who refuses to go out among the people, who refuses to be judged by the people, who is unwilling to lay his case before the people, can never be President of all the people.

The people want to see their President in person. They want to hear firsthand what he believes. They want to decide if he can act for them.

And unless the President goes to the people, unless he visits and talks with them, unless he senses how they respond as he discusses issues with them, he cannot do the President's job. The voice of the people will be lost among the clamor of divisions and diversities, and the Presidency will not become a clear beacon of national purpose.

As long as I hold it, I will keep the office of President always close to all the people. I think I know what it is the people want, and I make that as a solemn pledge. . . .

☆

. . . The office of the Presidency is the only office in this land of all the people.

Whatever may be the personal wishes or the preferences of any man who holds it, a President of all the people can afford no thought of self. At no time and in no way and for no reason can a President allow the integrity or the responsibility or the freedom of the office ever to be compromised or diluted or destroyed, because when you destroy it, you destroy yourselves.

I hope and I pray that by not allowing the Presidency to be involved in division and deep partisanship I shall be able to pass on to my successor a stronger office, strong enough to guard and defend all the people against all the storms that the future may bring us.

☆

ON LYNDON JOHNSON: *Testimony of Undersecretary of State Katzenbach on the President's Power to Conduct the War in Vietnam*

J. W. FULBRIGHT, Chairman (Senate Foreign Relations Committee): Does the department support or oppose the enactment of Senate Resolution 151? [The resolution stated that it is the sense of the Senate "that a national commitment by the United States to a foreign power necessarily and exclusively results from affirmative action taken by the executive and legislative branches of the United States government through means of a treaty, convention, or other legislative instrumentality specifically intended to give effect to such a commitment."]

MR. KATZENBACH: I could not support the resolution, Mr. Chairman, because it seems to me that it tries to do precisely what the Founding Fathers of this country declined to do in writing the Constitution, and that it purports to take a position, through a Senate resolution, on matters that it seems to me have worked out successfully, have worked out well in terms of distribution of functions between the executive branch and the Congress, and it seems to me that it could be interpreted to seek to join with the President on those matters which I think the President, in his capacity of conducting foreign relations of the United States has the constitutional authority to do. So in short I see no need for it.

Q. Well, let us see if we can develop a few of the specific points.

Nicholas de B. Katzenbach, Undersecretary of State in the Johnson Administration, presented this testimony at Hearings of the Senate Foreign Relations Committee on August 17, 1967. From *The Congressional Record*, August 21, 1967, pp. 11882–11884.

. . . You say: "his"—that is the President—"his is a responsibility born of the need for speed and decisiveness in an emergency. His is the responsibility of controlling and directing all the external aspects of the nation's power."

How do you fit this in with the constitutional provision as to the declaration of war by the Congress?

Yesterday we had one of the nation's leading authorities, Professor [Ruhl] Bartlett. He interprets the Constitution as meaning that the Congress has the exclusive power to initiate war.

A. I believe that the Constitution makes it very clear that on a declaration of war that it is the function of Congress to declare. I believe our history has been that the wars that we have declared have been declared at the initiative and instance of the executive.

The function of the Congress is one to declare. It is not one to wage, not one to conduct, but one simply to declare. That is the function of Congress as expressed in the Constitution.

The use of the phrase "to declare war" as it was used in the Constitution of the United States had a particular meaning in terms of those events, in terms of the practices which existed at that time, and which existed really until the United Nations organization, but it existed for a long time after that, to build on the structure that war was recognized to be an instrument of that policy, not in the climate today, which rejects that, which rejects the idea of aggression, which rejects the idea of conquest. It came in that context.

Now, it came for a function. As you rightly say, it was recognized by the Founding Fathers that the President might have to take emergency action to protect the security of the United States, but that if there was going to be a use of the armed forces of the United States, that was a decision which Congress should check the executive on, which Congress should support. It was for that reason that the phrase was inserted in the Constitution.

It would not, I think, correctly reflect the very limited objectives of the United States with respect to Vietnam. It would not correctly reflect our efforts there, what we are trying to do, the reasons why we are there. To use an outmoded phraseology, to declare war.

Q. You think it is outmoded to declare war?

A. In this kind of a context I think the expression of declaring a war is one that has become outmoded in the international arena, that is not correctly reflected. But I think there is, Mr. Chairman, an obligation on the part of the executive to give Congress the opportunity, which that language was meant to reflect in the Constitution of the United States, to give the Congress of the United States an opportunity to express its views with respect to this. In this instance, in the instance if you will of Vietnam, Congress had an opportunity to participate in these decisions. Congress ratified the SEATO treaty by an overwhelming vote, which expressed the security concerns, the general obligation of the United States in accordance with its constitutional process to attempt to preserve order and peace and defense against aggression in Southeast Asia. That was debated, that was discussed, and it was affirmed by two thirds of the Senate, and in fact confirmed by an overwhelming vote.

Q. You are talking about the SEATO treaty?

A. I am talking about the SEATO treaty. That is not all that happened.

Q. You mentioned that as a basis for the Tonkin Gulf resolution?

[The Resolution—approved by Congress on August 7, 1964—read as follows:

Whereas naval units of the Communist regime in Vietnam, in violation of the principles of the charter of the United Nations and of international law, have deliberately and repeatedly attacked United States naval vessels lawfully present in international waters, and have thereby created a serious threat to international peace;

Whereas these attacks are part of a deliberate and systematic campaign of aggression that the Communist regime in North Vietnam has been waging against its neighbors and the nations joined with them in the collective defense of their freedom;

Whereas the United States is assisting the peoples of Southeast Asia to protect their freedom and has no territorial, military, or political ambitions in that area, but desires only that these peoples should be left in peace to work out their own destinies in their own way;

Now, therefore, be it resolved, by the Senate and House of Representatives of the United States of America in Congress assembled:

Sec. 1. The Congress approves and supports the determination of the President, as Commander in Chief, to take all necessary measures to repel any armed attack against the forces of the United States and to prevent further aggression.

Sec. 2. The United States regards as vital to its national interest and to world peace the maintenance of international peace and security in Southeast Asia. Consonant with the Constitution and the Charter of the United Nations and in accordance with its obligations under the Southeast Asia Collective Defense Treaty, the United States is, therefore, prepared, as the President determines, to take all necessary steps, including the use of armed force, to assist any member or protocol state of the Southeast

Asia Collective Defense Treaty requesting assistance in defense of its freedom.

Sec. 3. This resolution shall expire when the President shall determine that the peace and security of the area is reasonably assured by international conditions created by action of the United Nations or otherwise, except that it may be terminated earlier by concurrent resolution of the Congress.]

A. Congress participated in that. As the situation there deteriorated, as American ships were attacked in the Tonkin Gulf, the President of the United States came back to Congress to seek the views of Congress with respect to what should be done in that area and with respect to the use of the military of the United States in that area, and on those resolutions Congress had the opportunity to participate and did participate. The combination of the two, it seems to me, fully fulfills the obligation of the executive in a situation of this kind to participate with the Congress, to give the Congress a full and effective voice, the functional equivalent, the constitutional obligation expressed in the provision of the Constitution with respect to declaring war.

Q. Well, it is quite true, not only literally, but in the spirit of it. You haven't requested and you don't intend to request a declaration of war, as I understand it.

A. As I explained—that is correct, Mr. Chairman, but didn't that resolution authorize the President to use the armed forces of the United States in whatever way was necessary? Didn't it? What could a declaration of war have done that would have given the President more authority and a clearer voice of the Congress of the United States than that did?

Q. The circumstances partook of an emergency, as an attack upon the United States, which could fall within the procedures or the principles developed in the last century of the temporary repelling of attacks as opposed to a full-fledged war, which we are in, and he [Professor Bartlett] was, I thought, quite critical of that, and the circumstances were such that we were asked to act upon this resolution very quickly. As a matter of fact, he [the President] had already, before the resolution, had responded to the attack by I think an attack upon the sources of the PT-boats.

It has been interpreted as equivalent to a declaration of war. I think this is a very critical difference as to how we regard it.

A. It seems to me that if your complaint is the drafting of the [Tonkin] Resolution of Congress, it ill becomes—

Q. That resolution was drafted by the executive and sent up here.

We didn't draft it, but we did, under the impeller of the emergency, accept it.

A. Mr. Chairman, it wasn't accepted without consideration.

Q. Yes, it was largely without any consideration.

A. Mr. Chairman, whether a resolution of that kind is or is not, does or does not perform the functions similar to a declaration of war must indeed depend upon what the language of that resolution is and what it says. Now the language of that resolution, Mr. Chairman, is a very broad language. . . . It was explained in the debate. You explained it, Mr. Chairman, as head of this committee.

Q. But I misinterpreted it.

A. You explained that bill and you made it clear as it could be what the Congress was committing itself to.

Q. I not only didn't make it clear, obviously, it wasn't clear to me, because I did make statements that I thought this did not entail nor contemplate any change in the then existing policy, and of course there has been great change in it.

It is the waging of war that really concerns us, together with commitments which are made which seem to entail and may eventually entail the waging of war. In this Tonkin Bay, the Tonkin Gulf Resolution, I think it illustrates this distinction that I think should be made clear between repelling of an attack and the waging of war as a matter of broad policy, and I think there was a certain confusion under the circumstances at that moment that at least helped in influencing the Congress in making the approval—

A. Mr. Chairman, the President didn't need such a broad authorization to repel an attack upon American ships in the Tonkin Bay.

Q. That is right.

A. And that isn't what the resolution says—you have authority to repel an attack against ships in the Tonkin Bay. The resolution goes on and that was the reason for the resolution and I do not think it is correct to characterize that resolution as something simply dealing with some PT-boats attacking. That was not the way you presented it, Mr. Chairman, it was not the way the Administration presented it. It was not the way the Congress understood it and it wasn't what it said.

Q. It seems to me that if the Administration had taken the position at the time that this was the equivalent of a declaration of war, in pursuance of the SEATO treaty, it might have made a difference. But it was a fact that at the time it was under consideration, the Administration position was it was not based upon the SEATO treaty. It was based upon repelling the attack, is that not so?

A. That is correct in the sense that at the time of that resolution the evidence with respect to the invasion of South Vietnam, the aggression of North Vietnam against South Vietnam was not so clear.

This is not the kind of thing that we are doing there. And I said that I thought that the reason for that was to give the Congress of the United States an opportunity to look at, to examine, to speak upon the use of armed forces of the United States, that that was the purpose of it.

It seems to me it is clear as anything can be to anyone who reads that resolution and reads the debate.

Q. Mr. Secretary, I don't wish to keep disagreeing with you, but I think it is anything but clear. I think the whole background of the situation then existing, the declarations not only by President Johnson but by President Kennedy before him that in Southeast Asia, in Vietnam, it was not the policy of this country to use American forces, that we were there only to help them. It wasn't our war. That the President shortly thereafter made many statements in which he didn't propose that American men would do the fighting of Asian youths, and so on. He emphasized this. It had been the same statement with President Kennedy, a very similar one.

In other words, the policy as expressed, the general policy, as to waging a war there was against it by the executive themselves. The resolution was in response to an emergency. It wasn't even based as you said upon SEATO, any considered treaty arrangement.

I think in all fairness the circumstances were we were responding to an attack. As you have said, the President didn't need this authority to respond to an attack. And I agree with that, under the previous decision. But we did resolve, we did act and I have said many times I think wrongly, precipitously, without due consideration, to giving authority far beyond that particular attack, that additional authority which the professor described yesterday. This was a mistake.

SENATOR GORE: Mr. Secretary, your presentation lends greater importance to this hearing than I had previously thought was involved. As I understand your statement, it is to the effect that the Tonkin Bay Resolution did in fact grant the broad authority which has been predicated upon it, and that if Congress acted without understanding such import, then that was the fault of the Congress. This may be true.

MR. KATZENBACH: I do not wish to be misunderstood as saying that the Tonkin Resolution was tantamount to a direct declaration of war, because I have given you the reasons why I think the phraseology "declaration of war," the use of that, would make it misunderstood, our objectives there. What I attempted to say was that the

Tonkin Gulf Resolution gave Congress a voice in this, and that they expressed their will and their voice in that.

They expressed that will, Senator, in the language of that resolution in extremely broad terms. They made reference to the obligations under the SEATO treaty, and it said: "The United States is, therefore, prepared as the President determines to take all necessary action, including the use of armed forces, to assist any member or protocol state in the Southeast Asia Collective Defense Treaty requesting assistance in defense of its freedom."

Now, my point in saying this is that that is an expression of congressional will in this regard. It is an authorization to the President, and in my judgment it is as broad an authorization of war so-called as could be in terms of our internal constitutional process.

Q. I accept that clarification. Nevertheless, the fact stands that a resolution was passed which the President has regarded as a commitment on the part of the Congress that, I have heard speak, understood at the time that they were authorizing the commitment of ground troops, combat troops in Vietnam by the President. I regard this as one of the most tragic mistakes in American history. I did not intend to authorize it. Now, I think it is clear that Congress is in large part at fault in not being precise.

The President has now directed planes to bomb targets within seconds of the most populous nation on earth. Do you think that the President should seek authorization of the Congress to undertake such provocation to run such risk of war between the largest industrial nation and the most populous nation in the world?

A. No.

Q. Do you think the Tonkin Bay Resolution is sufficient?

A. I think our obligations under the SEATO treaty referred to in the Tonkin Bay Resolution, the broad language of that resolution, are adequate. But I would make an additional point if I could, Senator.

In any event, when the Congress has authorized, whether by resolution of this kind, whether by declaration of war, however, the use of the armed forces of the United States, I do not believe that the Congress can then proceed, and I think this was very clear in the constitutional base, can then proceed to tell the President what he shall bomb, what he shall not bomb, where he shall dispose his troops, where he shall not.

Q. Mr. Secretary, if I may respectfully suggest, it appears to me that you are saying on the one hand that Congress is at fault in not sufficiently debating, in not drafting its resolution with sufficient precision to exercise its function in the formulation of policy, and in the extension of authority, but on the other hand, when I raise the question of provocation of possible war between two of the world's greatest nations, you say no, Congress should not be that precise.

Now just how should we operate in this field?

A. I see no fault of the Congress in this respect. I do not think there is any lack of precision in that. I think it expresses the will of Congress. I think they did authorize the use of the armed forces.

Q. It seems to me, Mr. Secretary, that you are now in a way of saying that this resolution authorized a war with China.

A. No, I think the resolution is quite precise in what it authorized. . . . Now in the course of that authorization, there can be risks, there can be risks taken. Other people could be involved. You could have that situation arise. It seems to me that it is very clear in what it says, and I am quite convinced that Congress knew what it was doing when it said it.

Q. You hold that this resolution authorized the use of the United States forces to bomb targets in Laos?

A. I think as far as—that would depend very much, Senator, on what was necessary in terms of coming to the aid of South Vietnam, but it also would depend on many of the facts and circumstances because I do not think that the Congress sought to authorize any action unless that action was justified in repelling an aggression.

Q. Will you please respond to the same question, but I use the word "China" instead of "Laos"?

A. I think that the resolution authorized—

Q. You would give the same answer?

A. The necessary defensive measures in this respect. Now it is in defense of South Vietnam. I think that if China were to invade South Vietnam, that that would present a very different factual situation than exists today. I think the limitation on it, Senator, is a limitation on what is necessary and proper in carrying out the statement, the authorization as was made there.

Now, I think there are risks in the situation, and I think the President has been extremely careful in his conduct of this to avoid those risks.

Q. Now, in the event we discovered that Chinese military advisers were in South Vietnam serving as cadres, organizers, assistants in training and advice in combat against our troops, in those circumstances would you interpret the extent of the authority of the Tonkin Resolution with respect to an attack on China?

A. I do not think—it is difficult for me in a hypothetical situation to attempt to deal with a situation like that. My judgment is so clear on it that the President of the United States would not run the risk of further involvement on those facts that it just becomes to me a purely hypothetical question that it would be hard for me to see that anybody could have contemplated and could have discussed under this situation. . . .

Q. You say it would be difficult for you to interpret this resolution in the light of the hypothesis. It was equally difficult for the Congress. I doubt if any congressman could foresee the bombing of targets within ten miles of China. Taking into consideration the speed of supersonic missiles, the provocation which is involved. Therefore, I come back to the thing about which I started. It seems to me that the thrust of your testimony is that it is incumbent upon the Congress hereafter to consider in detail and precision the grant of authority involved in its action.

☆

ON LYNDON JOHNSON: *from* The Exercise of Power
by Rowland Evans and Robert Novak

Unique among American statesmen and political leaders, Lyndon Baines Johnson has been near or at the center of power in Washington for all the great political events of our epoch. He arrived in the Capital in 1931, more than a year before Franklin D. Roosevelt, as a twenty-three-year-old secretary to a right-wing millionaire congressman from Texas. Increasingly, as the years went by and his power grew, he placed his own distinctive touch on each of those events. Among the truly powerful legislative leaders in our history, he is the only one since James Madison who has become the Chief Executive. He succeeded where Henry Clay, Thomas Brackett Reed, and Robert A. Taft failed.

No man in American history became President with a greater relish for power or with more experience in its exercise than did Johnson. Nor did any President assume the office with a prospect so spectacular in its opportunities and so difficult by the very nature of his assumption.

"Men . . . love their martyrs," Dostoevsky wrote, "and honor those whom they have slain." On November 22, 1963, Johnson became President, but it was the martyred John F. Kennedy and the Kennedy legend that men loved. Kennedy left Johnson a plan in domestic affairs that was only partially completed, and this plan, en-

Rowland Evans and Robert Novak are widely syndicated Washington political columnists. This selection is from *Lyndon B. Johnson: The Exercise of Power* (New York: New American Library, 1966), pp. 1–4. Copyright © 1966 by Rowland Evans and Robert Novak. Reprinted by permission of the publisher and the authors.

ergized by a national longing to atone for Kennedy's assassination, gave Johnson his matchless opportunity. With the same grasp of political genius that marked his earlier years as the Senate's Majority Leader, Johnson completed Kennedy's plan. Then, in unprecedented partnership with Congress, he carried it far forward with a plan of his own, the Great Society, a social and economic blueprint for a unified, prosperous America that excited and impressed the American people not only because of its audacious sweep but because so much of it became law.

The difficulty was the memory of Kennedy that still haunted Lyndon Johnson many months after he had been elected President in his own right. Thus, in the late spring of 1966, fully two and a half years after Kennedy's assassination, Johnson called several Senators to the White House to discuss a political matter. The business concluded, Johnson set off on a long monologue about the war in Vietnam. He quoted Senator Wayne Morse of Oregon, his most vitriolic Democratic critic on the war, as having said that "the Great Society is dead." When he heard about that verdict of Morse's, said Johnson, he ordered the Budget Bureau to give him a lengthy memorandum showing the spectacular increases in federal spending for education, health, poverty, and other Great Society programs above the Kennedy years.

The President reached on his desk for the Budget Bureau memorandum, read the statistics to the Senators, and then said: "They say Jack Kennedy had style, but I'm the one who's got the bills passed."

That was a typical Johnson reaction to criticism and it contained a flash of self-revelation, exposing several truths about Lyndon Johnson: his ego, his hypersensitivity, his intensely personal reaction to his critics, his lack of taste in slighting the dead President, and his fierce sense of competition with everybody—including John Kennedy.

But there was another, far different Lyndon Johnson. In February, 1965, the new President dropped in unexpectedly on a birthday luncheon at the Capitol for Senator George Aiken of Vermont, the much-beloved senior Republican of the Senate. All the Senate leaders were there, and for Johnson it was a triumphal homecoming.

"A few months ago," he told his colleagues, "we lost our beloved leader and colleague of many years, Jack Kennedy, in a terrible tragedy. He left partially finished many things he thought were in the best interests of our country. I happened to be called upon to pick up the torch that he had to leave. I want on behalf of this country, and on his behalf—watching us from Heaven—to thank every member here for your help in carrying on some of the things he was leading us toward, especially the leaders at this table. I know he thanks you."

There was nothing contrived in those words. They were, in fact, an essence of the sentiment that marks the other Lyndon Johnson, spoken in the direct and unsophisticated idiom of the Texas hill country. Johnson was *both* men: the detractor of Kennedy and the keeper of Kennedy's memory, and herein lies part of the secret of his command of power. Johnson has shed many tears for himself and he has shed tears for others. Johnson has cursed his friends behind their backs and showered them with presents. Johnson has unmercifully berated his closest White House aides in the presence of others, and has shown infinite tenderness when the occasion fit his mood.

Johnson is bigger than life—bigger in both the good and the bad. It is part of the contradiction that conceals the inner man. He hungers for affection, but his ego constantly intrudes. He preaches humility, but often subverts it with his own exuberant arrogance. In a deliberate exaggeration, one of his admiring counselors says: "90 per cent of what he does is right, and 90 per cent of the way he does it is wrong."

The conflict between objective and performance, between the public posture of the President and the private manipulations of the politician, is the essence of the Johnson paradox. The lofty goal and the hard use of power to achieve it are essential components for any successful Presidency, but Johnson often overstates the goal and overuses his power to achieve it. Sometimes these characteristics have been self-defeating for him; sometimes they have produced greater accomplishments than he had any right to expect.

But the road to those accomplishments has been a jagged one, twisting and turning to fit the shape of his shifting goals and objectives. In the spring of 1966, a friend gently chided Senator Richard B. Russell, the conservative Southern patriarch, about Lyndon Johnson. Why was it, asked the friend, that Lyndon Johnson, the President was so different from the Lyndon Johnson who had been Russell's protégé in the Senate. "I asked him that," Russell replied softly, "and he told me, 'Dick, I'm an older and a wiser man than I was then.' "

As one of the many political patrons of Johnson during his long career, Russell has had an enduring relationship with Johnson sustained by few other men and stretching over nearly two decades. But even Russell has felt the thrust and parry of Johnson's nature, receiving kindness and his scorn almost at the same time. The President telephoned Russell almost every day during Russell's long illness in 1965. But when Russell publicly predicted that Ho Chi Minh, the Communist leader of North Vietnam, would win any honest election in Vietnam, Johnson ridiculed him behind his back in the White

House. With heavy sarcasm, Johnson asked: "Since when did Dick Russell become an expert on elections in Southeast Asia?"

Yet, it was not surprising that Johnson would react harshly, even to an old and enduring friend and patron, on the subject of Vietnam. For the war in Vietnam had confounded his Presidency. It was the worst of all crises ever faced by Johnson. It was natural that Johnson instinctively lashed out at Russell's remarks in a personal fashion, for always, Johnson has placed himself at the center, with the world revolving around him. In 1964, he remarked to a Texas politician that "the trouble with de Gaulle is that he's got the biggest ego in the world." Johnson saw nothing inconsistent between this verdict and his words at a White House state dinner for a visiting prime minister. He introduced a member of the United States Supreme Court to his foreign guest this way: "Mr. Prime Minister, I want you to meet a member of *my* Supreme Court."

But a different Johnson went unexpectedly to the Indian Embassy in the spring of 1966 during the visit of Mrs. Indira Gandhi, the Indian Prime Minister, and stayed for dinner. He moved one guest, the wife of a Senator, close to tears with an unrehearsed after-dinner toast. In words both noble and awkward, he described his aspirations for the world. The contrast between the two leaders was vivid: Mrs. Gandhi, diminutive, patrician, the leader of a powerful, patriarchal Kashmiri family who spoke polished sentences in precise, Oxford English; and Johnson, ungainly in his vast bulk, a man from the stock of farmers in the remote back country of Texas. With simple dignity, Johnson drew the contrast between himself and Mrs. Gandhi. Here, the crass exhibitionism of a President boasting about "my" Supreme Court was nowhere to be seen. In its place was an unpretentious tenderness.

That tenderness connotes but one of the many Johnsons, through all of which there runs a common theme: the theme of power, unifying all his disparate sides. Whether exhibitionist or unpretentious, whether considerate or insensitive, the single thrust of his long career has been the acquisition and the use of power. Johnson was born with the instinct of power, and long before he reached the White House he knew exactly where it rested, how to obtain it, and, most important, how to exercise it—sometimes with restraint, sometimes without. This ponderous, protean Texan, with the forbidding look of a chain-gang boss, knows more about the sources of power in the political world of Washington than any President in this century. He can be as gentle and solicitous as a nurse, but as ruthless and deceptive as a riverboat gambler, with the veiled threat in his half-closed eyes. He has come a long way to the White House, and there is no harder road to travel anywhere in the world.

☆

RICHARD NIXON: *Campaign Speech on the Nature of the Presidency*

During the course of this campaign, I have discussed many issues with the American people. Tonight, I would like to talk with you about a subject often debated by scholars and the public, but seldom dealt with directly in a Presidential campaign: The nature of the Presidency itself.

What *kind* of leadership should a President give? Is the office too strong, or not strong enough? How can it be made more responsive? Should a President lead public opinion, or follow it? What are the priorities for Presidential attention, and the range of Presidential responsibilities?

Perhaps the best way to begin my own answer is with another question, one I am often asked as I travel around the country: "Why do you seek the office? With all the troubles that we have, why would *anyone* want to be President today?"

The answer is not one of glory, or fame; today the burdens of the office outweigh its privileges. It's not because the Presidency offers a chance to *be* somebody, but because it offers a chance to *do* something.

Today, it offers a greater opportunity to help shape the future than ever before in the nation's history—and if America is to meet its challenges, the next President must seize that opportunity.

We stand at a great turning point—when the nation is groping

Richard Milhous Nixon, the 37th President of the United States (1969–   ), delivered this speech on the CBS and NBC radio networks on September 19, 1968.

for a new direction, unsure of its role and its purposes, caught in a tumult of change. And for the first time, we face serious, simultaneous threats to the peace both at home and abroad.

In this watershed year of 1968, therefore, America needs Presidential leadership that can establish a firm focus, and offer a way out of a time of towering uncertainties. Only the President can hold out a vision of the future and rally the people behind it.

The next President must unite America. He must calm its angers, ease its terrible frictions, and bring its people together once again in peace and mutual respect. He has to take *hold* of America before he can move it forward.

This requires leadership that believes in law, and has the courage to enforce it; leadership that believes in justice, and is determined to promote it; leadership that believes in progress, and knows how to inspire it.

The days of a passive Presidency belong to a simpler past. Let me be very clear about this: The next President must take an activist view of his office. He must articulate the nation's values, define its goals and marshal its will. Under the Nixon Administration, the Presidency will be deeply involved in the entire sweep of America's public concerns.

The first responsibility of leadership is to gain mastery over events, and to shape the future in the image of our hopes.

The President today cannot stand aside from crisis; he cannot ignore division; he cannot simply paper over disunity. He must lead.

But he must bear in mind the distinction between forceful leadership and stubborn willfulness. And he should not delude himself into thinking that he can do everything himself. America today cannot afford vest-pocket government, no matter who wears the vest.

In considering the kind of leadership the next President should give, let us first consider the special relationship—the special trust— that has developed between President and people.

The President is trusted, not to follow the fluctuations of the public-opinion polls, but to bring his own best judgment to bear on the best *ideas* his administration can muster.

There are occasions on which a President must take unpopular measures.

But his responsibility does not stop there. The President has a duty to decide, but the people have a right to know why. The President has a responsibility to tell them—to lay out all the facts, and to explain not only why he chose as he did but also what it means for the future. Only through an open, candid dialogue with the people can a President maintain his trust and his leadership.

It's time we once again had an open administration—open to

ideas *from* the people, and open in its communication *with* the people—an administration of open doors, open eyes and open minds.

When we debate American commitments abroad, for example, if we expect a decent hearing from those who now take to the streets in protest, we must recognize that neither the Department of State nor of Defense has a monopoly on all wisdom. We should bring dissenters into policy discussions, not freeze them out; we should invite constructive criticism, not only because the critics have a right to be heard, but also because they often have something worth hearing.

And this brings me to another, related point: The President cannot isolate himself from the great intellectual ferments of his time. On the contrary, he must consciously and deliberately place himself at their center. The lamps of enlightenment are lit by the spark of controversy; their flame can be snuffed out by the blanket of consensus.

This is one reason why I don't want a government of yes-men. It's why I do want a government drawn from the broadest possible base—an administration made up of Republicans, Democrats and independents, and drawn from politics, from career government service, from universities, from business, from the professions—one including not only executives and administrators, but scholars and thinkers.

While the President is a leader of thought, he is also a user of thought, and he must be a catalyst of thought. The thinking that he draws upon—must be the best in America—and not only in government. What's happening today in America and the world is happening not only in politics and diplomacy, but in science, education, the arts—and in all areas a President needs a constant exposure to ideas that stretch the mind.

Only if we have an Administration broadly enough based philosophically to ensure a true ferment of ideas, and to invite an interplay of the best minds in America, can we be sure of getting the best and most penetrating ideas.

We cannot content ourselves with complacency, with an attiude that because something worked once before, it must be good enough for us now. The world is changing, America is changing, and so must our ideas and our policies change—and our pursuit of the new must be an unremitting pursuit of excellence.

When we think of leadership, we commonly think of persuasion. But the coin of leadership has another side.

In order to lead, a President today must listen. And in this time of searching and uncertainty, government must learn to listen in new ways.

A President has to hear not only the clamorous voices of the organized, but also the quiet voices, the *inner voices*—the voices that speak through the silences, and that speak from the heart and the conscience.

These are the voices that carry the real meaning and the real message of America.

He's got to articulate these voices so that they can be heard, rather than being lost in the wail and bellow of what too often passes today for public discourse. He must be, in the words of Woodrow Wilson, "the spokesman for the real sentiment and purpose of the country."

The President is the one official who represents every American —rich and poor, privileged and underprivileged. He represents those whose misfortunes stand in dramatic focus, and also the great, quiet forgotten majority—the non-shouters and the non-demonstrators, the millions who ask principally to go their own way in decency and dignity, and to have their own rights accorded the same respect they accord the rights of others. Only if he listens to the quiet voices can he be true to this trust.

This I pledge, that in a Nixon Administration, America's citizens will not have to break the law to be heard, they will not have to shout or resort to violence. We can restore peace only if we make government attentive to the quiet as well as the strident, and this I intend to do.

But what of the burdens of the Presidency? Have they, as some maintain, grown beyond the capacity of any one man?

The Presidency has been called an impossible office.

If I thought it were, I would not be seeking it. But its functions have become cluttered, the President's time drained away in trivia, the channels of authority confused.

When questions of human survival may turn on the judgments of one man, he must have time to concentrate on those great decisions that only he can make.

One means of achieving this is by expanding the role of the Vice President—which I will do.

I also plan a re-organized and strengthened Cabinet, and a stronger White House staff than any yet put together.

The people are served not only by a President, but by an Administration, and not only by an Administration, but by a government.

The President's chief function is to lead, not to administer; it is not to oversee every detail, but to put the right people in charge, to provide them with basic guidance and direction, and to let them do the job. As Theodore Roosevelt once put it, "the best executive is the one who has enough sense to pick good men to do what he wants done, and self-restraint enough to keep from meddling with them while they do it."

This requires surrounding the President with men of stature, including young men, and giving them responsibilities commensurate with that stature. It requires a Cabinet made up of the ablest men in America, leaders in their own right and not merely by virtue of appointment—men who will command the public's respect and the President's attention by the power of their intellect and the force of their ideas.

Such men are not attracted to an Administration in which all credit is gathered to the White House and blame parceled out to scapegoats, or in which high officials are asked to dance like puppets on a Presidential string. I believe in a system in which the appropriate Cabinet officer gets credit for what goes right, and the President takes the blame for what goes wrong.

Officials of a new Administration will not have to check their consciences at the door, or leave their powers of independent judgment at home.

Another change I believe necessary stems directly from my basic concept of government. For years now, the trend has been to sweep more and more authority toward Washington. Too many of the decisions that would better have been made in Seattle or St. Louis have wound up on the President's desk.

I plan a streamlined Federal system, with a return to the states, cities and communities of decision-making powers rightfully theirs.

The purpose of this is not only to make government more effective and more responsive, but also to concentrate Federal attention on those functions that can only be handled on the Federal level.

The Presidency is a place where priorities are set, and goals determined.

We need a new attention to priorities, and a new realism about goals.

We are living today in a time of great promise—but also of too many promises. We have had too much wishful imagining that all the ills of man could be set right overnight, merely by making a national "commitment."

A President must tell the people what cannot be done immediately, as well as what can. Hope is fragile, and too easily shattered by the disappointment that follows inevitably on promises unkept and unkeepable. America needs charts of the possible, not excursions into the impossible.

Our cause today is not a nation, but a planet—for never have the fates of all the peoples of the earth been so bound up together.

The tasks confronting the next President abroad are among the most complex and difficult ever faced. And, as Professor Clinton Rossiter has observed, "Leadership in foreign affairs flows today from the President—or it does not flow at all."

The whole structure of power in the world has been undergoing far-reaching changes. While these pose what may be our period of greatest danger, they open what also may be our greatest opportunity. This is a time when miscalculation could prove fatal; a time when the destructive power amassed by the world's great nations threatens the planet. But it is also a time when leaders both East and West are developing a new, sobering awareness of the terrible potential of that power and the need to restrain it.

The judgments of history can bestow no honor greater than the title of peacemaker. It is this honor—this destiny—that beckons America, the chance to lead the world at last out of turmoil and onto that plateau of peace man has dreamed of since the dawn of time. This is our summons to greatness. If we answer the call, generations yet unborn will say of this generation of Americans that we truly mastered our moment, that we at last made the world safe for mankind.

The President cannot stand alone. Today, more than ever in modern times, he must reach out and draw upon the strength of the people.

Theodore Roosevelt called the Presidency "a bully pulpit"; Franklin Roosevelt called it pre-eminently "a place of moral leadership." And surely one of a President's greatest resources is the moral authority of his office. It's time we restored that authority—and time we used it once again, to its fullest potential—to rally the people, to define those moral imperatives which are the cement of a civilized society, to point the ways in which the *energies* of the people can be enlisted to serve the *ideals* of the people.

What has to be done, has to be done by President and people together, or it won't be done at all.

In asking you to join this great effort, I am asking not that you give something *to* your country, but that you do something *with* your country; I am asking not for your gifts, but for your hands. Together, we can hardly fail, for there is no force on earth to match the will and the spirit of the people of America, if that will and that spirit are mobilized in the service of a common aim. . . .

Let me add a personal note. I made a point of conducting my campaign for the nomination in a way that would make it possible to unite the party after the convention. That was successful. I intend now to conduct my election campaign in a way that will make it possible to unite the nation after November. It is not my intention to preside over the disintegration of America or the dissolution of

America's force for good in the world. Rather, I want the Presidency to be a force for pulling our people back together once again, and for making our nation whole by making our people one. We have had enough of discord and division, and what we need now is a time of healing or renewal, and of realistic hope.

No one who has been close to the Presidency would approach its powers lightly, or indifferently, or without a profound sense of the awesome responsibility these powers carry.

Nor should the American people approach this time of challenge without a sense of the majesty of the moment.

Greatness comes from stepping up to events, not from sitting on the sidelines while history is made by others.

History will be made in these years just ahead—history that can change the world for generations to come. So let us seize the moment, and accept the challenge—not as a burden, and not in fear— but in the full confidence that no people has ever had such resources to meet its challenge. Ours is the chance to see the American dream fulfilled at last in the destiny of man. This is the role that history offers; this is the hope that summons us; this is our generation's call to greatness as a nation. This, today, is America's opportunity.

☆

ON RICHARD NIXON: The Private Presidency
by Robert B. Semple, Jr.

Whether the Nixon Presidency will be good or bad for the country remains to be seen. The evidence is fragmentary at best, and on some key issues even the direction is far from clear. But what we do know at this early juncture is that the Presidency has very clearly become *his* Presidency, conducted in a manner that in turn is defined by his own peculiarities of style, personality and philosophy of government.

Mr. Nixon's method of doing business is certainly different from his predecessor's, which is no accident. Stylistically, the opportunity to strike a politically profitable contrast was there, and he shrewdly seized it. Where President Johnson had been occasionally brusque and often tempestuous at his news conferences, Nixon would try to be deferential. Where Johnson had enjoyed surprises and secrecy, Nixon would invent a "director of communications" and—within reason, of course—urge him to open wide the books of government. Where Johnson had asserted his powers in every nook and cranny of the bureaucracy, Nixon would concern himself with the large questions and leave the details of policy formulation to others.

In time, more fundamental differences have gradually emerged. Johnson drew his strength from the people, whom he longed to touch and hear. Nixon tends to place his faith in the executive machinery of government and his own carefully contrived decision-making process. Johnson reached to his friends beyond government

Robert B. Semple, Jr., is White House correspondent for the *New York Times*. This selection is from "Nixon's Presidency Is a Very Private Affair," *The New York Times Magazine*, November 2, 1969. © 1969 by The New York Times Company. Reprinted by permission.

for advice and self-renewal; Nixon seeks nourishment within the system. Johnson relished the dust of battle, treating each crisis large or
small as a potential Armageddon; Nixon is more selective, thrusting
forward his press secretary, his Congressional spokesmen, and—with
mixed results—his Vice President to grapple with the intermediate
problems, husbanding his own energies for the long haul and releas-
ing them only when he feels it absolutely necessary, as when he suddenly surfaced, after weeks of isolation, to deliver a carefully timed
and spirited defense of Judge Haynsworth.

In other words: if Johnson's was in the familiar sense a free swing-
ing, often chaotic, occasionally sweaty and essentially *public* Presidency, Nixon's is not only cool and methodical but peculiarly private. . . .

[Mr.] Nixon's problems have not visibly ruffled the orderly
surface of his Presidency; neither have his successes, which he appears
to treat with the same cautious reserve. He luxuriated publicly in the
euphoria of the moon shot, but discounted privately the notion that
it would help him politically (which is not to say that he won't
claim at least a bit of credit for it in his next campaign). As his aides
were congratulating one another after the public unveiling of his welfare program, the President crisply advised: "Let's wait for the mail."
And at the moment of one of his earliest triumphs—the whirlwind
European tour in February—his friends sought out his judgment and
he replied: "Too soon. Too soon. A year from now and we will know
if it was a success."

Whether he will be able to sustain his orderly pace and his equanimity in the face of a truly major crisis is an unanswered question,
for he has yet to be seriously tested. The challenge to the President's
authority and stability have been both peaceable and dignified . . .
permitting him to set his own pace.

Kennedy suffered the Bay of Pigs, the Berlin wall and the Cuban
missile crisis early in the game; Johnson grappled with riots in the
cities, insurrections in Latin America, and Barry Goldwater. Meanwhile, Nixon has enjoyed a cool summer, the moon voyage, and few
foreign crises. There has been daily warfare but no Tet offensive
in Vietnam. On balance, he has been the beneficiary of unusual good
fortune.

Yet even in truly turbulent times, one suspects, the Nixon pattern
as established over the first 10 months of his Administration is likely
to prevail, if only because what he is doing and the way he is doing it
seem to spring so plainly from his personality. . . .

The decision-making apparatus constructed by his chief of staff,
H. R. Haldeman, has been designed to match [his] temperament and

satisfy the President's twin passions for order and solitude. Order, to insure that he receives a regular flow of the best advice his government can give him; solitude, to insure that when he receives his options he can safely disappear and, in an atmosphere of studied detachment, reach the decision he feels is best.

The staff system appears cumbersome on paper—Nixon maintains the largest White House staff in history, with 50 Presidential appointees and about 100 others who assist the appointees—but can be reduced to several rather simple elements. The State Department, the Defense Department and the national security staff churn up foreign-policy options, which are funneled through Kissinger; the Urban Affairs Council and the various executive agencies churn up domestic options, which undergo further screening by Ehrlichman. Ultimately, everything must pass through Haldeman, who regulates the flow of people and paper in and out of the President's office and zealously budgets the President's time.

Nixon vastly prefers to have the options presented to him in memorandum form. He feels that face-to-face confrontations with the advocates or opponents of a particular scheme can be impossibly time-consuming. But he still manages to spend a considerable amount of his energy in informal and freewheeling sessions with his Cabinet, his economic advisers, the Urban Affairs Council, the Environmental Quality Council, the Republican leaders and the other official advisory bodies that orbit in and out of his decision-making universe.

By all accounts, Nixon is a good moderator at these meetings. He enjoyed watching his Attorney General John Mitchell, and Robert H. Finch, his Secretary of Health, Education and Welfare, spar over the appropriate response to last spring's student disorders; he is said to welcome debate and he engages in neither the monologues nor endless silences of his predecessor. He is reported to be a thoughtful listener and perceptive interrogator. He peppered his Cabinet and urban-affairs staff with endless questions during the long and frequently turbulent debate over the welfare and antihunger programs —"Who are the working poor?" "Do we know whether poor food causes brain damage in kids?" "How many hungry people are there?" —and when he is unsure of a point raised in a meeting he will ask Haldeman to dispatch a memo to an aide to find an answer.

Daniel Patrick Moynihan, the Democrat who serves as Nixon's urban-affairs adviser, has made no attempt to conceal his admiration for Nixon's executive temperament.

"Let me say with absolute candor that I think he is the most civil man I have ever worked for. I have worked for some very great men who were not necessarily very civil. President Kennedy, you know, would do anything for you; but he could throw you out of the room. He knew you would bounce. But [President Nixon] really does have some sense of your own feelings.

"He is very methodical. He likes to get it on paper; he likes to get it in a big book. I think he is a lawyer. He goes off in a corner; he sits down; and he reads through it all. I wouldn't read through half the stuff that he gets; but he does."

Mr. Nixon's typical working day is carefully scripted in advance. John F. Kennedy, in the first 24 hours of his Presidency, cleaned his desk off in a few minutes, looked at the aides clustered expectantly around him, and laughed: "What do I do now?" Nixon had no such problem. Up at 6:45 on Jan. 21, he arrived in his office at 7:45, read the papers, conferred with his aides, entertained about 1,300 campaign workers in the East Room in midmorning, witnessed the swearing-in of 81 eager and conservatively attired members of his White House staff—Hugh Sidey of *Time* magazine counted sideburns that day, and found only one pair—held his first meeting with his National Security Council, and spent the afternoon absorbed with Kissinger.

The essential pattern of the President's day has varied little since then, although instead of the newspapers he relies largely for his news information on a 20-to-40-page summary compiled by Pat Buchanan, a facile and quick campaign speech writer who has a staff of six people working for *him*. The Buchanan summary—which includes not only a digest of the major news stories but also reprints and summaries of what the columnists, networks and magazines are saying—is delivered first thing every morning, and is further evidence of the President's penchant for organized, digested material. One of his first acts as head of state was to throw out Johnson's massive three-set television console (he gave it to Herb Klein, the Director of Communications); his second act was to throw out Johnson's chattering news tickers (he gave them to Buchanan). Lyndon liked his news in huge, raw quantities; his successor prefers the prepackaged variety.

(Nixon also pays less attention than did Johnson to the public-opinion polls, although his aides devour them. One recalls that Johnson, his popularity sagging at home, would pull wads of paper from his pockets and announce proudly that, according to Gallup, he ranked second only to Adenauer in Germany's affection and ahead of everybody but the Pope in Italy. Nixon keeps a close watch on the White House mail, but regards the polls with a skeptical and mildly fatalistic eye.)

Otherwise, Nixon's routine seldom varies: "Staff time" with

Ehrlichman, Haldeman and press secretary Ronald L. Ziegler from about 8:30 to 9, ceremonial occasions and courtesy calls from dignitaries in the mornings, advisory group meetings (the N.S.C., Cabinet, etc.) before noon, and a healthy chunk of "free time"—usually spent reading or with key staffers—in the afternoon.

When the meetings are over and the options in hand, the President leaves the field of debate and retires to make up his own mind —sometimes to his oval office, more often to his standby office in the Executive Office Building across West Executive Avenue (a pleasant place furnished with volumes about Teddy Roosevelt and mementos from the President's travels), or to the Lincoln sitting room in the family quarters of the East Wing. His aides are never sure what will emerge.

Nixon's decision to move ahead with a multibillion dollar assault on hunger, for instance, took most of his staff by surprise. This reporter recalls asking Steve Hess, Moynihan's deputy and an advocate of an antihunger program, to give his assessment of the program's prospects, and watching Hess shake his head sadly and say, "I think we've lost that one." Two days later, Nixon brought forth the program. The one man who said he wasn't surprised was Haldeman, who knew that a final decision had not been made and that Finch's advice —he had yet to register his opinion with any real force—might turn the tide. It did.

Similarly, Nixon's decision to name Warren Earl Burger to the Supreme Court was shielded from even his closest advisers, including —the President insists—the ubiquitous Haldeman. And when the time came to make a decision on whether to alter the 7 per cent business tax credit and the 10 per cent surcharge request inherited from Lyndon Johnson, aides were so uncertain of Nixon's mind after a 90-minute meeting in April that they prepared one announcement justifying changes in the surtax and another announcement justifying no changes at all.

Nixon's decisions have been known to surprise even his Cabinet members—indeed, the Cabinet is often the last to know. Some Cabinet members, of course, are better-informed than others about policymaking outside their own departments. There is hardly a thing that Attorney General Mitchell, Nixon's former law partner, doesn't know. And there are very few things that escape the scrutiny of Finch, Secretary of State William Rogers or Labor Secretary George Shultz, another favorite who rose rapidly in Nixon's esteem as a result of his efforts to reconcile the competing claims of Nixon's advisers in the welfare reform struggle.

But the others in the Cabinet do not know so much. Some political scientists regard the Cabinet as a relic, and in any case most modern Presidents have not quite known what to do with it. Nixon is no exception. He meets with it, consults with it and has given individual Cabinet members quite free rein with the press and in their own departments. But he does not regard it as the central decision-making body of his regime. More often, it is reduced to ratifying decisions already taken.

A case in point was the decision to move ahead with a program of welfare reform. Nixon first informed his Cabinet about the plan at a meeting at the Presidential retreat in Camp David, Md., only a few days before he was to announce it on nationwide television. One Cabinet member—aides refuse to identify him—denounced the program vehemently. Finally one of Nixon's closest advisers whispered to a colleague:

"Can't this man tell the President's made up his mind? If he keeps going on like that this may be his last Cabinet meeting."

The President's decision-making style is, in sum, distinguished by a process of progressive isolation and diminishing debate, beginning at the committee or Cabinet level, where the alternatives are reduced to manageable proportions, and ending with the President alone, determining his course.

It is hardly surprising, therefore, that such a system produces unexpected surprises for those who are not at the President's elbow; or that it yields decisions and policies that clearly bear the President's mark. Nixon has delegated some decisions to lesser officials, often to his later embarrassment; but he has reserved the important ones for himself, and as a rule they show it.

A quick rundown of his major pronouncements of the year illustrate the point. His controversial speech in Colorado Springs in June defending the military and excoriating the "neo-isloationists" in Congress was very much his own invention. He tried the idea out in May on a partly skeptical Cabinet, gave it a dry run during a brief visit to the naval yards in Virginia, ordered speechwriter Bill Safire to draw up a draft, and put on the finishing touches himself.

His stern talk to the students at General Beadle State College in North Dakota—wherein he accused college faculties of fostering student disturbances—was no less a personal document. He had asked Ray Price, another speechwriter, to draw up a tough speech, and added some stiff inserts of his own. Some of Nixon's toughest phrases were dropped during the editing process, but the President kept sticking them back in. One evening a couple of associates came upon him in his office, working with scissors and tape and muttering about "these good phrases of mine that people keep trying to take out."

It was the President, too, who finally determined to move ahead with deployment of the antiballistic missile system, and who chose the new approach to welfare after exhaustive internal debate.

"I don't know whether this is right," he told his Cabinet at Camp David, "but what I do know is that the present program is a mess and I refuse to go down that road any more."

The tightly structured staff system does not always function well. The President had trouble getting accurate readings of Congressional sentiment on the ABM issue and the tax surcharge proposal. In part this was because he got poor advice from the Democratic leaders in the House—notorious for their inability to count noses in their own ranks. But the main trouble was that he relied entirely on his own overworked staff of Congressional relations men, and seemed curiously reluctant to invite key Senators and Representatives in for the long chats that Johnson so usefully employed in times of legislative crisis.

Nixon is now said to be making a strenuous effort to correct this situation. The press office has always refused to give out the President's full schedule—it makes a distinction between a "private" and "public schedule"—so there is no clear way of telling who sees the President and when, but more and more Congressmen admit being invited to the White House for breakfast and to the President's yacht, the *Sequoia*, for moonlight cruises down the Potomac.

Similarly, Nixon's remoteness from the day-to-day concerns of his government can produce unexpectedly embarrassing episodes, and for this reason he is said to be still tinkering with his staff system. He prefers to concentrate on one issue at a time, letting lesser problems ride. And while the staff system may provide ideal protection for a President who wants time in which to mull over major issues, it has tended to insulate him from little things that have a way of developing into big things.

Already in his brief tenure, for example, he has been forced to rescind several unwise appointments that a President more intimately engaged in the lower reaches of policymaking might never have made in the first place. He unaccountably allowed the squabble over the appointment of John H. Knowles as Assistant Secretary of Health to fester into a major national issue; he watched with apparent unconcern as Spiro Agnew privately undercut some of his own tax proposals.

Despite the rosy portraits of equanimity drawn by his aides, these episodes are known to have rankled the President, who detests sloppy staff work, in part because he relies so heavily on it in making his judgments. He was disturbed during his San Clemente vacation when the State and Defense Departments began promoting contradictory assessment of the decline in enemy casualty rates; and Treasury Secretary Kennedy's suggestion last summer that the Administration might impose wage-and-price controls brought an even more vehement outburst. When Paul McCracken, chairman of the Council of Economic Advisers, told him about the Kennedy statement in late June, Nixon replied:

"Controls. Oh, my God, no! I was a lawyer for the O.P.A. [the Office of Price Administration] during the war and I know all about controls. They mean rationing, black markets, inequitable administration. We'll never go for controls."

His surveillance system, in other words, leaves something to be desired. Relying almost entirely on the advice of his Attorney General, he named Judge Haynsworth to the Supreme Court, later admitting that he probably wouldn't recognize the judge if he suddenly materialized in the middle of his oval office. Only later—after the storm broke—did he ask Ehrlichman, one of the few members who might have detected trouble, to review Haynsworth's qualifications. And Clark Mollenhoff, the investigative reporter hired by Ehrlichman to keep Nixon out of precisely this kind of trouble, was called in even later—and then to bolster the original judgment.

The President's passion for privacy extends even to the press, from whom he has isolated himself far more than Johnson, and there is some feeling that this, too, has hurt him. Although an occasional columnist has slipped in to see him privately, he has dealt with the press largely through Ziegler or in formal news conferences in the East Room. Many newsmen believe that this is an improvement over Johnson, who cultivated individual newsmen. They believe that the press is more likely to keep its independence if the President keeps himself at arm's length. But it also means that during the long periods between news conferences his policies are subject to misinterpretation and confusion. Nixon's subalterns at State and Defense, for example, have taken advantage of his extended silences to float various and often contradictory policy statements on the war in Vietnam, and until quite recently he has made no effort to reconcile them. . . .

Despite his troubles, Nixon has clearly enjoyed being President, which was true of both Kennedy and Johnson, less so of Eisenhower. There is one difference. Although he loved the Presidency and delighted in its power and pomp, Johnson advertised its responsibilities at every turn, and wore them heavily. In crisis he seemed to bear the weight of centuries; even in modestly good times, his face wore a mournful expression and his shoulders sagged under the weight of real or imagined burdens.

But his successor, spared serious crisis so far, has more candidly accepted the privileges of office, and indeed this may have caused some of the criticism in recent weeks. Americans expect their Presidents to work and give some hint of the pain of their efforts, but Nixon seems incapable of hiding the obvious pleasures he derives from his task. If Johnson sought to portray the Presidency as a lonely journey—and it was, at the end—Nixon romps openly through the fields of Presidential power.

"The Presidency has not yet become for me," he told the White House Correspondents Association earlier this year, "that awesome burden that some have described." . . .

What has Nixon brought to the Presidency so far? Most notably, a restrained view of his job—a fundamental conception of his role that, in combination with the traits of character and personality that govern his operations, does much to explain why his has so far been a peculiarly private Presidency. Senator Eugene McCarthy is credited with first planting the notion of an unheroic Presidency—"This is a good country if the President will just let it be," he once said—but Nixon has clearly taken it up.

He wants, as he told Ehrlichman, to use the great powers of his office to do something for the nation; yet he also seems to believe that he must first determine what the limits of those powers really are. His first response has been to lower his own profile and to speak modestly, if at all, about the capacity of the federal government to do good.

On the surface, he seems clearly to be contradicting himself. How can he use the great power of his office when he denies it? But Nixon, like McCarthy, seems to believe that in that contradiction lies the answer. It is time to admit, he seems to be saying, that Washington alone cannot clean up the problems of society and the more Washington tries the worse the problems get. Reformulated: The best way to realize the great power of the office is to ration it wisely and, if possible, give it to those who can use it.

At the heart of this conception lies an apprehension of his own limits as an emotional leader, an awareness that the country and the Congress are probably tired of prepackaged visions of the good life, but beyond that a recognition of the fact that while he may serve effectively within constitutional limits as Commander-in-Chief and as party leader, he cannot, in practical terms, function effectively as governor of all the states and mayor of all the cities. He said in his campaign, and obviously still believes, that the major problems are local and regional in nature, and thus the trick is to start power flowing back to the places where power is needed. He has therefore been anxious to strengthen the powers of states and cities, and from that concern has emerged the new strategies to decentralize welfare, revenue and manpower retraining.

This is not to say that Nixon's domestic motives are crystal clear —only that there is a visible and not widely recognized pattern to some of the things he has done. He seems clearly bent on getting government out of the business of providing people with services and providing them instead with income; and he seems determined to force the Federal apparatus to start delivering on some of its promises. He is, in short, reform-minded in the sense that he very much wants to make government work.

☆

RICHARD NIXON: *Two Interviews With The President*

MR. SMITH: . . . To me, the key formative fact about the Nixon Presidency is the fact that you were elected to lead the Nation but due to our system of separate elections you were not given the usual means of leadership. You got a popular mandate which was small; you are the first President in this century to be elected with both Houses of Congress in opposition; you said, I think, last week in an interview that in your situation, television, getting to the public by television, gave you the leverage you needed.

Well, now, that channel is menaced by what the columnists call the credibility gap, and the Gallup Poll said 7 out of 10 Americans don't believe what the Administration is saying.

How did the diminution of belief come about and what do you intend to do about it?

THE PRESIDENT. Well, I think first, Mr. Smith, with regard to what you call the credibility gap, that many observers, in fact, I think, I even recall something you said at one time, have pointed out that Presidents, particularly when they have difficult problems in foreign affairs, inevitably are going to acquire some credibility gap. This was true of Woodrow Wilson. I remember my mother voted for him because it was thought that if that was the case, if he became President, that he kept us out of war.

You will remember Franklin D. Roosevelt once made the state-

Richard M. Nixon, the 37th President of the United States, made these comments during a television interview with Howard K. Smith of the American Broadcasting Company on March 22, 1971, and in a press interview with Garnett Horner of the *Washington Star-News* on November 10, 1972.

ment in a speech before World War II, "I will not send your sons to fight on foreign shores." I think both Wilson and Franklin D. Roosevelt meant exactly what they said. They were not lying to the American people.

On the other hand, the great events made it necessary for them each to take the Nation into war.

Now, in my case, I found the Nation in war. I found it with 550,000 Americans abroad, with our casualties running at over 300 a week, with no plans to bring them home, with no plans to end the war or end America's involvement in it in a way that would allow South Vietnam to survive as an independent entity.

I have taken the Nation quite a ways since then. When I say I have, I shouldn't use that in such a, shall we say, arrogant fashion. I mean we have done that. We have done it with the assistance of many Democrats as well as Republicans in the House and Senate and, of course, of our fighting men abroad.

Now we are reaching the key point—the key point when we see that we are ending America's involvement in a war that has been the longest, the most bitter, the most difficult war in our Nation's history.

Once we go over that hump, once the American people are convinced that the plans that have taken so long to implement have come into effect, then I think the credibility gap will rapidly disappear.

It is the events that cause the credibility gap, not the fact that a President deliberately lies or misleads the people. That is my opinion. . . .

MR. SMITH: When President Johnson retired from politics, he confessed to an association of broadcasters that he felt he had deficiencies in communication. Well, you are obviously very articulate and clear. Can this be the possibility: Your former aide, Patrick Moynihan, has written an article in *Commentary* saying that we have entered an era in which it is fashionable and obligatory for the press to disparage Presidents, and he gives a host of reasons for that. Do you believe that to be true?

THE PRESIDENT. Well, Mr. Smith, you will remember that in 1962 I had my showdown with the press and I have avoided one since. I have respect for the press. It is true that of all the Presidents in this century, it is probably true, that I have less, as somebody has said, supporters in the press than any President. I understand that and I do not complain about it because it is philosophical.

MR. SMITH: Don't you think the press mistreated Lyndon Johnson more, and Harry Truman?

THE PRESIDENT. Yes, as a matter of fact, I think President Johnson did get a bad rap from the press and for the wrong reasons. His style, for example. Now, when you take a man on because of his accent and because he happens to be from Texas or something like that, that is the wrong reason. If you take a man on his policy, that is something else again.

Understand, I am not complaining about my treatment from the press. I think it is a philosophical difference. I have many friends in the press, personal friends, as you are quite aware.

I have never taken on a member of the press individually. I have never called a publisher since I have been President. I have never called an editor to complain about anything. I have never called a television station to complain about anything, and I never shall, as long as I have the opportunity to talk to the American people on a program like this directly. Then if I fail to communicate, it is my fault.

Getting back to your major question, what about the problem of Presidents communicating with the American people, getting across. I don't think we can blame the press, I don't think we can blame the media. I really don't think you can blame the President.

I think what it really gets down to is that the problems are enormous, and that the American people at the present time are frankly just frustrated. They are frustrated by having gone through Korea and then they are frustrated by having gone through Vietnam.

When I said in an interview that there is a new isolationism growing in the country, I understand it. I know why people feel that way, because they say after all of this sacrifice, after all of this war, for what? Why can't we have some peace? We don't start any wars. We don't want anything from anybody else. Why can't they just leave us alone?

So, for that reason, any President who tries to see to it, to take the long view, that we do not take that very, very inviting but dangerous road of peace at any price, sort of an instant peace, so to speak, any President who insists on giving that kind of leadership is going to have problems with communicating.

But I can also say this: Any President who didn't do it wouldn't be able to go to bed at night and sleep very well, knowing what he knows. You see, I know that if we fail, if we fail to meet America's commitment in the world, to be as strong as we need to be, to deter any major aggressor, and as strong as we need to be to help our friends with whom we have treaty alliances, and to have the will just at the time we are nearing the end to finish our involvement in Vietnam in a way that South Vietnam will be able to survive—that is what is on the line.

I think we can do it. I think we will. And I think that the American people will support me. Maybe the polls will go down, but I am not going to live or die by the polls. If I did, I wouldn't be here now.

MR. SMITH: Don't you think your job would be a lot easier if you carried Congress with you? Senator Fulbright has complained that Congress has absolutely no control over foreign affairs. Two major actions, Cambodia and Laos, were undertaken with little information to and without the advice of Congress. Doesn't he have a point?

THE PRESIDENT. Well, Senator Fulbright has a point with regard to himself, yes. But I should point out that if a majority of the Congress, Mr. Smith, disapproved of what the President was doing in Cambodia or in Laos, the majority of the Congress can act, and it can act by cutting off the funds. The majority of the Congress has not done that.

You may recall that the Supplemental Appropriation Bill of $1 billion at the end of last year was passed by both Houses of Congress. Those votes will be close. There is great debate in the Congress. I respect the Congress. I would like to be able to carry the Congress perhaps better than we have. I would like better understanding in the Congress.

But, on the other hand, it is the responsibility of the President of the United States, particularly when as Commander-in-Chief he has responsibility for the lives of American men, to make those decisions that are going to save those lives. Cambodia saved the lives of American men.

And may I say, too, that the thousands of North Vietnamese who were casualties in North Vietnam, the hundreds and millions of rounds of ammunition that were destroyed there, the time that was bought there, all of these things—that means that the risk to American lives is substantially reduced, and that is why the support of that operation was worthwhile, in my opinion.

MR. SMITH: The members of Congress obviously feel left out, feel they don't have much control, and a subsidiary complaint made by Senator Fulbright is that Congress has no access to White House aides who have played an ever larger role in advising on foreign affairs. *The New York Times* said the other day a coup d'etat could hardly deprive the people's elected representatives more completely of their constitutional powers than this gradual process of the White House without accounting taking over foreign affairs.

Is there something to that?

THE PRESIDENT. It is an old argument, Mr. Smith. As you know, from having studied many Presidents before this one, it has been raised with regard to virtually every Presidential advisor, and there is nothing to it.

I have Presidential advisors—Dr. Kissinger. I have my prime foreign policy advisors, the Secretary of State, with whom I just talked before coming on this program, and the Secretary of Defense for national security policy, with whom I just talked before coming on this program. Both of them, incidentally, have been testifying this week before the Congress; some in private and some in public session.

As far as a Presidential advisor is concerned, however, he cannot be hauled down before the Congress. Then you are going to have two Secretaries of State. You cannot have that, there being only one.

MR. SMITH: Aside from the fact that you have the responsibility, wouldn't it be simply politically prudent if you invited the Senate Foreign Affairs Committee here every month and had a talk with them and listened to their suggestions and explained your point of view to them informally and gave them a sense of participation?

THE PRESIDENT. I would have to go really further than that. I would have to take the Foreign Affairs Committee and the Armed Services Committee and the Appropriations Committees, all of which, of course, have some significant control over these policies.

At the time of Cambodia, as Senator Fulbright will recall, I did have the whole group down and we discussed some of these matters and I answered questions.

The possibility of having meetings on an informal basis with Committee members is something that I can consider. I see many of them individually.

For example, Senator Aiken, Senator Mansfield—I see him virtually every two to three weeks for breakfast as the Majority Leader. Any Senator who asks to see me usually gets in to see me. It is a question of time.

MR. SMITH: The story keeps recurring that access to you is difficult. *Newsweek* carries a story this week that Secretary Volpe is having a hard time seeing you, as Mr. Hickel complained he did. In the case of Senators, I will use names. A year ago Senator Javits, Republican, New York, the best vote-getter in the State for your Party, . . . said he had not been consulted by you on anything.

And Senator Dole, increasingly your spokesman, was heard to complain recently that he had been "shunned off" to lesser White House aides. Is that true?

THE PRESIDENT. I think there is no substitute, Mr. Smith, for seeing the man in the Oval Office, and yet while my schedule, as you probably are aware, due to a rather disciplined schedule unless I have a guest, I eat breakfast alone in five minutes, never have guests for lunch—I do that in five minutes, too. I perhaps put more time in in the day than any President could put in, and it is because it is my way and not bragging about it.

But in terms of the number of people I see, the number of Senators, the number of Cabinet officers, the number of appointments, I would say that it is probably a record. But the more you see naturally the more others who don't get in as often want to see you. It is not possible to meet this adequately, but the only way I can figure it out is to cut another hour off of my sleep, but then I wouldn't be as sharp on this program.

MR. SMITH: The kind of thing I am concerned about is I see— this is a prediction—the next two years being dominated by this political theme: The age-old conflict between the Executive and Congress, but in sharper form than ever. Resolutions are being prepared in the Senate to try and require your aides to testify and resolutions limiting your powers as Commander-in-Chief.

There is another assault coming from another quarter and I don't know whether you are aware of it. But tomorrow morning Senator Ervin begins hearings on the impounding of funds by you which had been appropriated by Congress. It is said that several billions of dollars that Congress is appropriating for things like dams and so on you have refused to spend, that this violates the Constitution and deprives Congress of its main power of the purse.

THE PRESIDENT. Mr. Smith, when I was a Senator and a Congressman, particularly when I was a Senator and a Congressman with a President in the other party in the White House, I played all of those games, too, with very little success.

These games are going to be played. The efforts will be made, it is true, by members of the Senate, members of the House and some of them with the very best of intentions to hamstring the Executive, the President. When it is the proper thing to do, it will be done.

But I think, generally speaking, you will find that in these great battles that have occurred through the years, between the President and the Congress, that sometimes the Congress wins, sometimes the President wins. But where the President's responsibility as Commander-in-Chief of the Armed Forces is concerned, and where the lives of American men are involved, usually the President wins and for good reason. You can have only one Commander-in-Chief.

We get back to this business of why not pass a resolution saying that we will get out of Vietnam by Christmas of this year. It is very easy to pass a resolution. It would be very popular for me, as a matter of fact, to sponsor it.

On the other hand, it is my judgment, as I have already indicated, that such a resolution would not be in the interest of the security of our own forces, not be in the interest of the negotiations, the possibility of negotiating the release of our prisoners and not in the interest of the United States long-run in terms of ending this war in a way that might discourage another war coming.

That is my judgment. I have to fight for that judgment. If the Congress determines to move in another direction, so be it. I don't think it will, though, and I don't think the American people will support the Congress whenever it fights the President in his honest effort to serve as Commander-in-Chief, in that service to protect the lives of American men and to, in addition, conduct policy in a way that will avoid those lives being lost, we hope, at some future time. . . .

MR. SMITH: We haven't talked about domestic affairs, and let me ask you a general domestic question. This is a cliché but a very vital cliché. I would like to hear you explain how it is that we can master the impossible, achieve perfection in 10,000 actions it takes to send the men to the moon, land them and bring them back safely, and we can't make New York City a clean, pleasant place to live. It is not size. I lived in greater London, which is bigger, for eleven years and everything works, mass transit, the police work, air pollution is declining. What are we doing wrong?

THE PRESIDENT. Well, this is the challenge of our time, Mr. Smith. That is why environment has been one of the six great goals that I have set out for the American people. We can clean up the air, we can clean up the water, we can also clean up the congestion. We can work on the problems of mass transit. But in order to do it we need what I have called a new American revolution.

The trouble with government today in this country—and I think I can summarize in a word—is this, that to the average person out there in New York, in California, in Florida, wherever he may live, to that average person he looks at government, all government and he is fed up with it, and the reason he is fed up with it is that it costs too much, it doesn't work and he can't do anything about it.

That is why our new revenue-sharing proposals, I think, have very, very great meaning, because they will reduce the cost of government, it will make it work better but more important, it is going to give people in New York and other places a chance to do something about it. As far as these programs are concerned, the other point that we have to bear in mind is whether it is education, whether it is welfare, whether it is health, what we need is reform, not simply pouring billions of more dollars into these old programs—we can't do that— but what we need to do is to reform all of these programs, and that is why this administration—and due to the fact that the problems of our foreign policy have not only in this administration but in the previous administration been so predominant, people have failed to recognize it—this administration has the most progressive proposals in the area of reform of any administration in this century. And it is needed, it is desperately needed.

We are either going to have to reform the machinery of government in the United States or it is going to break down completely

MR. SMITH: Sir, that is often cited as the great objection to revenue sharing, giving money without strings to states whose governments are not very good. . . . Don't you have to attach strings to them to make them return before you give them money?

THE PRESIDENT. Mr. Smith, I don't believe in that doctrine. I think it is repugnant to the American system, that only a bureaucratic elite at the top of the heap in Washington knows what is best for the people out in the sticks. Sure, there are people—there are dishonest people in government, but there are dishonest people in national government, too. There are dishonest people in state governments.

But the way to make people more responsible, the way to get better people in the government, is to give them, it seems to me, more responsibility.

What I mean by that is that if your people who are mayors, county officials and governors are simply errand boys for the purpose of disbursing the money that is handed out with strings, with all the decisions made by someone else, you are not going to get competent people to do the job.

But if, on the other hand, they have some responsibility to make their own decisions about how to clean up New York City, how to revise state government, you are going to get better governors, you are going to get better mayors, you are going to get better county officials.

Incidentally, on that point let me say that I just met with the Nation's governors. They are a pretty first-rate group of people and we are getting some fine governors in this country, and we can get better governors, better mayors, better county officials by giving them more responsibility, not by taking responsibility away from them.

MR. SMITH: Let me ask you just one question on civil rights.

It is clear after a generation of trial that the greatest block to integration of any form is segregated suburbs. I have asked you about that before and your answer has been that you oppose forced integration.

But does that mean, in effect, the perpetuation of discrimination in housing, and isn't that against the law?

THE PRESIDENT. Mr. Smith, when you have basically a situation that is caused by economic considerations rather than by racial decisions, I do not believe that you can say that that is a violation of the law, or certainly not of the law or of the Constitution, either in spirit or in letter.

Let's understand that as far as any suburb is concerned they all must be open. Any individual must have a right, a Constitutional right, to buy a house, rent a house, or a home, or an apartment, any place in this country, without regard to what his race or religion may be. That Constitutional right now is guaranteed and we will see that it is enforced.

On the other hand, if you have a situation where people are living in a certain area, people, say, who have purchased their homes—let us say they are $20,000 to $25,000 homes—then for the federal government to come in and say: We are going to insist that we will in effect, break up this community, break it up from an economic standpoint, because those homes are too expensive for some people to move into—it may happen that some of those people may be black people, they may be other minority people, they may be white people, but because they are too expensive we are going to put in a lower, low-cost federal government project in there—I do not believe that that kind of forced integration is Constitutional, and it certainly is not required by the law. Until it is required by the law, we are not going to do it.

MR. SMITH: Mr. President, we have got just a short time left. This is a very unfair question to put to you in a short time. But I have noticed so many of your opinions have changed lately in favor of deficit spending. When somebody attacked Mr. Yost for allegedly having a relationship with Alger Hiss, you defended him.

Do you think you have changed greatly? Whatever happened to the jut-jawed, aggressive young man who would fight at the drop of a hat over those things?

THE PRESIDENT. The jaw is still there. As my wife often said, there is not much I can do about my image. I was born with it.

But as far as the problems that we confront in this country are concerned, it is the responsibility of whoever reaches what Disraeli once referred to as the top of the greasy pole when he became Prime Minister, or whoever is in that Oval Office over there, he must see the problems of the world and the problems of his country in a very different perspective.

What is most important for the man who is President—I have often thought about it—is what would you look for? Of course, you want a man who is intelligent. You hope he is reasonably intelligent, a man with courage and a man who can give political leadership, maybe make a speech and that sort of thing.

But the most important single factor is that he must be one who has perspective and poise, what the Quakers call peace at the center, one who isn't knocked out of balance by the stories, the crises of the moment, one who having that peace at the center then will make decisions, decisions with regard to our foreign policy, decisions with regard to the lives of men as you have referred to, in a way that will be in the best interests of the country.

☆

. . . When we talk about philosophy, I am not saying we are going to be more conservative, more liberal. Maybe I can describe it this way: I think if you would look at it in terms of the great debates in the British system in the 19th century, I would say that my views, my approach, is probably that of a Disraeli conservative—a strong foreign policy, strong adherence to basic values that the nation believes in and the people believe in, and to conserving those values, and not being destructive of them, but combined with reform, reform that will work, not reform that destroys. . . .

Now, having said this, however, this does not mean that my position is over on the far right. Basically it means my position is simply in the center. In the field of foreign policy, I think most people would describe my position as being that of a centrist. In domestic policy, if you look at the Nixon proposals in the first four years— and I can assure you, that when you look at them over the next four years, this will be known as an Administration which advocated —and if we get proper support in the Congress after the election, was able to accomplish—more significant reform than any Administration since Franklin Roosevelt's in 1932; but reform in a different direction. Roosevelt's reforms led to bigger and bigger power in Washington. It was perhaps needed then. The country's problems were so massive they couldn't be handled otherwise.

The reforms that we are instituting are ones which will diffuse the power throughout the country and which will make government leaner, but in a sense will make it stronger. After all, fat government is weak, weak in handling problems. . . .

Let me say on the world scene I would change it just a little. Whether the United States, as the only nation powerful enough in the free world to play this role, steps up to its responsibility and leads the way to this new period of peace, this is the real issue: Whether we step up to it or turn isolationist.

That is why I thought that was one of the great issues of this campaign. A weaker America, turned inward, in my view wouldn't have been good for the people in this country at home. But that is debatable. It would have been a disaster for the world, because without the United States on the world scene, smaller nations would be living in terror, because where there is a power vacuum, that vacuum is filled.

The United States now has a relationship with the Soviet Union and the Chinese, one of whom is a superpower, the other who has the potential in the future, which is a healthy relationship, but it is one in which our strength must always be maintained until we have mutual agreement to reduce.

Now, on the domestic scene: I think that the tragedy of the 60's is that so many Americans, and particularly so many young Americans, lost faith in their country, in the American system, in their country's foreign policy. Many were influenced to believe that they should be ashamed of our country's record in foreign policy and what we were doing in the world; that we should be ashamed of what America did, and all.

Many Americans got the impression that this was an ugly country, racist, not compassionate, and part of the reason for this was the tendency of some to take every mole that we had and to make it look like a cancer.

Now, let us understand: This is not a perfect country. There is much that needs to be corrected. But I don't say this in any jingoistic sense—I have seen the world, and I don't know any young person abroad, if he had the chance, who wouldn't rather be here than someplace else.

What I think we have to do is not simply to reinstill in Americans a pride in country, a majority of the Americans do have a pride in country. You see how they respond.

But they must not do it on blind faith, "My country, right or wrong but my country." We want them to know why this country is right. Now, taking the foreign field, we want to make the American people feel proud of their country's role in the foreign field. I think the trips to Peking and Moscow helped in that respect. I think the people saw that the United States was leading the world in peace and that we were the only ones who could do it. They were proud of our country.

We are going to continue to exert that kind of leadership.

At home, as we move toward equality of opportunity, and it will not come overnight, but as we move toward equality of opportunity, as we move toward dealing with the problems of the environment, whether it is clean air, or a better health system, or improvement in education, as we make progress in all of these fields, I think that we will reinstill some of the faith that has been lost in the 60's.

. . . I think what we are talking about here is that we have passed through a very great spiritual crisis in this country—during the late 60's, the war in Vietnam by many was blamed for it totally. It was only part of the problem and in many cases it was only an excuse rather than a reason. But we saw a breakdown in frankly what I could call the leadership class of this country.

I am not saying that critically because many lost faith in many of our institutions. For example, the enormous movement toward permissiveness which led to the escalation in crime, the escalation in drugs in this country, all of this came as a result of those of us who basically have a responsibility of leadership not recognizing that above everything else you must not weaken a people's character. . . .

The average American is just like the child in the family. You give him some responsibility and he is going to amount to something. He is going to do something. If, on the other hand, you make him completely dependent and pamper him and cater to him too much, you are going to make him soft, spoiled and eventually a very weak individual.

So, I would simply sum it up by saying that when you are looking in the next four years at the domestic front and the international front, it will be an exciting period. Internationally, because of instead of withdrawing from the world, as our opponents advocated, in so many areas we are going to continue to play a great role in the world because that is the only way you can have the peace we talk about.

On the domestic front, it will be exciting because it is going to be a different approach. The approach that has always been considered to be the most certain vote-getter in the past has been who is going to promise the most to get the votes. In others, it was a question of how much you were going to promise, how much money were you going to promise to pay out for this program or that program. This is the first campaign in history, I think you see probably the first campaign of a candidate who didn't go out with a whole bag full of goodies.

I have stuck by the program I have and I haven't laid out a lot of new goodies. This is a case where the American people were confronted with a choice of one candidate who promised to spend billions more of their money, basically, as they put it, to help them, and the other candidate said, "No, we are not going to promise to do that; we are going to promise to give you the chance to help yourself."

The American people will speak on that issue. It is our responsibility to find a way to reform our government institutions so that this new spirit of independence, self-reliance, pride, that I sense in the American people can be nurtured. I think it is out there.

Now, I realize what I have just said in many quarters in Washington in which we live, and the Georgetown cocktail set, that will be tut-tutted by those who are living in another era. They honestly believe that the answer to the problem is always some new massive government program. I totally disagree with that. Sometimes a new program is needed. But what we need now, rather than more government, is better government. I realize that is a cliché, but rather than more it is better and many times the better is not the fatter, but the leaner.

We are going to change the way we are going to do this and

rather than government doing more for people and making people more dependent upon it, what I am standing for is government finding ways through the government programs to allow people to do more for themselves, to encourage them to do more for themselves; not only to encourage them, but to give them incentive to do more for themselves on their own without government assistance.

III

JUDICIAL VIEWS

IN THE AMERICAN governmental system, the last word on the scope of presidential power ostensibly belongs to the Supreme Court as the ultimate interpreter of the Constitution. But in fact the judiciary's role in defining executive authority has been quite limited. Under normal conditions, the Court seldom comes into direct conflict with the executive, since most legal challenges to governmental action are tests of legislative rather than executive power. And under crisis conditions, when presidential resort to inherent authority is most likely to cause constitutional concern, the sort of action usually involved—the making of executive agreements, threats of war, commitments of armed forces—is of such a nature that no justiciable issue can be raised.

On occasion important questions of presidential power do come before the Court. But the Justices have almost always evinced great reluctance to engage in battle with the executive. There have been periods—the New Deal is the best example—when the judicial branch has attempted to overrule the policies of a presidentially-dominated government, and there have even been direct confrontations—like the Steel Seizure Case of 1952—in which it has rebuked a President for exceeding his authority. But when vital issues of presidential power are involved, the judiciary's usual approach has been to delay or avoid decision and, when this has not been possible, to uphold the executive's exercise of power. Indeed even in those rare instances when it has ruled against the President, the Court has generally blunted the effect of its adverse decisions by using cautious, qualified, and ambiguous language. In short, the Supreme Court has consistently given Presidents a wide berth in judging the validity of their claims to power.

Despite the fact that most assertions of presidential authority are never subjected to judicial review, however, and notwithstanding the judicial restraint displayed in this highly-charged political field, Supreme Court decisions provide the only formal exposition of the Presidency's constitutional power. If they are less authoritative than American governmental mythology insists, still those decisions set the standards for presidential actions and provide American society with norms by which to judge their legitimacy. Recognizing all of the qualifications that reality imposes on the Supreme Court's reviewing authority, its opinions nonetheless represent the "constitutional concept" of presidential power.

The case excerpts presented here deal with judicial interpretation of the President's authority in a number of important problem areas: foreign relations, warmaking, crisis government, control over administrative policy, and the preservation of domestic peace. The first selection constitutes a major pronouncement on presidential power to conduct the nation's external affairs. In this case, *United States* v. *Curtiss-Wright Export Corporation*, the Court not only upheld a broad delegation of legislative authority to the President, it also expounded on his independent power in the field of greatest contemporary concern. Much of the decision was *obiter dicta*, but in adverting to "the very delicate, plenary and exclusive power of the President as the sole organ of the federal government in the field of international relations," the Court in effect constitutionalized this Hamiltonian conception of executive authority.

In the second selection, from the Civil War *Prize Cases*, the Court provided constitutional answers to two vital questions regarding the President's power under crisis conditions, as it accepted the view that he may both determine the existence of an emergency and take whatever measures he deems necessary to meet it. The President cannot "declare" war in the legal or constitutional sense, but as Commander in Chief he may nonetheless commit the nation to military action without congressional approval when the nation's survival is at stake. He has independent authority, in other words, to make "defensive war"—a concept which has been projected into the era of international crisis by several of Abraham Lincoln's more recent successors.

The next series of three readings deals with presidential power over individual liberty and private property in time of war. The excerpt from *Ex parte Milligan*, in which the Court declared unconstitutional Lincoln's establishment of martial rule during the Civil War, is a forceful rejection of the crisis doctrine of unlimited executive-military authority and an eloquent defense of constitutional principles. But the decision was handed down over a year after the war's end and the President's death; and its ringing insistence that "none of [the Constitution's] provisions can be suspended during any of the great exigencies of government" seems rhetorical in view of the extraconstitutional regime which Lincoln had instituted in his effort to preserve the nation. Indeed the next selection, from the World War II *Korematsu* decision, emphasizes the point. For in that case the Court put its constitutional imprimatur on just the sort of executive-military resort to power that the *Milligan* ruling had implicitly rejected. And though it tried to lessen the blow to constitutional standards by talking about the "war power of Congress and the Executive," in fact the World War II exclusion of Japanese-Americans from the West Coast was initiated under the authority of the President alone. Thus *Korematsu* is the leading example of the judiciary's reluctance to substitute its judgment of constitutionality for the executive's determination of necessity under wartime conditions. The third excerpt in this series is from the 1952 Steel Seizure Case and is the Supreme Court's most recent major decision regarding presidential power. Here the issue of executive authority to determine the existence of an emergency and to take steps in defense of the national security—seemingly established by *The Prize Cases*—was reopened. For despite a declaration of national emergency by President Truman, and although he insisted that seizure of the steel industry was necessary to assure continued production in support of the Korean War effort, the Court declared that the President had acted beyond his legitimate powers. There were many non-constitutional factors involved in this case—the absence of declared war, the President's lack of popular support, the Court's concern about projecting presidential emergency power into an era of recurrent emergencies—and it is significant that not even his concurring colleagues agreed with Justice Black's simplistic interpretation of the separation-of-powers principle as a check on presidential authority. But however qualified the ruling may have been, and whatever its merit or effectiveness as constitutional doctrine, *Youngstown Sheet & Tube Company* v. *Sawyer* remains a landmark decision as the only time the Supreme Court has struck down a resort to inherent executive power under wartime conditions.

The next selection is from a less spectacular but still important decision limiting presidential power. Here the issue was the scope of executive authority over the administrative agencies of government, and specifically in *Humphrey's Executor* v. *United States*, over those agencies established by Congress to operate as independent regulatory commissions. The Court handed down this opinion in the midst of its great struggle with President Roosevelt over the constitutional validity of the New Deal, and there is more than a little animosity in its statement that "one who holds his office only during the pleasure of another cannot be depended upon to maintain an attitude of independence against the latter's will." But the doctrine of *Humphrey's Executor* has been reiterated by later Courts, and its limitation on the President's power to implement policy through the removal of recalcitrant administrative officials remains in effect.

The final selection in this section, *In re Neagle*, involves the scope of the President's power under his constitutional duty "to take care that the laws be faithfully executed." Ostensibly this clause refers to laws passed by Congress, but in the *Neagle* decision, the Court broadened the concept to include "any obligation fairly and properly inferable" from the Constitution. The result was to provide a constitutional base for the President's power to protect "the peace of the United States." Arising out of a bizarre incident before the century's turn, this ruling gave the executive authority of undefined (and still largely unexplored) magnitude in domestic affairs. Resuscitated by Presidents Eisenhower and Kennedy in support of their efforts to enforce the law of the Constitution at Little Rock and Oxford, the idea of the President as protector of internal peace has important implications for contemporary American society.

Like the Presidents themselves, the Justices of the Supreme Court have adopted varying conceptions of presidential power. And like the presidential views, those of the judges have reflected the changing needs, demands, and moods of the nation and the world. But over the long course of American history, and particularly since the Roosevelt era, the Court has supported the development of a strong Presidency. In any event, it has never been an insurmountable obstacle to the exercise of presidential power. Indeed, one of the great issues that has confronted the judicial branch during crisis periods is whether it should acquiesce in extraordinary exercises of presidential authority and thereby legitimize actions whose constitutionality is doubtful.

Justice Jackson raised this problem in his dissent in *Korematsu*, when he declared that "a civil court cannot be made to enforce an order which violates constitutional limitations even if it is a reasonable exercise of military authority." But the weight of judicial opinion rejects the notion of distinguishing between necessity and constitutionality, and a consistent majority of the Court has accepted the view that any necessary exercise of presidential authority can be encompassed within the Constitution. While the result of this attitude has been to allow for the growth of executive power without precipitating a constitutional crisis, it has also raised the question of whether the constitutional provisions dealing with that power are infinitely interpretable and illimitably expansible. The Supreme Court's answer would be "no"; the answer of experience is "yes." But in any event, Justice Jackson's conclusion was correct: that for restraints on our national leaders we must ultimately look not to the Supreme Court but "to the political judgments of their contemporaries and to the moral judgments of history."

PRESIDENTIAL POWER IN FOREIGN AFFAIRS

☆

UNITED STATES V. CURTISS-WRIGHT EXPORT

CORPORATION

Mr. Justice Sutherland delivered the opinion of the Court:

On January 27, 1936, an indictment was returned in the court below, the first count of which charges that appellees, beginning with the 29th day of May, 1934, conspired to sell in the United States certain arms of war; namely, fifteen machine guns, to Bolivia, a country then engaged in armed conflict in the Chaco, in violation of the Joint Resolution of Congress approved May 28, 1934, and the provisions of a proclamation issued on the same day by the President of the United States pursuant to authority conferred by ¶ 1 of the resolution. In pursuance of the conspiracy, the commission of certain overt acts was alleged, details of which need not be stated. The Joint Resolution (chapter 365, 48 Stat. 811) follows:

"Resolved by the Senate and House of Representatives of the United States of America in Congress assembled, That if the President finds that the prohibition of the sale of arms and munitions of war in the United States to those countries now engaged in armed conflict in the Chaco may contribute to the re-establishment of peace between those countries, and if after consultation with the governments of other American Republics and with their cooperation, as well as that of such other governments as he may deem necessary, he makes proclamation to that effect, it shall be unlawful to sell, except under such limitations and exceptions as the President prescribes, any arms or munitions of war in any place in the United States to the countries now engaged in that armed conflict, or to any person, company, or association acting in the interest of

299 U.S. 304 (1936).

either country, until otherwise ordered by the President or by Congress. . . ."

It is contended that by the Joint Resolution the going into effect and continued operation of the resolution was conditioned (a) upon the President's judgment as to its beneficial effect upon the re-establishment of peace between the countries engaged in armed conflict in the Chaco; (b) upon the making of a proclamation, which was left to his unfettered discretion, thus constituting an attempted substitution of the President's will for that of Congress; (c) upon the making of a proclamation putting an end to the operation of the resolution, which again was left to the President's unfettered discretion; and (d) further, that the extent of its operation in particular cases was subject to limitation and exception by the President, controlled by no standard. In each of these particulars, appellees urge that Congress abdicated its essential functions and delegated them to the Executive.

Whether, if the Joint Resolution had related solely to internal affairs, it would be open to the challenge that it constituted an unlawful delegation of legislative power to the Executive, we find it unnecessary to determine. The whole aim of the resolution is to affect a situation entirely external to the United States, and falling within the category of foreign affairs. The determination which we are called to make, therefore, is whether the Joint Resolution, as applied to that situation, is vulnerable to attack under the rule that forbids a delegation of the lawmaking power. In other words, assuming (but not deciding) that the challenged delegation, if it were confined to internal affairs, would be invalid, may it nevertheless be sustained on the ground that its exclusive aim is to afford a remedy for a hurtful condition within foreign territory?

It will contribute to the elucidation of the question if we first consider the differences between the powers of the federal government in respect of foreign or external affairs and those in respect of domestic or internal affairs. That there are differences between them, and that these differences are fundamental, may not be doubted.

The two classes of powers are different, both in respect of their origin and their nature. The broad statement that the federal government can exercise no powers except those specifically enumerated in the Constitution, and such implied powers as are necessary and proper to carry into effect the enumerated powers, is categorically true only in respect of our internal affairs. In that field, the primary purpose of the Constitution was to carve from the general mass of legislative powers *then possessed by the states* such portions as it was thought desirable to vest in the federal government, leav-

ing those not included in the enumeration still in the states. That
this doctrine applies only to powers which the states had is self-
evident. And since the states severally never possessed international
powers, such powers could not have been carved from the mass of
state powers but obviously were transmitted to the United States
from some other source. During the colonial period, those powers
were possessed exclusively by and were entirely under the control of
the Crown. By the Declaration of Independence, "the Representatives of the United States of America" declared the United [not the
several] Colonies to be free and independent states, and as such to
have "full Power to levy War, conclude Peace, contract Alliances,
establish Commerce and to do all other Acts and Things which
Independent States may of right do."

As a result of the separation from Great Britain by the colonies,
acting as a unit, the powers of external sovereignty passed from the
Crown not to the colonies severally, but to the colonies in their
collective and corporate capacity as the United States of America.
Even before the Declaration, the colonies were a unit in foreign
affairs, acting through a common agency—namely, the Continental
Congress, composed of delegates from the thirteen colonies. That
agency exercised the powers of war and peace, raised an army,
created a navy, and finally adopted the Declaration of Independence.
Rulers come and go; governments end and forms of government
change; but sovereignty survives. A political society cannot endure
without a supreme will somewhere. Sovereignty is never held in
suspense. When, therefore, the external sovereignty of Great Britain
in respect of the colonies ceased, it immediately passed to the
Union. . . .

The Union existed before the Constitution, which was ordained
and established among other things to form "a more perfect Union."
Prior to that event, it is clear that the Union, declared by the Articles of Confederation to be "perpetual," was the sole possessor of
external sovereignty, and in the Union it remained without change
save in so far as the Constitution in express terms qualified its exercise. . . .

It results that the investment of the federal government with the
powers of external sovereignty did not depend upon the affirmative
grants of the Constitution. The powers to declare and wage war, to
conclude peace, to make treaties, to maintain diplomatic relations
with other sovereignties, if they had never been mentioned in the
Constitution, would have vested in the federal government as necessary concomitants of nationality. Neither the Constitution nor the
laws passed in pursuance of it have any force in foreign territory unless in respect of our own citizens . . . ; and operations of the nation

in such territory must be governed by treaties, international under-standings and compacts, and the principles of international law. As a member of the family of nations, the right and power of the United States in that field are equal to the right and power of the other mem-bers of the international family. Otherwise, the United States is not completely sovereign. . . .

Not only, as we have shown, is the federal power over external af-fairs in origin and essential character different from that over internal affairs, but participation in the exercise of the power is significan ly limited. In this vast external realm, with its important, complicatvd, delicate and manifold problems, the President alone has the power to speak or listen as a representative of the nation. He *makes* treaties with the advice and consent of the Senate; but he alone negotiates. Into the field of negotiation the Senate cannot intrude; and Congress itself is powerless to invade it. . . .

It is important to bear in mind that we are here dealing not a'one with an authority vested in the President by an exertion of legislative power, but with such an authority plus the very delicate, plenary and exclusive power of the President as the sole organ of the federal gov-ernment in the field of international relations—a power which does not require as a basis for its exercise an act of Congress, but which, of course, like every other governmental power, must be exercised in subordination to the applicable provisions of the Constitution. It is quite apparent that if, in the maintenance of our international re-lations, embarrassment—perhaps serious embarrassment—is to be avoided and success for our aims achieved, congressional legislation which is to be made effective through negotiation and inquiry within the international field must often accord to the President a degree of discretion and freedom from statutory restriction which would not be admissible were domestic affairs alone involved. Moreover, he, not Congress, has the better opportunity of knowing the conditions which prevail in foreign countries, and especially is this true in time of war. He has his confidential sources of information. He has his agents in the form of diplomatic, consular and other officials. Secrecy in re-spect of information gathered by them may be highly necessary, and the premature disclosure of it productive of harmful results. Indeed, so clearly is this true that the first President refused to accede to a request to lay before the House of Representatives the instructions, correspondence and documents relating to the negotiation of the Jay Treaty—a refusal the wisdom of which was recognized by the House itself and has never since been doubted. In his reply to the request, President Washington said:

"The nature of foreign negotiations requires caution, and their success must often depend on secrecy; and even when brought to a conclusion a full disclosure of all the measures, demands, or eventual concessions which may have been proposed or contemplated would be extremely impolitic; for this might have a pernicious influence on future negotiations, or produce immediate inconveniences, perhaps danger and mischief, in relation to other powers. The necessity of such caution and secrecy was one cogent reason for vesting the power of making treaties in the President, with the advice and consent of the Senate, the principle on which that body was formed confining it to a small number of members. To admit, then, a right in the House of Representatives to demand and to have as a matter of course all the papers respecting a negotiation with a foreign power would be to establish a dangerous precedent."

The marked difference between foreign affairs and domestic affairs in this respect is recognized by both houses of Congress in the very form of their requisitions for information from the executive departments. In the case of every department except the Department of State, the resolution *directs* the official to furnish the information. In the case of the State Department, dealing with foreign affairs, the President is requested to furnish the information "if not incompatible with the public interest." A statement that to furnish the information is not compatible with the public interest rarely, if ever, is questioned.

When the President is to be authorized by legislation to act in respect of a matter intended to affect a situation in foreign territory, the legislator properly bears in mind the important consideration that the form of the President's action—or, indeed, whether he shall act at all—may well depend, among other things, upon the nature of the confidential information which he has or may thereafter receive, or upon the effect which his action may have upon our foreign relations. This consideration, in connection with what we have already said on the subject, discloses the unwisdom of requiring Congress in this field of governmental power to lay down narrowly definite standards by which the President is to be governed. . . .

In the light of the foregoing observations, it is evident that this court should not be in haste to apply a general rule which will have the effect of condemning legislation like that under review as constituting an unlawful delegation of legislative power. The principles which justify such legislation find overwhelming support in the unbroken legislative practice which has prevailed almost from the inception of the national government to the present day. . . .

Practically every volume of the United States Statutes contains one or more acts or joint resolutions of Congress authorizing action by the President in respect of subjects affecting foreign relations, which either leave the exercise of the power to his unrestricted judgment, or provide a standard far more general than that which has always been considered requisite with regard to domestic affairs.

. . . A legislative practice such as we have here, evidenced not by only occasional instances, but marked by the movement of a steady stream for a century and a half of time, goes a long way in the direction of proving the presence of unassailable ground for the constitutionality of the practice, to be found in the origin and history of the power involved, or in its nature, or in both combined. . . .

We deem it unnecessary to consider, seriatim, the several clauses which are said to evidence the unconstitutionality of the Joint Resolution as involving an unlawful delegation of legislative power. It is enough to summarize by saying that, both upon principle and in accordance with precedent, we conclude there is sufficient warrant for the broad discretion vested in the President to determine whether the enforcement of the statute will have a beneficial effect upon the re-establishment of peace in the affected countries; whether he shall make proclamation to bring the resolution into operation; whether and when the resolution shall cease to operate and to make proclamation accordingly; and to prescribe limitations and exceptions to which the enforcement of the resolution shall be subject. . . .

PRESIDENTIAL POWER TO
MAKE WAR

☆

THE PRIZE CASES

Mr. Justice Grier delivered the opinion of the Court:

There are certain propositions of law which must necessarily affect the ultimate decision of these cases, and many others, which it will be proper to discuss and decide before we notice the special facts peculiar to each.

They are, 1st. Had the President a right to institute a blockade of ports in possession of persons in armed rebellion against the government, on the principles of international law, as known and acknowledged among civilized States? . . .

1. Neutrals have a right . . . to enter the ports of a friendly nation for the purposes of trade and commerce, but are bound to recognize the rights of a belligerent engaged in actual war, to use this mode of coercion, for the purpose of subduing the enemy.

That a blockade *de facto* actually existed, and was formally declared and notified by the President on the 27th and 30th of April, 1861, is an admitted fact in these cases.

That the President, as the Executive Chief of the Government and Commander in Chief of the Army and Navy, was the proper person to make such notification, has not been, and cannot be disputed.

The right of prize and capture has its origin in the *jus belli*, and is governed and adjudged under the law of nations. To legitimate the capture of a neutral vessel or property on the high seas, a war must exist *de facto*, and the neutral must have a knowledge or notice of the intention of one of the parties belligerent to use this mode of coercion against a port, city, or territory, in possession of the other.

2 Black 635 (1863).

Let us enquire whether, at the time this blockade was instituted, a state of war existed which would justify a resort to these means of subduing the hostile force.

War has been well defined to be, "That state in which a nation prosecutes its right by force."

The parties belligerent in a public war are independent nations. But it is not necessary to constitute war, that both parties should be acknowledged as independent nations or sovereign States. A war may exist where one of the belligerents claims sovereign rights as against the other.

Insurrection against a government may or may not culminate in an organized rebellion, but a civil war always begins by insurrection against the lawful authority of the government. A civil war is never solemnly declared; it becomes such by its accidents—the number, power, and organization of the persons who originate and carry it on. When the party in rebellion occupy and hold in a hostile manner a certain portion of territory; have declared their independence; have cast off their allegiance; have organized armies; have commenced hostilities against their former sovereign, the world acknowledges them as belligerents, and the contest a *war*. *They* claim to be in arms to establish their liberty and independence, in order to become a sovereign State, while the sovereign party treats them as insurgents and rebels who owe allegiance, and who should be punished with death for their treason. . . .

As a civil war is never publicly proclaimed, *eo nomine* against insurgents, its actual existence is a fact in our domestic history which the Court is bound to notice and to know.

The true test of its existence, as found in the writing of the sages of the common law, may be thus summarily stated: "When the regular course of justice is interrupted by revolt, rebellion, or insurrection, so that the Courts of Justice cannot be kept open, *civil war exists* and hostilities may be prosecuted on the same footing as if those opposing the government were foreign enemies invading the land."

By the Constitution, Congress alone has the power to declare a national or foreign war. It cannot declare war against a State, or any number of States, by virtue of any clause in the Constitution. The Constitution confers on the President the whole Executive power. He is bound to take care that the laws be faithfully executed. He is Commander in Chief of the Army and Navy of the United States, and of the militia of the several States when called into the actual service of the United States. He has no power to initiate or declare a war either against a foreign nation or a domestic State. But by the Acts of Congress of February 28th, 1795, and 3d of March, 1807, he is authorized to call out the militia and use the military and naval forces of the United States in case of invasion by foreign nations, and to suppress insurrection against the government of a State or of the United States.

If a war be made by invasion of a foreign nation, the President is not only authorized but bound to resist force by force. He does not initiate the war, but is bound to accept the challenge without waiting for any special legislative authority. And whether the hostile party be a foreign invader, or States organized in rebellion, it is none the less a war, although the declaration of it be *unilateral*. . . .

The battles of Palo Alto and Resaca de la Palma had been fought before the passage of the Act of Congress of May 13th, 1846, which recognized *a state of war as existing by the act of the Republic of Mexico*. This act not only provided for the future prosecution of the war, but was itself a vindication and ratification of the Act of the President in accepting the challenge without a previous formal declaration of war by Congress.

This greatest of civil wars was not gradually developed by popular commotion, tumultuous assemblies, or local unorganized insurrections. However long may have been its previous conception, it nevertheless sprung forth suddenly from the parent brain, a Minerva in the full panoply of *war*. The President was bound to meet it in the shape it presented itself, without waiting for Congress to baptize it with a name; and no name given to it by him or them could change the fact. . . .

Whether the President in fulfilling his duties, as Commander in Chief, in suppressing an insurrection, has met with such armed hostile resistance, and a civil war of such alarming proportions as will compel him to accord to them the character of belligerents, is a question to be decided *by him*, and this Court must be governed by the decisions and acts of the political department of the government to which this power was entrusted. "He must determine what degree of force the crisis demands." The proclamation of blockade is itself official and conclusive evidence to the Court that a state of war existed which demanded and authorized a recourse to such a measure, under the circumstances peculiar to the case. . . .

If it were necessary to the technical existence of a war, that it should have a legislative sanction, we find it in almost every act passed at the extraordinary session of the Legislature of 1861, which was wholly employed in enacting laws to enable the government to prosecute the war with vigor and efficiency. And finally, in 1861, we find Congress *ex majore cautela* and in anticipation of such astute objections, passing an act "approving, legalizing, and making valid all the acts, proclamations, and orders of the President, etc., as if they had been *issued and done under the previous express authority* and direction of the Congress of the United States."

Without admitting that such an act was necessary under the circumstances, it is plain that if the President had in any manner assumed powers which it was necessary should have the authority or sanction of Congress, that on the well-known principle of law, *omnis ratihabitio retrotrahitur et mandato equiparatu.*, this ratification has operated to perfectly cure the defect. . . .

On this first question therefore we are of the opinion that the President had a right, *jure belli*, to institute a blockade of ports in possession of the States in rebellion, which neutrals are bound to regard. . . .

Mr. Justice Nelson, dissenting:

. . . In the case of a rebellion or resistance of a portion of the people of a country against the established government, there is no doubt, if in its progress and enlargement the government thus sought to be overthrown sees fit, it may by the competent power recognize or declare the existence of a state of civil war, which will draw after it all the consequences and rights of war between the contending parties.

. . . But before this insurrection against the established government can be dealt with on the footing of a civil war, within the meaning of the law of nations and the Constitution of the United States, and which will draw after it belligerent rights, it must be recognized or declared by the war-making power of the government.

. . . Instead, therefore, of inquiring after armies and navies, and victories lost and won, or organized rebellion against the general government, the inquiry should be into the law of nations and into the municipal fundamental laws of the government. For we find there that to constitute a civil war in the sense in which we are speaking, before it can exist, in contemplation of law, it must be recognized or declared by the sovereign power of the State, and which sovereign power by our Constitution is lodged in the Congress of the United States—civil war, therefore, under our system of government, can exist only by an act of Congress, which requires the assent of two of the great departments of the government, the executive and legislative.

We have thus far been speaking of the war power under the Constitution of the United States, and as known and recognized by the law of nations. But we are asked, what would become of the peace and integrity of the Union in case of an insurrection at home or invasion from abroad if this power could not be exercised by the President in the recess of Congress, and until that body could be assembled?

[*The opinion proceeds to note the power of the President, under various Acts of Congress to call forth the militia in times of emergency.*]

It will be seen, therefore, that ample provision has been made under the Constitution and laws against any sudden and unexpected disturbance of the public peace from insurrection at home or invasion from abroad. . . .

[But the Acts referred to] did not, and could not under the Constitution, confer on the President the power of declaring war against a State of this Union, or of deciding that war existed, and upon that ground authorize the capture and confiscation of the property of every citizen of the State whenever it was found on the waters. The laws of war, whether the war be civil or *inter gentes*, as we have seen, convert every citizen of the hostile State into a public enemy, and treat him accordingly, whatever may have been his previous conduct. This great power over the business and property of the citizen is reserved to the legislative department by the express words of the Constitution. It cannot be delegated or surrendered to the Executive. Congress alone can determine whether war exists or should be declared; and until they have acted, no citizen of the State can be punished in his person or property, unless he has committed some offense against a law of Congress passed before the act was committed, which made it a crime, and defined the punishment. The penalty of confiscation for the acts of others with which he had no concern cannot lawfully be inflicted. . . .

Upon the whole, after the most careful consideration of this case which the pressure of other duties has admitted, I am compelled to the conclusion that no civil war existed between this government and the States in insurrection till recognized by the Act of Congress 13th of July, 1861; that the President does not possess the power under the Constitution to declare war or recognize its existence within the meaning of the law of nations, which carries with it belligerent rights, and thus change the country and all its citizens from a state of peace to a state of war; that this power belongs exclusively to the Congress of the United States, and, consequently, that the President had no power to set on foot a blockade under the law of nations, and that the capture of the vessel and cargo in this case, and in all cases before us in which the capture occurred before the 13th of July, 1861, for breach of blockade, or as enemies' property, are illegal and void, and that the decrees of condemnation should be reversed and the vessel and cargo restored.

PRESIDENTIAL POWER IN
TIME OF WAR

☆

EX PARTE MILLIGAN

Mr. Justice Davis delivered the opinion of the Court:

. . . The importance of the main question presented by this record cannot be overstated; for it involves the very framework of the government and the fundamental principles of American liberty.

During the late wicked rebellion, the temper of the times did not allow that calmness in deliberation and discussion so necessary to a correct conclusion of a purely judicial question. Then, considerations of safety were mingled with the exercise of power; and feelings and interests prevailed which are happily terminated. Now that the public safety is assured, this question, as well as all others, can be discussed and decided without passion or the admixture of any element not required to form a legal judgment. We approach the investigation of this case, fully sensible of the magnitude of the inquiry and the necessity of full and cautious deliberation. . . .

The controlling question in the case is this: Upon the facts stated in Milligan's petition, and the exhibits filed, had the military commission [established under presidential authority] mentioned in it jurisdiction, legally, to try and sentence him? Milligan, not a resident of one of the rebellious States, or a prisoner of war, but a citizen of Indiana for twenty years past, and never in the military or naval service, is, while at his home, arrested by the military power of the United States, imprisoned, and, on certain criminal charges preferred against him, tried, convicted, and sentenced to be hanged by a military commission, organized under the direction of the military commander of the military district of Indiana. Had this tribunal the legal power and authority to try and punish this man?

No graver question was ever considered by this court, nor one

4 Wallace 2 (1866).

which more nearly concerns the rights of the whole people; for it is the birthright of every American citizen when charged with crime, to be tried and punished according to law. . . . The Constitution of the United States is a law for rulers and people, equally in war and in peace, and covers with the shield of its protection all classes of men, at all times, and under all circumstances. No doctrine involving more pernicious consequences was ever invented by the wit of man than that any of its provisions can be suspended during any of the great exigencies of government. Such a doctrine leads directly to anarchy or despotism, but the theory of necessity on which it is based is false; for the government, within the Constitution, has all the powers granted to it which are necessary to preserve its existence; as has been happily proved by the result of the great effort to throw off its just authority.

Have any of the rights guaranteed by the Constitution been violated in the case of Milligan? and if so, what are they?

Every trial involves the exercise of judicial power; and from what source did the military commission that tried him derive their authority? Certainly no part of the judicial power of the country was conferred on them; because the Constitution expressly vests it "in one Supreme Court and such inferior courts as the Congress may from time to time ordain and establish," and it is not pretended that the commission was a court ordained and established by Congress. They cannot justify on the mandate of the President, because he is controlled by law, and has his appropriate sphere of duty, which is to execute, not to make, the laws; and there is "no unwritten criminal code to which resort can be had as a source of jurisdiction." . . .

It is claimed that martial law covers with its broad mantle the proceedings of this military commission. The proposition is this: that in a time of war the commander of an armed force (if, in his opinion, the exigencies of the country demand it, and of which he is to judge) has the power, within the lines of his military district, to suspend all civil rights and their remedies, and subject citizens as well as soldiers to the rule of his will; and in the exercise of his lawful authority cannot be restrained, except by his superior officer or the President of the United States.

If this position is sound to the extent claimed, then when war exists, foreign or domestic, and the country is subdivided into military departments for mere convenience, the commander of one of them can, if he chooses, within his limits, on the plea of necessity, with the approval of the Executive, substitute military force for, and to the exclusion of, the laws, and punish all persons, as he thinks right and proper, without fixed or certain rules.

The statement of this proposition shows its importance; for, if true, republican government is a failure, and there is an end of liberty regulated by law. Martial law, established on such a basis, destroys every guarantee of the Constitution, and effectually renders the "military independent of, and superior to, the civil power"—the attempt to do which by the King of Great Britain was deemed by our fathers such an offense, that they assigned it to the world as one of the causes which impelled them to declare their independence. Civil liberty and this kind of martial law cannot endure together; the antagonism is irreconcilable; and, in the conflict, one or the other must perish.

This nation, as experience has proved, cannot always remain at peace, and has no right to expect that it will always have wise and humane rulers, sincerely attached to the principles of the Constitution. Wicked men, ambitious of power, with hatred of liberty and contempt of law, may fill the place once occupied by Washington and Lincoln; and if this right is conceded, and the calamities of war again befall us, the dangers to human liberty are frightful to contemplate. If our fathers had failed to provide for just such a contingency, they would have been false to the trust reposed in them. They knew —the history of the world told them—the nation they were founding, be its existence short or long, would be involved in war; how often or how long continued, human foresight could not tell; and that unlimited power, wherever lodged at such a time, was especially hazardous to freemen. For this, and other equally weighty reasons, they secured the inheritance they had fought to maintain, by incorporating in a written Constitution the safeguards which time had proved were essential to its preservation. Not one of these safeguards can the President, or Congress, or the judiciary disturb, except the one concerning the writ of habeas corpus.

It is essential to the safety of every government that, in a great crisis like the one we have just passed through, there should be a power somewhere of suspending the writ of habeas corpus. In every war, there are men of previously good character, wicked enough to counsel their fellow-citizens to resist the measures deemed necessary by a good government to sustain its just authority and overthrow its enemies; and their influence may lead to dangerous combinations. In the emergency of the times, an immediate public investigation according to law may not be possible; and yet the peril to the country may be too imminent to suffer such persons to go at large. Unquestionably, there is then an exigency which demands that the government, if it should see fit, in the exercise of a proper discretion, to make arrests, should not be required to produce the persons arrested in answer to a writ of habeas corpus. The Constitution goes no further. It does not say after a writ of habeas corpus is denied a citi-

zen, that he shall be tried otherwise than by the course of the common law; if it had intended this result, it was easy by the use of
direct words to have accomplished it. The illustrious men who framed
that instrument were guarding the foundations of civil liberty against
the abuses of unlimited power; they were full of wisdom, and the
lessons of history informed them that a trial by an established court,
assisted by an impartial jury, was the only sure way of protecting the
citizen against oppression and wrong. Knowing this, they limited the
suspension to one great right, and left the rest to remain forever
inviolable. But, it is insisted that the safety of the country in time
of war demands that this broad claim for martial law shall be sustained. If this were true, it could be well said that a country, preserved at the sacrifice of all the cardinal principles of liberty, is not
worth the cost of preservation. Happily, it is not so.

It will be borne in mind that this is not a question of the power
to proclaim martial law, when war exists in a community and the
courts and civil authorities are overthrown. Nor is it a question what
rule a military commander, at the head of his army, can impose on
States in rebellion to cripple their resources and quell the insurrection. The jurisdiction claimed is much more extensive. The necessities of the service, during the late Rebellion, required that the loyal
States should be placed within the limits of certain military districts
and commanders appointed in them; and, it is urged, that this, in a
military sense, constituted them the theater of military operations;
and, as in this case, Indiana had been and was again threatened with
invasion by the enemy, the occasion was furnished to establish martial law. The conclusion does not follow from the premises. If armies
were collected in Indiana, they were to be employed in another
locality, where the laws were obstructed and the national authority
disputed. On her soil there was no hostile foot; if once invaded, that
invasion was at an end, and with it all pretext for martial law. Martial law cannot arise from a threatened invasion. The necessity must
be actual and present; the invasion real, such as effectually closes
the courts and deposes the civil administration.

It is difficult to see how the safety of the country required martial
law in Indiana. If any of her citizens were plotting treason, the power
of arrest could secure them, until the government was prepared for
their trial, when the courts were open and ready to try them. It was
as easy to protect witnesses before a civil as a military tribunal; and
as there could be no wish to convict, except on sufficient legal evidence, surely an ordained and established court was better able to
judge of this than a military tribunal composed of gentlemen not
trained to the profession of the law.

It follows, from what has been said on this subject, that there are occasions when martial rule can be properly applied. If, in foreign invasion or civil war, the courts are actually closed, and it is impossible to administer criminal justice according to law, then, in the theater of active military operations, where war really prevails, there is a necessity to furnish a substitute for the civil authority, thus overthrown, to preserve the safety of the army and society; and as no power is left but the military, it is allowed to govern by martial rule until the laws can have their free course. As necessity creates the rule, so it limits its duration; for, if this government is continued after the courts are reinstated, it is a gross usurpation of power. Martial rule can never exist where the courts are open, and in the proper and unobstructed exercise of their jurisdiction. It is also confined to the locality of actual war. . . .

If the military trial of Milligan was contrary to law, then he was entitled, on the facts stated in his petition, to be discharged from custody by the terms of the Act of Congress of March 3, 1863. The provisions of this law having been considered in a previous part of this opinion, we will not restate the views there presented. Milligan avers he was a citizen of Indiana, not in the military or naval service, and was detained in close confinement, by order of the President, from the 5th day of October, 1864, until the 2d day of January, 1865, when the circuit court for the district of Indiana, with a grand jury, convened in session at Indianapolis; and afterwards, on the 27th day of the same month, adjourned without finding an indictment or presentment against him. If these averments were true (and their truth is conceded for the purposes of this case), the court was required to liberate him on taking certain oaths prescribed by the law, and entering into recognizance for his good behavior. . . .

☆

KOREMATSU V. UNITED STATES

Mr. Justice Black delivered the opinion of the Court:

. . . In the light of the principles we announced in the Hirabayashi Case, we are unable to conclude that it was beyond the war power of Congress and the Executive to exclude those of Japanese ancestry from the West Coast war area at the time they did. True, exclusion from the area in which one's home is located is a far greater deprivation than constant confinement to the home from 8 P.M. to 6 A.M. Nothing short of apprehension by the proper military authorities of the gravest imminent danger to the public safety can constitutionally justify either. But exclusion from a threatened area, no less than curfew, has a definite and close relationship to the prevention of espionage and sabotage. The military authorities, charged with the primary responsibility of defending our shores, concluded that curfew provided inadequate protection and ordered exclusion. [The military actions were based on Executive Order 9066 issued by the President.] They did so, as pointed out in our Hirabayashi opinion, in accordance with congressional authority to the military to say who should, and who should not, remain in the threatened areas. . . .

Here, as in the Hirabayashi Case, "we cannot reject as unfounded the judgment of the military authorities and of Congress that there were disloyal members of that population, whose number and strength could not be precisely and quickly ascertained. We cannot say that the war-making branches of the government did not have ground for believing that in a critical hour such persons could not readily be isolated and separately dealt with, and constituted a menace to the national defense and safety, which demanded that prompt and adequate measures be taken to guard against it."

323 U.S. 214 (1944).

Like curfew, exclusion of those of Japanese origin was deemed necessary because of the presence of an unascertained number of disloyal members of the group, most of whom we have no doubt were loyal to this country. It was because we could not reject the finding of the military authorities that it was impossible to bring about an immediate segregation of the disloyal from the loyal that we sustained the validity of the curfew order as applying to the whole group. In the instant case, temporary exclusion of the entire group was rested by the military on the same ground. The judgment that exclusion of the whole group was for the same reason a military imperative answers the contention that the exclusion was in the nature of group punishment based on antagonism to those of Japanese origin. That there were members of the group who retained loyalties to Japan has been confirmed by investigations made subsequent to the exclusion. Approximately five thousand American citizens of Japanese ancestry refused to swear unqualified allegiance to the United States and to renounce allegiance to the Japanese Emperor, and several thousand evacuees requested repatriation to Japan.

We uphold the exclusion order as of the time it was made and when the petitioner violated it. In doing so, we are not unmindful of the hardships imposed by it upon a large group of American citizens. But hardships are part of war, and war is an aggregation of hardships. All citizens alike, both in and out of uniform, feel the impact of war in greater or lesser measure. Citizenship has its responsibilities as well as its privileges, and in time of war the burden is always heavier. Compulsory exclusion of large groups of citizens from their homes, except under circumstances of direst emergency and peril, is inconsistent with our basic governmental institutions. But when under conditions of modern warfare our shores are threatened by hostile forces, the power to protect must be commensurate with the threatened danger. . . .

It is said that we are dealing here with the case of imprisonment of a citizen in a concentration camp solely because of his ancestry, without evidence or inquiry concerning his loyalty and good disposition toward the United States. Our task would be simple, our duty clear, were this a case involving the imprisonment of a loyal citizen in a concentration camp because of racial prejudice. Regardless of the true nature of the assembly and relocation centers—and we deem it unjustifiable to call them concentration camps with all the ugly connotations that term implies—we are dealing specifically with nothing but an exclusion order. To cast this case into outlines of racial prejudice, without reference to the real military dangers which were presented, merely confuses the issue. Korematsu was not excluded from the Military Area because of hostility to him or his race. He *was* excluded because we are at war with the Japanese Empire, because the properly constituted military authorities feared an invasion of our West Coast and felt constrained to take proper security measures, because they decided that the military urgency of the situation demanded that all citizens of Japanese ancestry be segregated from the West Coast temporarily, and finally, because Congress, reposing its confidence in this time of war in our military leaders—as inevitably it must—determined that they should have the power to do just this. There was evidence of disloyalty on the part of some, the military authorities considered that the need for action was great, and time was short. We cannot—by availing ourselves of the calm perspective of hindsight—now say that at that time these actions were unjustified.

Mr. Justice Frankfurter, concurring:
. . . The provisions of the Constitution which confer on the Congress and the President powers to enable this country to wage war are as much part of the Constitution as provisions looking to a nation at peace. And we have had recent occasion to quote approvingly the statement of former Chief Justice Hughes that the war power of the Government is "the power to wage war successfully." Therefore, the validity of action under the war power must be judged wholly in the context of war. That action is not to be stigmatized as lawless because like action in times of peace would be lawless. . . .

Mr. Justice Jackson, dissenting:
. . . [It] is said that if the military commander had reasonable military grounds for promulgating the orders, they are constitutional and become law, and the Court is required to enforce them. There are several reasons why I cannot subscribe to this doctrine.

It would be impracticable and dangerous idealism to expect or insist that each specific military command in an area of probable operations will conform to conventional tests of constitutionality. When an area is so beset that it must be put under military control at all, the paramount consideration is that its measures be successful, rather than legal. The armed services must protect a society, not merely its Constitution. The very essence of the military job is to marshal physical force, to remove every obstacle to its effectiveness, to give it every strategic advantage. Defense measures will not, and often should not, be held within the limits that bind civil authority in peace. No court can require such a commander in such circumstances to act as a reasonable man; he may be unreasonably cautious and exacting. Perhaps he should be. But a commander in temporarily focusing the life of a community on defense is carrying out a military program; he is not making law in the sense the courts know the term. He issues orders, and they may have a certain authority as military commands, although they may be very bad as constitutional law.

But if we cannot confine military expedients by the Constitution, neither would I distort the Constitution to approve all that the military may deem expedient. . . .

In the very nature of things military decisions are not susceptible of intelligent judicial appraisal. They do not pretend to rest on evidence, but are made on information that often would not be admissible and on assumptions that could not be proved. Information in support of an order could not be disclosed to courts without danger that it would reach the enemy. Neither can courts act on communications made in confidence. Hence courts can never have any real alternative to accepting the mere declaration of the authority that issued the order that it was reasonably necessary from a military viewpoint.

Much is said of the danger to liberty from the Army program for deporting and detaining these citizens of Japanese extraction. But a judicial construction of the due process clause that will sustain this order is a far more subtle blow to liberty than the promulgation of the order itself. A military order, however unconstitutional, is not apt to last longer than the military emergency. Even during that period a succeeding commander may revoke it all. But once a judicial opinion rationalizes such an order to show that it conforms to the Constitution, or rather rationalizes the Constitution to show that the Constitution sanctions such an order, the Court for all time has validated the principle of racial discrimination in criminal procedure and of transplanting American citizens. The principle then lies about like a loaded weapon ready for the hand of any authority that can bring forward a plausible claim of an urgent need. Every repetition imbeds that principle more deeply in our law and thinking and expands it to new purposes. . . . A military commander may overstep the bounds of constitutionality, and it is an incident. But if we review and approve, that passing incident becomes the doctrine of the Constitution. There it has a generative power of its own, and all that it creates will be in its own image. . . .

I should hold that a civil court cannot be made to enforce an order which violates constitutional limitations even if it is a reasonable exercise of military authority. The courts can exercise only the judicial power, can apply only law, and must abide by the Constitution, or they cease to be civil courts and become instruments of military policy.

Of course the existence of a military power resting on force, so vagrant, so centralized, so necessarily heedless of the individual, is an inherent threat to liberty. But I would not lead people to rely on this Court for a review that seems to me wholly delusive. The military reasonableness of these orders can only be determined by military superiors. If the people ever let command of the war power fall into irresponsible and unscrupulous hands, the courts wield no power equal to its restraint. The chief restraint upon those who command the physical forces of the country, in the future as in the past, must be their responsibility to the political judgments of their contemporaries and to the moral judgments of history. . . .

☆

YOUNGSTOWN SHEET & TUBE COMPANY V. SAWYER

Mr. Justice Black delivered the opinion of the Court:

We are asked to decide whether the President was acting within his constitutional power when he issued an order directing the Secretary of Commerce to take possession of and operate most of the Nation's steel mills. The mill owners argue that the President's order amounts to lawmaking, a legislative function which the Constitution has expressly confided to the Congress and not to the President. The Government's position is that the order was made on findings of the President that his action was necessary to avert a national catastrophe which would inevitably result from a stoppage of steel production, and that in meeting this grave emergency the President was acting within the aggregate of his constitutional powers as the Nation's Chief Executive and the Commander in Chief of the Armed Forces of the United States. . . .

The President's power, if any, to issue the order must stem either from an act of Congress or from the Constitution itself. There is no statute that expressly authorizes the President to take possession of property as he did here. Nor is there any act of Congress to which our attention has been directed from which such a power can fairly be implied. . . .

Moreover, the use of the seizure technique to solve labor disputes in order to prevent work stoppages was not only unauthorized by any congressional enactment; prior to this controversy, Congress had refused to adopt that method of settling labor disputes. When the Taft-Hartley Act was under consideration in 1947, Congress

343 U.S. 579 (1952).

rejected an amendment which would have authorized such governmental seizures in cases of emergency. . . .

It is clear that if the President had authority to issue the order
he did, it must be found in some provision of the Constitution. And
it is not claimed that express constitutional language grants this
power to the President. The contention is that presidential power
should be implied from the aggregate of his powers under the Constitution. Particular reliance is placed on provisions in Article II
which say that "The executive Power shall be vested in a President
. . ."; that "he shall take Care that the Laws be faithfully executed";
and that he "shall be Commander in Chief of the Army and Navy
of the United States."

The order cannot properly be sustained as an exercise of the
President's military power as Commander in Chief of the Armed
Forces. The Government attempts to do so by citing a number of
cases upholding broad powers in military commanders engaged in
day-to-day fighting in a theater of war. Such cases need not concern
us here. Even though "theater of war" be an expanding concept, we
cannot with faithfulness to our constitutional system hold that the
Commander in Chief of the Armed Forces has the ultimate power
as such to take possession of private property in order to keep labor
disputes from stopping production. This is a job for the Nation's
lawmakers, not for its military authorities.

Nor can the seizure order be sustained because of the several
constitutional provisions that grant executive power to the President.
In the framework for our Constitution, the President's power to see
that laws are faithfully executed refutes the idea that he is to be a
lawmaker. The Constitution limits his functions in the lawmaking
process to the recommending of laws he thinks wise and the vetoing
of laws he thinks bad. And the Constitution is neither silent nor
equivocal about who shall make laws which the President is to execute. The first section of the first article says that "All legislative
Powers herein granted shall be vested in a Congress of the United
States. . . ." After granting many powers to the Congress, Article I
goes on to provide that Congress may "make all Laws which shall
be necessary and proper for carrying into Execution the foregoing
Powers, and all other Powers vested by this Constitution in the
Government of the United States, or in any Department or Officer
thereof."

The President's order does not direct that a congressional policy
be executed in a manner prescribed by Congress—it directs that a
presidential policy be executed in a manner prescribed by the
President. The preamble of the order itself, like that of many statutes, sets out reasons why the President believes certain policies

should be adopted, proclaims these policies as rules of conduct to be followed, and again, like a statute, authorizes a government official to promulgate additional rules and regulations consistent with the policy proclaimed and needed to carry that policy into execution. The power of Congress to adopt such public policies as those proclaimed by the order is beyond question. It can authorize the taking of private property for public use. It can make laws regulating the relationships between employers and employees, prescribing rules designed to settle labor disputes, and fixing wages and working conditions in certain fields of our economy. The Constitution does not subject this lawmaking power of Congress to presidential or military supervision or control.

It is said that other Presidents without congressional authority have taken possession of private business enterprises in order to settle labor disputes. But even if this be true, Congress has not thereby lost its exclusive constitutional authority to make laws necessary and proper to carry out the powers vested by the Constitution "in the Government of the United States, or any Department or Officer thereof."

The Founders of this Nation entrusted the lawmaking power to the Congress alone in both good and bad times. It would do no good to recall the historical events, the fears of power and the hopes for freedom that lay behind their choice. Such a review would but confirm our holding that this seizure order cannot stand.

Mr. Justice Frankfurter, concurring:
. . . The issue before us can be met, and therefore should be, without attempting to define the President's powers comprehensively.

. . . We must therefore put to one side consideration of what powers the President would have had if there had been no legislation whatever bearing on the authority asserted by the seizure, or if the seizure had been only for a short, explicitly temporary period, to be terminated automatically unless congressional approval were given. These and other questions, like or unlike, are not now here. I would exceed my authority were I to say anything about them.

The question before the Court comes in this setting. Congress has frequently—at least sixteen times since 1916—specifically provided for executive seizure of production, transportation, communications, or storage facilities. In every case it has qualified this grant of power with limitations and safeguards. This body of enactments demonstrates that Congress deemed seizure so drastic a power as to require that it be carefully circumscribed whenever the President was vested with this extraordinary authority.

Congress in 1947 was again called upon to consider whether

governmental seizure should be used to avoid serious industrial shutdowns. Congress decided against conferring such power generally and in advance, without special congressional enactment to meet each particular need. . . . In any event, nothing can be plainer than that Congress made a conscious choice of policy in a field full of perplexity and peculiarly within legislative responsibility for choice.

. . . Previous seizure legislation had subjected the powers granted to the President to restrictions of varying degrees of stringency. Instead of giving him even limited powers, Congress in 1947 deemed it wise to require the President, upon failure of attempts to reach a voluntary settlement, to report to Congress if he deemed the power of seizure a needed shot for his locker. The President could not ignore the specific limitations of prior seizure statutes. No more could he act in disregard of the limitation put upon seizure by the 1947 Act.

It cannot be contended that the President would have had power to issue this order had Congress explicitly negated such authority in formal legislation. Congress has expressed its will to withhold this power from the President as though it had said so in so many words. . . .

. . . The powers of the President are not as particularized as are those of Congress. But unenumerated powers do not mean undefined powers. The separation of powers built into our Constitution gives essential content to undefined provisions in the frame of our government.

To be sure, the content of the three authorities of government is not to be derived from an abstract analysis. . . . In short, a systematic, unbroken, executive practice, long pursued to the knowledge of the Congress and never before questioned, engaged in by Presidents who have also sworn to uphold the Constitution, making as it were such exercise of power part of the structure of our government, may be treated as a gloss on "executive power" vested in the President by § 1 of Art. 2. . . . [But no such] practice can be vouched for executive seizure of property at a time when this country was not at war, in the only constitutional way in which it can be at war. . . .

A scheme of government like ours no doubt at times feels the lack of power to act with complete, all-embracing, swiftly moving authority. No doubt a government with distributed authority, subject to be challenged in the courts of law, at least long enough to consider and adjudicate the challenge, labors under restrictions from which other governments are free. It has not been our tradition to envy such governments. In any event our government was designed to have such restrictions. The price was deemed not too high in view of the safeguards which these restrictions afford. I know no more impressive words on this subject than those of Mr. Justice Brandeis:

"The doctrine of the separation of powers was adopted by the Convention of 1787, not to promote efficiency but to preclude the exercise of arbitrary power. The purpose was, not to avoid friction, but, by means of the inevitable friction incident to the distribution of the governmental powers among three departments, to save the people from autocracy." . . .

Mr. Chief Justice Vinson, joined by Mr. Justice Reed and Mr. Justice Minton, dissenting:
Because we cannot agree that affirmance is proper on any ground, and because of the transcending importance of the questions presented not only in this critical litigation but also to the powers of the President and of future Presidents to act in time of crisis, we are compelled to register this dissent.

In passing upon the question of presidential powers in this case, we must first consider the context in which those powers were exercised.

Those who suggest that this is a case involving extraordinary powers should be mindful that these are extraordinary times. . . .

One is not here called upon even to consider the possibility of executive seizure of a farm, a corner grocery store or even a single industrial plant. Such considerations arise only when one ignores the central fact of this case—that the Nation's entire basic steel production would have shut down completely if there had been no government seizure. Even ignoring for the moment whatever confidential information the President may possess as "the Nation's organ for foreign affairs," the uncontroverted affidavits in this record amply support the finding that "a work stoppage would immediately jeopardize and imperil our national defense.". . .

Accordingly, if the President has any power under the Constitution to meet a critical situation in the absence of express statutory authorization, there is no basis whatever for criticizing the exercise of such power in this case.

. . . Admitting that the government could seize the mills, plaintiffs claim that the implied power of eminent domain can be exercised only under an Act of Congress; under no circumstances, they say, can that power be exercised by the President unless he can point to an express provision in enabling legislation. . . .

Under this view, the President is left powerless at the very moment when the need for action may be most pressing and when no one, other than he, is immediately capable of action. Under this view, he is left powerless because a power not expressly given to Congress is nevertheless found to rest exclusively with Congress. . . .

A review of executive action demonstrates that our Presidents have on many occasions exhibited the leadership contemplated by the Framers when they made the President Commander in Chief, and imposed upon him the trust to "take Care that the Laws be faithfully executed." With or without explicit statutory authorization, Presidents have at such times dealt with national emergencies by acting promptly and resolutely to enforce legislative programs, at least to save those programs until Congress could act. Congress and the courts have responded to such executive initiative with consistent approval.

[*The Chief Justice proceeded to review the occasions on which Presidents—from Washington to Roosevelt—exercised emergency power without congressional authorization.*]

This is but a cursory summary of executive leadership. But it amply demonstrates that Presidents have taken prompt action to enforce the laws and protect the country whether or not Congress happened to provide in advance for the particular method of execution. At the minimum, the executive actions reviewed herein sustain the action of the President in this case. And many of the cited examples of Presidential practice go far beyond the extent of power necessary to sustain the President's order to seize the steel mills. The fact that temporary executive seizures of industrial plants to meet an emergency have not been directly tested in this Court furnishes not the slightest suggestion that such actions have been illegal. Rather, the fact that Congress and the courts have consistently recognized and given their support to such executive action indicates that such a power of seizure has been accepted throughout our history. . . .

. . . Much of the argument in this case has been directed at straw men. We do not now have before us the case of a President acting solely on the basis of his own notions of the public welfare. Nor is there any question of unlimited executive power in this case. The President himself closed the door to any such claim when he sent his Message to Congress stating his purpose to abide by any action of Congress, whether approving or disapproving his seizure action. Here, the President immediately made sure that Congress was fully informed of the temporary action he had taken only to preserve the legislative programs from destruction until Congress could act.

The absence of a specific statute authorizing seizure of the steel mills as a mode of executing the laws—both the military procurement program and the anti-inflation program—has not until today been thought to prevent the President from executing the laws. Unlike an administrative commission confined to the enforcement of the statute under which it was created, or the head of a department when administering a particular statute, the President is a constitutional officer charged with taking care that a "mass of legislation" be executed. Flexibility as to mode of execution to meet critical situations is a matter of practical necessity. . . .

Plaintiffs place their primary emphasis on the Labor Management Relations Act of 1947, hereinafter referred to as the Taft-Hartley Act, but do not contend that that Act contains any provision prohibiting seizure.

. . . Plaintiffs admit that the emergency procedures of Taft-Hartley are not mandatory. Nevertheless, plaintiffs apparently argue that, since Congress did provide the eighty-day injunction method for dealing with emergency strikes, the President cannot claim that an emergency exists until the procedures of Taft-Hartley have been exhausted. This argument was not the basis of the District Court's opinion and, whatever merit the argument might have had following the enactment of Taft-Hartley, it loses all force when viewed in light of the statutory pattern confronting the President in this case. . . .

When the President acted on April 8, he had exhausted the procedures for settlement available to him. . . . Faced with immediate national peril through stoppage in steel production on the one hand and faced with destruction of the wage and price legislative programs on the other, the President took temporary possession of the steel mills as the only course open to him consistent with his duty to take care that the laws be faithfully executed. . . .

The diversity of views expressed in the six opinions of the majority, the lack of reference to authoritative precedent, the repeated reliance upon prior dissenting opinions, the complete disregard of the uncontroverted facts showing the gravity of the emergency and the temporary nature of the taking all serve to demonstrate how far afield one must go to affirm the order of the District Court.

The broad executive power granted by Article II to an officer on duty 365 days a year cannot, it is said, be invoked to avert disaster. Instead, the President must confine himself to sending a message to Congress recommending action. Under this messenger-boy concept of the Office, the President cannot even act to preserve legislative programs from destruction so that Congress will have something left to act upon. There is no judicial finding that the executive action was unwarranted because there was in fact no basis for the President's finding of the existence of an emergency for, under this view, the gravity of the emergency and the immediacy of the threatened disaster are considered irrelevant as a matter of law.

. . . Presidents have been in the past, and any man worthy of the Office should be in the future, free to take at least interim action necessary to execute legislative programs essential to survival of the Nation. A sturdy judiciary should not be swayed by the unpleasantness or unpopularity of necessary executive action, but must independently determine for itself whether the President was acting, as required by the Constitution, "to take Care that the Laws be faithfully executed.". . .

As the District Judge stated, this is no time for "timorous" judicial action. But neither is this a time for timorous executive action. Faced with the duty of executing the defense programs which Congress had enacted and the disastrous effects that any stoppage in steel production would have on those programs, the President acted to preserve those programs by seizing the steel mills. There is no question that the possession was other than temporary in character and subject to congressional direction—either approving, disapproving or regulating the manner in which the mills were to be administered and returned to the owners. The President immediately informed Congress of his action and clearly stated his intention to abide by the legislative will. No basis for claims of arbitrary action, unlimited powers or dictatorial usurpation of congressional power appears from the facts of this case. On the contrary, judicial, legislative, and executive precedents throughout our history demonstrate that in this case the President acted in full conformity with his duties under the Constitution.

PRESIDENTIAL POWER OVER ADMINISTRATIVE POLICY

☆

HUMPHREY'S EXECUTOR V. UNITED STATES

Mr. Justice Sutherland delivered the opinion of the Court:

. . . William E. Humphrey, the decedent, on December 10, 1931, was nominated by President Hoover to succeed himself as a member of the Federal Trade Commission and was confirmed by the United States Senate. He was duly commissioned for a term of seven years expiring September 25, 1938; and, after taking the required oath of office, entered upon his duties. On July 25, 1933, President Roosevelt addressed a letter to the commissioner asking for his resignation, on the ground "that the aims and purposes of the Administration with respect to the work of the commission can be carried out most effectively with personnel of my own selection," but disclaiming any reflection upon the commissioner personally or upon his services. The commissioner replied, asking time to consult his friends. After some further correspondence upon the subject, the President, on August 31, 1933, wrote the commissioner expressing the hope that the resignation would be forthcoming and saying:

"You will, I know, realize that I do not feel that your mind and my mind go along together on either the policies or the administering of the Federal Trade Commission, and, frankly, I think it is best for the people of this country that I should have a full confidence."

The commissioner declined to resign, and on October 7, 1933, the President wrote him: "Effective as of this date, you are hereby removed from the office of Commissioner of the Federal Trade Commission."

Humphrey never acquiesced in this action, but continued thereafter to insist that he was still a member of the commission, entitled

295 U.S. 602 (1935).

to perform its duties and receive the compensation provided by law at the rate of $10,000 per annum. Upon these and other facts set forth in the certificate which we deem it unnecessary to recite, the following questions are certified:

"1. Do the provisions of § 1 of the Federal Trade Commission Act, stating that 'any commissioner may be removed by the President for inefficiency, neglect of duty or malfeasance in office,' restrict or limit the power of the President to remove a commissioner except upon one or more of the causes named?

"If the foregoing question is answered in the affirmative, then—

"2. If the power of the President to remove a commissioner is restricted or limited as shown by the foregoing interrogatory and the answer made thereto, is such a restriction or limitation valid under the Constitution of the United States?"

The Federal Trade Commission Act . . . creates a commission of five members to be appointed by the President by and with the advice and consent of the Senate, and § 1 provides:

"Not more than three of the commissioners shall be members of the same political party. The first commissioners appointed shall continue in office for terms of three, four, five, six, and seven years, respectively, from the date of the taking effect of this act, the term of each to be designated by the President, but their successors shall be appointed for terms of seven years, except that any person chosen to fill a vacancy shall be appointed only for the unexpired term of the commissioner whom he shall succeed. The commission shall choose a chairman from its own membership. No commissioner shall engage in any other business, vocation, or employment. Any commissioner may be removed by the President for inefficiency, neglect of duty, or malfeasance in office.". . .

First. The question first to be considered is whether, by the provisions of § 1 of the Federal Trade Commission Act already quoted, the President's power is limited to removal for the specific causes enumerated therein. . . .

. . . The statute fixes a term of office in accordance with many precedents. The first commissioners appointed are to continue in office for terms of three, four, five, six, and seven years, respectively; and their successors are to be appointed for terms of seven years— any commissioner being subject to removal by the President for inefficiency, neglect of duty or malfeasance in office. The words of the act are definite and unambiguous.

The government says the phrase "continue in office" is of no legal significance, and moreover, applies only to the first commissioners. We think it has significance. It may be that, literally, its application is restricted as suggested; but it, nevertheless, lends support to a view contrary to that of the government as to the meaning of the entire requirement in respect of tenure; for it is not easy to suppose that Congress intended to secure the first commissioners against removal except for the causes specified and deny like security to their successors. Putting this phrase aside, however, the fixing of a definite term subject to removal for cause, unless there be some countervailing provision or circumstance indicating the contrary, which here we are unable to find, is enough to establish the legislative intent that the term is not to be curtailed in the absence of such cause. But if the intention of Congress that no removal should be made during the specified term except for one or more of the enumerated causes were not clear upon the face of the statute, as we think it is, it would be made clear by a consideration of the character of the commission and the legislative history which accompanied and preceded the passage of the act.

The commission is to be nonpartisan; and it must, from the very nature of its duties, act with entire impartiality. It is charged with the enforcement of no policy except the policy of the law. Its duties are neither political nor executive, but predominantly quasi-judicial and quasi-legislative. Like the Interstate Commerce Commission, its members are called upon to exercise the trained judgment of a body of experts "appointed by law and informed by experience.". . .

The legislative reports in both houses of Congress clearly reflect the view that a fixed term was necessary to the effective and fair administration of the law. . . .

The debates in both houses demonstrate that the prevailing view was that the commission was not to be "subject to anybody in the government but . . . only to the people of the United States," free from "political domination or control," or the "probability or possibility of such a thing"; to be "separate and apart from any existing department of the government—not subject to the orders of the President.". . .

Thus, the language of the act, the legislative reports and the general purposes of the legislation as reflected by the debates, all combine to demonstrate the congressional intent to create a body of experts who shall gain experience by length of service—a body which shall be independent of Executive authority, *except in its selection*, and free to exercise its judgment without the leave or hindrance of any other official or any department of the government. To the accomplishment of these purposes it is clear that Congress was of the opinion that length and certainty of tenure would vitally contribute. And to hold that, nevertheless, the members of the commission continue in office at the mere will of the President, might be to thwart, in large measure, the very ends which Congress sought to realize by definitely fixing the term of office.

We conclude that the intent of the act is to limit the executive power of removal to the causes enumerated, the existence of none of which is claimed here; and we pass to the second question.

Second. To support its contention that the removal provision of § 1, as we have just construed it, is an unconstitutional interference with the executive power of the President, the government's chief reliance is *Myers* v. *United States*, 272 U.S. 52. . . . Nevertheless, the narrow point actually decided was only that the President had power to remove a postmaster of the first class, without the advice and consent of the Senate, as required by act of Congress. In the course of the opinion of the court, expressions occur which tend to sustain the government's contention, but these are beyond the point involved, and therefore, do not come within the rule of stare decisis. In so far as they are out of harmony with the views here set forth, these expressions are disapproved. . . .

The office of a postmaster is so essentially unlike the office now involved that the decision in the Myers case cannot be accepted as controlling our decision here. A postmaster is an executive officer restricted to the performance of executive functions. He is charged with no duty at all related to either the legislative or judicial power. The actual decision in the Myers case finds support in the theory that such an officer is merely one of the units in the executive department and hence inherently subject to the exclusive and illimitable power of removal by the Chief Executive, whose subordinate and aid he is. Putting aside dicta, which may be followed if sufficiently persuasive but which are not controlling, the necessary reach of the decision goes far enough to include all purely executive officers. It goes no farther; much less does it include an officer who occupies no place in the executive department and who exercises no part of the executive power vested by the Constitution in the President.

The Federal Trade Commission is an administrative body created by Congress to carry into effect legislative policies embodied in the statute, in accordance with the legislative standard therein prescribed, and to perform other specified duties as a legislative or as a judicial aid. Such a body cannot in any proper sense be characterized as an arm or an eye of the executive. Its duties are performed without executive leave and, in the contemplation of the statute, must be free from executive control. In administrating the provisions of the statute in respect of "unfair methods of competition"—that is to say in filling in and administering the details embodied by the general standard —the commission acts in part quasi-legislatively and in part quasi-judicially. In making investigations and reports thereon for the information of Congress under § 6, in aid of the legislative power it acts as a legislative agency. Under § 7, which authorizes the commission to act as a master in chancery under rules prescribed by the court, it acts as an agency of the judiciary. To the extent that it exercises any executive function—as distinguished from executive power in the constitutional sense—it does so in the discharge and effectuation of its quasi-legislative or quasi-judicial powers, or as an agency of the legislative or judicial departments of the government.

If Congress is without authority to prescribe causes for removal of members of the Trade Commission and limit executive power of removal accordingly, that power at once becomes practically all inclusive in respect of civil officers, with the exception of the judiciary provided for by the Constitution. The Solicitor General, at the bar, apparently recognizing this to be true, with commendable candor agreed that his view in respect of the removability of members of the Federal Trade Commission necessitated a like view in respect of the Interstate Commerce Commission and the Court of Claims. We are thus confronted with the serious question whether not only the members of these quasi-legislative and quasi-judicial bodies, but the judges of the legislative Court of Claims, exercising judicial power . . . continue in office only at the pleasure of the President.

We think it plain under the Constitution that illimitable power of removal is not possessed by the President in respect of officers of the character of those just named. The authority of Congress, in creating quasi-legislative or quasi-judicial agencies, to require them to act in discharge of their duties independently of executive control, cannot well be doubted; and that authority includes, as an appropriate incident, power to fix the period during which they shall continue, and to forbid their removal except for cause in the meantime. For it is quite evident that one who holds his office only during the pleasure of another cannot be depended upon to maintain an attitude of independence against the latter's will.

The fundamental necessity of maintaining each of the three general departments of government entirely free from the control or coercive influence, direct or indirect, of either of the others, has often been stressed and is hardly open to serious question. So much is implied in the very fact of the separation of the powers of these departments by the Constitution, and in the rule which recognizes their essential co-equality. The sound application of a principle that makes one master in his own house precludes him from imposing his control in the house of another who is master there. . . .

The power of removal here claimed for the President falls within this principle, since its coercive influence threatens the independence of a commission, which is not only wholly disconnected from the executive department, but which, as already fully appears, was created by Congress as a means of carrying into operation legislative and judicial powers, and as an agency of the legislative and judicial departments.

In the light of the question now under consideration, we have re-examined the precedents referred to in the Myers case, and find nothing in them to justify a conclusion contrary to that which we have reached. . . .

The result of what we now have said is this: Whether the power of the President to remove an officer shall prevail over the authority of Congress to condition the power by fixing a definite term and precluding a removal except for cause will depend upon the character of the office. The Myers decision, affirming the power of the President alone to make the removal, is confined to purely executive officers. And as to officers of the kind here under consideration, we hold that no removal can be made during the prescribed term for which the officer is appointed, except for one or more of the causes named in the applicable statute. . . .

To the extent that, between the decision in the Myers case, which sustains the unrestrictable power of the President to remove purely executive officers, and our present decision that such power does not extend to an office such as that here involved there shall remain a field of doubt, we leave such cases as may fall within it for future consideration and determination as they arise.

PRESIDENTIAL POWER TO
PROTECT THE PEACE

☆

IN RE NEAGLE

Mr. Justice Miller delivered the opinion of the Court:

. . . Without a more minute discussion of this testimony, it produces upon us the conviction of a settled purpose on the part of Terry and his wife, amounting to a conspiracy, to murder Justice Field. And we are quite sure that if Neagle had been merely a brother or a friend of Judge Field, traveling with him, and aware of all the previous relations of Terry to the judge—as he was—of his bitter animosity, his declared purpose to have revenge even to the point of killing him, he would have been justified in what he did in defense of Mr. Justice Field's life, and possibly of his own.

But such a justification would be a proper subject for consideration on a trial of the case for murder in the courts of the State of California, and there exists no authority in the courts of the United States to discharge the prisoner while held in custody by the State authorities for this offense, unless there be found in aid of the defense of the prisoner some element of power and authority asserted under the government of the United States.

This element is said to be found in the facts that Mr. Justice Field, when attacked, was in the immediate discharge of his duty as judge of the Circuit Courts of the United States within California; that the assault upon him grew out of the animosity of Terry and wife, arising out of the previous discharge of his duty as Circuit Justice in the case for which they were committed for contempt of court; and that the deputy marshal of the United States, who killed Terry in defense of Field's life, was charged with a duty under the law of the United States to protect Field from the violence which Terry was inflicting, and which was intended to lead to Field's death.

135 U.S. 1 (1890).

To the inquiry whether this proposition is sustained by law and the facts which we have recited, we now address ourselves. . . .

We have no doubt that Mr. Justice Field when attacked by Terry was engaged in the discharge of his duties as Circuit Justice of the Ninth Circuit, and was entitled to all the protection under those circumstances which the law could give him.

It is urged, however, that there exists no statute authorizing any such protection as that which Neagle was instructed to give Judge Field in the present case, and indeed no protection whatever against a vindictive or malicious assault growing out of the faithful discharge of his official duties; and that the language of section 753 of the Revised Statutes, that the party seeking the benefit of the writ of habeas corpus must in this connection show that he is "in custody for an act done or omitted in pursuance of a law of the United States," makes it necessary that upon this occasion it should be shown that the act for which Neagle is imprisoned was done by virtue of an Act of Congress. It is not supposed that any special Act of Congress exists which authorizes the marshals or deputy marshals of the United States in express terms to accompany the judges of the Supreme Court through their circuits, and act as a bodyguard to them, to defend them against malicious assaults against their persons. But we are of opinion that this view of the statute is an unwarranted restriction of the meaning of a law designed to extend in a liberal manner the benefit of the writ of habeas corpus to persons imprisoned for the performance of their duty. And we are satisfied that if it was the duty of Neagle, under the circumstances, a duty which could only arise under the laws of the United States, to defend Mr. Justice Field from a murderous attack upon him, he brings himself within the meaning of the section we have recited. This view of the subject is confirmed by the alternative provision, that he must be in custody "for an act done or omitted in pursuance of a law of the United States or of an order, process, or decree of a court or judge thereof, or is in custody in violation of the Constitution or of a law or treaty of the United States."

In the view we take of the Constitution of the United States, any obligation fairly and properly inferable from that instrument, or any duty of the marshal to be derived from the general scope of his duties under the laws of the United States, is "a law" within the meaning of this phrase. It would be a great reproach to the system of government of the United States, declared to be within its sphere sovereign and supreme, if there is to be found within the domain of its powers no means of protecting the judges, in the conscientious and faithful discharge of their duties, from the malice and hatred of those upon whom their judgments may operate unfavorably. . . .

Where, then, are we to look for the protection which we have shown Judge Field was entitled to when engaged in the discharge of his official duties? Not to the courts of the United States; because, as has been more than once said in this court, in the division of the powers of government between the three great departments, executive, legislative and judicial, the judicial is the weakest for the purposes of self-protection and for the enforcement of the powers which it exercises. The ministerial officers through whom its commands must be executed are marshals of the United States, and belong emphatically to the executive department of the government. They are appointed by the President, with the advice and consent of the Senate. They are removable from office at his pleasure. They are subjected by Act of Congress to the supervision and control of the Department of Justice, in the hands of one of the Cabinet officers of the President, and their compensation is provided by Acts of Congress. The same may be said of the district attorneys of the United States, who prosecute and defend the claims of the government in the courts.

The legislative branch of the government can only protect the judicial officers by the enactment of laws for that purpose, and the argument we are now combating assumes that no such law has been passed by Congress.

If we turn to the executive department of the government, we find a very different condition of affairs. The Constitution, section 3, Article II, declares that the President "shall take care that the laws be faithfully executed," and he is provided with the means of fulfilling this obligation by his authority to commission all the officers of the United States, and, by and with the advice and consent of the Senate, to appoint the most important of them and to fill vacancies. He is declared to be Commander in Chief of the army and navy of the United States. The duties which are thus imposed upon him he is further enabled to perform by the recognition in the Constitution, and the creation by Acts of Congress, of executive departments, which have varied in number from four or five to seven or eight, the heads of which are familiarly called cabinet ministers. These aid him in the performance of the great duties of his office, and represent him in a thousand acts to which it can hardly be supposed his personal attention is called, and thus he is enabled to fulfill the duty of his great department, expressed in the phrase that "he shall take care that the laws be faithfully executed."

Is this duty limited to the enforcement of Acts of Congress or of treaties of the United States according to their express terms, or does it include the rights, duties, and obligations growing out of the Constitution itself, our international relations, and all the protection implied by the nature of the government under the Constitution? . . .

We cannot doubt the power of the President to take measures for the protection of a judge of one of the courts of the United States, who, while in the discharge of the duties of his office, is threatened with a personal attack which may probably result in his death, and we think it clear that where this protection is to be afforded through the civil power, the Department of Justice is the proper one to set in motion the necessary means of protection. . . .

But there is positive law investing the marshals and their deputies with powers which not only justify what Marshal Neagle did in this matter, but which imposed it upon him as a duty. In chapter fourteen of the Revised Statutes of the United States, which is devoted to the appointment and duties of the district attorneys, marshals, and clerks of the courts of the United States, section 788 declares:

"The marshals and their deputies shall have, in each State, the same powers, in executing the laws of the United States, as the sheriffs and their deputies in such State may have, by law, in executing the laws thereof."

If, therefore, a sheriff of the State of California was authorized to do in regard to the laws of California what Neagle did, that is, if he was authorized to keep the peace, to protect a judge from assault and murder, then Neagle was authorized to do the same thing in reference to the laws of the United States. . . .

That there is a peace of the United States; that a man assaulting a judge of the United States while in the discharge of his duties violates that peace; that in such case the marshal of the United States stands in the same relation to the peace of the United States which the sheriff of the county does to the peace of the State of California; are questions too clear to need argument to prove them. That it would be the duty of a sheriff, if one had been present at this assault by Terry upon Judge Field, to prevent this breach of the peace, to prevent this assault, to prevent the murder which was contemplated by it, cannot be doubted. And if, in performing this duty, it became necessary for the protection of Judge Field, or of himself, to kill Terry, in a case where, like this, it was evidently a question of the choice of who should be killed, the assailant and violator of the law and disturber of the peace, or the unoffending man who was in his power, there can be no question of the authority of the sheriff to have killed Terry. So the marshal of the United States, charged with the duty of protecting and guarding the judge of the United States court against this special assault upon his person and his life, being present at the critical moment, when prompt action was necessary, found it to be his duty, a duty which he had no liberty to refuse to perform, to take the steps which resulted in Terry's death. This duty was imposed on him by the section of the Revised Statutes which we have recited, in connection with the powers conferred by the State of California upon its peace officers, which become, by this statute, in proper cases, transferred as duties to the marshals of the United States. . . .

The result at which we have arrived upon this examination is, that in the protection of the person and the life of Mr. Justice Field while in the discharge of his official duties, Neagle was authorized to resist the attack of Terry upon him; that Neagle was correct in the belief that without prompt action on his part the assault of Terry upon the judge would have ended in the death of the latter; that such being his well-founded belief, he was justified in taking the life of Terry, as the only means of preventing the death of the man who was intended to be his victim; that in taking the life of Terry, under the circumstances, he was acting under the authority of the law of the United States, and was justified in so doing; and that he is not liable to answer in the courts of California on account of his part in that transaction. . . .

IV

EXPERT
VIEWS

PROFESSIONAL STUDENTS of government and poli-
tics have always been fascinated by the Presidency. Generations of
both foreign and American scholars have regarded the office as a
great experiment in constitutional-democratic leadership and have
watched its development closely. Each of these observers has had
his own ideas about the executive's proper role in American government and all have become engaged in the controversy over presidential power.

As with other commentators on the subject, the experts vary
widely in their views. Among the foreign observers, Alexis de Tocqueville at the beginning of the Jacksonian era despaired of an effective
executive because "All his important acts are directly or indirectly
submitted to the legislature; and where he is independent of it he
can do but little." In 1906, James Bryce voiced doubts about the
office because the American system did not tend to bring "the highest gifts to the highest place." But Harold Laski, writing in the
glow of Franklin Roosevelt's achievements, was hopeful that the
social and economic changes of the 1930s would produce a new
Presidency with power "commensurate to the functions he has to
perform." And in 1960 Denis Brogan noted "the present predomi-
nance of the President." On the whole, foreign—and particularly
British—students of the office, with their parliamentary proclivities,
have argued for strong presidential leadership and have been troubled
by those characteristics of American politics that tend to thwart the
establishment of such leadership.

Despite the cogency of these views from abroad, the readings
presented here are confined to the conceptions of Americans who
have observed (and in some cases been associated with) the Presi-

dency as professional students of the office and its power. Moreover, there is no attempt to include expert views from the inception of the office; rather, all the selections are related to the contemporary Presidency. The preceding selections have provided adequate historical material, and the purpose in this section is to focus on the major issue confronting the office as it is now constituted: whether today's Presidency has too much, too little, or sufficient power to meet the demands of our time.

All these readings share the view that the contemporary Presidency is a powerful institution. But each selection reflects a different attitude regarding the substance and effectiveness of presidential authority, as well as a different assessment of its necessity or desirability, and each is concerned from its own point of view with the future development of the office. The readings are divided into two groups, the first set being related in their emphasis on the *scope* of presidential power; the second in their emphasis on the *limits* of that power.

Among the ten authors presented here, only one—Edward S. Corwin—concludes that the Presidency as it emerged during Franklin Roosevelt's time is excessively and dangerously powerful. In his article tracing the growth of executive authority, Corwin expresses concern lest the Presidency become a "matrix of dictatorship," and he proposes institutional changes to prevent such a result. Clinton Rossiter is not unmindful of the problem Corwin raises, but after outlining the variety of roles in which the President functions and the authority which he exercises in each, Rossiter cautions against any major changes affecting the Presidency's focal position in American government. Aaron Wildavsky argues that since international affairs have become the nation's dominant concern, there is no alternative to virtually absolute presidential control over decision-making in the areas of defense and foreign policy. My own article presents the view that today's office is an institutionalized version of the enormously powerful Lincoln-Wilson-Roosevelt crisis Presidencies, and that in an age of continuing crisis it will probably grow even more powerful. But I believe that the Presidency will remain a position of democratic leadership and that it constitutes the nation's indispensable instrument in meeting the challenges of the nuclear age. James MacGregor Burns also rejects the notion that the success of presidential government will undermine American democracy. On the contrary, he contends that "the stronger we make the Presidency, the more we . . . can hope to realize modern liberal democratic goals." But he fears that with the achievement of its contemporary aims, the powerful Presidency may lose its dynamism and be unable to turn to new purposes.

Thus all these selections express the view that the contemporary

Presidency's vast power dominates the American political scene. And all but Corwin regard this development as both necessary and desirable. Rossiter would maintain the office as it is now constituted; Wildavsky regards presidential dominance in foreign affairs as inevitable in today's world; I see the Presidency's power as being essential to meet the problems confronting us, and I believe the scope of that power should be expanded to meet new challenges. Burns would argue for a conscious attempt to increase executive authority in order to perfect presidential government and sustain its vitality.

Each of the second group of expert observers agrees that the contemporary Presidency is in form and under certain (crisis) conditions a tremendously powerful institution. And all believe that such an institution is needed to meet the problems facing American society. But at least one, Arthur Schlesinger, Jr., is particularly troubled by the absence of restraints on the President's authority in the area of foreign policy and warmaking, while the entire group is concerned with the limitations imposed on the executive's power by a variety of factors which diminish or deny its effectiveness in domestic affairs. The initial selection is a pioneer effort by Richard E. Neustadt to describe the office in terms of the manner in which it actually operates on a problem-by-problem, decision-to-decision basis. Analyzing the array of pressures that impinge upon a President's freedom to choose and to act, Neustadt concludes that the Presidency's power is primarily "the power to persuade," not to command. Focusing on executive-legislation relations, Nelson Polsby cautions against overestimating the extent of conflict between the President and Congress. He agrees that such conflict limits presidential power, but argues that the result has been neither politically nor historically fatal. Louis W. Koenig reviews the manifold political and legislative obstacles to sustained presidential leadership and makes a number of specific recommendations that, in his view, would strengthen the office and enable the President to "stay with the race" against change and emergency. Schlesinger, contending that the President is "notably weaker in dealing with internal than with international problems," asks whether ways can be found to increase his authority over domestic policy while restraining his warmaking power. Finally, Sidney Warren notes the limitations imposed on the contemporary Presidency by the complex considerations of international, as well as domestic, affairs. The President's power is today unprecedented says Warren, but paradoxically in the nuclear age it is more circumscribed than ever before in American history.

The common theme of all the selections in this second set of readings is that the power of the Presidency is less available, less usable, and less effective than it often appears to be; that it is not fixed, but is dependent on events, personalities, and the vagaries of the political systems (global as well as national) within which it operates. With all of this the first group of expert observers would agree. Conversely, all of the second group would endorse the concept of presidential power expounded by their colleagues. The two groups differ primarily in their methods of analyzing executive authority and in their general orientations to the subject. But taken as a whole the readings in this final section reflect the attempt by students of the office to find both the form and the substance of a Presidency equal to the great challenges that now confront it.

THE SCOPE OF
PRESIDENTIAL POWER

☆

EDWARD S. CORWIN: *The Aggrandizement of*
Presidential Power

It is a common allegation that the terms in which the President's
powers are granted are the loosest and most unguarded of any part
of the Constitution, and this is true when Article II is read by
itself. But what warrant is there for reading it thus, rather than in
its context, the Constitution as a whole? When it is read in this
way the net impression left is quite different.

"The Executive power shall be vested in a President of the
United States of America"; "the President shall be Commander in
Chief of the Army and Navy"; with the advice and consent of
the Senate he shall make treaties and appoint to office; he shall
have power to "grant reprieves and pardons for offenses against the
United States"; he shall recommend to Congress "such measures as
he shall judge necessary and expedient"; and so on and so forth.
Yet, in order to exercise any of these powers—in order, indeed, to
subsist—he must have money, and can get it only when and if
Congress appropriates it. Likewise, he is dependent on Congress for
the very agencies through which he must ordinarily exercise his
powers, and Congress is the judge as to the necessity and propriety
of such agencies. Again, he is bound to "take care that the laws"
which Congress enacts are "faithfully executed"—for this purpose
all his powers are in servitude; and Congress has the power to investigate his every official act, and can, by a special procedure, if it

Edward S. Corwin was McCormick Professor of Jurisprudence at Princeton
University. This selection on "Some Aspects of the Presidency" is from *The
Annals*, November, 1941, pp. 122–131. Copyright 1941 by the American Acad-
emy of Political and Social Sciences. Reprinted by permission.

finds him guilty of "high crimes and misdemeanors," impeach him and throw him out of office. Moreover, by the standard set by the prerogative of the British monarch in 1787, his "Executive power" and his power to protect that power were both seriously curtailed. The power to "declare war" was vested in Congress; the Senate was made a participant in his diplomatic powers; he was given a veto upon all legislative acts, but one which the houses may override by a two-thirds vote, whereas the supposed veto of the British monarch was absolute.

TWO CONSTITUTIONAL CONCEPTIONS

In short, the Constitution itself reflects not *one* but *two* conceptions of executive power: the conception that it exists for the most part to serve the legislative power, wherein resides the will of society, and the conception that it ought to be within generous limits autonomous and self-directory. The source of this dualism was the eighteenth-century notion of a *balanced constitution*; its consequence has been a constantly renewed struggle for power between the political branches. Nor has the struggle ceased to this day, although its total result has been, especially within recent years, the vast aggrandizement of the Presidency.

The Constitution was hardly set going when an indicative and decisive event occurred to head the Presidency toward its destiny. "The Executive power shall be vested in a President of the United States," was originally intended merely to settle the issue whether the National Executive should be single or plural and to baptize the office. Yet when the question arose in the first Congress as to how nonjudicial officers appointed by the President and Senate should be removed, Congress, under the leadership of Madison, took action which, in reliance on the clause just recited, attributed this power to the President alone; and 137 years later the Supreme Court, speaking by a Chief Justice who had himself been President, ratified this "practical construction of the Constitution" as the theoretically correct one. Likewise Hamilton, in justifying Washington's course in 1793 in issuing a Proclamation of Neutrality in view of the outbreak of war between France and England, appealed to the "Executive power" clause, which in effect he construed as endowing the President with the complete prerogative of the British monarch in the conduct of foreign affairs except only the "power to declare war," that having been transferred by specific provision of the Constitution to Congress. This time Madison took a brief on the other side; yet who can doubt that Hamilton's view has in the main won out?

In the case of the "fifty destroyer" deal in 1940 the President violated statutes which had been enacted by Congress in the uncontroverted exercise of its specifically delegated powers, and was justified by his Attorney General in so doing, by an argument which empowers the President, as Commander in Chief—and as organ of foreign relations—to ride high, wide, and handsome over the legislative powers of the Nation whenever he deems it desirable to do so. Yet I have heard of no impeachment proceedings being initiated in Congress against either the President or the Attorney General. Quite to the contrary, the attainments of the latter as a constitutional lawyer have been recently proclaimed to the Nation by his elevation to the Supreme Court.

But this confrontation of Hamilton and Madison in 1793 is of importance for a second reason; it signalized the early differentiation of what may be termed the quasi-monarchical and the ultra-Whig conceptions of the Presidency. Under the first two Presidents the former conception prevailed as of course. The Presidency at once furnished what Walter Bagehot would have termed the "dignified element of government" and also directed the legislative process to a notable extent, although without diminishing in the least the spontaneous legislative initiative of the houses themselves—exactly as in contemporary Britain before the younger Pitt, the legislative initiative was divided. The famous Judiciary Act of 1789 was elaborated in the Senate; the acts creating the great executive departments came from the House; Hamilton's financial measures exemplified the legislative leadership of the executive.

JEFFERSON'S VIEW

Jefferson's conception of executive power, on the other hand, was more Whig than that of the British Whigs themselves in subordinating it to "the supreme legislative power." At the time when the presidential election of 1800 was pending in the House, John Marshall predicted that if Jefferson was chosen he would "embody himself in the House of Representatives, and by weakening the office of President" would "increase his personal power. He will . . . become the leader of that party which is about to constitute the majority of the legislature." Better political prophecy has rarely been recorded.

In Jefferson we encounter for the first time a President who is primarily a party leader, only secondarily Chief Executive. The tone of his messages is uniformly deferential to Congress. His first one closes with these words: "Nothing shall be wanting on my part to inform, as far as in my power, the legislative judgment, nor to carry that judgment into faithful execution." His actual guidance of Congress' judgment was none the less constant and unremitting even while often secret and sometimes furtive. The chief instruments of his leadership were the party caucus, which enabled the party membership to present on the floor a united front and over which he himself is alleged to have presided now and then, and his Secretary of the Treasury, Albert Gallatin, whose own influence with Congress was also enormous. At the same time, it should be noted that the principal issues with which Congress was asked to deal legislatively were issues of foreign policy. Nor was the flow of power all in one direction. Both in the enactment of the famous Embargo Act of 1807 and in its subsequent repeal at Congress' insistence, we have an outstanding example of departmental collaboration in the diplomatic field.

What, then, of Marshall's prophecy that Jefferson would weaken the office of President? This, too, was justified by events when the Ulysses' bow of party leadership passed to feebler hands. With the practical disappearance of the Federalist Party the Republican caucus became "the congressional caucus," by which Madison and Monroe were each in turn put in nomination for the Presidency, while the younger Adams was virtually elected by it, through the election being thrown into the House. Thus, for twenty years the plan rejected by the framers, of having the President chosen by Congress, was substantially in operation. During this period the practice grew up of each succeeding President's continuing a considerable part of his predecessor's Cabinet in office; and when he convened them in council the Chief Executive counted the votes of the heads of departments as of equal weight with his own. Hardly more than *primus inter pares* in his own sight, he was glad if Congress accorded him that degree of deference. In short, the Presidency was in commission.

JACKSON'S VIEW

With Jackson's accession this enfeebling tendency was checked as decisively as it was abruptly. Jackson's Presidency was, in truth, no mere revival of the office—it was a remaking of it. The credit, however, should not go to Jackson alone. He contributed an imperious temper, a military reputation, and a striking personality; and he had the good luck to have an admiring public in the shape of a new and ignorant electorate. But the lasting impact of the Jacksonian Presidency upon American constitutional practice also owed much to the constructive skill of his political lieutenants, and particularly to their invention of the National Nominating Convention. When

Jefferson retired in 1809 his party began at once to dissolve into local or personal followings. That the same thing did not happen on Jackson's retirement was due to the rise of the national convention and the political devices which cluster about it.

Backed by a party organization which reached far beyond the halls of Congress, indeed eventually penetrated the remotest corners of the Union, Jackson became the first President in our history to appeal to the people over the heads of their legislative representatives. At the same time, the office itself was thrust forward as one of three *equal* departments of government and to each and every one of its powers was imparted new scope, new vitality. The Presidency became tridimensional, and all of the dimensions underwent more or less enlargement. Jackson was a more dominant party leader than Jefferson; his claim to represent the American people as a whole went to the extent of claiming to embody them; his claim to be one of three *equal* departments inferred the further claim that *all* his powers were autonomous, even his purely executive powers.

The logical implications of Jackson's position, as stated in his famous Bank Veto Message of July 10, 1832, were not exaggerated by his Whig critics, although its practical effects were. "I look upon Jackson," Kent wrote Story early in 1834, "as a detestable, ignorant, reckless, vain, and malignant tyrant. . . . This American elective monarchy frightens me. The experiment, with its foundations laid on universal suffrage and our unfettered press, is of too violent a nature for our excitable people." "The President," thundered Webster in the Senate, "carries on the government; all the rest are subcontractors. . . . A Briareus sits in the center of our system, and with his hundred hands touches everything, controls everything." "We are in the midst of a revolution," lamented Clay, "hitherto bloodless, but tending rapidly towards a total change of the pure republican character of the Government, and to the concentration of all power in the hands of one man."

Actually, prior to the Civil War, the supposed menace was more apparent than real. For this there were several reasons. In the first place, while magnifying the powers of the Presidency, Jackson subscribed to the states' rights doctrine of strict construction of Congress' powers. His legislative role consequently was chiefly negative, being confined for the most part to a vigorous use of the veto power. In the second place, even though it had been otherwise, the further development in the houses since Jefferson's day of the committee system interposed obstacles in the way of presidential participation in legislation which had not existed at first. But a circumstance which contributed even more to the temporary declension of the Jacksonian Presidency was the emergence after 1846 of the issue of slavery in the territories. For the handling of this highly charged question by the devices of negotiation and compromise, Congress, and especially the Senate, offered a far better theater than the Presidency. So the forces making for compromise systematically depressed the Presidency by taking care that only secondary and manageable personalities should be elevated to it. Lastly, the recently enunciated Monroe Doctrine had asserted a restraining principle upon presidential adventuring in the foreign field which gradually became invested with all the moral authority of the Constitution itself—an eminence it was to retain till 1898.

LINCOLN'S VIEW

The last important contribution to the theory of the Presidency until recent decades was Lincoln's, whose ultimate conception of the office was as much an expression of temperament as was Jackson's. A solitary genius who valued the opportunity for reflection above that for counsel, Lincoln came to regard Congress as a more or less necessary nuisance and the Cabinet as a usually unnecessary one. Nor could it have escaped Lincoln's intuition—especially after Buchanan's Message of December 3, 1860—that, if the Union was to be saved, recourse must be had to some still untested source of national power, one which had not become entangled, as had Congress', in the strangulating sophistries of states' rights. So, for a double reason, Lincoln turned to the "Commander in Chief" clause, from which, read in conjunction with the "Executive power" clause, he drew the conclusion that "the war power" was his. Originally, it is true, he appears to have assumed that his power was a simple emergency power whose ad interim decisions Congress must ratify if they were to be permanently valid. But, as the problems of Emancipation and then of Reconstruction loomed, he shifted ground, and his final position was "that as President he had extraordinary legal resources which Congress lacked," and which it could not control.

The long-run effect of Lincoln's Presidency on conceptions of the office would be difficult to exaggerate. Here two points need to be specially noted. The first is that Lincoln's course, fortified by the Supreme Court's dictum in the Prize Cases, that insurrection is "war," affords a strong warrant for any President, called upon to deal with a widespread condition of violence in the country, to ignore all constitutional and statutory restraints in favor of personal liberty. The other is that presidential spokesmen have repeatedly turned to Lincoln's acts as if they supported the thesis of presidential autonomy—in other words, presidential autocracy—in all fields of presidential power, which of course they are far from doing.

Moreover, the immediate effect of Lincoln's incumbency was little short of calamitous for the office. A frontiersman, his conception of the requirements of sound administration were no less naive than Jackson's, whose record as a spoilsman he far surpassed; while except for an ineffectual endeavor to interest Congress in the subject of compensated emancipation, he left the task of procuring necessary legislation to his Cabinet secretaries, and especially to Chase and Stanton, theirs being the departments most concerned. The outcome in the latter case was the creation of a direct relationship between the War Department and the congressional Committee on the Conduct of the War which under Johnson brought the Presidency to the verge of disaster.

JOHNSON'S THEORY OF THE PRESIDENCY

Final appraisement of Johnson's incumbency for the theory of the Presidency is, nevertheless, not easy. Johnson escaped dismissal from office by the High Court of Impeachment by a single vote, but he *escaped!* What is more, it was during his Administration that the Supreme Court confessed its inability, in *Mississippi* v. *Johnson*, to enjoin a President from exceeding his constitutional powers or to order him to perform his constitutional duties. The principle which Marshall had stated in *Marbury* v. *Madison* as applicable to the President's "important political powers," that "in their exercise he is to use his own discretion, and is accountable only to his country in his political character, and to his own conscience," was thus extended *even to the President's duty to enforce the law.* Furthermore, whatever of popular glamour the office had lost under Johnson was promptly restored to it when "the man from Appomattox and its famous apple tree" became President.

Reflecting upon all this, Henry C. Lockwood, in his *The Abolition of the Presidency*, which appeared in 1884, advanced the thesis that only by replacing the President with an executive council after the Swiss model could American liberty be preserved. He wrote:

> The tendency of all people is to elevate a single person to the position of ruler. The idea is simple. It appeals to all orders of intellects. It can be understood by all. Around this center all nationality and patriotism are grouped. A nation comes to know the characteristics and nature of an individual. It learns to believe in the man. Certain contingencies are likely to take place.

It does not require a great amount of political knowledge to form an opinion as to the course of their favorite statesman, whose character they have studied. Under these circumstances, let a person be chosen to an office, with power conferred upon it equal to that of the Presidency of the United States, and it will make but little difference whether the law actually gives him the right to act in a particular direction or not. He determines a policy. He acts. No argument that the law has been violated will avail. He is the chief officer of the nation. He stands alone. He is a separate power in himself. The lines with which we attempt to mark the limits of his power are shadowy and ill-defined. A party, real or imaginary, stands back of him demanding action. In either event, the President acts. The sentiment of hero worship, which to a great extent prevails among the American people, will endorse him. Under our form of government, we do not think so much of what Congress may do. A great multitude declared: "Give us President Grant! We know him. He is strong! He will rule!"

It is interesting to lay alongside Mr. Lockwood's words the contention advanced by Mr. Kemler, in his recently published *Deflation of American Ideals*, that our only escape from totalitarianism is to make the President a perpetual hero!

ABANDONMENT OF LAISSEZ FAIRE

The great accessions to presidential power in recent years have been due in part to an enlarged foreign policy, and in part to the replacement of the laissez faire theory of government with the idea that government should make itself an *active, reforming* force in the field of economic enterprise, which has meant, necessarily, that the *National Government* should be active in this way, inasmuch as the field in question has long since come to transcend state lines.

The result for the Presidency of the latter development has been twofold. On the one hand, Presidents have made themselves spokesmen of the altered outlook, have converted their parties to it—a conversion not infrequently accompanied by backsliding—and, with the popular support thus obtained, have asserted a powerful legislative initiative. On the other hand, Congress, in responding to the President's leadership in its own peculiar field, has found it convenient to aggrandize his executive role enormously, by delegating to him the power to supplement its measures by a type of sublegislation called "administrative regulations." Not all this delegated power, it is true, has gone to the President, but a vast proportion of it has;

and it constitutes a realm of presidential power of which the framers had little prevision, although it began to appear in the field of foreign relations even as early as Washington's second Administration.

The first exponent of the new Presidency was Theodore Roosevelt, whose achievement was to some extent negated by faults of method. Woodrow Wilson was enabled by the advantage of having critically observed his predecessor, by his knowledge of political methods abroad, by a taste for institution building, which was later to divert him into an abortive effort at world organization, and finally by the opportunity afforded by our entrance into the First World War, to illustrate on an unprecedented scale both the new roles of the President—that of legislative leader and that of recipient of delegated legislative power. Our war with Germany was prosecuted for the most part under laws which were drafted under the appraising eye of the President and which conferred upon him far greater powers than those which Lincoln had exercised as Commander in Chief.

To be sure, the war being ended, some degree of reaction to earlier, conventional views of the relations of President and Congress ensued; but the really surprising thing is that the reaction was so slight. Candidate Harding announced that while as President he would recommend a program, as the Constitution required him to do, legislation would be the work of Congress; but there is good reason to believe that he later regretted the promise thus implied. His ultimate failure to lead was apparently due much less to lack of willingness than of will. Although to Mr. Coolidge's ingrained conservatism legislation was in itself thoroughly distasteful, he nevertheless asserted it to be "the business of the President as party leader to do the best he can to see that the declared party platform purposes are translated into legislative and administrative action." Mr. Hoover was rather less articulate regarding his views on the subject, but according to Mr. Luce, an excellent authority, "he sent drafts of several important proposals to the Capitol to be introduced by leaders." And thanks to his inaction at the time of framing the Hawley-Smoot tariff, he has had in retrospect the doubtful satisfaction of being responsible for the supreme legislative monument to the futility of the gospel of "hands off."

FRANKLIN D. ROOSEVELT'S PRESIDENCY

While President Franklin D. Roosevelt's accomplishment as legislator has surpassed all previous records, yet the story of it, so far as it is of interest to the student of constitutional practice, offers little of novelty. Old techniques have been sharpened and improved, sometimes with the aid of modern gadgets—radio, for instance. The President, said one columnist in 1933, "has only to look toward a radio to bring Congress to terms." And there are certain lessons for the future which the record underlines. Yet except for two features, the pleasure afforded by its study is—to employ Henry James's classification—that of recognition rather than of surprise.

The first of these features is Mr. Roosevelt's consistent championship of the demands of certain groups, especially Agriculture and Labor. Congressional legislation meant to promote the general welfare via the welfare of particular groups is, of course, as old as Congress itself. The element of novelty presented by the New Deal legislation in this respect is furnished by the *size and voting strength of the groups served by it*. The tendency of this development to aid the party in power to remain in power is obvious.

The second exceptional feature of Mr. Roosevelt's legislative achievement is its dissolving effect on the two great structural principles of the Constitution—the principle of the Separation of Powers and the principle of Dual Federalism. The Supreme Court's decisions sustaining the New Deal legislation all turn on the one essential idea, even when it is not distinctly stated, that the reserved powers of the states do not afford a valid constitutional test of national legislation. As to the Separation of Powers doctrine, I have already pointed out how the President today takes toll at both ends of the legislative process, by pressing a legislative program upon Congress and by rounding out Congress' completed work with administrative regulations.

Is the Presidency of today a potential matrix of dictatorship? The dictatorship theme is a familiar one in the history of the Presidency—Jefferson was a dictator, Jackson was a dictator, Lincoln was a dictator, Theodore Roosevelt was a dictator, and so was Wilson. Nevertheless, it seems we still have rights and free institutions to be menaced.

That a disturbing case can today be made out for regarding the President as a potential despot has to be conceded. By *Mississippi v. Johnson*, as I mentioned earlier, the President has no judicially enforceable responsibility either for nonperformance of his duties or for exceeding his powers. Impeachment is, as Jefferson discovered much earlier, a "scarecrow," and to galvanize this scarecrow into life would be to run the risk of reducing the Presidency to a nullity, as almost happened in 1868. Congress has, to be sure, the power of the purse, and could not be deprived of it except by a coup d'état; but the President dominates Congress by the hold which fat relief rolls give him over millions of votes, and so a vicious circle is created whereby Congress pays for its own slow enslavement. Moreover, within recent times, propaganda, once the casual art of a gifted few, has been converted into a skilled technique, which is supplemented by the most ingenious gadgets of mechanical science. Today the President of the United States can at any time request that the Nation's broadcasting channels be cleared that he may chat with the people, and the request will be granted pronto, all the available frequencies being allocated to companies by a federal license which terminates every six months.

Then there is the role of the President as organ of foreign relations, the potential menace of which to American democracy has been pointed out by writers many times. By virtue of his powers in the diplomatic field, wrote Professor Pomeroy as far back as 1871, the President holds in his keeping "the safety, welfare, and even permanence of our internal and domestic institutions." And the Marquis de Chambrun, writing at the same period, voiced his concurrence in this judgment, for, said he, "An active and energetic foreign policy necessarily implies that the executive who directs it is permanent and clothed with powers in proportion to his vigor of action." And both these warnings, be it noted, were written at a time when the acknowledged field of American foreign policy was still limited in the main to the Western Hemisphere.

Finally, we must not forget what occurred in November 1940, when the most generally understood, most widely accepted usage of the Constitution was tossed casually into the discard. It is true that what occurred was by the approval of the American electorate, but that is precisely why the occurrence was so disturbing a portent, for the electorate in question contained millions of voters who were recipients of governmental bounty and other hundreds of thousands who were on the government's payroll, and the number of both classes seems likely to increase indefinitely. And surely it is not necessary to cite Aristotle to prove that the very processes of democracy, and the electoral process in particular, can be, and have been, used in times past to overthrow democracy.

The picture is somewhat overdrawn. Nevertheless, I doubt very much if it would be worth while to point out meticulously just wherein the exaggeration lies. Even after all the words of reassurance were spoken, important counts would remain unanswered. The real refutation of the above jeremiad is that it deals with *symptoms*, not with *causes*. The menace today of the Presidency to "liberty" and "democracy," as these have been conceived in the past, consists in the fact that the enlarged role of the President is the product for the most part of conditions which appear likely to continue operative for an indefinite future. The first of these conditions is the international crisis; the other is the persuasion of the American electorate that government does not exist primarily to supplement and reinforce private economic superiority, but ought on the contrary to correct and improve the operation of economic forces in the interest of the masses. And both these conditions spell one thing—increased and increasing governmental activity, which means, of course, increased activity and hence increased power for the National Government. The only question therefore which can be profitably raised from the point of view of those whose concern for "liberty" and "democracy" I have voiced is whether or not all this increased power is to go to the President; and if it is not, how such outcome is to be obviated.

NEED FOR CONSTITUTIONAL REFORM

My answer to this question, or rather to the latter part of it, is that *the present enlarged position of the President in the constitutional system requires of the American people a deliberate effort at constitutional reform*, though this need not mean resort to the formal process of constitutional amendment. The reform demanded, however, must have for its purpose not merely the preservation of "liberty" in the conventional sense of *liberty against government*, but also—and indeed primarily—the enhanced *responsiveness* of government to public opinion. Bearing this qualification in mind, I suggest that under the existing constitutional setup the solution must take the form of providing some method of equating easily and without constant jar to society the political forces which Congress at any time represents with those which the President represents at the same time, and of putting the relationship of the two branches on a *durable* and *understood* basis. And for this purpose I suggest a reconstruction of the Cabinet to include the principal leaders of Congress, men who do not owe their political salt to presidential bounty, and so can bring an independent judgment to bear upon presidential projects betimes.

The objection will no doubt be forthcoming that it is constitutionally impossible for an individual to be a member of Congress and to hold office at the same time. The answer is that membership in the Cabinet is not as such an office, though headship of a department is. The Cabinet as a body is as little known to the Constitution as is a "kitchen cabinet" or a "brain trust." All three comprise persons whom the President chooses to consult, the only difference being that the latter two are more apt to contain his real advisers, while the Cabinet goes neglected or is consulted only because Cabinet meetings have become an understood part of presidential routine.

More pauseworthy is the objection that such an arrangement could not long be adhered to, otherwise it must at times cut athwart the two-party system, and so weaken the political responsibility of the President. The objection has reference to the possibility that the President would belong to the party which was a minority in Congress. Actually, the supposed situation has obtained comparatively rarely—only twice, I believe, in the last seven Administrations, or four years out of twenty-eight. What is more to the point, the objection overvalues the importance of so-called "political responsibility," which operates in the main only *ex post facto*, that is, after the damage is done, *whereas the problem is to prevent the damage from being done in the first place*. Nor does cooperation between the President and Congress under present arrangements invariably stop at the party line, or even generally do so when conditions of crisis arise; and why should it require a crisis to bring forth the best methods? Suppose one takes the position that government is normally a species of *nation keeping*; then it is clear that much of the fuss and fury of politics is really factitious and a sheer waste to the community; that the chief objective to be sought in political discussion, whether carried on in Cabinet council, on the floors of Congress, or elsewhere, is *consensus* or compromise—in what light does the above proposal then appear?

Finally, it may be objected that the arrangement I propose would put the President as organ of foreign relations in leading strings to Congress. The answer is, that the Constitution itself already puts him there. Contrary to a common, but quite mistaken impression, no President has a mandate from the Constitution to conduct our foreign relations according to his own sweet will. If his power in that respect is indefinite, so is Congress' legislative power; and if he holds the "sword," so does Congress hold the "purse strings." Simply from constitutional necessity, therefore, the actual conduct of American foreign relations is a joint affair, and to my mind this is an altogether desirable arrangement which should be lived up to in spirit. Thanks especially to the bad tradition of secrecy which surrounds foreign policy and which ministers to the self-importance of State Departments and diplomats, there is no field where presidential whim has been more rampant or its solicitations for popular support more misleading and dangerous. But why not a foreign policy based on candor and a real attempt at securing popular understanding of its motivation, rather than on bamboozlement and hysteria? And would not frank recognition by the President that Congress is an equal in this field of power, and not a mere servitor, be apt to eventuate in just such a policy?

CONCLUSION

The Presidency of this present year of grace, in terms of power, is the product of the following factors: (1) social acceptance of the idea that government should be active and reformist, rather than simply protective of the established order of things; (2) the breakdown of the principle of dual federalism in the field of Congress' legislative powers; (3) the breakdown of the principle of the separation of powers as defining the relation of President and Congress in lawmaking; (4) the breakdown of the Monroe Doctrine and the enlarged role of the United States in the international field.

To repeat what I said before, it is my belief that the growth of presidential power within recent years confronts the American people with a problem of deliberate constitutional reform; otherwise what was the result of democracy may turn out to be democracy's undoing. And it is my further belief that the reform must consist in stabilizing by means of a reconstructed Cabinet the relationship between President and Congress, for there today lies the center of gravity of our constitutional system, therein lies enfolded the secret of our democracy's future.

The problem of the alleged undue influence of the President on public opinion, of course, remains. For that, I suspect, there is under our system no remedy except an unshackled public opinion itself. When the self-renewing stream of public opinion ceases to provide a cure for its own humors, free institutions fail of their main support and their main purpose, and the democratic process withers away for want of the juices of life. For while democracy implies leadership, it also implies criticism of that leadership, criticism outspoken and unremitting. Leadership immune from criticism is the very definition of totalitarianism. Mr. Kemler to the contrary notwithstanding, no President should be regarded as hero ex officio unless it is at the same time recognized that even heroes have their off days.

☆

CLINTON ROSSITER: *The Presidency as the*
Focus of Leadership

No American can contemplate the Presidency without a feeling of
solemnity and humility—solemnity in the face of a historically unique
concentration of power and prestige, humility in the thought that he
has had a part in the choice of a man to wield the power and enjoy
the prestige.

Perhaps the most rewarding way to grasp the significance of this
great office is to consider it as a focus of democratic leadership. Freemen, too, have need of leaders. Indeed, it may well be argued that
one of the decisive forces in the shaping of American democracy has
been the extraordinary capacity of the Presidency for strong, able,
popular leadership. If this has been true of our past, it will certainly
be true of our future, and we should therefore do our best to grasp
the quality of this leadership. Let us do this by answering the essential question: For what men and groups does the President provide
leadership?

First, the President is *leader of the executive branch*. To the extent that our federal civil servants have need of common guidance,
he alone is in a position to provide it. We cannot savor the fullness
of the President's duties unless we recall that he is held primarily
accountable for the ethics, loyalty, efficiency, frugality and respon-

Clinton Rossiter is John L. Senior Professor of American Institutions at Cornell University. The first part of the selection is from "The Presidency: Focus of
Leadership," *New York Times Magazine*, November 11, 1956, p. 26. © 1956 by
The New York Times Company. Reprinted by permission. The second part is
from *The American Presidency* (New York: Harcourt, Brace, 1960), pp. 257–
262. Copyright © 1956, 1960 by Clinton Rossiter. Reprinted by permission of
the publisher and the author.

siveness to the public's wishes of the two and one-third million Americans in the national administration.

Both the Constitution and Congress have recognized his power to guide the day-to-day activities of the executive branch, strained and restrained though his leadership may often be in practice. From the Constitution, explicitly or implicitly, he receives the twin powers of appointment and removal, as well as the primary duty, which no law or plan or circumstances can ever take away from him, to "take care that the laws be faithfully executed."

From Congress, through such legislative mandates as the Budget and Accounting Act of 1921 and the succession of Reorganization Acts, the President has received further acknowledgment of his administrative leadership. Although independent agencies such as the Interstate Commerce Commission and the National Labor Relations Board operate by design outside his immediate area of responsibility, most of the government's administrative tasks are still carried on within the fuzzy-edged pyramid that has the President at its lonely peak; the laws that are executed daily in his name and under his general supervision are numbered in the hundreds.

Many observers, to be sure, have argued strenuously that we should not ask too much of the President as administrative leader, lest we burden him with impossible detail, or give too much to him, lest we inject political considerations too forcefully into the steady business of the civil service. Still, he cannot ignore the blunt mandate of the Constitution, and we should not forget the wisdom that lies behind it. The President has no more important tasks than to set a high personal example of integrity and industry for all who serve the nation, and to transmit a clear lead downward through his chief lieutenants to all who help shape the policies by which we live.

Next, the President is *leader of the forces of peace and war*. Although authority in the field of foreign relations is shared constitutionally among three organs—President, Congress, and, for two special purposes, the Senate—his position is paramount, if not indeed dominant. Constitution, laws, customs, the practice of other nations and the logic of history have combined to place the President in a dominant position. Secrecy, dispatch, unity, continuity and access to information—the ingredients of successful diplomacy— are properties of his office, and Congress, needless to add, possesses none of them. Leadership in foreign affairs flows today from the President—or it does not flow at all.

The Constitution designates him specifically as "Commander in Chief of the Army and Navy of the United States." In peace and war he is the supreme commander of the armed forces, the living guarantee of the American belief in "the supremacy of the civil over military authority."

In time of peace he raises, trains, supervises and deploys the forces that Congress is willing to maintain. With the aid of the Secretary of Defense, the Joint Chiefs of Staff and the National Security Council—all of whom are his personal choices—he looks constantly to the state of the nation's defenses. He is never for one day allowed to forget that he will be held accountable by the people, Congress and history for the nation's readiness to meet an enemy assault.

In time of war his power to command the forces swells out of all proportion to his other powers. All major decisions of strategy, and many of tactics as well, are his alone to make or to approve. Lincoln and Franklin Roosevelt, each in his own way and time, showed how far the power of military command can be driven by a President anxious to have his generals and admirals get on with the war.

But this, the power of command, is only a fraction of the vast responsibility the modern President draws from the Commander in Chief clause. We need only think back to three of Franklin D. Roosevelt's actions in World War II—the creation and staffing of a whole array of emergency boards and offices, the seizure and operation of more than sixty strike-bound or strike-threatened plants and industries, and the forced evacuation of 70,000 American citizens of Japanese descent from the West Coast—to understand how deeply the President's authority can cut into the lives and liberties of the American people in time of war. We may well tremble in contemplation of the kind of leadership he would be forced to exert in a total war with the absolute weapon.

The President's duties are not all purely executive in nature. He is also intimately associated, by Constitution and custom, with the legislative process, and we may therefore consider him as *leader of Congress*. Congress has its full share of strong men, but the complexity of the problems it is asked to solve by a people who still assume that all problems are solvable has made external leadership a requisite of effective operation.

The President alone is in a political, constitutional and practical position to provide such leadership, and he is therefore expected, within the limits of propriety, to guide Congress in much of its law-making activity. Indeed, since Congress is no longer minded or organized to guide itself, the refusal or inability of the President to serve as a kind of prime minister results in weak and disorganized government. His tasks as leader of Congress are difficult and delicate, yet he must bend to them steadily or be judged a failure. The

President who will not give his best thoughts to leading Congress, more so the President who is temperamentally or politically unfitted to "get along with Congress," is now rightly considered a national liability.

The lives of Jackson, Lincoln, Wilson, and the two Roosevelts should be enough to remind us that the President draws much of his real power from his position as *leader of his party.* By playing the grand politician with unashamed zest, the first of these men gave his epic administration a unique sense of cohesion, the second rallied doubting Republican leaders and their followings to the cause of the Union, and the other three achieved genuine triumphs as catalysts of congressional action. That gifted amateur, Dwight D. Eisenhower, has also played the role for every drop of drama and power in it. He has demonstrated repeatedly what close observers of the Presidency know well: that its incumbent must devote an hour or two of every working day to the profession of Chief Democrat or Chief Republican.

It troubles many good people, not entirely without reason, to watch the President dabbling in politics, distributing loaves and fishes, smiling on party hacks, and endorsing candidates he knows to be unfit for anything but immediate delivery to the county jail. Yet if he is to persuade Congress, if he is to achieve a loyal and cohesive administration, if he is to be elected in the first place (and re-elected in the second), he must put his hand firmly to the plow of politics. The President is inevitably the nation's No. 1 political boss.

Yet he is, at the same time if not in the same breath, *leader of public opinion.* While he acts as political chieftain of some, he serves as moral spokesman for all. It took the line of Presidents some time to sense the nation's need of a clear voice, but since the day when Andrew Jackson thundered against the Nullifiers of South Carolina, no effective President has doubted his prerogative to speak the people's mind on the great issues of his time, to serve, in Wilson's words, as "the spokesman for the real sentiment and purpose of the country."

Sometimes, of course, it is no easy thing, even for the most sensitive and large-minded of Presidents, to know the real sentiment of the people or to be bold enough to state it in defiance of loudly voiced contrary opinion. Yet the President who senses the popular mood and spots new tides even before they start to run, who practices shrewd economy in his appearances as spokesman for the nation, who is conscious of his unique power to compel discussion on his own terms and who talks the language of Christian morality and the American tradition, can shout down any other voice or chorus of voices in the land. The President is the American people's one authentic trumpet, and he has no higher duty than to give a clear and certain sound.

The President is easily the most influential leader of opinion in this country principally because he is, among all his other jobs, our Chief of State. He is, that is to say, the ceremonial head of the Government of the United States, the *leader of the rituals of American democracy.* The long catalogue of public duties that the Queen discharges in England and the Governor General in Canada is the President's responsibility in this country, and the catalogue is even longer because he is not a king, or even the agent of one, and is therefore expected to go through some rather undignified paces by a people who think of him as a combination of scoutmaster, Delphic oracle, hero of the silver screen and father of the multitudes.

The role of Chief of State may often seem trivial, yet it cannot be neglected by a President who proposes to stay in favor and, more to the point, in touch with the people, the ultimate support of all his claims to leadership. And whether or not he enjoys this role, no President can fail to realize that his many powers are invigorated, indeed are given a new dimension of authority, because he is the symbol of our sovereignty, continuity and grandeur as a people.

When he asks a Senator to lunch in order to enlist his support for a pet project, when he thumps his desk and reminds the antagonists in a labor dispute of the larger interests of the American people, when he orders a general to cease caviling or else be removed from his command, the Senator and the disputants and the general are well aware—especially if the scene is laid in the White House—that they are dealing with no ordinary head of government. The framers of the Constitution took a momentous step when they fused the dignity of a king and the power of a Prime Minister in one elective office—when they made the President a national leader in the mystical as well as the practical sense.

Finally, the President has been endowed—whether we or our friends abroad like it or not—with a global role as a *leader of the free nations.* His leadership in this area is not that of a dominant executive. The power he exercises is in a way comparable to that which he holds as a leader of Congress. Senators and Congressmen can, if they choose, ignore the President's leadership with relative impunity. So, too, can our friends abroad; the action of Britain and France in the Middle East is a case in point. But so long as the United States remains the richest and most powerful member of any coalition it may enter, then its President's words and deeds will have a direct bearing on the freedom and stability of a great many other countries.

Having engaged in this piecemeal analysis of the categories of presidential leadership, we must now fit the pieces back together into a seamless unity. For that, after all, is what the Presidency is, and I hope this exercise in political taxonomy has not obscured the paramount fact that this focus of democratic leadership is a single office filled by a single man.

The President is not one kind of leader one part of the day, another kind in another part—leader of the bureaucracy in the morning, of the armed forces at lunch, of Congress in the afternoon, of the people in the evening. He exerts every kind of leadership every moment of the day, and every kind feeds upon and into all the others. He is a more exalted leader of ritual because he can guide opinion, a more forceful leader in diplomacy because he commands the armed forces personally, a more effective leader of Congress because he sits at the top of his party. The conflicting demands of these categories of leadership give him trouble at times, but in the end all unite to make him a leader without any equal in the history of democracy.

I think it important to note the qualification: "the history of democracy." For what I have been talking about here is not the Fuehrerprinzip of Hitler or the "cult of personality," but the leadership of free men. The Presidency, like every other instrument of power we have created for our use, operates within a grand and durable pattern of private liberty and public morality, which means that the President can lead successfully only when he honors the pattern—by working toward ends to which a "persistent and undoubted" majority of the people has given support, and by selecting means that are fair, dignified, and familiar.

The President, that is to say, can lead us only in the direction we are accustomed to travel. He cannot lead the gentlemen of Congress to abdicate their functions; he cannot order our civil servants to be corrupt and slothful; he cannot even command our generals to bring off a coup d'état. And surely he cannot lead public opinion in a direction for which public opinion is not prepared—a truth to which our strongest Presidents would make the most convincing witnesses. The leadership of free men must honor their freedom. The power of the Presidency can move as a mighty host only with the grain of liberty and morality. . . .

☆

. . . The strong Presidency is the product of events that cannot be undone and of forces that continue to roll. We have made our decisions for the New Economy and the New Internationalism, and in making them we have made this kind of Presidency a requisite for the effective conduct of our constitutional system. No government can exercise the supervision that ours does over the economy at home or honor the bargains that ours has made abroad unless it has a strong, unified, energetic executive to lead it.

I do not mean to say—I have not meant to say—that "strength" in the Presidency is to be equated with "goodness" and "greatness." A strong President is a bad President, a curse upon the land, unless his means are constitutional and his ends democratic. . . . We honor the great Presidents of the past, not for their strength, but for the fact that they used it wisely to build a better America. And in honoring them we recognize that their kind of Presidency is one of our chief bulwarks against decline and chaos.

In point of fact, the struggle over the powers of the Presidency, fierce though it may seem, is only a secondary campaign in a political war, now pretty well decided, over the future of America. Few men get heated up over the Presidency alone. Their arguments over its powers are really arguments over the American way of life and the direction in which it is moving. The strong Presidency is an instrument and symbol of the 1960s; the weak Presidency is an instrument and symbol of the 1920s. Those who truly yearn to "go home again," like John T. Flynn and Clarence Manion and the Daughters of the American Revolution, are right in thinking that a reduction in the power of the Presidency would be an excellent first step to the rear, although it would be only a first step. It should be clearly understood that an attack on the Presidency like the Bricker amendment is aimed beyond the Constitution at America's position in the world. The backers of this amendment may be greatly worried about the potential dangers of "presidential autocracy," but they are even more worried about the present consequences of the New Internationalism. Conversely, many voices that are raised for an even stronger Presidency are really raised for an even bigger government with even more control of society.

We should not look with equanimity on the Presidency and its huge arsenal of authority. We should be careful about giving the President additional powers, alert to abuses of those he already holds, cognizant that the present balance of the Constitution is not a cause for unlimited self-congratulation. But we can look on it with at least as much equanimity—each of us according to his own blend of blood, bile, phlegm, and melancholy—as we do upon the present state of the Union. For the strength of the Presidency is a measure of the strength of the America in which we now live. Those who reject this America and are alarmed by the course we are taking reject the strong Presidency angrily. Those who accept this America and do not fear the one that is coming accept the strong Presidency soberly.

As I look back, I detect a deep note of satisfaction, although hardly of complacency, with the American Presidency as it stands today. A steady theme seems to have run all through this final review of its weaknesses and problems, a theme entitled (with apologies to the genius of Thurber) "Leave Your Presidency Alone!" This feeling of satisfaction springs, I am frank to admit, from a political outlook more concerned with the world as it is than as it is said to have been by reactionaries and is promised to be by radicals. Since this outlook is now shared by a staggering majority of Americans, I feel that I am expressing something more than a personal opinion. If we accept the facts of life in the 1960s, as we must, and if we shun the false counsels of perfection, as we do, then we are bound to conclude that we are richly blessed with a choice instrument of constitutional democracy. Judged in the light of memory and desire, the Presidency is in a state of sturdy health, and that is why we should not give way easily to despair over the defects men of too much zeal or too little courage claim to discover in it. Some of these are not defects at all; some are chronic in our system of government; some could be cured only by opening the way to others far more malign.

This does not mean that we should stand pat with the Presidency. Rather, we should confine ourselves to small readjustments— I have noted a dozen or more that might be worth a try—and leave the usual avenues open to prescriptive change. We should abolish the electoral college but leave the electoral system to pursue its illogical but hitherto effective way. We should plan carefully for mobilization in the event of war but take care that the inherent emergency power of the President—the power used by Lincoln to blockade the South, by Wilson to arm the merchantmen, and by Roosevelt to bring off the Destroyer Deal—be left intact and untrammeled. We should experiment with a joint executive-legislative council and the item veto but be on our guard against the urge to alter radically the pattern of competitive coexistence between Congress and President. We should give the President all the aides he can use but beware the deceptively simple solution of a second and even third Vice President for executive purposes. And we should tinker modestly with the President's machinery but wake from the false dream of perfect harmony in high places, especially in the highest place of all. For if the Presidency could speak, it would say with Whitman:

> Do I contradict myself?
> Very well then I contradict myself.
> (I am large, I contain multitudes.)

"Leave Your Presidency Alone": that is the message of this chapter, and I trust I have made clear why I transmit it so confidently. To put the final case for the American Presidency as forcefully as possible, let me point once again to its essential qualities:

It strikes a felicitous balance between power and limitations. In a world in which power is the price of freedom, the Presidency, as Professor Merriam and his colleagues wrote in 1937, "stands across the path of those who mistakenly assert that democracy must fail because it can neither decide promptly nor act vigorously." In a world in which power has been abused on a tragic scale, it presents a heartening lesson in the uses of constitutionalism. . . . The quest of constitutional government is for the right balance of authority and restraint, and Americans may take some pride in the balance they have built into the Presidency.

It provides a steady focus of leadership: of administration, Congress, and people. In a constitutional system compounded of diversity and antagonism, the Presidency looms up as the countervailing force of unity and harmony. In a society ridden by centrifugal forces, it is, as Sidney Hyman has written, the "common reference point for social effort." The relentless progress of this continental republic has made the Presidency our one truly national political institution. There are those who would reserve this role to Congress, but as the least aggressive of our Presidents, Calvin Coolidge, once testified, "It is because in their hours of timidity the Congress becomes subservient to the importunities of organized minorities that the President comes more and more to stand as the champion of the rights of the whole country." The more Congress becomes, in Burke's phrase, "a confused and scuffling bustle of local agency," the more the Presidency must become a clear beacon of national purpose.

It is a priceless symbol of our continuity and destiny as a people. Few nations have solved so simply and yet grandly the problem of finding and maintaining an office of state that embodies their majesty and reflects their character. Only the Constitution overshadows the Presidency as an object of popular reverence, and the Constitution does not walk about smiling and shaking hands. "The simple fact is," a distinguished, disgruntled Briton wrote at the end of the "Royal Soap Opera" of 1955, "that the United States Presidency today is a far more dignified institution than the British monarchy." In all honesty and tact we must quickly demur, but we can be well satisfied with our "republican king."

It has been tested sternly in the crucible of time. Our obsession with youth leads us to forget too easily how long our chief instruments of government have been operating in unbroken career. The

Presidency is now the most venerable executive among all the large nations of the earth, and if one looks back beyond 1787 to "times of ancient glory and renown," he will find that the formula has worked before. "The truth is," Henry Jones Ford wrote with grace and insight,

> that in the presidential office, as it has been constituted since Jackson's time, American democracy has revived the oldest political institution of the race, the elective kingship. It is all there: the precognition of the notables and the tumultuous choice of the freemen, only conformed to modern conditions. That the people have been able . . . to make good a principle which no other people have been able to reconcile with the safety of the state, indicates the highest degree of constitutional morality yet attained by any race.

It is, finally, an office of freedom. The Presidency is a standing reproach to those petty doctrinaires who insist that executive power is inherently undemocratic; for, to the exact contrary, it has been more responsive to the needs and dreams of giant democracy than any other office or institution in the whole mosaic of American life. It is no less a reproach to those easy generalizers who think that Lord Acton had the very last word on the corrupting effects of power; for, again to the contrary, his doctrine finds small confirmation in the history of the Presidency. The vast power of this office has not been "poison," as Henry Adams wrote in scorn; rather, it has elevated often and corrupted never, chiefly because those who held it recognized the true source of the power and were ennobled by the knowledge.

The American people, who are, after all, the best judges of the means by which their democracy is to be achieved, have made the Presidency their peculiar instrument. As they ready themselves for the pilgrimage ahead, they can take comfort and pride in the thought that it is also their peculiar treasure.

☆

AARON WILDAVSKY: *The Two Presidencies*

The United States has one President, but it has two presidencies; one presidency is for domestic affairs, and the other is concerned with defense and foreign policy. Since World War II, Presidents have had much greater success in controlling the nation's defense and foreign policies than in dominating its domestic policies. Even Lyndon Johnson has seen his early record of victories in domestic legislation diminish as his concern with foreign affairs grows.

What powers does the President have to control defense and foreign policies and so completely overwhelm those who might wish to thwart him?

The President's normal problem with domestic policy is to get congressional support for the programs he prefers. In foreign affairs, in contrast, he can almost always get support for policies that he believes will protect the nation—but his problem is to find a variable policy.

Whoever they are, whether they begin by caring about foreign policy like Eisenhower and Kennedy or about domestic policies like Truman and Johnson, Presidents soon discover they have more policy preferences in domestic matters than in foreign policy. The Republican and Democratic parties possess a traditional roster of policies, which can easily be adopted by a new President—for example, he can be either for or against Medicare and aid to education. Since existing domestic policy usually changes in only small steps, Presi-

Aaron Wildavsky is Professor of Political Science and Dean of the Graduate School of Public Policy at the University of California, Berkeley. The selection is from "The Two Presidencies," in *Trans-action*, December, 1966. © by Trans-action, Inc., New Brunswick, New Jersey. Reprinted by permission of the publisher and the author.

dents find it relatively simple to make minor adjustments. However, although any President knows he supports foreign aid and NATO, the world outside changes much more rapidly than the nation inside —Presidents and their parties have no prior policies on Argentina and the Congo. The world has become a highly intractable place with a whirl of forces we cannot or do not know how to alter.

THE RECORD OF PRESIDENTIAL CONTROL

It takes great crises, such as Roosevelt's hundred days in the midst of the depression, or the extraordinary majorities that Barry Goldwater's candidacy willed to Lyndon Johnson, for Presidents to succeed in controlling domestic policy. From the end of the 1930's to the present (what may roughly be called the modern era), Presidents have often been frustrated in their domestic programs. From 1938, when conservatives regrouped their forces, to the time of his death, Franklin Roosevelt did not get a single piece of significant domestic legislation passed. Truman lost out on most of his intense domestic preferences, except perhaps for housing. Since Eisenhower did not ask for much domestic legislation, he did not meet consistent defeat, yet he failed in his general policy of curtailing governmental commitments. Kennedy, of course, faced great difficulties with domestic legislation.

In the realm of foreign policy there has not been a single major issue on which Presidents, when they were serious and determined, have failed. The list of their victories is impressive: entry into the United Nations, the Marshall Plan, NATO, the Truman Doctrine, the decisions to stay out of Indochina in 1954 and to intervene in Vietnam in the 1960's, aid to Poland and Yugoslavia, the test-ban treaty, and many more. Serious setbacks to the President in controlling foreign policy are extraordinary and unusual.

Table 1, compiled from the Congressional Quarterly Service tabulation of presidential initiative and congressional response from 1948 through 1964, shows that Presidents have significantly better records in foreign and defense matters than in domestic policies. When refugees and immigration—which Congress considers primarily a domestic concern—are removed from the general foreign policy area, it is clear that Presidents prevail about 70 per cent of the time in defense and foreign policy, compared with 40 per cent in the domestic sphere.

WORLD EVENTS AND PRESIDENTIAL RESOURCES

Power in politics is control over governmental decisions. How does the President manage his control of foreign and defense policy? The

TABLE 1

Congressional Action on Presidential Proposals from 1948–1964

Policy Area	Congressional Action % Pass	% Fail	Number of Proposals
Domestic policy (natural resources, labor, agriculture, taxes, etc.)	40.2	59.8	2499
Defense policy (defense, disarmament, manpower, misc.)	73.3	26.7	90
Foreign policy	58.5	41.5	655
Immigration, refugees	13.2	86.0	129
Treaties, general foreign relations, State Department, foreign aid	70.8	29.2	445

Source: Congressional Quarterly Service, *Congress and the Nation,* 1945–1964 (Washington, 1965).

answer does not reside in the greater constitutional power in foreign affairs that Presidents have possessed since the founding of the Republic. The answer lies in the changes that have taken place since 1945.

The number of nations with which the United States has diplomatic relations has increased from 53 in 1939 to 113 in 1966. But sheer numbers do not tell enough; the world has also become a much more dangerous place. However remote it may seem at times, our government must always be aware of the possibility of nuclear war.

Yet the mere existence of great powers with effective thermonuclear weapons would not, in and of itself, vastly increase our rate of interaction with most other nations. We see events in Assam or Burundi as important because they are also part of a larger worldwide contest, called the cold war, in which great powers are rivals for the control or support of other nations. Moreover, the reaction against the blatant isolationism of the 1930's has led to a concern with foreign policy that is worldwide in scope. We are interested in what happens everywhere because we see these events as connected with larger interests involving, at the worst, the possibility of ultimate destruction.

Given the overriding fact that the world is dangerous and that small causes are perceived to have potentially great effects in an unstable world, it follows that Presidents must be interested in relatively "small" matters. So they give Azerbaijan or Lebanon or Vietnam huge amounts of their time. Arthur Schlesinger, Jr., wrote of Kennedy that "in the first two months of his administration he probably spent more time on Laos than on anything else." Few failures in domestic policy, Presidents soon realize, could have as disastrous consequences as any one of dozens of mistakes in the international arena.

The result is that foreign policy concerns tend to drive out domestic policy. Except for occasional questions of domestic prosperity and for civil rights, foreign affairs have consistently higher priority for Presidents. Once, when trying to talk to President Kennedy about natural resources, Secretary of the Interior Stewart Udall remarked, "He's imprisoned by Berlin."

The importance of foreign affairs to Presidents is intensified by the increasing speed of events in the international arena. The event and its consequences follow closely on top of one another. The blunder at the Bay of Pigs is swiftly followed by the near catastrophe of the Cuban missile crisis. Presidents can no longer count on passing along their most difficult problems to their successors. They must expect to face the consequences of their actions—or failure to act— while still in office.

Domestic policy-making is usually based on experimental adjustments to an existing situation. Only a few decisions, such as those involving large dams, irretrievably commit future generations. Decisions in foreign affairs, however, are often perceived to be irreversible. This is expressed, for example, in the fear of escalation or the various "spiral" or "domino" theories of international conflict.

If decisions are perceived to be both important and irreversible, there is every reason for Presidents to devote a great deal of resources to them. Presidents have to be oriented toward the future in the use of their resources. They serve a fixed term in office, and they cannot automatically count on support from the populace, Congress, or the administrative apparatus. They have to be careful, therefore, to husband their resources for pressing future needs. But because the consequences of events in foreign affairs are potentially more grave, faster to manifest themselves, and less easily reversible than in domestic affairs, Presidents are more willing to use up their resources.

THE POWER TO ACT

Their formal powers to commit resources in foreign affairs and defense are vast. Particularly important is their power as Commander-in-Chief to move troops. Faced with situations like the invasion of South Korea or the emplacement of missiles in Cuba, fast action is required. Presidents possess both the formal power to act and the knowledge that elites and the general public expect them to act. Once they have committed American forces, it is difficult for

Congress or anyone else to alter the course of events. The Dominican venture is a . . . case in point.

Presidential discretion in foreign affairs also makes it difficult (though not impossible) for Congress to restrict their actions. Presidents can use executive agreements instead of treaties, enter into tacit agreements instead of written ones, and otherwise help create *de facto* situations not easily reversed. Presidents also have far greater ability than anyone else to obtain information on developments abroad through the Departments of State and Defense. The need for secrecy in some aspects of foreign and defense policy further restricts the ability of others to compete with Presidents. These things are all well known. What is not so generally appreciated is the growing presidential ability to *use* information to achieve goals.

In the past Presidents were amateurs in military strategy. They could not even get much useful advice outside of the military. As late as the 1930's the number of people outside the military establishment who were professionally engaged in the study of defense policy could be numbered on the fingers. Today there are hundreds of such men. The rise of the defense intellectuals has given the President of the United States enhanced ability to control defense policy. He is no longer dependent on the military for advice. He can choose among defense intellectuals from the research corporations and the academies for alternative sources of advice. He can install these men in his own office. He can play them off against each other or use them to extend spheres of coordination.

Even with these advisers, however, Presidents and Secretaries of Defense might still be too bewildered by the complexity of nuclear situations to take action—unless they had an understanding of the doctrine and concept of deterrence. But knowledge of doctrine about deterrence has been widely diffused; it can be picked up by any intelligent person who will read books or listen to enough hours of conversation. Whether or not the doctrine is good is a separate question; the point is that civilians can feel they understand what is going on in defense policy. Perhaps the most extraordinary feature of presidential action during the Cuban missile crisis was the degree to which the Commander-in-Chief of the Armed Forces insisted on controlling even the smallest moves. From the positioning of ships to the methods of boarding, to the precise words and actions to be taken by individual soldiers and sailors, the President and his civilian advisers were in control.

Although Presidents have rivals for power in foreign affairs, the rivals do not usually succeed. Presidents prevail not only because they may have superior resources but because their potential opponents are weak, divided, or believe that they should not control foreign policy. Let us consider the potential rivals—the general citizenry, special interest groups, the Congress, the military, the so-called military-industrial complex, and the State Department.

COMPETITORS FOR CONTROL OF POLICY

The Public. The general public is much more dependent on Presidents in foreign affairs than in domestic matters. While many people know about the impact of social security and Medicare, few know about politics in Malawi. So it is not surprising that people expect the President to act in foreign affairs and reward him with their confidence. Gallup Polls consistently show that presidential popularity rises after he takes action in a crisis—whether the action is disastrous as in the Bay of Pigs or successful as in the Cuba missile crisis. Decisive action, such as the bombing of oil fields near Haiphong, resulted in a sharp (though temporary) increase in Johnson's popularity.

The Vietnam situation illustrates another problem of public opinion in foreign affairs: it is extremely difficult to get operational policy directions from the general public. It took a long time before any sizable public interest in the subject developed. Nothing short of the large-scale involvement of American troops under fire probably could have brought about the current high level of concern. Yet this relatively well-developed popular opinion is difficult to interpret. While a majority appear to support President Johnson's policy, it appears that they could easily be persuaded to withdraw from Vietnam if the administration changed its line. Although a sizable majority would support various initiatives to end the war, they would seemingly be appalled if this action led to Communist encroachments elsewhere in Southeast Asia. . . .

Although Presidents lead opinion in foreign affairs, they know they will be held accountable for the consequences of their actions. President Johnson has maintained a large commitment in Vietnam. His popularity shoots up now and again in the midst of some imposing action. But the fact that a body of citizens do not like the war comes back to damage his overall popularity. We will support your initiatives, the people seem to say, but we will reserve the right to punish you (or your party) if we do not like the results.

Special Interest Groups. Opinions are easier to gauge in domestic affairs because, for one thing, there is a stable structure of interest groups that covers virtually all matters of concern. The farm, labor, business, conservation, veteran, civil rights, and other interest groups provide cues when a proposed policy affects them. Thus people who identify with these groups may adopt their views. But in foreign policy matters the interest group structure is weak, unstable, and thin rather than dense. In many matters affecting Africa and Asia, for example, it is hard to think of well-known interest groups. While ephemeral groups arise from time to time to support or protest particular policies, they usually disappear when the immediate problem is resolved. In contrast, longer-lasting elite groups like the Foreign Policy Association and Council on Foreign Relations are composed of people of diverse views; refusal to take strong positions on controversial matters is a condition of their continued viability.

The strongest interest groups are probably the ethnic associations whose members have strong ties with a homeland, as in Poland or Cuba, so they are rarely activated simultaneously on any specific issue. They are most effective when most narrowly and intensely focused—as in the fierce pressure from Jews to recognize the state of Israel. But their relatively small numbers limits their significance to Presidents in the vastly more important general foreign policy picture—as continued aid to the Arab countries shows. Moreover, some ethnic groups may conflict on significant issues such as American acceptance of the Oder-Neisse line separating Poland from what is now East Germany.

The Congress. Congressmen also exercise power in foreign affairs. Yet they are ordinarily not serious competitors with the President because they follow a self-denying ordinance. They do not think it is their job to determine the nation's defense policies. Lewis A. Dexter's extensive interviews with members of the Senate Armed Services Committee, who might be expected to want a voice in defense policy, reveal that they do not desire for men like themselves to run the nation's defense establishment. Aside from a few specific conflicts among the armed services which allow both the possibility and desirability of direct intervention, the Armed Services Committee constitutes a sort of real estate committee dealing with the regional economic consequences of the location of military facilities.

The congressional appropriations power is potentially a significant resource, but circumstances since the end of World War II have tended to reduce its effectiveness. The appropriations committees and Congress itself might make their will felt by refusing to allot funds unless basic policies were altered. But this has not happened. While Congress makes its traditional small cuts in the military budget, Presidents have mostly found themselves warding off congressional attempts to increase specific items still further.

Most of the time, the administration's refusal to spend has not been seriously challenged. However, there have been occasions when individual legislators or committees have been influential. Senator

Henry Jackson in his campaign (with the aid of colleagues on the Joint Committee on Atomic Energy) was able to gain acceptance for the Polaris weapons system and Senator Arthur H. Vandenberg played a part in determining the shape of the Marshall Plan and so on. The few congressmen who are expert in defense policy act, as Samuel P. Huntington says, largely as lobbyists with the executive branch. It is apparently more fruitful for these congressional experts to use their resources in order to get a hearing from the executive than to work on other congressmen.

When an issue involves the actual use or threat of violence, it takes a great deal to convince congressmen not to follow the President's lead. James Robinson's tabulation of foreign and defense policy issues from the late 1930's to 1961 (Table 2) shows dominant influence by Congress in only one case out of seven—the 1954 decision not to intervene with armed force in Indochina. In that instance President Eisenhower deliberately sounded out congressional opinion and, finding it negative, decided not to intervene—against the advice of Admiral Radford, chairman of the Joint Chiefs of Staff. This attempt to abandon responsibility did not succeed, as the years of American involvement demonstrate.

The Military. The outstanding feature of the military's participation in making defense policy is their amazing weakness. Whether the policy decisions involve the size of the armed forces, the choice of weapons systems, the total defense budget, or its division into components, the military have not prevailed. Let us take budgetary decisions as representative of the key choices to be made in defense policy. Since the end of World War II the military has not been able to achieve significant (billion dollar) increases in appropriations by their own efforts. Under Truman and Eisenhower defense budgets were determined by what Huntington calls the remainder method: the two Presidents estimated revenues, decided what they could spend on domestic matters, and the remainder was assigned to defense. The usual controversy was between some military and congressional groups supporting much larger expenditures while the President and his executive allies refused. A typical case, involving the desire of the Air Force to increase the number of groups of planes is described by Huntington in *The Common Defense*:

> The FY [fiscal year] 1949 budget provided 48 groups. After the Czech coup, the Administration yielded and backed an Air Force of 55 groups, in its spring rearmament program. Congress added additional funds to aid Air Force expansion to 70 groups. The Administration refused to utilize them, however, and in the gathering economy wave of the summer and fall of 1948, the Air

TABLE 2

Congressional Involvement in Foreign and Defense Policy Decisions

Issue	Congressional Involvement (High, Low, None)	Initiator (Congress or Executive)	Predominant Influence (Congress or Executive)	Legislation or Resolution (Yes or No)	Violence at Stake (Yes or No)	Decision Time (Long or Short)
Neutrality Legislation, the 1930's	High	Exec	Cong	Yes	No	Long
Lend-Lease, 1941	High	Exec	Exec	Yes	Yes	Long
Aid to Russia, 1941	Low	Exec	Exec	No	No	Long
Repeal of Chinese Exclusion, 1943	High	Cong	Cong	Yes	No	Long
Fulbright Resolution, 1943	High	Cong	Cong	Yes	No	Long
Building the Atomic Bomb, 1944	Low	Exec	Exec	Yes	Yes	Long
Foreign Services Act of 1946	High	Exec	Exec	Yes	No	Long
Truman Doctrine, 1947	High	Exec	Exec	Yes	No	Long
The Marshall Plan, 1947–48	High	Exec	Exec	Yes	No	Long
Berlin Airlift, 1948	None	Exec	Exec	No	Yes	Long
Vandenberg Resolution, 1948	High	Exec	Cong	Yes	No	Long
North Atlantic Treaty, 1947–49	High	Exec	Exec	Yes	No	Long
Korean Decision, 1950	None	Exec	Exec	No	Yes	Short
Japanese Peace Treaty, 1952	High	Exec	Exec	Yes	No	Long
Bohlen Nomination, 1953	High	Exec	Exec	Yes	No	Long
Indo-China, 1954	High	Exec	Cong	No	Yes	Short
Formosan Resolution, 1955	High	Exec	Exec	Yes	Yes	Long
International Finance Corporation, 1956	Low	Exec	Exec	Yes	No	Long
Foreign Aid, 1957	High	Exec	Exec	Yes	No	Long
Reciprocal Trade Agreements, 1958	High	Cong	Cong	Yes	No	Long
Monroney Resolution, 1958	High	Exec	Exec	Yes	No	Long
Cuban Decision, 1961	Low	Exec	Exec	No	Yes	Long

Source: James A. Robinson, *Congress and Foreign Policy-Making* (Homewood, Illinois, 1962).

Force goal was cut back again to 48 groups. In 1949 the House of Representatives picked up the challenge and appropriated funds for 58 groups. The President impounded the money. In June, 1950, the Air Force had 48 groups.

The great increases in the defense budget were due far more to Stalin and modern technology than to the military. The Korean War resulted in an increase from 12 to 44 billions and much of the rest followed Sputnik and the huge costs of missile programs. Thus modern technology and international conflict put an end to the one major effort to subordinate foreign affairs to domestic policies through the budget.

It could be argued that the President merely ratifies the decisions made by the military and their allies. If the military and/or Congress were united and insistent on defense policy, it would certainly be difficult for Presidents to resist these forces. But it is precisely the disunity of the military that has characterized the entire postwar period. Indeed, the military have not been united on any major matter of defense policy. The apparent unity of the Joint Chiefs of Staff turns out to be illusory. The vast majority of their recommendations appear to be unanimous and are accepted by the Secretary of Defense and the President. But this facade of unity can only be achieved by methods that vitiate the impact of the recommendations. Genuine disagreements are hidden by vague language that commits no one to anything. Mutually contradictory plans are strung together so everyone appears to get something, but nothing is decided. Since it is impossible to agree on really important matters, all sorts of trivia are brought in to make a record of agreement. While it may be true, as Admiral Denfield, a former Chief of Naval Operations, said, that "On nine-tenths of the matters that come before them the Joint Chiefs of Staff reach agreement themselves," the vastly more important truth is that "normally the *only* disputes are on strategic concepts, the size and composition of forces, and budget matters."

Military-Industrial. But what about the fabled military-industrial complex? If the military alone is divided and weak, perhaps the giant industrial firms that are so dependent on defense contracts play a large part in making policy.

First, there is an important distinction between the questions "Who will get a given contract?" and "What will our defense policy be?" It is apparent that different answers may be given to these quite different questions. There are literally ten of thousands of defense contractors. They may compete vigorously for business. In the course of this competition, they may wine and dine military officers, use retired generals, seek intervention by their congressmen, place ads in trade journals, and even contribute to political campaigns. The famous TFX controversy—should General Dynamics or Boeing get the expensive contract?—is a larger than life example of the pressures brought to bear in search of lucrative contracts.

But neither the TFX case nor the usual vigorous competition for contracts is involved with the making of substantive defense policy. Vital questions like the size of the defense budget, the choice of strategic programs, massive retaliation vs. a counter-city strategy, and the like were far beyond the policy aims of any company. Industrial firms, then, do not control such decisions, nor is there much evidence that they actually try. No doubt a precipitous and drastic rush to disarmament would meet with opposition from industrial firms among other interests. However, there has never been a time when any significant element in the government considered a disarmament policy to be feasible.

It may appear that industrial firms had no special reason to concern themselves with the government's stance on defense because they agree with the national consensus on resisting communism, maintaining a large defense establishment, and rejecting isolationism. However, this hypothesis about the climate of opinion explains everything and nothing. For every policy that is adopted or rejected can be explained away on the grounds that the cold war climate of opinion dictated what happened. Did the United States fail to intervene with armed force in Vietnam in 1954? That must be because the climate of opinion was against it. Did the United States send troops to Vietnam in the 1960's? That must be because the cold war climate demanded it. If the United States builds more missiles, negotiates a test-ban treaty, intervenes in the Dominican Republic, fails to intervene in a dozen other situations, all these actions fit the hypothesis by definition. The argument is reminiscent of those who defined the Soviet Union as permanently hostile and therefore interpreted increases of Soviet troops as menacing and decreases of troop strength as equally sinister.

If the growth of the military establishment is not directly equated with increasing military control of defense policy, the extraordinary weakness of the professional soldier still requires explanation. Huntington has written about how major military leaders were seduced in the Truman and Eisenhower years into believing that they should bow to the judgment of civilians that the economy could not stand much larger military expenditures. Once the size of the military pie was accepted as a fixed constraint, the military services were compelled to put their major energies into quarreling with one another over who should get the larger share. Given the natural rivalries of the military and their traditional acceptance of civilian rule, the

President and his advisers—who could claim responsibility for the broader picture of reconciling defense and domestic policies—had the upper hand. There are, however, additional explanations to be considered.

The dominant role of the congressional appropriations committee is to be guardian of the treasury. This is manifested in the pride of its members in cutting the President's budget. Thus it was difficult to get this crucial committee to recommend even a few hundred million increase in defense; it was practically impossible to get them to consider the several billion jump that might really have made a difference. A related budgetary matter concerned the planning, programming, and budgeting system introduced by Secretary of Defense McNamara. For if the defense budget contained major categories that crisscrossed the services, only the Secretary of Defense could put it together. Whatever the other debatable consequences of program budgeting, its major consequence was to grant power to the secretary and his civilian advisers.

The subordination of the military through program budgeting is just one symptom of a more general weakness of the military. In the past decade the military has suffered a lack of intellectual skills appropriate to the nuclear age. For no one has (and no one wants) direct experience with nuclear war. So the usual military talk about being the only people to have combat experience is not very impressive. Instead, the imaginative creation of possible future wars—in order to avoid them—requires people with a high capacity for abstract thought combined with the ability to manipulate symbols using quantitative methods. West Point has not produced many such men.

The State Department. Modern Presidents expect the State Department to carry out their policies. John F. Kennedy felt that State was "in some particular sense 'his' department." If a Secretary of State forgets this, as was apparently the case with James Byrnes under Truman, a President may find another man. But the State Department, especially the Foreign Service, is also a highly professional organization with a life and momentum of its own. If a President does not push hard, he may find his preferences somehow dissipated in time. Arthur Schlesinger fills his book on Kennedy with laments about the bureaucratic inertia and recalcitrance of the State Department.

Yet Schlesinger's own account suggests that State could not ordinarily resist the President. At one point, he writes of "The President, himself, increasingly the day-to-day director of American foreign policy." On the next page, we learn that "Kennedy dealt personally with almost every aspect of policy around the globe. He knew more about certain areas than the senior officials at State and probably called as many issues to their attention as they did to his." The

President insisted on his way in Laos. He pushed through his policy on the Congo against strong opposition within the State Department. Had Kennedy wanted to get a great deal more initiative out of the State Department, as Schlesinger insists, he could have replaced the Secretary of State, a man who did not command special support in the Democratic party or in Congress. It may be that Kennedy wanted too strongly to run his own foreign policy. Dean Rusk may have known far better than Schlesinger that the one thing Kennedy did not want was a man who might rival him in the field of foreign affairs.

Schlesinger comes closest to the truth when he writes that "the White House could always win any battle it chose over the [Foreign] Service; but the prestige and proficiency of the Service limited the number of battles any White House would find it profitable to fight." When the President knew what he wanted, he got it. When he was doubtful and perplexed, he sought good advice and frequently did not get that. But there is no evidence that the people on his staff came up with better ideas. The real problem may have been a lack of good ideas anywhere. Kennedy undoubtedly encouraged his staff to prod the State Department. But the President was sufficiently cautious not to push so hard that he got his way when he was not certain what that way should be. In this context Kennedy appears to have played his staff off against elements in the State Department.

The growth of a special White House staff to help Presidents in foreign affairs expresses their need for assistance, their refusal to rely completely on the regular executive agencies, and their ability to find competent men. The deployment of this staff must remain a presidential prerogative, however, if its members are to serve Presidents and not their opponents. Whenever critics do not like existing foreign and defense policies, they are likely to complain that the White House staff is screening out divergent views from the President's attention. Naturally, the critics recommend introducing many more different viewpoints. If the critics could maneuver the President into counting hands all day ("on the one hand and on the other"), they would make it impossible for him to act. Such a viewpoint is also congenial to those who believe that action rather than inaction is the greatest present danger in foreign policy. But Presidents resolutely refuse to become prisoners of their advisers by using them as other people would like. Presidents remain in control of their staff as well as of major foreign policy decisions.

HOW COMPLETE IS THE CONTROL?

Some analysts say that the success of Presidents in controlling foreign policy decisions is largely illusory. It is achieved, they say, by anticipating the reactions of others, and eliminating proposals that would run into severe opposition. There is some truth in this objection. In politics, where transactions are based on a high degree of mutual interdependence, what others may do has to be taken into account. But basing presidential success in foreign and defense policy on anticipated reactions suggests a static situation which does not exist. For if Presidents propose only those policies that would get support in Congress, and Congress opposes them only when it knows that it can muster overwhelming strength, there would never be any conflict. Indeed, there might never be any action.

How can "anticipated reaction" explain the conflict over policies like the Marshall Plan and the test-ban treaty in which severe opposition was overcome only by strenuous efforts? Furthermore, why doesn't "anticipated reaction" work in domestic affairs? One would have to argue that for some reason presidential perception of what would be successful is consistently confused on domestic issues and most always accurate on major foreign policy issues. But the role of "anticipated reactions" should be greater in the more familiar domestic situations, which provide a backlog of experience for forecasting, than in foreign policy with many novel situations such as the Suez crisis or the Rhodesian affair.

Are there significant historical examples which might refute the thesis of presidential control of foreign policy? Foreign aid may be a case in point. For many years, Presidents have struggled to get foreign aid appropriations because of hostility from public and congressional opinion. Yet several billion dollars a year are appropriated regularly despite the evident unpopularity of the program. In the aid programs to Communist countries like Poland and Yugoslavia, the Congress attaches all sorts of restrictions to the aid, but Presidents find ways of getting around them.

What about the example of recognition of Communist China? The sentiment of the country always has been against recognizing Red China or admitting it to the United Nations. But have Presidents wanted to recognize Red China and been hamstrung by opposition? The answer, I suggest, is a qualified "no." By the time recognition of Red China might have become a serious issue for the Truman administration, the war in Korea effectively precluded its consideration. There is no evidence that President Eisenhower or Secretary Dulles ever thought it wise to recognize Red China or help admit her to the United Nations. The Kennedy administration viewed the matter as not of major importance and, considering the opposition, moved cautiously in suggesting change. Then came the war in Vietnam. If the advantages for foreign policy had been perceived to be much higher, then Kennedy or Johnson might have proposed changing American policy toward recognition of Red China.

One possible exception, in the case of Red China, however, does not seem sufficient to invalidate the general thesis that Presidents do considerably better in getting their way in foreign and defense policy than in domestic policies.

THE WORLD INFLUENCE

The forces impelling Presidents to be concerned with the widest range of foreign and defense policies also affect the ways in which they calculate their power stakes. As Kennedy used to say, "Domestic policy . . . can only defeat us; foreign policy can kill us."

It no longer makes sense for Presidents to "play politics" with foreign and defense policies. In the past, Presidents might have thought that they could gain by prolonged delay or by not acting at all. The problem might disappear or be passed on to their successors. Presidents must now expect to pay the high costs themselves if the world situation deteriorates. The advantages of pursuing a policy that is viable in the world, that will not blow up on Presidents or their fellow citizens, far outweigh any temporary political disadvantages accrued in supporting an initially unpopular policy. Compared with domestic affairs, Presidents engaged in world politics are immensely more concerned with meeting problems on their own terms. Who supports and opposes a policy, though a matter of considerable interest, does not assume the crucial importance that it does in domestic affairs. The best policy Presidents can find is also the best politics.

The fact that there are numerous foreign and defense policy situations competing for a President's attention means that it is worthwhile to organize political activity in order to affect his agenda. For if a President pays more attention to certain problems he may develop different preferences; he may seek and receive different advice; his new calculations may lead him to devote greater resources to seeking a solution. Interested congressmen may exert influence not by directly determining a presidential decision, but indirectly by making it costly for a President to avoid reconsidering the basis for his action. For example, citizen groups, such as those concerned with a change in China policy, may have an impact simply by keeping their proposals on the public agenda. A President may be compelled to reconsider a problem even though he could not overtly be forced to alter the prevailing policy.

In foreign affairs we may be approaching the stage where knowledge is power. There is a tremendous receptivity to good ideas in Washington. Most anyone who can present a convincing rationale for dealing with a hard world finds a ready audience. The best way to convince Presidents to follow a desired policy is to show that it might work. A man like McNamara thrives because he performs; he comes up with answers he can defend. It is, to be sure, extremely difficult to devise good policies or to predict their consequences accurately. Nor is it easy to convince others that a given policy is superior to other alternatives. But it is the way to influence with Presidents. For if they are convinced that the current policy is best, the likelihood of gaining sufficient force to compel a change is quite small. The man who can build better foreign policies will find Presidents beating a path to his door.

☆

ROBERT S. HIRSCHFIELD: *The Power of the*

Contemporary Presidency

In general terms the Presidency at the beginning of the 1960s is easily
described: It is the focus of both the American governmental system
and the free world coalition, an office of great authority and commensurate responsibility. Resting firmly on the twin supports of
democratic election and the necessities of a critical era, it is now a
permanently strong office, an institutionalized version of the "crisis
presidencies" of Lincoln, Wilson, Roosevelt, and Truman. And like
the regimes from which it stems, the outstanding feature of the
executive office today is its power.

The purpose of this article is to outline the power of today's
Presidency—to describe and analyze the kinds of authority which it
includes, the real sources from which it springs, and the system of
restraints to which it is subject. The result intended is a better understanding of the Presidency's full dimensions in a time of protracted
crisis, and of the opportunities for effective leadership open to the
new President.

THE KINDS OF PRESIDENTIAL AUTHORITY

Although the power of the Presidency is today so vast as to defy
precise definition, it may be divided into three major categories of
authority: statutory, constitutional, and extraconstitutional.

Much of the President's authority is delegated to him by Acts of

This selection is from "The Power of the Contemporary Presidency," *Parliamentary Affairs*, Summer, 1961, pp. 353–377. Reprinted by permission of the
Hansard Society for Parliamentary Government.

Congress. In this manner he may be empowered to reorganize the Executive Branch of the government, raise or lower tariffs, exercise control over the nation's atomic resources, federalize the National Guard, or halt labor-management disputes. In fact, virtually all major domestic legislation includes grants of power to the executive so that he may effectuate national policies. In addition—and most significant under contemporary conditions—Congress, either on its own initiative or at the President's request, may delegate authority enabling the President to meet extraordinary situations abroad, as in the Formosa Resolution of 1954 or the Near East Resolution of 1956. In such cases, however, there is often a question regarding the necessity for congressional action, and the delegations may be viewed, at least by the President, as a way of indicating congressional support for a presidential policy already undertaken, rather than as a means for extending his authority. Wilson, Roosevelt, Truman, and Eisenhower all sought and received this kind of legislative approval in dealing with emergency situations abroad. All of them insisted, as Mr. Eisenhower did in the 1956 Near East crisis, that since the President already possessed all the power required to meet such situations there was no constitutional need for congressional action; but all nonetheless agreed that Congress should be consulted whenever possible so that there would be no doubt regarding the nation's unity.

Power delegated prospectively for discretionary use by the President in the event of a foreign emergency, though designed as an indication of legislative confidence in the executive and as a warning to potential aggressors, may in effect authorize or put a congressional seal of approval on presidential warmaking. The Lend-Lease Act of 1941 was of this nature, and so was the Near East Resolution. Conversely, the delegatory process may be used as a device for according retroactive legislative assent to actions already taken by the President on his own initiative. Thus the Congress which convened on July 4, 1861, sanctioned the crisis regime instituted by Lincoln, though in fact this amounted simply to its recognition of a *fait accompli.*

Whatever the reasons for congressional grants of authority, statutory delegations are an important part of a President's reservoir of power, and in the absence of overriding considerations which make resort to other forms of authority seem more desirable, he will utilize such grants. Indeed Presidents will occasionally try to justify their actions by citing delegatory statutes which are defunct or inapplicable in order to maintain a semblance of normal procedure (FDR, for example, resurrected the Trading with the Enemy Act of 1917 to support his closing of the banks in 1933). But usually it is not too difficult to find a relevant statute, since emergency measures have a way of remaining on the books after the crisis which impelled their enactment has passed. Although an Attorney General must some-times use ingenuity to find the proper reference, with the hundreds of accumulated emergency provisions now on hand the task can ordinarily be accomplished. In any event, Presidents have never had great difficulty in persuading Congress to legitimize their indepen-dent actions or to make additional power available under crisis conditions.

The second kind of presidential authority is constitutional: power vested in the President by the basic law and exercisable by him on his own initiative. And because problems of interpretation become greater when the Constitution itself is involved, this is a trickier area than that which deals with statutory law.

The extent of the President's constitutional authority has been the subject for continuing national debate, and the dispute between "broad" and "strict" construction of the powers barely outlined in Article II is as old as the Republic. In this debate virtually every President of note has joined. The crescendo passages have been reached, of course, during the terms of those who acted most "strongly"—Washington, Jefferson, Jackson, Polk, Lincoln, Theodore Roosevelt, Wilson, Franklin Roosevelt, and Truman. However, only the first Roosevelt (whose impetuous autonomy gave rise to much controversy, though he never had a really serious crisis to test his vigor) ever propounded a "theory" of broad presidential power, by asserting that it was limited only by "specific restrictions and pro-hibitions appearing in the Constitution or imposed by the Congress under its Constitutional powers." In TR's view the President is the "steward of the people," having not only the right but the duty to do whatever the needs of the nation demand, unless such action is forbidden "by the Constitution or the laws."

Emphasizing the President's tribunate character, this "steward-ship theory" places the executive in the center of the American governmental system, but it does not help very much in defining just what the obviously vast residue of power not constitutionally or legally forbidden to the President includes. And indeed it is only by reference to what Presidents have actually done (or gotten away with) that Article II takes form. For the great builders of the power-ful Presidency have been the powerful Presidents themselves. The State of the Union message, for example, was not an element of power until Woodrow Wilson made it the instrument for announc-ing his legislative program to the nation as well as Congress. It was Lincoln who molded the Chief Executive and Commander in Chief clauses into a combination strong enough to save the Union. And every powerful President has helped to develop the Hamiltonian conception of executive primacy in the conduct of foreign relations.

Much scholarship has been devoted to discovering the content of the President's constitutional power, with the result that many of its aspects have been spelled out. The President is, constitutionally, Head of State, Chief Executive, Head of Administration, Chief Foreign Policymaker, Commander in Chief, and Legislative Leader. Under these titles, he has independent power to perform, among many others, such varied and significant functions as recognizing new governments, enforcing legislative enactments and judicial decisions, subdelegating presidential authority, making executive agreements which have the force of treaties, deploying the armed forces, and recommending or vetoing legislation. These and all the other activities which flow from the Constitution either by direct sanction or reasonable implication comprise an impressive array of powers even if exercised by a President whose conception of the office is modest. When placed in the hands of a strong President they take on overwhelming proportions. And it is the strong view which is today the accepted one. Indeed this acceptance has resulted in a theory of the office that attributes to it "inherent" power which is virtually unlimited.

It is at this point, however, that the President's authority under the Constitution, no matter how broadly interpreted, must give way to yet another kind of power. For constitutionalism means limitation on governmental power, including that wielded by the President, and no matter how far his authority under the basic law may be pushed, it cannot transcend the concept of limitation and remain constitutional. He cannot, in short, have "constitutional" power to do *anything* which the needs of the nation require, and any theory of the Presidency which projects executive power into this limitless range of action, by definition goes beyond the bounds of constitutionality.

When Presidents in meeting emergencies have assumed extraordinary power on their own initiative, they have invariably sought to legitimize their actions by reference to the Constitution, relying on the "inherent power" concept and generally using the magic formula: "By virtue of authority as President of the United States and Commander in Chief of the armed forces under the Constitution and the laws." But while this formula undoubtedly covers a lot of ground, it cannot be made to include exercises of power which ignore or violate the basic law even though their use is necessary to defense of the nation and notwithstanding the fact that their ultimate purpose is to preserve that law.

There is a third kind of presidential power, therefore, and it is *extraconstitutional:* the American manifestation of that executive authority which John Locke defined as the power to act "according to discretion for the public good, without the prescription of the laws, and sometimes even against it." And it is this kind of power which forms the unique ingredient of presidential authority today—a kind of power which has been resorted to by every crisis leader, and which must be more clearly identified and understood in our time.

Extraconstitutional presidential prerogative is the most difficult to assay, however, because it is unacknowledged in our political theory and unrecognized in our jurisprudence. Unwilling to face the dilemma created by exercises of power which transcend the established bounds of legitimate authority, our public law has refused to distinguish between necessity and constitutionality in judging presidential actions. Jurists and political scientists have, instead, equated these two very different bases of action, with the result that while Presidents have in fact exceeded their legal and constitutional authority in every instance of major national emergency, it remains a dogma of our system that the Constitution is "equal to any of the great exigencies of government."

Among the Presidents who have resorted to extraconstitutional power, only Abraham Lincoln—whose dictatorial regime at the beginning of the Civil War remains the clearest example of reliance on such authority—ever admitted the true nature of his actions, expressing the hope that "measures otherwise unconstitutional might become lawful by becoming indispensable to the preservation of the Constitution through the preservation of the Nation." The Civil War President exceeded his constitutional authority in many instances, from the independent raising of an army to the unauthorized expenditure of public funds. Yet, when Woodrow Wilson used indirect sanctions to gain compliance with his war agencies' directives; when Franklin Roosevelt closed the banks, traded destroyers for bases, threatened to repeal existing legislation, and interned citizens solely because of their racial descent; and when Harry Truman committed the nation to war on his own initiative—all were acting in the Lincolnian tradition.

That tradition is at the core of the strong Presidency, and it flows from a conception of the office legitimized through public approval: that the President, as the "sole representative of all the people," possesses unlimited authority to preserve, protect, and defend the nation which gives the Constitution life and meaning. He may suspend the basic law in order to assure its ultimate survival, and the only standard by which the validity of his actions can be measured is necessity, not constitutionality. Regardless of what American political theory and jurisprudence may hold, history demonstrates clearly that the executive does possess extraconstitutional power, and its existence as an essential part of the office must be acknowledged if we are to understand the Presidency of our time.

THE SOURCES OF PRESIDENTIAL POWER

Although theoretically the twin fountainheads of executive power are the "Constitution and the laws," in fact the sources of this prodigious authority are now democracy and necessity.

The Presidency, like all offices of government, is only a paper institution until the political process supplies the personality which brings it to life. And Article II, though it outlines a potentially powerful executive office, has no effect until its words are translated into action. The real foundations of presidential power, therefore, are those forces which elevate the executive to a focal position in government, allowing him to interpret his authority broadly and to exercise it boldly.

The most important of these forces lies in the democratic nature of the modern Presidency. Not only constitutionally, but also politically and psychologically, the President is *the* leader of the nation. "His," as Woodrow Wilson said, "is the only national voice in affairs. Let him once win the admiration and confidence of the country, and no other single force can withstand him, no combination of forces will easily overpower him. His position takes the imagination of the country. He is the representative of no constituency, but of the whole people." Whether the explanation for the unique popular response to the Presidency be put in politico-constitutional terms (the election process and the singular form of the office) or in psycho-sociological terms (the desire for a father-image and the need for a symbol of national unity), the fact remains that its power flows from and is primarily dependent on its tribunate character.

The personality and political philosophy of the President are closely related to his democratic leadership. All of our strongest Presidents have had charismatic personalities, and all have been power-oriented in their philosophy of government, for it is the combination of popular attraction to the person and popular support for his political principles which makes the President's power effective. Thus his role as Popular Tribune is basic to the exercise of whatever authority may be latent in the Constitution and the laws. Neither Lincoln nor Roosevelt could have acted with such spectacular independence in meeting the challenges that confronted them had they lacked solid popular support, but with that support, they could push their powers to the limits of constitutionality and beyond. Indeed a number of strong Presidents have received object lessons regarding the dependence of power upon popular support: Truman in the 1952 steel dispute, Wilson during the League fight, Roosevelt when he presented the Court-packing plan, and Lincoln's successor after the Civil War's end. Extending one of Woodrow Wilson's observations, the President can dominate American government (Wilson said "his party") by being "spokesman for the real sentiment and purpose of the country, by giving direction to opinion, by giving the country at once the information and the statements of policy which will enable it to form its judgments alike of parties and of men."

All strong Presidents have recognized the importance of maintaining a close relationship with their major source of power. Jackson's election, heralding the era of mass democracy, established the popular Presidency, and Lincoln made clear its significance under crisis conditions. Wilson, following the lead of Theodore Roosevelt, gave the conception further impetus by his practice of "going to the people" on important issues. And Franklin Roosevelt, through masterful use of modern communications media, brought the tribunate Presidency to its contemporary form. Radio, television, and the press conference have made possible the development of a relationship between the President and the people which is exceedingly close. As a result of this intimate—almost familial—bond, the President's constitutional role as symbol of national unity has become an instrument of tremendous power, making him the center of our governmental system, and creating the basis for his leadership both at home and abroad.

The other, and no less important, source of presidential power is necessity. Not only the psychological need for clearly identifiable and deeply trusted authority, but also the governmental necessity for centralized leadership and decisive action in times of crisis.

Ours is a system constitutionally attuned to the requirements of the eighteenth century, and it is mainly through the development of the Presidency that the system has been adapted to the demands of the twentieth. The separation of powers, federalism, even the Bill of Rights and the rule of law, must sometimes be transcended under conditions of grave national emergency. Even under less pressing circumstances, the need for purposeful and efficient government is increasingly evident. But the legislative process—complex, deliberative, cumbersome, and designed to assure the compromise of manifold local interests—is ill-suited to meet these challenges. Only the President, possessing (as Alexander Hamilton noted) both unity and energy, can meet the demand for leadership under critical conditions.

Again, every strong President has recognized this fact and acted in accordance with it. Lincoln arrogated to himself all the powers of government during his eleven-week "dictatorship" in 1861 on the ground that "whether strictly legal or not" his actions were ventured upon "under what appeared to be a popular demand and a public necessity." In the atmosphere of world war, Congress accepted Wilson's leadership and delegated theretofore unprecedented power to the President. Similarly, it was the pressure of economic catastrophe which elevated FDR to the dominant position he occupied during the first hundred days of the New Deal administration, and the existence of an even greater emergency which made him supreme commander of the nation during the Second World War. Likewise, Truman's war-making power sprang from the need for decisive action to halt aggression. Necessity creates power, and presidential power has always been commensurate with the nation's needs.

Most significant for our time, however, is the fact—clearly demonstrated by the Korean conflict and other events since the end of World War II—that the Communist challenge has created a permanent demand for strong leadership and extraordinary power. Because crisis has become the normal condition of our times, the vast authority available to former Presidents only occasionally has today become a permanent part of the executive office.

Thus the needs of the nation and the support of its citizens are the real sources of presidential power, unlocking all the authority hidden in the Constitution and the laws, as well as availing the executive of powers which go beyond even the broadest interpretation of that prodigious combination. The modern President can draw upon extraordinary power because he is the democratic symbol of national unity and the necessary instrument of national action, because it is to him that the nation turns for crisis leadership and because he alone can supply that leadership. As a result, under critical conditions there are no effective constitutional or governmental limits on executive power, for democracy and necessity allow the President to transcend the limitational principle and assert his full authority as trustee of the nation's destiny.

THE RESTRAINTS ON PRESIDENTIAL POWER

In our society there are ostensibly many restraints on presidential power. The federal system, for example, establishes fifty centers of local authority to contend with the national executive. The nation's socio-economic "power elite" represents another potential element of countervailing force. Even within the executive branch itself there is the kind of restraint which flows from administrative inertia or obstruction. But whatever limitations appear to reside in these areas, basically there are three major forms of external restraint on presidential power: judicial supervision, legislative control, and public opinion.

Judicial restraint. Of these the least effective—despite its vaunted reputation—is judicial review of executive acts. And the basic reason is clear: in a showdown the President's power is greater than the Supreme Court's. The judicial branch has generally recognized this fact and either avoided conflict with the executive when possible or accepted his assertions of authority when forced to reach a decision. Indeed the Court has established a consistent pattern of acquiescence in judging presidential exercises of extraordinary power. This acquiescent attitude is not automatic, but in only one instance of direct conflict between the two branches during an emergency period has an important exercise of independent presidential authority been effectively overturned, and then the actual holding was so narrow as to have little permanent value. It is the lesson of history that where exercises of extraordinary power are involved, the Court restrains itself and not the President.

The occasion for the single effective declaration against presidential authority was Truman's seizure of the steel industry during the Korean War, and the Court's hesitancy in breaking even temporarily from its own tradition was apparent in the fact that each of the six majority justices wrote his own opinion. All six agreed that the President had acted *ultra vires* in the particular case, but a majority of this "majority" (four justices) seemed to accept the dissenting view that the President does have "inherent power" to take extraordinary actions in time of crisis—and this was the crucial point. For these four members of the Court, the decision turned on the fact that Congress had explicitly eliminated seizure and provided an alternative procedure (the emergency provisions of the Taft-Hartley Act) for dealing with the type of dispute involved, and that in these circumstances the President, at least initially, could not act in a manner contrary to the clearly expressed legislative will.

Thus the decision was abundantly qualified, and though the steel mills had to be returned, it is more significant that seven members of the Court were unprepared to deprive the President of ultimate authority to meet emergencies. Indeed had there not been such widespread disapproval of the President's action—from Congress, the press, and the general public—or had the Korean situation seemed more critical (truce talks were already underway) it is doubtful that the four majority justices would have written even the cautious opinions that they did. But in the circumstances they evidently seized the opportunity to admonish the President, Congress, and the nation against indiscriminate use of inherent presidential power.

In this sense the Steel Case is very much like the first great decision in the area of presidential emergency power, *Ex parte Milligan*. For in that often cited but no more meaningful Civil War case, the Court, by declaring Lincoln's establishment of martial rule unconstitutional, also attempted to restore the basic law to its normal operation after a crisis. But the issue had been avoided during the war, and the decision did not come until both the emergency and the President had passed from the scene. The Milligan Court spoke the strongest language of limitation—and its words have been quoted against independent exercises of presidential authority on a number of occasions since—but in view of the Court's actual crisis behavior that language was embarrassingly unsubstantial. As most of the judiciary's blasts against the executive, the decision is more quotable than applicable.

Probably the most effective exercise of judicial restraining power was its use to invalidate the early New Deal, though the issue involved was not simply presidential authority but rather the power of the combined political branches of government. In any event, even on that occasion the Court's "victory" was short-lived if not pyrrhic. For the final result of the struggle which reached its climax in the Court-packing plan of 1937 was judicial capitulation to President Roosevelt's demand that economic disaster be viewed as seriously as war and that the Court cease to obstruct governmental efforts to meet the crisis.

The judiciary is always placed in a difficult position by conditions which allow a strong President to assume extraordinary power. Compelled to acknowledge that the law of necessity is superior to the law of the Constitution, and lacking the kind of popular support which is accorded the political leader, it must accept many actions which under normal conditions would be outside the realm of legitimate power. The Court's infrequent *ex post facto* pronouncements regarding the limits of presidential authority have little direct effect in any case, and since no judicial decision is self-enforcing they are always essentially lectures rather than injunctions. The Court's primary function in checking a strong President is to act as a symbol of restraint, a moral force, and a constant reminder of established principles—a function which is by no means unimportant—but with regard to executive power, Article II of the Constitution is what the President, and not what the Court, says it is.

Legislative restraint. In our governmental system Congress is traditionally viewed as the President's principal antagonist and most effective restrainer. The constitutional separation of powers with its mechanism of checks and balances was designed to encourage an executive-legislative power struggle which would prevent either branch from gaining dominant authority. And the local orientation of congressional politics supposedly provides a counterweight to the national purview of the Presidency. But despite all this, Congress cannot easily control the exercise of presidential power. In fact, both the constitutional structure of the government, with its separation of the branches, and the nature of American politics, with its emphasis on local interest representation, often tend to make that task more rather than less difficult.

The separation of powers doctrine can become both a shield and a sword in the hands of a strong President. He can use it to ward off alleged congressional encroachments on executive authority, as Lincoln did in combating the Committee on the Conduct of the (Civil). War and as Wilson did in preventing the establishment of a similar body. Or he can use the doctrine to support his resort to independent authority, the approach adopted on so many occasions by the Civil War President (who achieved the greatest concentration of power in our history by insisting on the separation principle), as well as by every other strong executive who has relied on that principle in assuming extraordinary power on his own initiative.

As the separation of powers principle often creates a constitutional power-vacuum which the executive can fill, so too does the nature of congressional politics give rise to conditions which may enhance rather than limit presidential authority. The local orientation of Congress assures the representation of all the significant interests in our society, but at the same time it results in legislative fragmentation, leaving Congress without a cohesive majority or effective leadership. And this political power-vacuum the President may also enter. Indeed it is increasingly evident that if he does not assume the role of legislative leader, Congress cannot move on important and controversial issues. Attuned to the process of continuing compromise rather than to the achievement of definite goals, Congress must always give way to the executive when events demand unity of purpose and decisive action.

Congress itself knows this and looks increasingly to the President for leadership, not only with regard to matters of national defense and foreign affairs, but in other areas as well, like domestic economic policy and civil rights. It is in time of actual or impending emergency, however, that this need for presidential initiative is most clearly evident and most readily acknowledged by Congress, as it quickly accepts the President's direction in delegating to him whatever authority he requests. Despite the separation of powers principle, executive leadership of the legislature has become an established feature of our system, though the effect of Congress's reliance on presidential initiative and of its delegations of authority to the executive is to enhance his domination over the legislative process and to increase his freedom from legislative control.

Congress's difficulty in restraining presidential power is also a result of the tremendous range and complexity of contemporary governmental problems, and of its own inability to deal with them. Neither the individual legislator nor the Congress as a whole possesses the information-gathering and problem-evaluating apparatus of the Presidency, particularly in the foreign affairs and defense areas, but in others as well. Congress is increasingly dependent, therefore, upon members of the executive branch—department heads, military officers, economic and scientific advisers—for the technical information essential to its own activity. Thus, while information may be acquired through congressional inquiry or investigation (and despite the fact that the President's subordinates do not always accept his policy determinations), to a large extent the effectiveness of legislative supervision depends upon the executive's willingness to cooperate.

Further detracting from the legislature's ability to contend with the President is his control over formulation of the budget, since this function gives the executive a dominant position in determining the final plan for governmental expenditures. Indeed the congressional power over the executive traditionally assumed to be the greatest— the power of the purse—is often ineffectual. The President may present Congress with a situation which does not permit the withholding of funds, as Theodore Roosevelt did by sending the Great White Fleet on its famous global journey without enough coal to get it back home, and as other Presidents have done by more serious dispositions of the armed forces. Congress may even be forced to appropriate money without knowing the reason for the expenditure, as it did in supporting the secret, multi-billion dollar development of the atomic bomb. And Lincoln simply paid out $2,000,000 of public funds on his own initiative. Despite its celebrated reputation, therefore, even the restraining power of the purse is subject to suspension when the need for secrecy or speed is of the essence.

The most important limitation on Congress as a presidential restrainer, however, is public support for the executive. While the localism of congressional politics makes legislators peculiarly responsive to the desires of particular groups, it also leaves the advantage increasingly with the President in mobilizing the general public behind national policies. For with regard to such policies Congress can never present a single view or project a definite image to the country, while the President can do so forcefully. Emphasizing his roles as head of state and sole national representative, and utilizing all the media of mass communication, he is able to generate pressure which Congress cannot easily withstand.

Of course Congress is not impotent in exercising control over the President. The political longevity of congressional leaders and the absence of party discipline allow for displays of legislative independence which can and do check, embarrass, or inhibit the executive. Legislative debate and investigation—techniques which have been used to harass every strong President—can focus attention on alleged maladministration or misconduct in the executive branch. And widespread congressional hostility makes even the strongest President somewhat cautious in his exercises of power. But under emergency or semi-emergency conditions congressional antagonism is largely sublimated, and attempts to limit the President are generally more irritating than effective. Despite legislative fulmination, no crisis executive has ever been deterred by the legislature from accomplishing his major purposes.

Indeed, confronted with a strong President, Congress generally finds the task of imposing restraints both thankless and frustrating. For the public is likely to equate opposition to the President with obstruction of his efforts in the nation's behalf, and moreover there is the hard fact that a popular crisis President who encounters difficulties or delays in Congress—particularly in matters of foreign policy—may simply bypass the legislature and present it with a *fait accompli* by resort to his independent authority. Congress is certainly a more formidable check on presidential power than the courts, but in our time it does not and cannot fulfill the restraining function traditionally ascribed to it.

Popular restraint. As the President's principal source of power is public support, so too can popular opinion be the most important restraint on that power. So long as the nation's approval is firm and evident, his authority cannot be challenged effectively, but conversely, in order to use his full powers a President must continue to have such approval. His personal relationship with the public and his ability to guide popular opinion are the mainstays of his dominant position in government.

Some of our strongest Presidents discovered this truth the hard way. Franklin Roosevelt lost the Court-packing battle (though he ultimately won the war against judicial obstructionism) because the same public which had just given him the greatest electoral mandate in history refused to support his attempt to invade judicial independence. Woodrow Wilson failed to meet his own test of success in the League campaign, and the absence of popular support played a major role in Harry Truman's defeat on the steel seizure issue. Moreover, Congress quickly reflects public hostility to the President, and, though less immediately, so may the Court. Thus FDR could not assert his legislative leadership once his opponents in Congress sensed that Court-packing lacked popular support, and the Supreme Court was encouraged to act with dispatch to invalidate Truman's unpopular assertion of power in the steel dispute.

The major instrumentalities for mobilizing public support against the President are the opposition political party, organized pressure groups, and the press or other communications media. But under critical conditions particularly, the same factors that limit the efficacy of the formal (legislative and judicial) restraints also apply to these three informal restraining forces. The President's political opponents —often including members of his own party—must beware of boomerangs; pressure groups represent only single rather than national interests; and the media, perhaps the most important of the three, fear that by combining their reportorial and editorial functions in opposing the President, they may lose the public trust, limit their wide area of freedom, and cut off their best source of news. The press, radio, and television report and comment on opposition to the executive, but even when the diverse elements of the communications system agree with this opposition, they seldom attempt to incite public disapproval of his actions.

While popular support may, on rare occasions, be mobilized against the President, the opposite is the rule. For he is the principal molder of public opinion, and as a result, even this most important instrument of restraint is not often effective. The same psychology that creates a desire for presidential leadership in critical times assures the executive of popular support for the policies which he pursues. Moreover, it is important to recognize that this "crisis psychology" which elevates the President to a dominant position is itself partly created by the President. For, given the framework of objective facts surrounding a critical situation, it is largely the crisis leader's own reaction to those facts—the extent to which he emphasizes and dramatizes the situation's seriousness—that determines the form of public response. The fact of Southern secession was no less serious in 1860 than 1861, but where Buchanan's equivocation clouded the issue, Lincoln's action mobilized the nation to meet it. Similarly, the depression did not begin when Roosevelt took office, but it was FDR who marshalled opinion behind a program to overcome the economic disaster. Most significantly, it was Wilson, Roosevelt, and Truman who made the nation aware that foreign aggression constituted a threat to domestic security. And conversely, in the immediate past, the country did not face up to the dangers confronting it largely because President Eisenhower failed to impress upon the public the urgency of the international situation.

Whatever the objective facts may be, it is the President himself who plays a central role in defining the issues and creating the popular attitudes which make possible his own exercises of extraordinary power. Moreover, all of this is especially true in our own time, not only because the means by which the President may influence opinion have improved so greatly, nor because his ability to use those means is so far superior to that of any other person or group in the society, but because even that segment of the public which is not politically indifferent finds it increasingly difficult to make independent judgments regarding the significance or seriousness of particular events. That international Communist aggression poses a threat to American security and world peace is perhaps generally recognized, but is economic penetration of Afghanistan or the fomenting of revolution in Iraq or infiltration of the Cuban government aggression? Adequate military defense is an acknowledged necessity, but to achieve it do we require planes or missiles, and if missiles, are domestic launching facilities sufficient or must we also have overseas bases? Support for those who seek their independence from colonial rule is in keeping with American principles, but should we favor strong central governments or federal unions in the newly-established nations?

Confronted with fantastically complex problems and asked to determine the wisdom of policies involving all the areas of the world, even the responsible and informed citizen often ends up placing his trust in God and the President. In the sense of its direct influence on decision-making, therefore, public opinion is less a limitation on presidential power than the key to its full utilization—a fact which every strong President has recognized by placing the greatest emphasis on his position of popular leadership.

Effective restraints. But if public opinion is ultimately no more effective than legislative or judicial restraint, are there no real limitations on the Presidency? There does exist in our political system one factor which can generally be counted on to minimize the possibility of arbitrary executive rule, and that is the process by which the President is selected. Not merely the element of choice in voting, though that is important, but rather the complex procedure by which candidates are selected in party conventions, and even more, the personal attributes of those who are finally chosen to seek the highest office.

Because the Presidency (along with the Vice Presidency) is the only national elective office in an exceedingly diverse society, it is open only to those who are attuned to the virtues of political compromise and moderate in their political philosophy. The parties will nominate only such men, and though this tends to exclude from consideration many competent people whose views are too definite, it also acts as a "safety valve" against those who might disregard the welfare of significant segments of our population. A new President may reveal or find within himself the capacity for bold and decisive leadership, but the basic personality, shaped by the same forces that open the way to the office, remains, and even in his assertions of extraordinary power he will not depart essentially from the conservative, evolutionary, and pragmatic tradition of American government and politics.

The Presidency reflects this tradition with remarkable accuracy in its consistent rejection of dogmatism, of the Left and of the Right alike. It is not a position for radical or reactionary autocrats, or for demagogues, and none of our strong Presidents, despite their claims to power, has given any evidence of desiring to establish a permanent dictatorship. Nor has any of them ever attempted to use temporary powers to achieve fundamentally different forms of social or political organization. Some Presidents have assumed dictatorial authority to meet crises, but none has ever *been* a dictator. In power they may sometimes violate basic principles of the constitutional system temporarily, even unnecessarily—as Wilson did by allowing overzealous subordinates to engage in witchhunting during World War I, and as Roosevelt did in permitting the denial of basic rights to a racial minority during World War II—but in the final analysis all have displayed a deep attachment to, and a high regard for, those principles.

It is at least partly because of their personal commitment to constitutional democratic processes that crisis Presidents have always attempted to justify their extraordinary actions by reference to the basic law, and that whenever possible they have sought to include Congress as a partner in crisis government. For legitimacy is important to the President, as it is to the Presidency, and presidential self-restraint, reflecting both innate personal qualities and real concern for the opinion of the public and of history can be as meaningful a restraining force as countervailing power. Thus, while constitutional and political methods of restraining the executive may not always be effective, the Presidency has auto-limitational features which tend to mitigate those dangers to our system of government which are inherent in its vast power.

THE PRESIDENCY IN THE SIXTIES

The scope and effect of executive power are today so broad as to make valid Henry Jones Ford's observation that in the presidential office American democracy has revived "the oldest political institution of the race, the elective kingship." In fact, considering the absence of external restraints on this power, the question arises as to whether the contemporary Presidency is not, potentially, a "matrix for dictatorship."

The answer is certainly "no" if by dictatorship is meant absolute and arbitrary authority which denies the opportunity for political opposition and rejects the possibility of free, nonpolitical activity. But it is just as clear that the Presidency today is unquestionably the dominant organ of American government, an office permanently and inherently strong, reflecting the institutionalization of crisis concepts established by precedent, legitimized by public acceptance, and sustained by the abnormality of international affairs.

The Presidency has always mirrored the facts of our national life, and under present conditions there is no alternative to a strong executive. Because ours is an age of crisis, it is an age of executive government, and this political truth applies no less surely to the United States than it does to virtually every other country in the world. The powerful American Presidency is part of a global pattern —as evident in the West as in the East—characterized by the expansion and centralization of governmental authority; it is a modern form of a more primitive kind of rule, developed to meet extraordinary challenges and perpetuated while the search for peaceful normalcy continues.

Despite its present eminence, however, the Presidency during the decade ahead will most likely become an even more powerful institution. And not only in the event of war, nor only in the field of foreign affairs. For the '60s will be a critical period, both at home and abroad, even in the absence of armed conflict, and executive authority may have to be exercised in new ways to meet new challenges. Indeed, to a significant degree the outcome of the struggle between communism and democracy, as well as the resolution of important domestic issues, will depend on the actions of the President. "Without leadership alert and sensitive to change," as Franklin Roosevelt said, "we are bogged up or lose our way," and in our rapidly changing world there is a pressing need for such leadership on both the national and the international scenes.

There are many new ways in which the power of the Presidency may have to be exercised during the decade ahead. Should the ultimate crisis of thermonuclear war occur, the President would necessarily have to assume dictatorial authority over every aspect of whatever remained of our national existence. His power would be total, to meet the totality of the disaster, and the regimes of Lincoln, Wilson, and Roosevelt would seem pale in comparison. But aside from the dread possibility of an atomic emergency, there will probably be at least three major problems in the '60s requiring strong executive action: the occurrence or threat of limited war in various parts of the globe, increasing political and economic competition with the Soviet camp, and the perfection of democracy within the United States itself.

With regard to the problem of limited armed conflict, Mr. Truman broke new ground in the exercise of presidential power when he committed the nation—and its allies—to a major war in Korea entirely on his own initiative, and a future President might well have to act with similar boldness in defense of the national interest. In fact, the President's responsibility is no longer limited to the maintenance of American security; it now embraces the security of all the free nations. Nor is his new role limited to sporadic instances of military aggression; because of the more subtle threat of Communist political, social, and economic competition, it is a permanent position. In a very real sense, the American President has become the executive of the entire Western Coalition, and the major instrument for assuring peace and order throughout the world.

To play this expanded executive role will require that the President lead in the formulation of common Western policy and that he assume the task of articulating the basic principles on which the Western Coalition is established. In the struggle for the nations of Asia and Africa, his will be the crucial job of presenting the case for democracy and of capturing the imagination of the uncommitted peoples. This job really starts at home, for the President must first create a climate of public opinion which will support a bold program of international leadership. To meet the challenge of Communist competition will require an effort much greater than that which was made to save Western Europe from collapse after World War II, but it will require a similar sense of urgency and a similar kind of vision and vitality in the executive office.

The major domestic problem which the President will have to meet in the '60s is related to the achievement of our foreign policy goals, since he cannot be an effective spokesman for democracy abroad so long as equality in civil rights is denied to colored citizens within the United States. The law of the Constitution is now clear with regard to this matter, but only the President has the prestige and the power to help make that law meaningful. The civil rights issue is not regional but national, and its resolution will depend largely on presidential initiative in mobilizing national sentiment behind the responsible leaders of both races.

In these new and as yet largely unexplored areas of presidential activity lies much of the future development of executive power. The precise form which that development may take cannot be foretold, but its general direction during the years immediately ahead seems clear. For the new President has already expressed an intention to act in the tradition of his "strong" predecessors, viewing his authority broadly and exercising it boldly. Thus he has recognized that the power of the contemporary Presidency is the nation's principal weapon for meeting the extraordinary challenges which now confront it. And though a President's determination to provide effective leadership cannot alone decide the nation's destiny, it nonetheless constitutes our best hope that those challenges will be met successfully.

☆

JAMES M. BURNS: *Presidential Government*

. . . The Presidency today is at the peak of its prestige. Journalists describe it as the toughest job on earth, the presiding office of the free world, the linchpin of Western alliance, America's greatest contribution to the art of self-government. Foreigners are fascinated by the Presidency, just as they are appalled by Congress and perplexed by party and election shenanigans. Scholars describe it as the most popular and democratic—and withal the most elevated and even most elitist—part of American government. They lovingly dissect the Presidency, slicing up its essentially indivisible power into that of Chief Executive, Chief of State, Chief Legislator, and so on. And they worry about its infirmities even as they marvel at its strength.

Even so, we may have underestimated the long-term impact of presidential government on the whole structure of American government. Past trends and current tendencies may permit some guarded speculations as to the future.

Conservatives have long held that the Presidency, as idealized and operated by liberals and internationalists, was imperialistic and exploitative and hence that it would eventually overpower the other branches of government. They are substantially right. For almost a century now, the Presidency has been warding off forays against its own constitutional domain and drawing other governmental and political institutions into the orbit of its influence. At least since the days of President Grant the defense and expansion of the office have

James MacGregor Burns is James Phinney Baxter Professor of History and Public Affairs at Williams College. The selection is from *Presidential Government: The Crucible of Leadership* (Boston: Houghton Mifflin, 1965), pp. 313–335. Copyright © 1965 by James MacGregor Burns. Reprinted by permission of the publisher and the author.

been conducted not only by the strong Presidents but by "weak" ones; hence we can say that the growth of the Presidency has been in part an institutional tendency and not one turning merely on the accident of crisis and personality.

As we have noted earlier, Hayes successfully withstood a vigorous effort by the Senate to dominate his major appointments and thus to exercise direct influence over the executive establishment. Cleveland refused to give in to Senate demands that he submit to that body executive papers relating to the nomination of federal officials. The Tenure of Office Act, "designed to transfer control of the public service from the President to the Senate, and thus to strike a vital blow both to executive power and to the capacity of a President to maintain a coordinate position with the legislative branch," was hamstrung under Grant and Hayes and repealed under Cleveland. Hayes overcame an attack on the President's legislative power when he vetoed an appropriation bill to which House Democrats had attached a rider relating to reconstruction policy in the South.

All this was good defense; and it confirmed the President's formal control of the executive department. The President in recent decades has seemed to bring the Cabinet more certainly under his personal influence than was often the case in the nineteenth century. Lincoln's famous episode of "seven noes, one aye—the ayes have it" would be impossible today; Cabinet members would not dare risk such a posture of opposition to the chief. The Vice Presidency also has been tucked securely into the executive establishment. Some agencies, such as the Federal Bureau of Investigation, remain classic examples of the limitations of the President's control, but this independence is in part a product of unique personality and will probably diminish in time.

Presidential aggrandizement has been even more marked in the sphere of party politics. There was a time when conventions refused to renominate incumbent Presidents, when the national chairman was independent of presidential control, when the national party apparatus was dominated by competing leaders or factions. Things are very different now. The most important change affecting the nominating process since 1896 in the party in power, according to David, Goldman, and Bain, "has been the rising position of the Presidency and the increased recognition accorded the President as party leader. Other circles of influence continue to exist; but the group consisting of the President and his immediate associates has become the innermost inner circle; the others can now be regarded as a loose constellation of groups surrounding the White House as the center of power." Recently the national party chairman has been simply one more political lieutenant of the President's and one who often has less power than political aides in the White House. The President's party influence does not run much beyond the scope of the presidential party; but the scope of the presidential party may be expanding too, depending in part on the President's influence over other sectors of the whole government.

Perhaps the most extraordinary but least remarked expansion of presidential government lies in the extension of its influence to the Supreme Court. Prior to the modern presidential epoch, successive Presidents held sharply different doctrines and hence put men of varying viewpoints on the bench. Judicial appointees of a Theodore Roosevelt versus a Taft, of a Wilson versus a Harding, of a Hoover versus a Franklin Roosevelt, could hardly be expected to agree in their socioeconomic doctrine, and generally their decisions reflected their differences. This does not mean that Presidents always appointed men who slavishly expressed the presidential line. Indeed, they sometimes chose men who in time diverged widely from the President's basic doctrine, as in the case of Wilson's appointment of James C. McReynolds. But inescapably the type of appointment, and the appointee's social and economic doctrine on the bench, were affected by the general set of ideas, as well as by the political interrelationships, of a presidential administration. Thus it was not surprising that the Supreme Court of 1933–37, composed mainly of appointees of Republican Presidents, rejected major New Deal legislation. Since 1937, however, the Supreme Court has not invalidated a major piece of national social legislation. The Court is composed of men who respond to the same general ideas of freedom and equality as have recent Presidents. Eisenhower's appointees are almost indistinguishable on social and economic legislation from Roosevelt's and Kennedy's; indeed, Eisenhower's major appointee, Earl Warren, has led the Court in some of its historic egalitarian decisions, notably the *Brown* school desegregation case. The election of Barry Goldwater, and the kind of judicial appointments he would have made, would of course have disrupted the harmony between the two branches, at least if Goldwater could have put enough of his own men on the bench, but Goldwater's rejection diminishes the likelihood of a sharp presidential-judicial break in the foreseeable future. As long as we elect liberal Presidents from either of the presidential parties we can anticipate a generally liberal Court.

Federalism has also felt the impact of presidential government. Modern Presidents have overturned old doctrines and practices of states' rights by extending their policy-making power into the urban areas of the nation. Historically the growth of cities has brought more need for public regulation and control and hence the growth of government. This tendency has been evident in public health, public transportation, social welfare services, traffic and crime control, and many other sectors. These developments in turn have produced financial crises in many cities; as the burden on city government has increased, its fiscal resources have proved inadequate. City officials have had to go cup in hand to state legislatures. But the states too have been struggling with financial limitations, and rurally dominated state legislatures have not been eager to hand out money to their city brethren. So the cities have turned to Washington. But here too they often have met frustration, for Congress too is heavily influenced by the rurally based congressional party coalition, especially in the appropriations committees. So the mayors head for the White House.

And the President is there to welcome them. Whatever his political party, the modern President must be sensitive to the needs of the cities. The alliance between the President and the cities is one of the oldest facts of American politics. As far back as 1800, a presidential candidate foresaw that his success might turn on the vote in New York City. In that year Jefferson wrote to Madison: "If the city election of New York is in favor of the Republican ticket, the issue will be Republican; if the federal ticket for the city of New York prevails, the probabilities will be in favor of a federal issue because it would then require a Republican vote both from New Jersey and Pennsylvania to preponderate against New York, on which we could not count with any confidence." The spread of urbanization and the electoral college "gerrymander" have made New York and the other big urban states "preponderate" in most recent presidential elections.

Thus the man in the White House has become the President of the Cities; he has become the Chief Executive of Metropolis. He has provided the main motive power for shaping legislation needed by the cities; he pushes through the federal money bills with their provision for matching grants; he commands the executive departments—Labor, Justice, Health, Education and Welfare—that work closely with metropolitan governments; he appoints the heads of promotional and regulatory agencies for housing, urban renewal, transportation, communication, that affect the city. The President of course extends aid to the cities with strings attached—strings in the form of presidentially approved standards, procedures, safeguards, and the like. But the community of doctrine and interest between presidential government and big-city government is so close that major conflicts of politics and policy do not arise. More often the President and the mayors are allied against hostile or indifferent officials in other parts of the "marble cake" of federalism—against state legislators, county officials, congressional appropriations committees and subcommittees, even Governors.

It is dangerous to generalize about such a complex set of governmental interrelationships as these. But the population explosion in metropolitan areas, the President's sensitivity to urban needs, the proliferation of urban and suburban areas cutting across county and state lines, the fiscal parsimony of municipalities, counties, and state legislatures, and the modern liberal assumption that government is an effective tool for realizing freedom and equality—all these forces are powerful ones that will operate for years to come. As a vital force behind the President's political and legislative leadership, the cities constitute a lasting foundation of presidential government. Inevitably, as presidential government cuts across and deranges the old formal division between local, state, and national authority, it will dominate policy making in and around metropolis.

Thus the Presidency has absorbed the Cabinet, the executive departments, the Vice Presidency. It has taken over the national party apparatus. Through consistently liberal appointments over the years it has a powerful influence on the doctrine of the Supreme Court. It has transformed the federal system. What about its impact on Congress, historically and constitutionally the great counterforce to the presidential office?

Here the change may be the most profound of all, at least in the long run. Our speculations need not be overly influenced by short-run developments, such as President Johnson's ·great success with Congress in his first two years in office. This success, coming on the heels of the congressional deadlock over many of Kennedy's major proposals, was largely due to some special circumstances: Johnson's standing on Capitol Hill, his particular legislative experience, the consolidation of presidential support after the rout of the Goldwater forces, and a congressional and popular urge to honor the late President's memory by supporting some of his major proposals. We must consider more basic and continuing forces that shape the relations of Congress and President as institutions.

One such force is reapportionment. The granting of greater representation in the House (and in state legislatures) to urban and suburban areas will bring the presidential and congressional constituencies into closer approximation and hence diminish some of the structural forces making for divergent policy. This shift may take longer than some expect, because it is the one-party district rather than the malapportioned district that lies at the heart of congressional party power on Capitol Hill. But in the long run reapportionment, along with the spread of heterogeneous urban and suburban population into presently rural districts, will diversify one-party areas and stimulate competitive two-party politics.

Another tendency that may bring Congress more into the presidential orbit is continuing congressional reform. Some of this might consist of formal change in organization and procedures, such as the strengthening of the Speaker early in 1965. Other changes will be less obvious, embracing the distribution of prestige and informal influence in the structure of both houses. The elected party leadership in Congress tends to support a President of the same party, as in the case of Senator Robert Taft lining up behind Eisenhower (just as the elected congressional leadership tends to diverge from the presidential party when the Presidency is in opposition hands). As the elected leadership continues to gain strength in Congress as compared to the committee chairmen—as in the long run I believe it will—the President will gain added influence over the legislature.

The most powerful force for unifying President and Congress will be the continuing and probably increasing consensus over freedom and equality. As long as the nation was deeply and closely divided over these goals, Congress with its bias toward conservatism was bound to be at odds with a President biased toward liberalism, except in times of crisis. Without a broad consensus it was impossible to mobilize steady congressional majorities behind presidential proposals for social welfare and other egalitarian measures. Congress has been slow to act when only a bare popular majority seemed to support Fair Deal or New Frontier programs, as suggested by the fate of major presidential proposals in Congress following the close popular majorities won by Truman in 1948 and Kennedy in 1960. Kennedy liked to quote Jefferson's remark that "great innovations should not be forced on slender majorities." They have not been, in Congress. Often a three-fifths or two-thirds majority of the electorate supporting liberal programs has been necessary to produce a dependable straight majority behind those programs in Congress, because of the distortions in congressional representation. But judging from polls, election data, and other indices, about three-fifths or two-thirds of the American voters have come to uphold in a general way federal welfare and regulatory measures at home and policies designed to support freedom and equality abroad. This consensus is bound to show in Congress.

This is not to predict joyous harmony between President and Congress. Relations will continue to be marked by misunderstanding, jealousies over status and protocol, and differences over policy. Oscillations between presidential and congressional power will continue, though probably with the balance of power continuing to shift toward the executive over the long run. Conflict will probably be especially acute in the fiscal sector, for the conservative grip on the spending and taxing committees and machinery of Congress will not soon be relaxed. But it is precisely in the fiscal sector of policy that the President will be under the greatest pressure to meet the claims of freedom and equality. The question will be whether the President has enough power to channel funds into federal programs for health, education, urban development, housing, and the like; whether he has the funds to staff effectively promotional, regulatory, and control agencies in civil rights and related fields. If congressional conservatives could not thwart passage of social legislation, they still might try to starve or cripple its implementation.

But even here the big guns seem to be on the President's side. The same consensus over freedom and equality that now pervades Congress as a whole should affect its fiscal policy making too in the long run. If in the short run fiscal conservatives in Congress are able to stymie presidential programs, the White House can retaliate by mobilizing interests that favor spending, dramatizing the social and economic ills that need to be attacked, returning to Congress for deficiency and emergency appropriations, using discretionary funds of the President, and other devices. The President has already been granted significant latitude in the use of funds to influence policy; the most notable example is the Civil Rights Act of 1964, which granted him power to withhold federal funds from any program or activity receiving direct or indirect federal assistance, in which racial discrimination was found to exist. President Kennedy asked Congress for presidential authority to change tax ratios within certain limits, in order to strengthen the arsenal of anti-recession weapons; Congress balked at granting this power, but may well change its mind in the future, especially in the face of a deepening economic recession. The actual coming of a recession would precipitate an even speedier and more drastic shift of fiscal authority to the White House, for no President today can afford to bear the political burden of a slump. In March 1933, Roosevelt warned that unless Congress acted in the economic emergency, "I shall ask the Congress for the one remaining instrument to meet the crisis—broad Executive power to wage a war against the emergency, as great as the power that would be given to me if we were in fact invaded by a foreign foe." No President could ask for less than this in a future crisis; he probably would ask for more. And no modern Congress could resist him, for part of the nation's consensus over freedom and equality is a commitment to federal action against depression and poverty. And because that commitment first and foremost binds the President and will do so indefinitely, it is part of the edifice of presidential government. . . .

The increasing dominance of the Presidency over the rest of the government, its embodiment of the national purpose, its symbolic expression of the nation's glory and solidarity, its tremendous impact on Americans during their most formative years—what does all this imply for the future of the nation and of the Presidency?

The old and accepted fears of presidential power, I have contended, do not seem justified on the basis of actual experience. Increased authority and scope have not made the Presidency a tyrannical institution; on the contrary, the office has become the main governmental bastion for the protection of individual liberty and the expansion of civil rights. The office "represents" the electorate at least as effectively and democratically as does Congress, though in a different way. The office has attracted neither power-mad politicians nor bland incompetents but the ablest political leaders in the land, and these leaders in turn have brought the highest talent to the White House. We must, under modern conditions, reassess the old idea that the *main* governmental protection of civil liberty, social and economic rights, and due process of law lies in the legislature or the courts or state and local government. The main protection lies today in the national executive branch. As a general proposition the Presidency has become the chief protector of our procedural and substantive liberties; as a general proposition, the stronger we make the Presidency, the more we strengthen democratic procedures and can hope to realize modern liberal democratic goals.

The danger of presidential dominance lies in a different and more subtle tendency. It lies not in presidential failure but in presidential success. It lies not in the failure to achieve our essential contemporary goals of freedom and equality but in their substantial realization and in the incapacity of presidential government to turn to new human purposes.

The prospects seem good that presidential government will continue to help broaden equality of opportunity at the same time that it protects our basic freedoms. All the Presidencies since that of Hoover have made some kind of commitment to this goal; they have aroused strong expectations; they have perfected the governmental machinery necessary to realize the goals; and we can expect that the contest between the presidential parties on domestic issues will turn mainly on the incumbent Administration's successes and failures in combating poverty, expanding opportunity, and enlarging civil rights, especially for Negroes. In foreign policy the election tests will be the efficient management of crisis plus the long-run effectiveness of military and economic programs abroad designed to strengthen the foundations of freedom and equality in other nations.

Given the harmony between ends and means—between the ends of freedom and equality and the means of presidential government—we can expect that well before the end of this century, and perhaps much sooner, we will have achieved substantial equality of opportunity in this nation. We need not expect equality of *condition*, nor full equality of opportunity, for gray areas of deprivation and discrimination will remain. Some of the old tension between equality and freedom will always be found in a diverse and changing society. But to the extent that public and private measures can realize freedom and equality, the goals will be substantially achieved.

And precisely here lies the problem. As freedom and equality are achieved presidential government will exhaust the purpose for which it has been such an eminently suited means. The great machinery of government that has been shaped to distribute welfare and overcome poverty and broaden opportunity and protect liberty will become devoted to increasingly automatic tasks. The passion will long since have disappeared, and increasingly the compulsion of purpose will be dissipated. Purpose will no longer be toughened in conflict; creativity will no longer rise from challenge and crisis. As the ends of government become increasingly agreed upon among the people, between the parties, between President and Congress, between national and state and local governments, issues will resolve mainly around questions of technique. And the more humdrum these matters become, the more the President will turn to his ceremonial and symbolic role to provide circuses to the people—the bread already being in abundance.

According to Morgenthau, we are already facing this problem, even with the goals of freedom and equality not yet achieved. In this nation there have been purposes, he reminds us, to which we could pledge our lives, our fortunes, and our sacred honor. "There is no such issue today. None of the contemporary issues of domestic politics of which the public at large is aware commands for its alternative solutions those loyalties out of which great political conflicts are made. There are divergent opinions and interests, to be sure; but there is no great issue that men deem worthy of sacrifice and risk. In consequence, the integrating principle of American society has lost both its dynamic and its substantive qualities. . . . The American consensus, which in the past was monistic in form and pluralistic in substance, has become monistic in both respects. In consequence, conformism now extends to the substance of policies and constitutional arrangements. Since no issue is any longer worth fighting over, a position must be 'moderate,' and what was once a compromise between seemingly irreconcilable positions now transforms itself into the adjustment of positions differing only in degree.

Since the purpose of America seems to have been achieved—the need for improvement notwithstanding—the *status quo* tends to become as sacred as the purpose itself, and an attack upon the *status quo* almost as unpalatable as dissent from the purpose. Since there is nothing left to fight for, there is nothing to fight against. . . ." Morgenthau was writing during the Eisenhower Administration, and he did not anticipate the force of Kennedy's challenge to Republicanism and of the Nergoes' revolt against the status quo in the early 1960s. But he was right in a broader sense, for it was precisely Eisenhower's acceptance of the purposes of the New Deal and the Fair Deal, and his blandness in his methods of realizing them, that made his administration an ominous indication of the likely nature of late twentieth-century politics in America.

Many would reject any call today for high purposes and fighting issues. They prefer a polity that is not rent by great issues, scarred by savage conflict, absorbed in passionate controversy, or even distracted by political problems. Considering the nature of the early and middle epochs of the twentieth century, they would cherish a period of calm in which people could indeed, in John Adams' words, turn to painting, poetry, music, architecture, statuary, tapestry, and porcelain. The very realization of the grand aims of freedom and equality, they believe, would create a basis on which people could turn to the enduring problems of the richness of quality of life, and could forsake some of the old ideological quarrels.

Those who spurn ideology will contend, moreover, that progress emerges not from the pursuit of central, synoptic visions or plans or purposes, but from the pursuit of a wide range of alternative policies, from flexible methods, from refusal to make an ultimate commitment to any means or any end, from incremental and adjustive tactics that permit day-to-day reconciliation of differences. Such an approach, they hold, produces innovation, creativity, and excitement. It rejects the grand formulations of interrelated ends and means in favor of special angles of vision, sharpened individual or group motivation, the social dynamics of a loosely articulated, highly accessible, and open-ended polity. The incrementalists would proceed step by step, renouncing passion and commitment in favor of prudence and calculation.

Yet many who have lived through the decades of traumatic and even bloody political conflict, at home or abroad, will wonder about a nation in which the great issues have dwindled to matters of technique. They will worry first about a people so bored by the relatively trivial political issues of the day that they have become largely absorbed in the minutiae of their private lives. They will doubt whether in the long run even architecture and poetry can be kept out of politics. They will worry that people might fall into adjustment, conformity, undiscriminating tolerance, and aimless, time-filling activities, and that this will lead to the acceptance of mediocrity and a compulsive togetherness rather than the pursuit of excellence and individuality.

They will be concerned about the governors as well as the governed. For a government agreed on the larger issues and proceeding by calculation and adjustment is likely to attract to its service the little foxes who know many little things—the operators, the careerists, the opportunists, the technicians, the fixers, the managers. Some of these men may be resourceful, zealous, dedicated, flexible, and adjustable. But they will be so absorbed in technique that it will be difficult for them to separate issues of policy from questions of their own immediate self-enhancement. Certainly there would be little room for the Churchills who give up office in the pursuit of broader principles, or even for the administrative innovators who wish to create something more exalted than a better administrative mousetrap. Thus the governors too would lose their way, become lost in technique, would become absorbed in private motives, would substitute means for ends.

For this is the corruption of consensus—the attempt to find universal agreement on so many issues that great public purposes are eroded by a torrent of tiny problems solved by adjustment and adaptation. Ways and means are more and more rationally elaborated by increasing numbers of technicians for a society having less and less human purpose. In government this would mean Hamiltonianism gone wild; in the Presidency it would mean the submergence of the nation's supreme political decision-maker in an ever widening tide of incremental adjustments. The President might still be a hero to most of his people, but his policy and program would not be heroic, only his image. He would still seem a potent figure to children—and grownups—but his actual influence over events would be dwindling. He would still be visible as he mediated among the technicians and occasionally coped with crises; but it would be the visibility of the tightrope walker whom the great public watches with emotional involvement but without actual participation. The defeat of presidential government would be inherent in its very success. Having taken over the Cabinet and the rest of the government, presidential government would finally have taken over the President.

THE LIMITS OF
PRESIDENTIAL POWER

☆

RICHARD E. NEUSTADT: *The Reality of*
Presidential Power

There are many ways to look at the American Presidency. It can be
done in terms juridical or biographical, political or managerial: the
office viewed primarily as a compendium of precedents, a succession
of personalities, a fulcrum for party politics, a focus for administrative management. This essay denies the relevance of none of these
approaches and makes use, incidentally, of them all, but aims at
observation from a rather different point of view. This is an effort
to look at the Presidency *operationally*, in working terms, as an instrument of governance in the middle years of the twentieth century; as man-in-office, that is to say, in a time of continuing "cold
war," spiralling atomic discovery (and vulnerability), stabilized "big
government," and stalemated partisan alignment—the *policy* environment capsuled by Clinton Rossiter as "new economy" and
"new internationalism"; the *political* environment billed by Samuel
Lubell as "politics of twilight." . . .
   [The] modern Presidency's powers and responsibilities—the
"what," that is to say—are widely known, however we may differ
on their import for our form of government, and anyone in doubt
has only to review numerous recent writings in the field. But the
"how" is relatively unexplored terrain for which there are no ready

Richard E. Neustadt is Director of the Institute of Politics of the John Fitzgerald Kennedy School of Government at Harvard University. The selection is
from "The Presidency at Mid-Century," from a symposium, *The Presidential Of-*
fice, appearing in *Law and Contemporary Problems*, Vol. 21, Autumn, 1956, pp.
609–645, published by the Duke University School of Law, Durham, North
Carolina. Copyright, 1956, by Duke University. Reprinted by permission of the
publisher and the author.

references outside the realm of selective particulars in press reports, case studies, memoirs, and the like. Granting the President his modern "roles," how does the work get done? What are his means? How may these be employed? Under what limitations? At what cost? With what effect? In what degree sufficient to the Presidency's purposes?

These are the central questions I should like to pose—to pose, note, not to "answer." . . .

There is, though, a prerequisite: If one would focus on the doing of the presidential job, one needs a characterization of the job, as such, that lends itself to operational appraisal; a characterization that defines what need be done in terms approaching those in which the doer does it. . . . For working purposes, the President is never "many men," but one; the Presidency, as an instrument of government, is indivisible; the White House has no separate rooms for the "Chief Legislator," "Chief of Party," "Chief Administrator," et al. Observations on the doing of the job must build upon a statement of what exists to be done in terms other than these.

Hence, having stressed an emphasis on means and advertised its claims, I must begin where everyone begins, with a review of presidential powers—a review of the Presidency's place, that is to say, in the contemporary governmental scene.

THE PRESIDENCY IN GOVERNMENT

"His is the vital place of action in the system," wrote Woodrow Wilson of the President toward the close of TR's term. And this, a new discovery for Wilson's generation, is now, at mid-century, a matter of course. Presidential leadership is now a matter of routine to a degree quite unknown before the Second World War. If the President remains at liberty, in Wilson's phrase, "to be as big a man as he can," the obverse holds no longer: he *cannot* be as small as he might choose.

Once, TR daringly assumed the "steward's" role in the emergency created by the great coal strike of 1902; the Railway Labor Act and the Taft-Hartley Act now make such interventions mandatory upon Presidents. Once, FDR dramatically asserted personal responsibility for gauging and guiding the American economy; now, the Employment Act binds his successors to that task. Wilson and FDR became chief spokesmen, leading actors on a world stage at the height of war; now UN membership, far-flung alliances, the facts of power, prescribe that role continuously in times termed "peace." Through both World Wars, our Presidents grappled experimentally with an emergency-created need to "integrate" foreign and military and domestic policies; the National Security Act now takes that need for granted as a constant of our times. FDR and Truman made themselves responsible for the development and first use of atomic weapons; the Atomic Energy Act now puts a com parable burden on the back of every President. In instance after instance, the one-time personal initiatives, innovations of this century's "strong" Presidents, have now been set by statutes as requirements of office. And what has escaped statutory recognition has mostly been absorbed into presidential "common law," confirmed by custom, no less binding: the unrehearsed press conference, for example, or the personally-presented legislative program.

The "vital place of action" has been rendered permanent; the *forms* of leadership fixed in the cumulative image of *ad hoc* assertions under Wilson and the two Roosevelts; past precedents of personality and crisis absorbed into the government's continuing routines. For the executive establishment and for the Congress, both, the Presidency has become the regular, accustomed source of all major initiatives: supplier of both general plans and detailed programs; articulator of the forward course in every sphere of policy encompassed by contemporary government. Bold or bland, aggressive or conciliatory, massive or minimal, as the case may be, the lead is his.

Thus, we have made a matter of routine the President's responsibility to take the policy lead. And at the same time, we have institutionalized, in marked degree, the exercise of that responsibility. President and Presidency are synonymous no longer; the office now comprises an officialdom twelve-hundred strong. For almost every phase of policy development, there is now institutional machinery engaged in preparations on the President's behalf: for the financial and administrative work plan of the government, the Budget Bureau; for the administration's legislative program, the White House counsel and the Budget's clearance organization; for programing in economic and social spheres, the Council of Economic Advisers (and to some degree the cabinet, Eisenhower-style); in foreign and military fields, the National Security Council; in spheres of domestic preparedness, the Office of Defense Mobilization; these pieces of machinery, among others, each built around a program-making task, all lumped together, formally, under the rubric, "The Executive Office of the President," an institutional conception and a statutory entity less than two decades old.

These are significant developments, this rendering routine, this institutionalizing of the initiative. They give the Presidency nowadays a different look than it has worn before, an aspect permanently "positive." But the reality behind that look was not just conjured up by statutes or by staffing. These, rather, are *responses* to the impacts of external circumstance upon our form of government; not causes but effects.

Actually or potentially, the Presidency has always been—at least since Jackson's time—a unique point of intersection for three lines of leadership responsibility: "executive" and partisan and national. The mandates of our Constitution, the structure of our political parties, the nature of the President's electorate, fused long ago to draw these lines together *at that point and there alone*: the Presidency at once the sole nationally elective office, independently responsible to a unique constituency; sole centralizing stake of power, source of control, in each party (as a glance at either party out of power shows); sole organ of foreign relations and military command; sole object of the "take care" clause and of the veto power; and with all this, sole crown-like symbol of the Union.

By Wilson's time, that combination, in the context of world power stakes and status, had brought a fourth line of leadership into play, a line of leadership abroad, its only point of intersection with the other three the White House, once again. Since then, there have been revolutionary changes in the world and in American society and in the character of government's commitments toward both; changes productive of fast-rising expectations and requirements for leadership transmitted toward the Presidency along each line— four streams of action impulses and obligations converging on the President, whoever he may be, their volume and their rate of flow varying with events, a source which never, nowadays, runs dry.

The contemporary President, in short, has *four constituencies*, each with distinctive expectations of him and demands upon him. One of these is his "government" constituency, comprising the great group of public officers—congressional as well as executive— who cannot do their own official jobs without some measure of performance on his part. A second is his "partisan" constituency, comprising at once his own party's congressional delegation, and its organization leaders, workers, even voters, all those whose political fortunes, interests, sentiments, are tied, in some degree, to his performance. A third is his "national" constituency, comprising all those individuals and groups among Americans who look to him, especially when crises come, for an embodiment and an expression of government's relationship to its citizenry, for a response to their needs, purposes, endeavors. And fourth, is his "overseas" constituency, comprising not alone the officers of foreign governments, but the political oppositions, the opinion molders, even the plain citizens to some degree, in every country where our power, policies, or postures have imposed themselves upon domestic politics.

In respect to the first three of these constituencies, membership is not a mutually exclusive matter. A number of American officials —among them cabinet officers and congressmen, are members of all three. And most Americans hold membership in two, as at once partisans and citizens. But whatever its effects on individual or group behavior, multiple membership does not preclude distinctly differentiated sets of Presidency-oriented expectations and demands, identifiable with each constituency, arising in the circumstances of mid-century from the pervasive needs of each for governmental action.

In these terms, it appears no accident that at a time when stakes of government are high for all the President's constituents, to him has passed, routinely, the continuing initiative in government. That role is both assured him and required of him by the very uniqueness of his place at the only point of intersection, the sole juncture, of those four lines of leadership responsibility and the constituencies they represent.

Yet, the demands and expectations pressing in upon the President propel him not alone toward enunciation, but delivery. Executive officials want decisions, congressmen want proposals, partisans want power, citizens want substance, friends abroad want steadiness and insight and assistance on their terms—all these as shorthand statements of complex material and psychological desires. These things are wanted *done*; given our Constitution and our politics, that means done by, or through, or with assistance from, or acquiescence of, the President. The very factors that contribute to his unique opportunities—and routinized responsibilities—as an initiator, make him essential also as protector, energizer, implementor, of initiatives once taken. His special place in government requires of him, indeed, thrusts upon him, a unique responsibility—and opportunity—to oversee and assure execution.

But while responsibility for the initiative has now been routinized and even institutionalized, authority to implement the courses set remains fragmented in our system. In most respects and for most purposes, the President lacks any solid base of assured, institutionalized support to carry through the measures he proposes. His four constituencies are capable of constant pressure, but not of reliable response to downward leads. The "executive" is not a unity with a firm command-and-subordination structure, nor is the Government, nor is the political party, in Congress or out, nor is the nation, nor the alliance system overseas. All these are feudalities in power terms; pluralistic structures every one of them. Our Constitution, our political system, our symbolism, and our history make certain that the President alone assumes, in form, the leadership of each; and guarantee, no less, that he will not have systematic, unified, assured support from any. Indeed, precisely the conditions vesting him alone with leadership responsibility for all prevent the rendering of any one of them into tight-welded followings. The constitutional separation of powers—really, of institutions sharing powers—the federal separations of sovereignty, hence politics, the geographic separations of electorates, these and their consequences at once have helped the Presidency to its special place and hindered the creation of a strong supporting base. And, at a time when the executive establishment has grown too vast for personal surveillance, when Congress is controlled in form by narrow, shifting partisan majorities, in fact by factional coalition, weighted against the President's electorate, the hindrances are bound to be enhanced. Ours is that sort of time.

This does not mean that Presidents are powerless; far from it. Their four-way leadership position gives them vantage points aplenty for exerting strength in Government, in party, in the country, and abroad; collectively, by all odds, an array of strong points quite unmatched by any other single power-holder in our system. It does mean, though, that presidential power must be exercised *ad hoc*, through the employment of whatever sources of support, whatever transient advantages can be found and put together, case by case. It means the President can never choose a policy with certainty that it will be approximated in reality or that he will not have it to unmake or make again. It means he cannot, as he pleases, moderate, adjust or set aside the rival, overlapping, often contradictory claims of his constituencies. *He has no option but to act, at once, as agent of them all, for their conjunction in his person is the keystone of his potency*; none is dispensable, hence the demands of none are automatically disposable at his convenience. Events, not his free choices, regulate their pressures and condition his response.

Dilemmas, consequently, are the Presidency's daily bread. The President must now initiate specific policies and programs for all fields of federal action; he has become the focus for all forward planning in our system; whatever leads the government and country and his party (and indeed, the opposition, also) are to have, will stem from him. Yet, not his preferences only, but events in an inordinately complex world, not his reasoning alone, but his constituencies' felt requirements, contradictory as they may be, mold his determinations, limit his choices, force his hand. What he initiates he must attempt to implement. He must try so to manage the executive establishment, and Congress, and his party oligarchs, and the other party's also, and "public opinion," and overseas support, that the essential things get done—so far at least as government can do them—to keep administration reasonably competent, the country reasonably prosperous, the cold war reasonably cold, and his party in the White House; objectives which will seem to him synonymous (no President in memory, Mr. Eisenhower naturally not excluded, has ever thought his policies could best be carried forward by the other party's men). Yet, none of these agencies of action, of execution, are subject to his management by fiat; not even those closest to home, his own administration, his own party, are constructed to provide him with assured support. Rarely can he order, mostly must he persuade. And even were his controls taut and sharp, there would remain, of course, those agencies beyond his power to command, events.

No doubt, in times of great emergency, sharp crisis seen and felt as such throughout the country, the Presidency's measure of assured support from public, party, and administration tends to increase dramatically, if temporarily, while "politics as usual" abates, at least until the sharpness wanes; witness the situation circa 1942. But it is characteristic of our circumstances at mid-century—in all the years since the Second World War—that while our government's responsibilities retain a trace of every prior crisis, no comparable sense of national emergency pervades our politics. If this is an "era of permanent crisis," it is one in which Presidents must manage without benefit of crisis consensus.

Given the underlying situation here described, the balance of this paper is, perforce, a study of dilemmas; dilemmas nurtured by disparities between the Presidency's obligation to initiate and its capacity to achieve, the one nailed down, the other relatively tenuous, both bound to be so by the nature of our institutional adjustment, up to now, to the complexities of governing this country at mid-century.

What, currently, is the American Presidency? A cat on a hot tin roof.

THE PRESIDENT IN THE PRESIDENCY

So far in this discussion, "President" and "Presidency" have been used almost interchangeably; the man and his office equated in an effort at capsule characterization. But since it is our purpose to appraise the man *in* office, the *President* at work, we must now differentiate between the individual and his official tasks, between the work done by the White House occupant and that performed by others in his name.

What does the President, himself, contribute to the conduct of the Presidency? What, in an office now so institutionalized that it encompasses six hundred "professional" aides, has he, himself, to do? What, in a government of vast and complicated undertakings, in a substantive environment demanding every sort of expertise, can there be *left* for him to do? To put the case in current terms, what is there that no "chief of staff" can do without him? . . .

[The] President's own specialties within the Presidency, the contributions none can make without him, consist of acts of choice and of persuasion; choices not in foreign policy alone, but in all spheres of action and of men as well as measures; persuasion not only of congressmen, but of administrative officers and politicians, of private interests and "the public" generally, of foreign governments and their publics; choice and persuasion exercised, in short, throughout the range of problems and of persons covered by his four constituencies.

These things are his to do because he is the sole, accountable human embodiment of an office which, in turn, is uniquely the center of responsibility and motive-power in our system. No President, of course, takes to himself more than a fraction of the choices, efforts at persuasion, made on his authority and in his name. But beyond a certain point—a point, of course, that varies case by case—choice-making and persuasion become personalized, of necessity, because his aides and auditors insist that it be so; because no one will accept others' choices, because no one will heed others' persuasions, because no others dare or care to run his risks on their discretion or their risks on his authority. Beyond another point—which may or may not coincide—persuasive acts and choices become ripe for his personal attention as a matter of desirability in his own interest, because his personal perceptions of that interest are ultimately untransferable; because save secondhand, by empathy, not even Harry Hopkins, Sherman Adams, can know fully what it feels like to sit where he sits (endowed with his intelligence, his temperament) at the solitary juncture of his four constituencies, "President of the United States"—hence, no one else can bring to bear precisely his own "feel" for risks to him, to the totality of his unique position, inherent in alternatives of doing and not doing.

If a look at the Presidency without a working President shows choices and persuasion as the man's own occupation, that impression cannot be strengthened by a glance at what takes up his time when on the job. Nowadays, the normal presidential working week revolves around a series of fixed sessions: one set meeting apiece with the National Security Council, and the Cabinet, and (when Congress is on hand) the legislative leaders, and the press, each preceded and followed by appropriate staff briefings, consultations;

one set appointment apiece with the Secretary of State, the Secretary of Defense, the Chairman of the Joint Chiefs of Staff, and (an Eisenhower innovation, now suspended) the Chairman of the Council of Economic Advisers. Truman had, besides, a daily morning conference with his principal staff aides to make *ad hoc* assignments and receive routine reports; such sessions Sherman Adams has conducted under Eisenhower.

When one includes the chores of getting ready, cleaning up, these regularly scheduled consultations pre-empt a substantial portion of the President's own working hours, week by week. In the case of a President like Eisenhower, who finds these mechanisms to his taste and uses them to the exclusion of much else, that share of hours occupied mounts high. And what is the object of this outlay of his time? Such sessions serve, in part, as occasions for others to put their concerns, their views before him; partly as occasions for him to impress his personality and attitudes *on* others. Which of these parts has major place will vary with each sort of session, influenced by subject matter, membership, and *his* proclivities. But whatever their variation, the components are the same: one part material for choice-making, the other part the stuff of personal persuasion.

As for the balance of the presidential working week, the bulk of it is turned to comparable account; the documents signed, the persons seen, the places filled, the arguments resolved, the messages sent, the speeches made, the ceremonies held, all these are characteristically acts of choice or efforts at persuasion, often both at once—even the formal ceremonials contributing a portion of his power to persuade, even their performance contingent on his choice.

The preoccupations of the presidential week will vary with the seasons of the presidential year, from budget and message seasons in the fall, through early, middle, and late stages of the legislative season, through the rush of adjournment and enrollments, to that precious period, the post-adjournment lull (if any), season for recovery and repairs, and so to fall again—a round, successively, of planning to decision, campaigning to compromise, recuperating to resumption; a peacetime rhythm set primarily to legislative tasks but liable constantly to interruptions on account of mishaps and emergencies in operating spheres. Inevitably, presidential choices, efforts at persuasion, reflect in their intensities, their objects, and their scope these swings of emphasis throughout the year. And even more may they reflect swings in the cycle of the presidential term, from early groping through a first consolidation and a forward push up to the test at midterm, then regrouping and a second forward effort dwindling toward hiatus in the final year. But whatever their application in a given context, choice-making and persuasion remain the components of the President's own work; comprising what he does himself, both on the insistence of others and at his own inner promptings.

These are, in short, his means; the means by which he, personally, exercises influence within his office and upon the course of government; the means by which he makes his own mark on the tasks of office sketched above. As such, these "means" are not for him mere instruments employed at will to carry out those tasks. Rather they are the concrete manifestations of the tasks themselves, applying to him personally; the work he has to do, no act of will required. In literary terms, one may say that he sets the tone, provides the lead in government by choosing and persuading. In operating terms, though, one must put it in reverse: that acts of choice and of persuasion cumulated over time produce an ultimate effect of tone and lead which may or may not correspond to any prior blueprint, purpose, or intention. Such is the consequence of disentangling the President from the Presidency.

That ultimate resultant labeled "leadership" will be compounded of two types of actions by the President: those he may reach for in his own discretion and those thrust on him of necessity; the one type, opportunities, the other, compulsions. And, as the compound will be viewed by his constituents and history, more than these enter in; the multifarious things done or left undone by others in his name, or the government's, and happenings beyond the government's discretion, plain events.

No President is free to concentrate upon his opportunities at the expense of his compulsions; he can but hope to find room for the things he may do amidst all things he must. Nor is he free to wave away those other actors on the scene; he can but hope to channel and deflect their impacts on his audience. To the extent he wants to make his own will dominate the conduct of his office, his regime, he has no recourse but to choices and persuasion exercised within these narrow limits. The purposeful President, his face set against drift (and any President, these days, will so regard himself), is thus confronted by an operating problem of immense complexity and large proportions, or more precisely by two problems tightly linked: Given those limits and in furtherance of his own purposes, how is he to maximize the efficiency of his choice-making? How maximize the efficacy of his power to persuade?

The proportions and complexities of these two connected problems it now becomes our object to explore.

THE FREEDOM TO CHOOSE

If Presidents were free to choose the matters they made choices on, their problems of choice-making would be relatively simplified; but Presidents are not. The flow of issues they must face cannot be turned off like a water tap; to know that, one has but to note its sources.

Why do men in government and politics (and in the country and the world) bring issues to a President, invoke his act of choice? To amplify the foregoing analysis, it may be said that they do so for one, or another, or all of three reasons. First, there are matters that by law or custom require some sort of personal performance on his part, his signature, his presence or his voice. Second, there are matters on which others, theoretically competent to act, want the loan of his potency or the cover of his prestige, his impetus behind their preferences, his brand on their performance. Third, there are the matters he himself wants made his own, that on his own initiative he has marked "count me in," matters on which he exercises the discretion we have already discussed. And in the circumstances of mid-century, no President will lack for quantities of matters of each sort.

In the first of these three categories, volume is adjustable, at least to a degree. . . .

As for the second category, the most a President seriously can hope to do is slow the rate of flow, shut out the marginal case. . . .

There remains the third category, where interventions come at *his* initiative. There, he has the option, theoretically, of moving not at all. But this is fatal; also quite impracticable. No doubt, some Presidents may relish, others shy away from forcing matters into their own hands. No doubt, each will evolve some special preferences according to his particular competences, interests. But every President will find some issues that he wants to seize and ride— Truman on Point Four, Eisenhower on Atoms for Peace—and each will find a plenitude he feels *impelled* to take upon himself. . . .

Since acts of choice are often negative, there are, of course, more instances of such "enforced" discretion than will appear in current press reports: Eisenhower choosing time and again, as Donovan records, *not* to blast McCarthy; Truman choosing—as he sometimes did—not to leap, guns blazing, into loyalty cases that aroused his ire; so forth, *ad infinitum.* The "I don't know about that" in press conference is deceptive as a guide to presidential doings. In most such cases, this would remain the expedient response, assuming he did know. Yet every President, one may suppose, will now go out of office wishing that in some respects he had pushed further still, discretion *un*enforced, toward taking over at times and in places where contemporary happenings did not push him.

One wonders whether Truman never wished that he had intervened more actively in the affairs of his Attorneys General. One wonders whether Eisenhower may not come to wish that he had done the same regarding some of *his* department heads. No President finds pleasure in waiting upon "messes" for his cue to intervene. But none can be sure, either, that initiatives of others will suffice to flash a warning to him in good time. There is an obverse of the second category named above: those issues men bring to the President out of their fears, uncertainties, are matched by those kept from him out of confidence, or cussedness, or independent power (even ignorance). . . . . Far from reducing his discretionary range, a President is bound to end by wishing he could widen it.

But time stands in his way. He cannot afford to do nothing at his own discretion; but neither can he manage to do everything. Priority of place on his choice-making production line belongs of sheer necessity to matters with *deadlines* attached. And in most days of his working week, most seasons of his year, a President has quite enough of these to drain his energy, crowd his attention regardless of all else. It is not "policy" but pressure that determines what comes first.

What makes a "deadline"? For one thing, constitutional or statutory obligations: the President must send his annual messages to Congress, must sign or veto its enactments. Or, for another, items on political agendas all across the country: the nomination and election contests over offices, both partisan and public, the distribution of the patronage, the management of national conventions and campaigns. Or, for a third, turns of events in diplomacy or war: the approach to the "summit" spurring a disarmament departure, "open skies"; the outbreak in Korea forcing a new Formosan policy. Or, for a fourth, "outside" events at home: a sharpened economic trend (whether up or down), a dragged-out strike, a natural disaster, a race riot; not necessarily the great things only but the small-with-bite, as when a Texas waitress would not serve the Indian Ambassador. Or, finally, for a fifth, such operational disorders in administration, day by day, as dot the preceding pages—plus, of course, their congressional counterparts. Dates-certain make for deadlines, so does heat; dates generated by our laws, our politics, and our diplomacy; heat generated by events impacting on the needs and expectations of presidential constituents. Singly or together—though most readily inflammable combined—dates and heat start the fires burning underneath the White House.

The President, of course, has influence on deadline-making and unmaking, but only to a limited degree. He sets or evades dates when he voluntarily decides upon a message or a meeting or a speech. He turns heat on when he permits himself to arouse expectations, as Eisenhower did in his press conferences before Geneva. He turns heat aside, if not off, when he finds plausible grounds, proper-looking means for "further study," as was done so notably in 1953. But these are marginal endeavors relative to the totality of dates and heat potentially imposed upon him from outside. And even these are usually reactions or responses to pressures not intrinsically his own. For the most part, even deadlines self-imposed are only nominally self-engendered. Save in rare instances, a mid-century President, however talented, simply has not time to man both ends of the choice-generating process.

The result is to put him in a paradoxical position anent the whole discretionary range of his choice-making. To reach out and take over *before* the dates are nigh or the heat on—publicly at least—can be crucially useful in his interest; yet, he always has to deal first with deadlines already at his desk. As has been said above, he cannot count on the initiatives of others to spur him into interventions timely in *his* terms; yet he is poorly placed to be his own self-starter. He needs to be an actor, yet he is pre-eminently a reactor, forced to be so by the nature of his work and its priorities. Since Eisenhower made Atoms for Peace his response to the heat expressed by cries for "candor" and to the dates required for a UN presentation in 1953, one may suppose he has not been entirely happy with its slowness to get off the ground. One may suppose, besides, that had he arrogated to himself all implementing choices and given them first call upon his time, the matter might have moved a little faster. Similarly, in the case of Truman and Point Four: had he, not State and Budget, implemented his inaugural's fourth point and made of this his first priority (as it never was for them), the sixteen months after his 1949 inauguration might have produced more results than one meager piece of legislation newly on the books. But whatever these Presidents might have done differently or "better" than they actually did, one thing they could *not* do: accord that hypothetical priority in terms of their own time.

Washington correspondents frequently complain that Eisenhower talks a better line than his administration takes; that he proposes better than his own regime disposes. Complaints of the same sort were made in Truman's time, oftener than not by the same corre-

spondents. And these complaints—along with the realities behind
them—symptomize the underlying problem here described. For in
a time of routinized responsibility to take the policy lead, a President himself will have few deadlines more compelling than those
clustering around the choice of measures to *propose*, of policies to
state. Except, perhaps, in general war or comparable emergency,
these gain and take his time more surely and more regularly than
the general run of operating choices bound to follow in their wake.
The weight which Robert Donovan's book gives to the *proposing*
side of Eisenhower's "story," presumably reflects that skewing of
the latter's workaday preoccupations. And if there is an implication
that the White House sometimes came to look on messages and
speeches as ends in themselves, delivery equated with accomplishment, such is a natural by-product, one not unknown in Truman's
time, a point of view, indeed, by no means wholly unrealistic.

Ideally, a President concerned for the efficiency of his own choice-
making in furtherance of his own purposes as *he* conceives them,
should have free rein in choosing what to choose—and when—
within the range of matters subject to his choice at his discretion. In
practice, though, that is precisely what he *cannot* have. His discretionary range, while not a sham, is nowhere near as open as the
term implies. Only his compulsions are potentially unbounded; his
opportunities are always limited. Ideals apart, he is in no position
to do more than seek some finite widening of those confines; he
has no chance to break them down. But paradoxically, the only
practical direction which his search can take—given the conditions
here described—is toward some means of putting pressure on himself, *of imposing new deadlines on himself*, to come to grips with
those things he would want to make his own if only he had time
to contemplate the world about him, interfering at his leisure. And
it is ironic that the very measures that a President may take to
spare himself for "bigger things" by staffing out the "small," tend
to work in the opposite direction. Of this, more later.

The limitations upon "what" and "when" which so restrict freedom of choice are reinforced by certain other limits of a different
sort: limits on the substance of alternatives in choices actually made.
The President's discretion is restricted by these limits also; they,
too, are features of his landscape subject to some rearrangement but
beyond his power to remove. What are these limitations on alternatives? Mainly three: limits of presentation, of substantive complexity, and of effectuation, each term loosely descriptive of a whole
array of complications worth a chapter to themselves, though necessarily denied it here.

By "presentation" is meant time, form, and manner in which

issues reach a President for his determination. If his desk is where the buck stops, as Truman liked to say, by the same token, it is the *last* stop on the line. Most matters reach him at a late stage of their evolution into issues calling for his choice; and many when they reach him warrant action fast. Wherever they occur, lateness and urgency—singly or combined—are bound to narrow options and to curtail chances for fresh looks or second thoughts. As for the *form* which issues take, the *context* of their presentation to a President, his settling of a budget sum, or phrasing of a speech, or soothing of a legislator, each in its own terms may mean disposal of an issue multi-faceted in terms of but one facet, thereby foreclosing options anent others. There is no counting the occasions on which Presidents have backed themselves—or been backed—into corners by this route. Moreover, those who brief a President, who can appeal to him, who can argue before him, have interests of their own which grow remote from his with every increment of organizational distance, institutional independence. Rarely will they see an issue wholly in his terms; oftener in some hybrid of his and theirs, sometimes in theirs alone. And Presidents are no less vulnerable than others (rather more so, in the circumstances) to the lure of wrong answers rightly put.

A tracing out of many of the illustrations posed above would show the workings of these presentation limits; signs of their presence are, of course, no novelty to readers of *The New York Times*. Nothing is intrinsically new about them nowadays, nor anything particularly obscure, though they are none the easier for being old and obvious. But when it comes to limits raised by substantive complexity, the case is rather different. Though not by any means a mid-century invention unknown to earlier times, the magnitude (and durability) of complications in the substance of issues with which Presidents must deal, these days, is greater in degree, to some extent in kind, than we have known before.

Take the question of the military budget which has haunted Eisenhower as it haunted Truman. That budget represents more than half the dollars of federal outlay year by year, four-fifths of the persons on all federal payrolls, half the government's civilian personnel. It represents a mainstay of deterrence and recourse in the cold war, a bed-rock stabilizer in the national economy. Its annual determination raises issues of strategy, of economics, politics, administration, and (emphatically) technology; none of which is really manageable in annual or financial terms (the limit of form, again); none of which is really soluble by reference to anybody's certain knowledge, for nothing is certain save uncertainty in these spheres. To estimate what the American economy can "stand" is not to answer what Congress and interest groups will "take" (or what would be required to equate the two). To estimate what new weapons may do is not to answer what may be demanded of them, or opposed to them, years hence. To estimate the Russians' *capabilities* is not to answer what are their *intentions*.

Yet, on some sorts of "answers" to these questions must military budgets now be built. And limited in terms of what is knowable, a President has no recourse but to select among the "guesstimates" of others—or to compound a compromise among them—by way of searching for his answer-substitutes. In such a search, the signs most readily discerned are bound to be those rendered most concrete by visibility, or pressure, or personal proclivities, or "common sense." No doubt a President needs better signposts in times of cold war, technological revolution; but given the uncertainties these generate, whence are such signs to come?

Parenthetically, it may be said that whatever the answer to that question, the "experts" are unlikely candidates. For if the real technicians see far more than a President can see, the record up to now suggests that they, least of all, show a capacity to ask themselves, out of their expertise, the questions pertinent to him; to translate their vision (and language) into his terms. Shifting the illustration, one thinks in this connection of an aspect of the thermonuclear "crash-program" controversy during 1949, as rendered by the transcript in the Oppenheimer case: that for weeks AEC's consulting scientists debated what the President should do in terms rendered obsolete, for him, by the mere fact of their debate.

Finally, there is the problem of effectuation, the third of the stated factors limiting alternatives in choice. How is a President to make "no" stick; to translate "yes" into performance, actuality? He is not bound to make each choice dependent on his response to these questions, but in the normal course he cannot fail to ask them and to give the answers weight. When Truman chose intervention in Korea, it happened that the necessary military means lay near at hand across the Sea of Japan; a factor, surely, in his choice. The obverse holds, of course, for our passivity in the last days of Dienbienphu; the means that *were* at hand were scarcely suited to the circumstance. But to cite instances of capability in military terms is to belittle the complexity of the how-to-do-it factor; in other terms, there are few choices blessed by aspects so nearly absolute or so readily calculable. Mostly the problem for the President is both more tenuous and more complex in character: how far can he hope to carry matters by persuading those whom he cannot command to do those things he lacks capacity to compel?

"I sit here all day," Truman used to remark, "trying to persuade people to do the things they ought to have sense enough to do without my persuading them." And on each posed alternative, in every act of choice, the question becomes whether to that workload he should add one thing more; with what prospect, at what risk. That question asked and answered may suffice to cancel options of all sorts; the President's choice-making ultimately interlocking with his power to persuade.

THE POWER TO PERSUADE

Concrete acts of choice engender concrete efforts at persuasion. Persuasion of whom? In general, of the President's constituencies, any or all as the case may be. In particular, of those who do the daily chores of governing this country: administrators, congressmen, and organization politicians. To these one might add certain foreign notables and private persons prominent at home, on whom the government depends for something in particular, a boost, a service or a sacrifice; but since such dependence is *ad hoc*, intermittent, their case can be ignored for present purposes.

In the main, day by day, it is the public officers and party politicians whom a President must reach to get his choices rendered into government performance. He may move toward them indirectly through public or interest-group opinion, sometimes his only routes, but they remain his objects because they, not the "public," do the close work; his preferences conditioned on their doing. To influence these men at work, he has at his disposal a quantity of instruments —refined and crude in varying degree—derived from his prerogatives of office as filtered through his personality.

Those instruments of influence, tools of persuasion, are common knowledge, no mystery about them and none pretended here: There is the aura of his office, coupled to the impact of his person and prestige, such as they may be. There are the varied forms of help, concrete and psychological, that congressmen want from the White House in dealing, as they must, with the executive establishment. There are, in turn, the various assistances desired by executive officialdom in dealing with the Congress. There are also the loyalties, varying in depth, of administrators to their chief, of party members to the boss, of congressmen (and citizens) to the head of State and Government. In party terms, there are, at once, supplies of federal patronage, such as it is, a presidential record which no party nowadays can shake, the prospect of a renewed candidacy (for first termers, anyway), and—save for Democrats, perhaps—a constantly replenished campaign chest, centrally controlled. These things, among others, are available to Presidents for use, reversibly, as carrots and as sticks in aid of their persuasion.

This listing has a formidable ring. In theory, it deserves it. For if a President could bring to bear that whole array effectively and all at once upon a given point, one may presume he would be irresistible. But practically speaking, such conjunctions are not easily arranged; far from it. Oftener than not, one or another of these tools will turn out ineffective of itself or in the hands of its prospective user, unsuited to use, by him, in any combination of resources he contrives. Why should this be so? What dulls their cutting edge and limits their employment? These questions become our immediate concern. Full answers would run far beyond the compass of this essay; no more can be attempted here than a suggestion of some factors that seem specially significant in the contemporary setting.

First among these factors—in order of discussion, not importance—is the uncertainty of a President's own hold upon his instruments of influence. They may attach to his office but can slip away from *him*. One doubts that at any time since 1935, or thereabouts, and not often before, have Presidents got half the mileage out of patronage the textbooks advertise. One doubts that Eisenhower can be sure from day to day of his control over the stockpile of administrative actions sought by congressmen. Most of these, certainly, are not under his sole lock and key. Others than he have the arts of persuasion to practice, and keys of their own. The story is told that a powerful House Democrat was traded off the same dam twice; once in Truman's time and once in Eisenhower's. If so, the Budget Bureau ought to be commended for its careful husbanding of presidential trading-stock. But such care is by no means universal in this Government (not even in the Budget). Moreover, a supply of trading-stock may prove insufficient just when the need is greatest. Appetites are insatiable and fears short-lived; a situation summed up in the phrase "What have you done for me lately," as amplified by "or *to* me."

In addition, sources of supplies to aid persuasion on one front may be endangered by the very effort at persuasion on another. A great share of a President's potential trading-stock with Congress is actually in the hands of the executive departments: jobs, expertise, publicity, administrative actions of all sorts. No less a share of his potential leverage with the departments is actually in the hands of his congressional supporters: protection or defense, consideration or support, in every sort of legislative situation. Too many sticks applied too often on the Hill may tend to uproot the supply of carrots growing there for use downtown, and vice versa.

A second factor is the tendency of certain presidential tools to cut in opposite directions, thereby impairing their simultaneous employment. It is not easy for a President to combine partisan approaches with attempts to crystallize support around the symbol of his office. He courts trouble when he tells his party's congressmen that his proposals will help them at the polls and simultaneously exhorts the other party's men to do their patriotic duty by their President. He courts trouble when he tries to draw upon the loyalties of subordinate officials and at the same time offers up their kind as human sacrifices on the altar, say, of adequate appropriations for their work. Such troubles come in infinite varieties; in every instance, they will tend to limit hypothetical effectiveness of each paired instrument. To say this is not to suggest, of course, that all these troubles are escapable. Carrying water on both shoulders—plus, perhaps, in both hands, also strapped around the waist—is frequently imperative for Presidents, a natural resultant of their four-way leadership position. But the complications are no less for often being unavoidable. So Truman found on many memorable occasions and even Eisenhower, now and then, especially in those first years of turmoil over "cleaning out the Communists" and Senator McCarthy.

A third factor complicating the persuasion process can be stated, most simply, as general dissatisfaction with the product to be "sold." It is difficult, in other words, to press a course of action intrinsically lacking much appeal to *any* of the persons whose support is being sought. Instruments of influence, however handled, are poor substitutes for genuine enthusiasm on the part of somebody among the movers and shakers in the case. And if the substitution must be made, as not infrequently occurs, the limits on the efficacy of persuasive tools will tend to be severe. The President's health-reinsurance scheme of 1954 is very much in point. So is the complex struggle over foreign aid in the 1956 session of Congress. There, Eisenhower pitted his own personal prestige, plus other sorts of pressure, against the disappointments, disenchantments, irritations, and forebodings which had penetrated every corner of both Houses. The result was a sharp check to the President—how serious in program terms one cannot know from the outside—a check administered, moreover, by traditional supporters of his course among the Democrats, together with a great proportion of *his* party's membership, election year or no. It is quite conceivable, in all the circumstances, that another President, in another year, might have done worse. But why did this President in this year not do better?

No doubt, his ileitis operation and its aftermath blunted Eisenhower's own persuasive influence at a crucial time. Perhaps there were things poorly done or left undone at other times as well. But

however healthy and adroit he might have been last summer, there
are no indications—not, anyway of public record—that by then his
persuasion could have bettered the result in any *marked* degree.
For the great lack, apparently, was not of influence in mechanistic
terms, but of program in substantive respects. A sense of changing
world relationships pervaded the debates, providing ammunition for
old enemies of Mutual Security and worries for old friends. Yet,
the administration's program appeared cast from the same mold as
all its predecessors back to 1951, when the world wore a very different look. And Eisenhower's troubles in July seem, by hindsight,
an inevitable outcome of his choices in December; the efficacy of
persuasive instruments conditioned, in their turn, upon the exercise
—and limits—of choice-making.

Alongside these three factors there is need to place a fourth,
which looms at least as large under mid-century conditions: the
factor of too many things at once, as represented, classically, by
FDR's fight for reorganization powers amidst controversy over his
"court-packing" plan. In that instance, Roosevelt was criticized for
moving for his management reform at a time when his influence
was mortgaged to another cause. Perhaps he had an option then—
though that can be debated—but not so his successors. In 1956, in
a relatively quiet time at home and abroad, the Eisenhower influence has been demanded in three closely spaced, competing, legislative fights of first importance to his regime—farm, education, foreign
aid—to say nothing of those headed off, like tax reduction, or of
the many other issues on which White House labels were affixed
to controversial aspects: Hells Canyon, highway aid, social security
amendments, the civil rights commission, and numbers more. In
Truman's time, the list was often longer, the controversial aspects
sharper, the presidential temperature higher, and, besides, in many
of his years, such legislative struggles were accompanied by operational involvements—military, diplomatic, economic, or administrative—also calling his persuasion into play on a grand scale.

A President's tools of persuasion are put under great strains
when used on many projects simultaneously. Look at the tools
themselves, and that becomes quite obvious. Yet, such use is the
normal practice, nowadays; often mandatory, always wanted. No
more as persuaders than as choice-makers are contemporary Presidents at liberty, discretion unconfined, to choose the "what" and
"when" of their endeavors to persuade.

Four factors have been named, so far, as limiting the efficacy of
persuasive instruments. But there remains a fifth, a factor so important as to dominate the rest, continually affecting the dimensions
of all four. This is the element of "setting" in persuasion, a matter

not of instruments, as such, but of the *background* against which they are employed. As a rough rule, it may be said that for a fraction of the persons on whom Presidents depend, continuing exposure to the White House and its occupant provides a background favoring—though not, of course, determining—effective exercise of presidential influence upon them. The bigger the "staff system," the smaller the fraction; but even an open door could not enlarge it into a preponderance. For most officials, both public and partisan, a favorable background will be differently derived. Derived from what? To this we may now turn.

In the case of executive officials, all sorts of variables of time, place, situation, substance, tend to affect actual responses to a particular pressure from the President. But there would seem to be one variable always present, always influential: their own instinctive estimate of his prestige with Congress, his potency on Capitol Hill. This may not square with visions conjured up by the tag "Chief Executive"; it is, however, entirely natural. For Congress, day in and day out, means life or death to programs, institutions, personnel. Putting the matter in its crudest terms (and thus rather larger than life): if Presidents can make much difference in these respects, either way, their own officialdom will be well disposed toward their wishes; if not, so much the worse for them; many a bureaucrat, like many a congressman, was there before and will be after.

Of course, such bureaucratic estimates of presidential prowess will vary from time to time. George Kennan once remarked that diplomats must rethink foreign policy each morning; so bureaucrats must reappraise their attitudes toward a President, and so they do, day after day. Such estimates will vary, also, from place to place. The weaker an agency, in terms of institutional entrenchment, program support, the more its officials will tend to view the President as a resource, no matter what the state of his congressional relations; thus Labor is traditionally a "tame" department. And every agency, however "strong," will make its calculations with reference, mainly, to those elements in Congress and those issues before Congress that affect it the most; even as between Army and Air the President is not appraised alike.

This does not mean that there is any one-to-one relationship between a President's congressional prestige and agency compliance with his wishes—though sometimes, certainly, the correlation is that close—but rather that a favorable background for persuasive efforts at his end of Pennsylvania Avenue is markedly dependent, over time, upon his prestige at the other end, with Congress. And in precisely the same sense—no more, no less—a favorable background for persuasion of the Congress is provided by his prestige

with the country. As in the bureaucratic case, Senators and congressmen differently situated, institutionally and electorally, will not see
that matter all alike; place, time, party, and electorate make for differing appraisals, though by no means along strict party lines: witness Republican and Democratic attitudes in the Eighty-fourth
Congress. No more than with the bureaucrats are estimates of this
sort to be taken as controlling the congressional response in given
instances of presidential pressure, but there can be no doubt that
they contribute most significantly to the background against which
such pressure is applied.

As for a President's own party's politicians outside Congress, they
are quite comparably circumstanced, with the important qualification
that at certain moments in the cycle of his term, their own enforced
commitment to his record and his name may enhance their responsiveness regardless of his momentary popular prestige; a qualification
applicable, equally, to certain of their brethren on the Hill.

In short, the President's persuasive power with those who do the
daily chores of governing, is influenced by a sort of *progression of
prestige*, a sequence culminating in the regard of the "general public," the country-at-large. Woodrow Wilson once wrote, in an aca-
demic vein, that a President "may be both the leader of his party
and the leader of the nation or he may be one or the other." Whatever the case fifty years ago, no such option is open to him now. He
must endeavor to lead "party" (for which read public officers as
well), since "nation" does not run the government machine, cannot
itself effectuate his choices. But if he is to manage those who make
the wheels go 'round, he needs public opinion at his back, must seek
consensus as his context for persuasion. And in that dual compulsion
lies the *ultimate dilemma* of the presidential operation at mid-century.

How describe this dilemma? One may begin by pointing to the
sources of that popular prestige which so affects the President's own
power to persuade. His general public—in our terms, national and
partisan constituencies combined—actually comprises a diversity of
presidential publics, their expectations nurtured variously by claims
on him as "government," by respect for his office, or by ties to his
personality: "interest" publics, "capacity" publics, and "personal"
publics, each subdivided many times, all linked by the crisscrossing
lines of overlapping membership, collectively encompassing the
country, or that part of it which cares about the President.

His national prestige, therefore—which congressmen and politicians watch and weigh—is simply the net balance of favorable response these many groups, in sum, accord their varied images of him
(a matter always to be gauged, not scientifically determined, the

result influenced, of course, by the affiliation of the gauger). Those images and the responses to them are not static; they can and do vary over time. And what are the determinants of variation? Happenings, mainly, or the appearance of happenings, ascribable—or anyway ascribed—to him: the reward or frustration of a bread-and-butter want, an ethical attitude, a psychological identification; to such as these his publics will react wherever and in whatever degree they see his office or his person as the cause. Inevitably, every concrete choice he makes, both positive and negative, and every effort at persuasion will set off some reactions of the sort, and not all of one kind; if somebody is pleased, then someone else is bound to be offended.

For the President to give offense is to risk blurring his own image in the eyes of those offended, hence to risk lowering their favorable response to him. But on a maximum of such response, as aggregated all across the country, must he depend for the effectuation of his choices. And on choice-making he depends for the impression of his person on the product of his office. But the conduct of office is liable to require policy initiatives in all directions, not as free will, but as constituency pressures and events decree. Hence, acts of choice and of persuasion become mandatory, inescapable. Yet, they are bound to give offense.

This, then, is the ultimate dilemma, the vicious circle Presidents must tread by virtue of their unique placement in our system, the personal equivalent for them, as individuals, of that disparity which haunts their office, routinely responsible for programming without assured support to carry through. No President, of course, is wholly helpless in this situation. He gains from office when he enters it a sizable initial fund of favorable response; if he is fortunate enough to be an Eisenhower, he brings still more *to* office. Once installed, his actions bring him gains as well as losses. Approbation, no less than offense, is bound to follow, from some quarter, everything he does or fails to do. And nobody in government is better placed than he to focus public interest and attention where he wants it, to foster certain images, obscuring others, to make desired happenings occur, to give events a nudge.

These are not insignificant resources. Particularly in a time of sharp emergency—which a preponderance of publics see or can be made to see as such—their use with skill, accompanied by luck, should help a President to break out of that circle altogether, in a fashion advantageous to his person and his cause; enabling him to gain from what he does far more by way of favorable response than negative reaction. For such a time, a crisis-time, tends to put premiums on affirmative action, to make the very act of doing almost its own reward, not doing almost its own penalty; so Hoover found to his discomfiture and Roosevelt to his taste a quarter-century ago. Of course, if circumstances are precisely opposite and times all peace and quiet, the outcome may be no less advantageous for a President; so Coolidge made a virtue of *not* doing and was well rewarded for it.

But our situation at mid-century fits neither of these models; the years since the Second World War have neither been perceived, widely, as crisis-times, nor have they been, in fact, peace-times in any familiar sense. And nowadays, the things that Presidents must do and those they may be called upon to do expose them regularly to the penalties of *both* such times with no assurance that they can gain the rewards of either. These days, both doing and not doing give offense in indeterminate proportion to offsetting approbation; almost all actions now *tend* to produce a negative reaction more concrete than favorable response. Both forms of action are abrasive; from neither can our Presidents now *count* upon a bonus of response. Yet, they are constantly impelled to actions of both sorts and so it has to be, these days, their preferences notwithstanding.

Consider what a President must do in times we now call "peace": keep taxes relatively high, armed forces relatively large, the budget "swollen," the bureaucracy "outsize"; inject himself into labor disputes just when tempers grow highest, into defense of overseas constituents just when they seem, at home, most irritating or unwise. And so the list goes on. Consider, also, what a President now may be called upon to do: intervene with arms in Korea, Indo-China; intervene with counsel in ·Southern school segregation; back the Benson plan for aid to farmers; endorse the Hobby plan for aid to schools; accept the Rockefeller plan for aid abroad; impose the New York Bar committee plan for personnel security; keep Nixon or take Herter; choose silence on McCarthy or attack; these among others. Such "musts" and "mays," as manifested in his acts of doing or not doing, are bound to outrage some among his publics (and anger may last long), to be accepted grudgingly by many as unpleasant facts of life, to warm the hearts of an uncertain number whose warmth may be short-lived. Whichever way he acts, his penalties may outrun his rewards in prestige terms. And rarely can he calculate with certainty, in advance, the net balance either way. Yet act he must.

By virtue of his unique place in government, a President gains unequaled opportunities to mold the images his publics have of him. But, for these opportunities, he pays a heavy price. Even for Eisenhower, immune, so far, to many of the payments levied on his predecessors, there is now the real price his illnesses exact: the issue of his health in the 1956 campaign; an issue taking its dimensions from the nature of his office at mid-century. . . .

PROSPECTS AND PROPOSALS

"Mid-century" will not endure forever. If the cold war holds its present course and if our national economy continues, generally, to climb, we may face six, eight, even ten years, perhaps more, that will bear an affinity, in presidential terms, to the decade just past. Beyond another decade, though, our population, science and resources, our industrial development, urbanization, regional realignments, will have brought us to such a point that even if affairs abroad held constant—which they cannot do—what has been described here may be wholly out of date. Even a decade may turn out too long a period to bracket as a portion of "our times." But there is likelihood, at least, that the next two, perhaps three, presidential terms will have much in common with the three since the Second World War.

How then might the next few Presidents be helped to ease the likely operating problems of the office? The answer, plainly, is that nothing fundamental can be done to help them. Nothing short of really revolutionary party centralization bids fair to eliminate that basic and dilemma-nurturing disparity between the Presidency's obligation to initiate and its capacity to achieve. Of course, were our parties fully nationalized and centralized, the party oligarchs might well command the capacity and would tend to assume the obligation, relieving the Presidency, as such, both of burdens and of unique place. But it has been six years now since a committee of the American Political Science Association summoned the revolution to commence, and I am prepared to predict that our parties will endure, for one more decade anyway, substantially unnationalized as in the last.

Barring fundamentals, one can try to nibble at the fringes of the Presidency's problems via piecemeal structural reforms. But those a President might find most fun cannot be had, as a practical matter: witness the item veto. And those most certain to affect him for the worse are only too likely to be thrust upon him: as now we have the two-term amendment and still might find ourselves some day with Bricker's or with Mundt's. As for the many proposed statutory changes which fit neither of these two extremes, opinions differ; their proponents, though, would be well advised to reflect upon Rossiter's admonition: "Leave Your Presidency Alone." In my own view, that caution makes great sense and applies equally to all proposals of a structural and statutory sort. For all of them—all, anyway, of which I am aware—incur a common risk: that they will produce *wayward side-effects*, however unintended by their sponsors, which may make matters worse, or at least put new problems in the place of old. Even the twentieth amendment, widely heralded as an essen-

tial modernization, made matters difficult for Eisenhower his first
year, and scarcely would have aided FDR, and easily might have
been ruinous in Lincoln's time, the classic case of grave emergency
it is intended to relieve. This is not to suggest we should repeal the
"Lame Duck" amendment, or even alter its required starting-dates
for the congressional and presidential terms; the point, rather, is
that if so logical and seemingly so slight a change produces wayward
side-effects, it might be well to avoid others more complex or more
obscure.

Some risks, of course, accompany all change; this is no argument
for never changing anything. But when one can foresee a wayward
consequence, however unintended by proponents, then is the time,
it seems to me, to move on their proposals very cautiously indeed.
So, in the legislative cabinet scheme, as recently revived by Professors
Corwin and Koenig, one is confronted with the prospect, all other
things aside, that formal cabinet rank for leading Senators would
transfer from an Eisenhower to Knowland, say, and Bridges, some
part of his privacy, prestige, and nominal authority, without in any
way diminishing their independent power base, or guaranteeing him
improvement in the quality of counsel and advice they have provided
up to now. If there should be a President who wished to try this
one-way transfer, he could find means without a statute. The privilege
remains his; why then impose a mandate? Of course, if one's concern
is less with easing operational dilemmas than with checking arbitrary
power, the matter wears a wholly different look. But if the Presidency
now is dangerously powerful, this essay's premises and argument are
all awry.

In terms of easing burdens, hence of strengthening the President,
by means externally imposed, there is but one proposal that in all
good conscience I could urge without equivocation, a proposal once
made (but not patented) by a former Roosevelt aide: to guarantee
new Presidents a solid partisan majority in both Houses of Congress,
composed of men dependent on the President's own electorate. But
in the circumstances of mid-century, this, above all, is never to be
guaranteed; indeed it is not even to be hoped for.

Where does this leave us then? It leaves us with the Presidents
themselves, with what they might do for themselves in their own
self-defense, within the confines and environs of their office.

To make suggestions to them, without knowing them or their
specific situations, imposes certain limitations on would-be suggestors,
one limit above all: that each suggestion be adaptable for use by an
incumbent, whatever his work-habits and his style; that each be
usable by men so various in those respects as Eisenhower, Truman,
FDR. Truman's White House rather resembled a senatorial estab-

lishment, writ large: the staff informal, almost family-like, assignments shifting casually among jacks-of-all-trades, organization plastic, hierarchy slight, and anything liable to be mulled over with the President. Eisenhower, one supposes, could not have abided it. But no more could Truman have abided—much less politically afforded —the military sort of staff system as adapted and on display in Eisenhower's White House. Yet this is the way Eisenhower works and that was the way Truman worked and the next President may want to work like one, or the other, or like neither. There is no point in urging upon any of them a suggestion he could not adopt without foregoing his accustomed way of work.

To illustrate the sort of thing thereby put out of bounds, a number of observers assert that the current regime is a "regency" and urge that Eisenhower should dispense with Sherman Adams. But if this were a regency, then Eisenhower and not Adams must be presumed First Regent. The military have their rules for chiefs of staff, and those who cannot keep them do not long retain the place. There is no evidence that Eisenhower lacks acquaintance with these rules or that his principal assistant has not learned to work within them. If Adams were to vanish overnight, no doubt there would soon appear in his place another such abrasive, intense concentrator. That is the Eisenhower way, and so it was long before 1953. In terms of personal performance, we might as well accept the moral and forbear to debate here whether Eisenhower's system, in the abstract, is a good thing or a bad. Some Presidents will find they cannot stand it, others that they cannot get away with it politically, while others, still, may try to proceed much as he has done.

I have stressed Eisenhower's case because among those of all recent Presidents his most restricts the range of the suggestible. Our need is for things Presidents might do to help themselves, on their initiative, at their discretion. Suggestions that seem reasonably practicable for a man of military background, entrenched behind the paraphernalia of elaborate staff, are likely to be usable, as well, by those schooled in more fluid, personalized, working-ways of civil government and politics, whence one supposes the next Presidents will come. But having so delimited the field of search, what remains to be found? In such a narrow ground, what is there to discover that may help a President resolve—or live with—his dilemmas? Tentatively, I would hazard the following response.

First, the fewer a President's illusions about the limitations on his power stakes and status in our system, the better his performance on the job. The more nearly he sees his power problem as I have endeavored to describe it here, the greater his chance to master his circumstances or at least hinder them from overwhelming him. Of course, a man wants the illusions that sustain him at his work, and if he needs to look upon the world in terms other than jungle, then so he must. It might help, though, if Presidents who felt impelled to find identification with a forerunner, would look to Lincoln, not as myth or symbol, but as man-in-office. For in their wartime crises, FDR and Wilson seem more removed from our mid-century state than Lincoln does, despite the fact of war. In its operational dilemmas, his was a very modern Presidency, contrasts notwithstanding. And should they seek such parallels, I suggest that the image of his operating burdens and his power problem, rather than, say, Washington's (or Jackson's or a Roosevelt's), be graven on the minds of our next Presidents.

Second, of all the self-perceptions that can help a President, nothing helps so much as an awareness of his absolutely unique place—of his aloneness at the only juncture of his four constituencies—and an alertness, consequently, to the fact that he can count on no one else in Government to sense his interests in precisely his own terms. To stress the "team" and teamwork is a fine thing for morale and useful, too, in binding others to one's cause. But any President who regards the blithe spirit all-for-one-and-one-for-all as a reality which may assume full right-and-title to his interests is assured disenchantment and distortion of his aims.

It follows that he needs to widen, so far as he can, the confines of his own freedom to choose what he himself would think he were well advised to make choices on and undertake persuasion on and when. As we have seen, he cannot hope to widen these confines more than a little; how might even that little be accomplished? On the one hand, I would suggest, by rendering the regular assistance he receives more representative of the totality of his constituencies; on the other hand, by building into government and his own staff the sorts of competitions which will create "deadlines" for him at times and on issues useful in his terms.

Perhaps we do not recognize sufficiently the deep distortions, in constituency terms, of staff assistance now officially available to a President. Without exception, his department heads and institutional staff aides are tightly linked to, actually are part of, his "government" constituency. The same thing can be said for his legislative leaders and for such White House aides as he may draw from agency or congressional sources to help with liaison in both directions. Many of these people also represent, in varying degree, some portions of his "partisan" constituency; so, of course, does the National Committee Chairman, whose office is more or less part of presidential staff facilities. And all of them can claim to be in some sense representative of "national" constituency as well. But taking them together as a collectivity, their representative character is decidedly different than his own; greatly overweighing the governmental element, especially its executive side, while relatively slighting partisan, underweighing national, and virtually ignoring overseas components. Even in the White House staff, none but the Press Secretary is free of institutionalized routines which pull particularly in the government direction (perhaps explaining why that post becomes so powerful when manned by a superb technician).

To compensate for these distortions, Presidents must break out of their official families and so they do, with ceremonials and visitors, with trips, and tête-à-têtes, with consultations and with confidants, each in his fashion. But I submit that these are frail reliances which need the utmost buttressing by Presidents themselves in conscious, purposeful awareness of official insufficiencies. And not the means but that awareness becomes crucial in this case; if that be strong enough, the man makes his own means. His aides, of course, can help and so they will, provided his insistence is incessant, but their reach is no *substitute* for his, nor their awareness either.

As for the matter of "created" deadlines, this was a specialty with FDR which, suitably adapted, I commend to his successors. Roosevelt is commonly supposed a "poor" administrator; lines of authority confused, the same assignments in the hands of numerous subordinates, doors opening and closing unpredictably, nobody knowing everything of anybody's business and everybody horning in on everything. Yet with all this and *by* it, he kept in his own hands more power of judgment and decision than most Presidents before or since. In the administration of the Presidency, what could be more important? This is not to suggest that future Presidents should try to play by ear, *ad hoc*, in Roosevelt's special way. They cannot if they would—nor could he either, at the end—for government has grown too big, its scope too broad, their own responsibilities too routinized, their office far too institutionalized. What is suggested, rather, is a search for substitutes compatible with their more complex circumstances. The building-in of competition seems to me the key.

Without attempting an exhaustive exploration, let me mention two means by which competitive relations might be fostered: namely appointments and reorganizations. The President who wishes to enhance his prospects for free choices in an area of policy will do well to arrange that opposed attitudes in country or in Congress, or in his own mind are represented among appointees charged institutionally with its consideration *and* administration. By "represented" is meant not in form alone, but in a balance that suffices to force underlying issues on the table, up the line, and in good time, without exhausting institutional support for a decision *either* way. Thus,

Eisenhower seems to run tremendous risks of foreclosed freedom in
the sphere of foreign aid, when all the posts of massive institutional
power are held by men reportedly conservative in view, with "balance" furnished mainly by a brace of White House aides.

One sympathizes with the wish of both of Roosevelt's successors
to avoid such unseemly public struggles as were carried on from inside
his regime. But foreclosed freedom can be harder on a President
than struggling subordinates. Indeed, unless they are sufficiently
well-matched to carry controversies to the press, he loses one among
the early warning signals built-in-competitions can provide. If he is
lucky and adroit and granted a respectful opposition, perhaps he can
hold down the public outcries though he keep his fighters matched,
and can devise internal signals as a substitute. But if, to keep the
public peace, he rigs fights overmuch, he pays an exorbitant price,
or so it seems to me. Indeed, under the circumstances of mid-century,
an outward look of total harmony in a regime might well be taken
as itself a warning sign.

As for reorganization, it is obviously useful, often essential, as a
supplement to the appointive power in building or in equalizing
institutionalized competitions. There is one disability, however: my
colleague, Wallace Sayre, has propounded the sound "law" that any
benefits of a reorganization are immediate, while disadvantages are
cumulative over time. To this I would append the simple corollary
that as for a President's own freedom, gains are short-range, risks
long-run. And this applies with greater force the closer one approaches his own person. The moral appears plain. It cannot be
enough to reorganize, one must keep on with it. In their relations
to each other and the President, his official associates need stirring
up; not with such frequency that they shrink into immobility, but
just enough so that they are never absolutely confident in unchecked
judgment of their chief's own judgment, or of their colleagues' either.

With that I would conclude. These several imprecise suggestions
of what Presidents might do in their own self-defense are neither
very bold nor very new; assuredly, they are neither my own last
testament nor anybody's. In that regard, one final word: if we, as
citizens, cannot rescue our Presidents from their dilemmas but must
leave them to help themselves as best they can, there is one thing
that we, as students and observers, might do to render their self-help
a little easier. We might take more care in the future than sometimes
in the past, lest we foster stereotypes and expectations not within
their capacities or even their own interests to fulfill.

In the two decades since the report of the President's Committee
on Administrative Management, great numbers of experts, in universities and out, have been hard at work seeking solutions for the

managerial dilemmas of the federal government. And whether the focus be on budgeting, on organization, or on personnel—in order of prevailing fashion, then to now—the outcome tends to be the same: "The President, himself, must take command."

Faster than perhaps we realize, the frame of reference underlying such investigations, such solutions, becomes popularized (and over-simplified), eventuating in those plain truths nobody learns but everybody knows: "The President, of course! As in business, so in government; the title is the same and so should be the function." Perhaps it would not be amiss to remind the managerial enthusiasts of Woodrow Wilson's wise prognosis half a century ago: ". . . as the business of government becomes more and more complex and extended . . . the President is becoming more and more a political and less an executive officer . . . incumbents will come more and more [*to be*] directors of affairs and leaders of the nation—men of counsel and of the sort of action that makes for enlightenment."

For so it has turned out; these and not management are the great objects of their work and sources of their troubles at mid-century.

☆

NELSON W. POLSBY: *Conflict Between the President and Congress*

It is possible to identify many sources of conflict between Congress and the President. One has to do with differences in the constituencies over-represented by each.

I have already outlined characteristics peculiar to the presidential coalition, and explained why it is predominantly liberal, activist, and urban in its orientation, and especially attentive to the needs of interest groups and large minorities in densely populated, two-party states. This coalition may be contrasted with typical winning coalitions in Congress, which depend so heavily on seniority and expertise. There are clear advantages in this system for congressmen and senators from one-party states with small electorates. The attention of these men is not so constantly diverted from legislative business; their ties back home are easier to maintain and their chances of falling by the wayside in massive party turnovers are of course much less than their brethren from competitive two-party areas. And so they rise to positions of power in the all-important committee system of Congress.

Malapportionment—the unequal populations of congressional districts and of states—also works to the advantage of sparsely populated areas, and provides interests which dominate in these areas with especially advantageous access to Congress.

The interests which dominate in sparsely populated and one-party

Nelson W. Polsby is Professor of Political Science at the University of California, Berkeley. This selection is from *Congress and the Presidency* (Englewood Cliffs, New Jersey: Prentice-Hall, Inc., 1964), pp. 102–13. © 1964 by Prentice-Hall, Inc. Reprinted by permission of the publisher and the author.

areas—tobacco and potato growers, and segregationist white south-erners, for example—are quite different from those which dominate in urban, two-party areas—such as laborers employed in manufactur-ing, and racial and ethnic minorities. Thus the germ of conflict over policy is contained in the very rules by which congressmen, senators, and Presidents are elected and sustained in office.

Once in office, certain *institutional* factors further facilitate con-flict between the two branches; at least three such conflicts have their roots in differing institutional positions and may drive a wedge between Presidents and even those men in Congress who were elected as supporters of presidential programs from constituencies like the President's own.

Perhaps the most fundamental of these institutional sources of conflict can be described as a difference in the time perspective of members of the two branches. Consider the "efficient minority" of congressmen—both liberals and conservatives—who regard Con-gress as their vocation and who have risen in the hierarchies of the House or Senate sufficiently to have a noticeable impact on legis-lative outcomes. The unit of time to which a member of this group is most attentive in gauging the consequences of his behavior is the career. The questions he must continually pose to himself are: How will my behavior today affect my standing in this house tomorrow, the next day, and in years to come? How may I act so as to enhance my esteem in the eyes of my colleagues? How may I lay up the trea-sures of obligation and friendship against my day of need? Or, if he is oriented to public policy: How may I enhance the future chances of policies I favor?

In contrast, the President and his agents must perforce focus on the presidential term of office as the unit of time most relevant to them. Eight years is the very most they have to do what they want to do. Subtract one year as a lame-duck period. Discount the period of time just before and just after elections—especially the critical period just prior to the decision whether there is to be a second term or not. And finally, subtract whatever time has elapsed already. How much time remains? Not very much, and yet there are so many pro-grams which they may want to advocate, so many policies which they desire to put into practice.

The conflict which arises from the difference in time perspectives even between responsible, loyal, and decent members of the two branches is this: The President is intent on the problem of the mo-ment, which is to press high-priority items in his program. He asks his congressional allies to spend power in behalf of his goal. The congressman, who has to worry about the possibility of a future transfer to a desirable committee or a private bill that may mean political life or death some time in the future, is naturally inclined to hoard power or to invest it so as to increase his future stock of resources. Meanwhile, the President's opponents in Congress are not so constrained. If they are of the opposition party, they may content themselves with simple party regularity. If they are of the President's party, they need only refrain from bestirring themselves. Or if they fight, they can fight in behalf of their own preferences or those of their district—but not necessarily those of the President.

A second institutional dilemma which strains presidential-congressional relations is the age-old strategic problem: "Help Thy Friends or Woo Thine Enemies?" No matter which horn of the dilemma the President chooses to confront, the other is bound to cause him grief. . . .

Presumably the ideal way to handle the problem is for the President to keep both his friends and his enemies happy. But then the question is bound to arise whether the President's friends are being sufficiently differentiated from his enemies. What profit accrues to a congressman who regularly sticks his neck out for the administration, if congressmen who do not are amply rewarded, the same as he is? In practice, limits on the time and other resources available to the President and his aides set boundaries on the extent to which *either* activity is pursued. Mistakes are bound to occur.

A third institutional factor encumbering presidential-congressional relations concerns the gains and costs of uncertainty to both. Congressmen and senators often find it useful to refrain from committing themselves on legislation in order to bargain with interest groups and within the House or Senate, or perhaps simply in order to avoid potentially dangerous controversy. The President, on the other hand, has a stake in knowing the lay of the land as early as possible, so he can see what he needs to do to win. And so the conflict between secrecy and disclosure can be added to the ones already mentioned.

All these various ingrained forces were amplified during the Kennedy Administration by the substantial gap that existed between White House and Executive Department legislative liaison personnel on one hand and Capitol Hill people on the other, in age, background, and personal styles. A White House aide once went so far in public to describe this gap as a "mutuality of contempt." Clearly the difficulties of the relatively youthful, hard-nosed, college-educated corps of new frontiersmen with older, more slow-moving, more elaborately courteous and folksier congressmen were real enough. . . .

Relations between President's men and the men of Congress have seldom been easy; one recalls widespread congressional resentment in former administrations of Harry Hopkins, Dean Acheson, and Sherman Adams. One way for people in the White House to avoid problems with Congress is to ask far less of them in the way of performance, and clearly some Presidents have taken this tack. But this course of action—or rather inaction—hazards the displeasure of the President's natural allies among interest groups. If carried to an extreme, it may even jeopardize the President's control of his own administration and his own or his party's chances of retaining the Presidency itself.

An indication that President Johnson is concerned with the problem of legislative liaison operations is provided by the fact that Mr. Johnson early in his Presidency rescinded the ban that Mr. Kennedy had imposed on organized fund-raising by the congressional campaign committees of the Democratic party. The attempt by President Kennedy and his aides to distribute nationally collected funds entirely through the Democratic National Committee mostly to congressmen and senators who were friendly to Kennedy Administration policies led to resentment on Capitol Hill. But even if Mr. Johnson is able to ease some of the superficial strains between the White House and congressmen, the various institutional factors I have mentioned will work cumulatively to exacerbate them.

INSTRUMENTS OF CONFLICT

The means that Congress and the President have available with which they can express disagreements and induce cooperation—in short, their weapons in the intramural political struggle of Washington politics—are probably well enough known to demand only a brief recapitulation.

The President can veto legislation desired by congressmen. He can prevent the spending of funds appropriated by Congress for purposes he does not approve. And he has an enormous range of discretion over the activities of the Executive Branch. This includes his power of appointment, a power which reaches into every state and locality, embracing postmasterships, U.S. attorneys, federal judges, and collectors of ports. Other appointments made mostly at presidential discretion include appointment to the Supreme Court, to independent regulatory commissions, to top managerial posts, to the various departments and agencies of the government, and to honorific boards and commissions—some of them *ad hoc*, such as the Presidential Commission on Intergovernmental Relations, and some more permanent, like the Fine Arts Commission that advises on the design of public buildings in Washington, D.C.

A President can create good will and forge alliances by prudent use of his appointment powers. He has the obligation, in order to protect his own political position, to find appointees who are com-

petent and also politically acceptable to others. Normally, these matters proceed on a state-by-state basis; some attempt is made to
strengthen the hand of the party and distribute rewards in states
where the party leaders are allies of the President's.

Sometimes "clearance" with state party leaders is quite formal
and elaborate, sometimes not. Minor appointments, such as post-
masters, are traditionally delegated to the congressman from the district involved, if he is of the President's party. This congressional
patronage helps to build a bridge between the President and his party
members in Congress. In like manner, senators of the President's
party clear the federal judgeships and most of the other important
federal appointments made to citizens of their respective states.

When senatorial confirmation is required by law, as it is in the
case of the more important appointments, senators employ a coopera-
tive device to ensure clearance. This is senatorial "courtesy," so called.
When a senator from the President's own party announces that a
nominee to high office from his state is personally obnoxious or
embarrassing to him, the Senate customarily refuses to confirm. This
is a powerful weapon, but is used sparingly; senators prefer to encourage clearance by less visible means, by arranging for delays in
the confirmation process while appropriate apologies, or even more
concrete tokens of contrition, are proffered.

Presidential discretion does not end with the appointment process.
All the manifold programs of the government have differential impacts on the various geographical areas of the nation, and so it is
possible to reward and punish congressional friends and foes quite
vigorously. Small Business Administration and Area Redevelopment
Administration loans to certain areas may get more and more difficult
to obtain, as applications fail to "qualify." Pilot programs and demonstration projects may be funneled here rather than there. Defense
contracts and public works may be accelerated in some areas, retarded
in others. Administrative decisions may be made to open branches or
consolidate operations of various federal agencies. All these activities
are indispensable to the running of any large administrative apparatus; and it may be a matter of indifference administratively
whether an installation is opened in Dallas or Houston, whether a
regional headquarters is in Portland or Seattle. But these administrative decisions have great political impact because they affect the
prosperity of areas where they are put into effect and they are often
of acute concern to local political leaders. And so they can become
weapons in the hands of a politically astute President.

The sheer high status of the Presidency is of course a formidable
weapon. Only the crustiest and most independent congressmen and
senators fail to warm to considerate personal treatment by a President

of the United States. A private breakfast, a walk in the rose garden, an intimate conference, all duly and widely reported in the press, gives a man a sense of importance which may not only flatter his ego but may also remind him of his responsibilities as a national legislator, as a trustee of the common weal. He may then moderate his opposition, or stiffen his resolve to support the President. . . .

Another way of exploiting the prestige of the Presidency is the gambit of "going to the people." This process is usually described in a misleading way. What a President does when he goes to the people is to try to focus the attention of the mass media and relevant interest groups on an issue. It is not really possible in the course of one or a few fireside chats to provoke a groundswell of opinion change that promises to rearrange the composition of Congress unless congressmen knuckle under forthwith. The ties that congressmen and senators have back home are typically multiple, strong, and of long standing. It is hard for a President to change all this over television, while explaining the intricacies of a particular issue. He can, however, communicate his concern about the issue. He can increase its general visibility, stir up interest-group activity, and to a certain extent set the terms in which it will be debated.

Congressional weapons have to a substantial degree been covered earlier. They include the power to delay and to fail to act, the power to cut appropriations and thus to curtail programs, the power to require the Executive agencies to comply with stringent requirements, either by writing technical and specific laws or by legally requiring frequent reports and repeated authorizations.

Senatorial courtesy is a significant constraint on the presidential appointment power. Throughout the legislative labyrinth, different congressmen and senators are strategically placed to delay, modify, or defeat legislation and appropriations. There is also the power of impeachment, which has only been used once against a President (in 1868), but that once almost succeeded in deposing President Andrew Johnson. The power is now moribund, however. It is an extreme constitutional safeguard; its employment, or even its serious consideration, would signal a severe breakdown of the political system and its constraints on behavior as we know it today.

One other weapon in the congressional arsenal deserves brief consideration—the power to investigate. This is a significant congressional activity, although one which has perhaps suffered from a surfeit of publicity. Investigations may move in many directions. Perhaps the most famous of these in recent years have been the Kefauver and McClellan investigations of crime and racketeering, various House Committee on Un-American Activities investigations of communism in the United States, and the Army-McCarthy hearings of 1954. Of these, only the last involved any sort of congressional scrutiny of the Executive Branch, and this was also an inquiry into the practices of a senator and a sub-committee of the Senate itself under his leadership.

The President and his Executive Office are immune from congressional investigations; the precedents for this stretch back to George Washington. But Congress may inquire minutely into the workings of the Executive Branch, may probe for conflict of interest, may seek to reconstruct the bases on which decisions were made, may ferret out inter-office disagreements and expose all to the glare of publicity. Insofar as the President needs the various departments and agencies of the Executive Branch to execute his policies, this power of Congress to investigate constrains him.

So, finally, does the congressional power of post-audit. The General Accounting Office, an agency of Congress, continuously audits the expenditure of federal funds after they are made to ascertain that they have been spent in accordance with law. This office may disallow expenditures and require restitution.

THE LEGITIMACY OF CONFLICT

Let us now examine the legitimacy of conflict between Congress and the President. Curiously, the fact of conflict itself has a very bad name with writers on political questions. In behalf of the President and his policies, Congress is charged with willful parochialism, with neglect of national needs, with a variety of immoral, illegal, and undignified activities—all of which are indicative, it is often held, of an overriding need for general reform of the Legislative Branch. In the words of a few book titles, Congress is "on trial," a sink of "corruption and compromise," responsible for the "deadlock of democracy." One author asks: "Can representative government do the job?"

In behalf of Congress, it is urged that the country is, as Congress is, "essentially moderate." The President is trying to impose a tyranny of the majority. He wishes to go "too far, too fast." He cares not for the Constitution, for public order, for the American way. His actions verge on usurpation. Nobody, however, suggests in this connection that the Presidency be weakened as an institution; rather, it is urged that incumbents pull up their socks and act less like Presidents.

In the light of our constitutional history, however, conflict between the two branches should come as no surprise; indeed, the system was designed so that different branches would be captured by different interests and they would have to come to terms with one another peaceably in order to operate the system at all. This theory is explicitly stated in *The Federalist* (1788), which is the authoritative commentary on the Constitution by the Founding Fathers:

> To what expedient, then, shall we finally resort, for maintaining in practice the necessary partition of power among the several departments, as laid down in the Constitution . . . ? By so contriving the interior structure of the government as that its several constituent parts may, by their mutual relations, be the means of keeping each other in their proper places. . . . In order to lay a due foundation for that separate and distinct exercise of the different powers of government, which to a certain extent is admitted on all hands to be essential to the preservation of liberty, it is evident that each department should have a will of its own. . . . The great security against a gradual concentration of the several powers in the same department, consists in giving to those who administer each department the necessary constitutional means and personal motives to resist encroachments of the others. . . . Ambition must be made to counteract ambition.

Indeed, if the Constitution can be said to grant legitimacy to anything, surely it legitimizes conflict between Congress and the President.

It is often argued, however, that majoritarian principles are violated by one or another of the two great branches. A presidential veto may render ineffectual congressional majorities in both houses. Or an administration bill may be stalled somewhere in the toils of the legislative process by a small minority. Aside from any general skepticism one may harbor that majority rule is always a good thing, there is in any case often a problem in identifying a relevant majority whose decisions are to be regarded as legitimate.

Different doctrines suggest different solutions. There is, for example, the doctrine of *party responsibility*. According to this doctrine, the will of the majority party within Congress, if it is the same as the President's party, should prevail. On the other hand, a doctrine of *congressional responsibility* would hold that the will of the majority within Congress as a whole should prevail.

As it happens, in present-day American politics, these two majorities are generally at loggerheads. The majority within Congress as a whole is frequently composed of a coalition of Republicans and southern Democrats. Northern and western Democrats, who make up a clear majority of the majority party, often cannot command a majority on the floor. . . .

One way to resolve this dilemma would be to regard the relevant majority as existing in the electorate. Those for whom the majority of people vote, nationwide, should prevail. Now it is true that the President is elected on a nationwide basis and congressmen and senators individually are not, but congressmen and senators act in concert; collectively, they are elected on a national basis.

At this point, the argument must become intricate. The legitimacy of the presidential majority may be impugned, first, because the Electoral College in effect nullifies the votes accruing to presidential candidates that lose states by narrow margins. Even when this does not actually deprive the winner of the popular vote of public office—as it did once (in 1876)—this system can lead to the election of a President who receives less than a majority of all the popular votes. This in fact has happened at least 12 times, most recently in 1960, when John F. Kennedy received 49.9 per cent of the votes and Richard M. Nixon received 49.7 per cent, the rest going to other candidates.

The legitimacy of the congressional majority can be questioned on at least two grounds. Malapportionment in the states, it can be argued, forbids the expression of true majority sentiment in electing congressmen and senators. And, what is more, after they are elected, various characteristics of decision-making processes in the respective houses make the expression of the will of the majority of even these truncated representatives difficult and on some occasions impossible.

All of these charges, it should be said, are perfectly true. It appears that nobody enters into the arena of national policy-making with an absolutely clean and unsullied right to have his will prevail because he was elected by majority sentiment. For who knows why men are elected to public office? Most people vote the way they do out of party habit, not because they endorse any particular set of campaign promises or projected policies. Typically, small minorities care about selected policies. But it is perfectly possible for a candidate to be elected by a majority which disagrees with *all* his policy preferences. It is also perfectly possible for a particular electorate to elect a President, a senator, and a congressman, none of whom agree with one another to a significant extent about any public policies. And so an attempt to justify particular policies advocated by congressmen or Presidents based on their supposed link to the electorate seems dubious.

What about reforms? Would it be possible to change a few features of the political system so that Congress and the President could at least claim legtimacy for their actions if not on the grounds that they expressed accurately the will of a majority, then on the grounds that they represented more closely the majority choice of their respective electorates?

On the presidential side, this would entail at least scrapping the Electoral College and substituting direct popular election. In some quarters the move would be popular. It would probably have the effect of loosening the present hold that the current presidential coalition has on the office. But the incentives to interest groups in the large, two-party states to give up their present access to the Presidency are of course not very great so long as they are at a severe disadvantage in the other parts of the system.

And so, presidential election reform is probably, for practical purposes, tied in some way or another to congressional reform. Here, there are many complications. First, the long-term effects of Baker v. Carr, a Supreme Court decision that will probably force the reapportionment of a good many state legislatures, seem to point toward the slow liberalization of Congress, without any concessions by the presidential coalition. Already one moderate congressman, from Atlanta, Georgia, has replaced a conservative who was kept in office by the operations of a county unit system that Baker v. Carr indirectly invalidated. But reapportionment is a long, long road that never really ends. And whether or not congressional districts are equitably apportioned within the states will always be a matter of some controversy, even where district populations are substantially equal. Recent Supreme Court decisions require substantial equality of populations; but standards of contiguity and especially compactness are harder to formulate, and leave room for political maneuver.

A second set of congressional reforms looks toward changing Congress' internal decision-making procedures. It would be instructive to list all such proposals, to see how many of them would cancel out in their effects. It is not certain, for example, that a joint committee on the budget would lead either to a comprehensive congressional overview or to a congressional appropriations process more sympathetic to presidential programs.

In general, reform proposals seeking to bring congressional policymaking more closely into line with presidential preferences suggest procedures to bring measures to the floor easily, and to weaken the grip of the committees on them. These proposals identify Congress as a great forum for debate.

The difficulties with suggestions of this kind are substantial. Insofar as congressmen weaken their committees, they weaken the one device they have to scrutinize legislative proposals on their merits. Committees encourage specialization and technical sophistication, even expertise. They are convenient agencies through which bridges can be built to the Executive Branch, making possible a flow of information so that Congress can act intelligently.

Typically, suggestions for congressional reform have their beginnings in modest dissatisfactions over the President's inability to persuade Congress to enact parts of his program. But like the comedian
who begins by tugging at a stray thread and ends up unraveling his
entire wardrobe, congressional reformers soon find themselves dis-
mantling the entire political system in their mind's eye, and suggesting instead a system modeled on the British government where the
Legislature takes orders from the Cabinet, and the Cabinet from the
Prime Minister. This vision of tidiness is, however, not well-suited
to a nation where conflict is a legitimate feature of the day-to-day
processes of governing, where sectional traditions are strong, and
where a substantial variety and number of interest groups have
learned to expect that one or another part of the government will
always be accessible to them.

Most specific proposals for reform would, however, if enacted, fall
far short of provoking a constitutional crisis. They are not adopted
primarily because they require the assent of leaders whose powers
they would curb. Thus it seems highly improbable that a proposal in
the Senate to make it a bit easier to close off filibusters would not
itself be subjected to the filibuster. A resolution changing the Rules
of the House so as to clip the wings of the Rules Committee must
be reported in the first instance by the Rules Committee. Proposals
to curtail the powers of committee chairmen seem likely to be opposed by committee chairmen, with all the skills, rewards and penalties they command. It may be that better government in some
meaningful sense would emerge if many of the specific reforms that
have been offered were adopted. But few of them are likely to be
adopted. . . .

Congress and the Presidency are like two gears, each whirling at
its own rate of speed. It is not surprising that, on coming together,
they often clash. Remarkably, however, this is not always the case.
Devices which harmonize their differences are present within the
system; the effects of party loyalty and party leadership within Congress, presidential practices of consultation, the careful restriction of
partisan opposition by both congressional parties, and the readily
evoked overriding patriotism of all participants within the system
in periods—which nowadays, regrettably, come with some frequency
—universally defined as crises.

With all the snags and thickets that complicate relations between
Congress and the Presidency, it is worth noting that cooperation between the two branches does take place. This remarkable fact can
be explained only in part by referring to incentives built into the
machinery of the system. In addition, the underlying political culture
discourages ideological extremism and fanatical intransigence and

places a premium on the political skills of negotiation, maneuver, and accommodation. These permit Congress and the President to get along in spite of their differences, to unite in times of national emergency, and yet to return another day to disagree.

☆

LOUIS W. KOENIG: *More Power to the President*

. . . When the realities of presidential power are examined more
closely, they reveal an office far less strong than those who attack it
would lead us to suppose. A considerable chasm stretches between
the Presidency that its critics speak of—or imagine—and the Presidency of reality.

That the Presidency should be a limited office was part of the
original conception. Distrustful of power in human hands, the
Founding Fathers wrote the principles of checks and balances and
separation of powers into the Constitution. Neither Congress nor
the executive was to become dominant, but each shared powers of
the other, whether making laws, appointments or treaties, and each
therefore could check the other (and the Supreme Court could
check both).

The President cannot long maintain important policies, domestic
or foreign, without congressional support in the form of laws or
money. But whereas a British Prime Minister, with an absolute
majority in the House of Commons operating under an altogether
different political arrangement can count on legislative enactment
of 100 per cent of his proposals, the President does well (except in
time of crisis, when he does far better) to average between 50 and
60 per cent.

He will sustain defeats on key measures, as Lyndon Johnson did
in 1964 on health care for the aged under Social Security and aid
for the depressed Appalachian region. John Kennedy, at the time of

Louis W. Koenig is Professor of Government at New York University. The
selection is from "More Power to the President (Not Less)" in *The New York
Times Magazine*, January 3, 1965, p. 7. © 1965 by The New York Times Company. Reprinted by permission of the publisher and the author.

his death, still was deprived of legislation he deemed of highest importance—public school aid, civil rights, Medicare, a Cabinet-level urban affairs department and stand-by authority to lower income taxes. Even with a slender majority of four votes, Harold Wilson launched in the first weeks of his Prime Ministership an ambitious and controversial foreign and domestic program, while simultaneously surviving votes of confidence.

The President has no dependable way, as the British Prime Minister does, to command the legislature's support. A complex of forces prompts Congress to resist or oppose the President much of the time. Because the method of electing the President differs from the method of electing congressmen, their constituencies and therefore their concerns and viewpoints differ.

The President and Vice President alone are chosen by the nation. Senators and congressmen are essentially local officers responsible to the voters of a single state or congressional district. Congress neither chooses the President nor is chosen by him, and is therefore not beholden to him, and cannot be bullied by him.

Only once in four years are the President and members of the House of Representatives elected simultaneously, and even then only one-third of the Senate is elected. At the President's midterm, the House and another one-third of the Senate are chosen, usually with local issues predominating. The outcome more often than not worsens the President's own party support in both congressional houses. At no point in any four-year term does the President face a Senate wholly elected during his tenure, owing to the Senate's six-year term and staggered elections. Presidents come and go, but the most powerful legislators—the chairmen of the standing committees—stay on, often for a third of a century and more.

The likelihood is that a President who seeks important—and therefore controversial—social and economic legislation will face a hard wall of opposition from legislative leaders of his own party. These are the committee chairmen who have great seniority because they come from "safe" districts, situated chiefly in Southern and in rural and small-town areas. . . .

Although the Founding Fathers did not foresee political parties, their rise has not hampered in any significant way the intended effect of checks and balances. President Eisenhower once perceptively observed, "Now let's remember there are no national parties in the United States. There are . . . state parties."

Our parties function effectively as national organizations only when control of the White House is at stake. Otherwise, a party is a loose confederation of state and local organizations, with sectional cleavages and factional differences commonplace. The President and the legislators, although they wear the same party label, are nominated by different party organizations and are chosen by different electorates, an arrangement that hardly works for unity.

There is no common standard of party loyalty, and no party caucus, as in Great Britain, which joins the executive with the legislators of his party in common support of a program. Even in the crisis of an election, which presumably would bring the party and its members into closest unity, differences between the President and his congressional party colleagues may rush to the surface.

The lengths to which the maladies may go is suggested by an episode midway in Eisenhower's second term, during the congressional elections of 1958. Richard M. Simpson of Pennsylvania, then chairman of the Republican Congressional Campaign Committee, went so far as to counsel Republican candidates for the House of Representatives to forget about Eisenhower's favor and support and "make known" to voters any "disagreement with the President's policies." Simpson, a conservative Republican, often opposed the President's "modern Republicanism."

Checks and balances and the President's legislative and party weaknesses affect his other functions. Although political science textbooks like to refer to him as "administrative chief," Congress too has powers over administration which it can use with the same independence that it exercises over legislation.

It can vest authority in subordinate officials to act independently of higher leadership, stratify a department's internal organization and require Senate confirmation of bureau chiefs. It can create independent regulatory commissions, such as the Interstate Commerce Commission and the Federal Reserve Board, rather far-removed from the President's control. Congress establishes the missions of departments, authorizes and amends their programs and provides money in such amounts and with such strings attached as it chooses.

Even where his authority is presumably great, in foreign affairs and as Commander in Chief, the President depends on congressional support. He often encounters resistance; George F. Kennan, surveying his tenure as Ambassador to Yugoslavia, was driven to remonstrate that "without the support of Congress, it was impossible to carry out an effective policy here."

The requirement that two-thirds of the Senate approve treaties makes the President vulnerable to concessions and reservations and puts him to the difficult test of winning support from the opposition party. Significantly, it was at the request of the Senate Republican leader, Everett Dirksen, that President Kennedy sent a letter to the Senate, when the test ban treaty was in its hands, giving a series of "assurances" to win over uncertain votes.

That the Presidency, for all the chains it wears, has served us well is not in question. It has waged and won wars, checked depressions, spread social justice and spurred the nation's growth. But the great crises in the nation's past have tended to come singly and intermittently, and fortunately have been of limited duration.

Our future promises to be quite another matter. It does not require a crystal ball to see that the United States will be engrossed over the next several decades in a simultaneous confrontation of at least three kinds of revolutions: the human rights revolution, the automation revolution, and the weapons revolution. None will be short-term. All are enduring phenomena, capable of spawning innumerable subrevolutions; all are apt to be sources of pervasive change for the world, the nation and the lives of each of us.

The human rights revolution is only beginning. President Johnson's announced dedication to equal opportunity for all Americans, regardless of race, will require deep transformations of long prevailing realities in fields such as employment, health, education, housing, and recreation. Merely one clue to the magnitude of this task is the fact that nearly 45 per cent of the nation's Negro citizens live in poverty—that is, they have yearly incomes of under $2,000.

We must be prepared to face the possibility that the automation revolution, whose marvels are already well apparent, may, as it gains momentum, increase unemployment to such a degree that the traditional link between jobs and income will be broken. The electronic computer and the automated, self-regulating machine may largely invalidate the general mechanism that undergirds our rights as consumers. Social attitudes toward work and leisure and the basis of individual compensation will need to undergo fundamental revisions.

No less initiative will be required in foreign affairs to make reason prevail over the horrendous alternative of nuclear war. The severity of the problem is already emerging in clear outline with Secretary of Defense McNamara's prediction of a steadily increasing spread of nuclear weapons capability among the nations in coming decades. The clear likelihood is that the adequacy of alliances and the United Nations, and the utility of national sovereignty in such a world, will be brought into serious question.

In the face of these and other possible revolutions, the task of future American leadership is clear. Peoples must be aroused, Congress moved, the bureaucracy stirred and alliances redirected. Only the President can do it.

To enable the Presidency to stay with the race, and to provide the nation, the world and mankind creative and forceful responses for the towering problems of the nineteen-sixties and beyond, several things might well be done to strengthen the office.

1. The present uneven terms of the President, Senate, and House might be replaced by the simultaneous election of all three for an identical term of four years. Past elections suggest that an election so conducted might produce a President and two houses of Congress in better harmony on party and policy outlook than the present fragmented elections permit.

2. The President should be given the item veto for appropriation bills. The item veto would equip him with powerful new bargaining strength which he could employ widely to advance his policies on Capitol Hill. He could conceivably engage in a kind of "log-rolling," exchanging his acceptance of appropriation items for support of his own measures by legislators individually and in blocs. The item veto might give the President a truly commanding influence in legislative affairs.

3. The seniority principle of choosing committee chairmen, which almost assures that a preponderance of those eminences will oppose much of the President's program, urgently needs to be modified. Chairmen might well be chosen by secret ballot of a majority of the entire committee at the beginning of each new Congress. The Speaker might have restored his former power to appoint the chairman and members of the House Rules Committee. A time limit might be placed on the number of weeks or months committees might consider and "bottle up" bills.

4. If the treaty power were revised to require the approval of only a majority of Senators present, rather than two-thirds, the President would be less vulnerable to pressures for concessions and reservations in the treaty's development and approval.

5. The Twenty-second, or two-term, Amendment should be repealed.

6. More frequent national party conventions, a national party council or cabinet, the stimulation of regional rather than local organizations, steps toward greater national party financing, all would capitalize on several trends afoot toward stronger national party organizations.

7. Future Presidents might continue what Kennedy began in subordinating party and congressional politics to urban politics. Kennedy pitched his policies, such as civil rights, education, housing, and the like, to urban, racial, national, and economic groups. Thereupon he could confidently cultivate state and local party leaders who determine the selection of and the support given to congressional candidates. Local leaders, whose business it is to win elections, presumably would choose congressional candidates responsive to the policy needs of urban groups. Kennedy, had he lived to follow his formula through, doubtless would have lighted bonfires under con-

gressmen and Senators, finding his fuel in the urban groups and local party chieftains.

These proposals will require constitutional amendments, creative presidential maneuver and serious congressional reform and party reorganization, all of which admittedly is a very large order. We can console ourselves that other American generations have mastered great problems with bold measures; and we can take a long stride forward and ease the remainder of our task if we disabuse ourselves of the notion that the President has too much power.

☆

ARTHUR M. SCHLESINGER, JR.: *Strengthening and Restraining the President*

The Presidency of Lyndon B. Johnson had its impact, of course, on the nation and on the world. It has also had a marked impact on thinking about the American Presidency itself. For it compelled American historians and political scientists to begin to question their traditional and rather uncritical acceptance of the virtues of a strong Presidency. After all, so far as the theory of presidential power is concerned, Lyndon Johnson's leadership in connection with the war in Vietnam was an exemplary case of presidential activism. It represented a splendid rejection of the theory that the Presidency was an office of limited and enumerated powers—the Whig theory of the Presidency or, as Theodore Roosevelt liked to call it, the Buchanan-Taft theory. It represented a bold use of the spacious powers that strong Presidents such as TR, Woodrow Wilson, and Franklin Roosevelt had perceived in the Presidency and added to it.

Yet, many historians and political scientists—this writer included —who had previously been what Professor Edward S. Corwin had presciently termed in 1951 "high-flying prerogative men," found themselves deeply troubled fifteen years later by the way in which President Johnson was applying the thesis of a strong Presidency to Vietnam. Invoking honored doctrine, he sent half a million American fighting men halfway around the world to enter a war that seemed to bear no overpowering relation to the vital interests of the

Arthur M. Schlesinger, Jr. is Regents Professor of the Humanities at the City University of New York. The selection is from "The Limits and Excesses of Presidential Power" in *Saturday Review*, May 3, 1969. © 1969 Arthur M. Schlesinger, Jr. Reprinted by permission of the publisher and the author.

United States. Moreover, he did so without giving either Congress or the electorate any clear sense that they had been consulted about the decisions which had deepened the commitment and escalated the war. (To do President Johnson justice, probably a majority of both were in favor of escalation until 1968. To do Congress and the electorate justice, they might not have been had they received an accurate picture of what was going on in Vietnam.)

Moreover, the executive appeared to be swallowing up vital powers of decision as a matter not only of practice but of principle. When a former Attorney General, later an Under Secretary of State, told the Senate Foreign Relations Committee that the declaration of war, expressly reserved in the Constitution for Congress, had become "outmoded in the international arena," and that the SEATO agreement and the Gulf of Tonkin resolution were together the "functional equivalent" of a declaration of war, the Committee formally concluded that "the intent of the framers of the Constitution with respect to the exercise of the war power has been virtually nullified." President Johnson himself carried the supposed usurpation even further when he said at Omaha on June 30, 1966, "There are many, many who can recommend, advise, and sometimes a few of them consent. But there is only one that has been chosen by the American people to decide." Everett M. Dirksen added a senatorial —and Republican—blessing: "It is a rather interesting thing," he told the Senate on October 3, 1967, "I have run down many legal cases before the Supreme Court, [and] I have found as yet no delimitation on the powers of the Commander-in-Chief under the Constitution."

The Vietnam experience thus provided an unexpected demonstration that a strong Presidency might have its drawbacks. It consequently forced scholars to face a disturbing question: Had they promoted the cult of the strong Presidency simply because, up to 1965, strong Presidents had mostly been doing things which historians and political scientists had mostly wanted done? The spectacle of a strong President doing things they mostly did not want done suddenly stimulated many of us to take a fresh look at the old problem of presidential power.

Then Senator Eugene McCarthy in the 1968 campaign gave powerful expression to this rising doubt about the virtues of a strong Presidency. "The New Politics," he said, "requires a different conception of the Presidency." He declared his opposition to "the sort of presidential power which extends itself in a personal way into every institution of government." He asked: "Has the integrity of Congress, of the Cabinet, and of the military been impinged upon by undue extension of the executive power?" The powers of the Presidency, he argued, should be decentralized. As against the idea of a strong Presidency on the Jackson-FDR model, Senator McCarthy offered instead a revival of the Whig theory of a passive Presidency, though he proposed to adapt this theory to progressive purposes. "This is a good country," he once said, "if the President will just let it be." The next President, he said, "should understand that this country does not so much need leadership. . . . He must be prepared to be a kind of channel." The President's duty is to "liberate individuals so that they may determine their own lives." In a variety of ways McCarthy made clear his fear of strong presidential leadership and his faith in greater independence among the units of the national government and greater initiative in the localities. He was the first liberal this century to run *against* the Presidency.

This was one of his major differences with Robert F. Kennedy. Kennedy retained the more traditional liberal belief in a strong Presidency. He saw affirmative presidential leadership as an indispensable means of welding disparate groups together into a common cause. He knew that Franklin Roosevelt, for example, had forged his coalition and held it together through precisely the sort of presidential leadership McCarthy condemned. Roosevelt had been able to persuade the working classes of the Thirties to go along with him on issues outside their daily concern—such as foreign policy, civil liberties, and equal rights—not because they had more enlightened views on such issues than their counterparts have today, but because they had a confidence in Roosevelt founded in his leadership on the issues that *were* part of their daily concern and because, for this and other reasons, they trusted and loved him. I think that Kennedy supposed that today's white, low-income groups were similarly composed of decent, if confused, people, and that they could be similarly reclaimed for political rationality.

Kennedy saw a strong Presidency as essential not just to unite the country but to enable the country to meet its problems. Certainly President Johnson had abused his power in foreign affairs. But a general cutback in presidential power, Kennedy feared, would only increase the nation's impotence in the face of deep and angry national division. He believed that as a country we were heading into perilous times, that the ties which had precariously bound Americans together were under almost intolerable strain, and that reducing presidential authority could be a disastrous error when only a strong President could rally us to meet our most difficult and urgent internal issue: racial justice. The President, in Kennedy's view, had to be the active protector of the alienated groups, the tribune of the disinherited and the dispossessed; he had to be the active champion both of racial justice and of civil peace (and he could only be the second if he had demonstrated that he was the first); and, if any President renounced these obligations, the country might well break up.)

McCarthy and Kennedy thus might agree that the Vietnam war revealed a dangerous concentration of power over war and peace in the hands of the man in the White House. But they disagreed in the conclusions they drew from this situation. McCarthy concluded that the situation demanded a general limitation of the Presidency, with all functions questioned and all powers reduced. Kennedy advocated a selective approach to the question of presidential power. He feared that if the American people recoiled indiscriminately against abuses of presidential authority in foreign affairs, they ran the risk of inviting a new period of weak Presidents—as in the dreary years from Taylor through Buchanan—at a time when only a strong President could serve as the center of action and purpose to hold the country together.

The problem of the future of the Presidency therefore resolves itself, in one of its aspects, into the question whether, if presidential power is excessive, it is unitary and must be diminished across the board, or whether presidential powers are separable—whether the President has too much power in foreign policy but conceivably not enough in domestic policy.

The argument is persuasive, it seems to me, that the problem of the American Presidency in domestic affairs is not that he has too much power but that he has too little. He does not have in internal matters, for example, the same constitutional authority he has in foreign policy. The Supreme Court in the Curtiss-Wright case spoke of "the very delicate, plenary, and exclusive power of the President as the sole organ of the federal government in the field of international relations," adding that this power is "in origin and essential character different from that over internal affairs." Nor can a President in domestic affairs so easily shield and enhance his authority by wrapping the flag around himself, invoking patriotism, and national unity, and claiming life-and-death crisis.

He is therefore much more at the mercy of Congress. From 1938 to 1968 a series of strong Democratic Presidents sought congressional approval for social programs which, had they been enacted, might have greatly alleviated some of the tensions presently convulsing our national community. But in these thirty years a coalition, predominantly rural, of Republicans and Southern Democrats in the House of Representatives blocked or whittled down most of the presidential proposals—except for a period of two years, 1965–67, when, as a result of the Goldwater fiasco, enough Northern Democrats were elected to create a short-lived but effective liberal majority in the House. Where a parliamentary Prime Minister can be reasonably sure that anything he suggests will become law in short order, the President of the United States cannot even be sure that *his* proposals will get to the floor of Congress for debate and vote. And no executive in any other democratic state has so little control over national economic policy as the American President.

In recent years, a second factor has arisen to limit presidential power: the growth of the executive bureaucracy. The expansion of governmental functions under the New Deal produced the modern bureaucracy—a development which the conservatives of the time, with their customary wisdom, regarded with consternation. The New Deal bureaucrats, in the demonology of the right, were the forerunners of radical revolution. Of course, as any sensible person should have expected, the government bureaucracy has turned out to be a conservatizing rather than a liberalizing force, at least against innovating Presidents. Its basic loyalty is to the established way of doing things, and, with age and size, it has acquired an independence which enables it to ignore or circumvent presidential initiative.

The rise of the modern bureaucracy has divided the executive branch between the presidential government and the permanent government. In this complex relationship, the presidential government has preferences and policies backed by a presumed mandate from the electorate. But the permanent government has preferences and policies of its own. It has vested interests of its own in programs; it has alliances of its own with congressional committees, lobbies, and the press; it has its own particular, and not seldom powerful, constituencies. Also, it is around longer. We now have, in consequence, four branches of government. An activist President may have quite as much trouble with the federal bureaucracy as with the legislative or judicial branches.

A third limitation on the Presidency in domestic affairs is the fact that nearly every President, who has enlarged the power of the White House, has provoked a reaction toward a more restricted idea of the Presidency, even if the reaction never quite cuts presidential power back to its earlier level. Thus Jackson and Polk were followed by a parade of weak Presidents. When Lincoln expanded presidential power, Congress took out its frustrations by impeaching his successor and establishing a generation of congressional government. Theodore Roosevelt begot Taft; Wilson begot Harding; Franklin Roosevelt and Truman begot Eisenhower. FDR, in addition, was posthumously punished by the Twenty-second Amendment for the offense of having been elected President four times.

All these considerations make the President notably weaker in dealing with internal than with international problems. If this is so, the next question is whether it is possible to think up devices that would strengthen his hand in domestic matters and restrain his hand in foreign matters.

A number of such devices have been proposed. There would seem no convincing reason why, for example, the President and the congressional leadership should not agree that all significant presidential proposals would go to the floor for debate and vote. This would not be a guarantee of enactment, but it would be a guarantee that proposals deemed vital to the nation by the President could no longer be filed away in committee and denied consideration by the whole. Such an arrangement, incidentally, would spare the Senate the perennial row over Rule XXII [cloture]. Similarly, there would seem to be no convincing reason why the President should not have the right of item veto; even the Confederate Constitution gave Jefferson Davis authority to "approve any appropriation and disapprove any other appropriation in the same bill." There would seem to be no reason why the President should not have the authority to adjust tax rates within a specified range in order to deal with economic fluctuations, or that he should not have greater discretion in reorganizing the executive branch or in moving funds from one program to another.

Congress resists such proposals out of conditioned institutional reflexes. It has the visceral fear that structural reform will transfer further power to the executive. Yet, the era of what Wilson called "congressional government" did not fade away at the end of the nineteenth century because of structural reform. It faded away for the simple reason that through so much of the twentieth century, Presidents have seemed right and Congress wrong on issues. The people, anxious to have necessary things done, welcomed Presidents who saw the necessity of doing these things—even if the Roosevelts and Wilson thereby increased the power of the Presidency at the expense of the power of Congress. So long as Congress falls behind Presidents in the perception of the needs of the nation, so long it may expect to lose ground in the war of attrition. And the only way that Congress will reclaim lost powers is by being right on issues when the executive is wrong—as the Senate Foreign Relations Committee proved in the case of Vietnam.

The best hope for Congress lies, not in withholding from the President powers which would benefit the nation, but in modernizing itself and thereby enabling it to compete with the Presidency on judgments of policy. The place to begin, of course, would be the seniority system. Contrary to congressional impression, this system was not handed down at Mount Sinai. Many state legislatures get along very well indeed without it. Its effect in Washington is to give disproportionate influence to men born in another century and shaped by small town or rural experience—hardly men qualified to deal with the problems of young people or of black people in an urban and industrial society.

Structural revisions of this sort would help both the President and the Congress to deal more intelligently with the accumulating troubles of our national community. Are there countervailing structural revisions on the international side which would prevent the President from running away with all initiative and decision in the conduct of foreign policy? This is the area which creates the real problem of presidential power. For, as Richard Neustadt has pointed out, acts in domestic policy are generally reversible; they are subject to revision and recall through democratic processes. But acts in foreign policy are often irreversible. President Kennedy used to say that domestic policy can only defeat us; foreign policy can kill us. Moreover, the nuclear age makes this quality of irreversibility more fateful than ever before. And foreign policy decisions very often are made in emergency contexts, real, imagined, or contrived, and this fact encourages the flow of power to the White House. Is it possible through structural reform to secure for Congress, and the people, an authoritative and continuing voice in the basic decisions of war and peace?

The Senate Foreign Relations Committee thought hard about this question and came up, in 1967, with Senate Resolution 187. This resolution declared it as "the sense of the Senate" that American armed forces could not be committed to hostilities on foreign territory for any purpose other than to repel an attack on the United States or to protect American citizens or property without "affirmative action by Congress specifically intended to give rise to such commitment." This or comparable resolutions must surely pass two tests: They must offer a plausible hope that (1) they will not tie the hands of the executive in a case of genuine national emergency; and (2) they will effectively prevent a step-by-step movement from marginal to major involvement.

These questions must be considered in specific situations; the answer one fears, is that SR 187 would probably have prevented President Roosevelt from taking his actions in 1941 in defense of American security, but that it would not have prevented President Johnson from pursuing his course of gradual military escalation in Vietnam. The reason for this is that Roosevelt would have found it difficult to put together a congressional majority for his North Atlantic policy, while, as the Gulf of Tonkin example showed, Johnson would have encountered little difficulty in getting congressional endorsement for his Vietnam policy before 1968.

This year, the Committee came up with a broader resolution declaring it the sense of the Senate that "a national commitment by the United States to a foreign power necessarily and exclusively results from affirmative action taken by the executive and legislative branches of the United States Government through means of a treaty, convention, or other legislative instrumentality specifically designed to give effect to such a commitment." On the face of it, this resolution would outlaw executive agreements. The executive agreement, of course, has been an indispensable device of foreign policy since at least the Rush-Bagot agreement of 1817 limiting naval forces on the Great Lakes; the Supreme Court, in decision after decision, has endowed the executive agreement with the same legal force as a treaty. If the principle behind the resolution had prevailed in 1940, Franklin Roosevelt could not have transferred the over-age destroyers to Great Britain without seeking congressional approval. He most probably could not have obtained that approval; in any case, the debate would have been angry and protracted, leading to a filibuster as bitter as the one by which the "little group of willful men" blocked Wilson's policy of arming merchant vessels in 1917, and the subsequent history of the world might have been very different.

These examples suggest, I believe, the futility of trying to solve substantive problems by structural means. The probable result of efforts to limit presidential power through institutional contrivance would be to introduce dangerous rigidities into our system of national decision which would stop Presidents from doing good as well as from doing harm, and which would ultimately cause more trouble than benefit.

The solution to the problem of excessive presidential power in foreign affairs lies, I would conclude, in the political and educational realm. The fundamental strength of the Congress in this area springs from its capacity to raise issues and thereby to shape national opinion —a proposition demonstrated in the revolt against the Vietnam policy in 1967–68. Next to the events in Vietnam themselves, the interpretation of these events provided by the dissident Senators under the leadership of Senator Fulbright and the Foreign Relations Committee and transmitted to the electorate was probably the major factor in turning the balance of opinion against the escalation policy.

In particular, Congress is well placed to assail the myth with which every foreign office seeks to silence critics: that only those who see the top secret cables know enough to make intelligent judgments on questions of foreign policy. As one who has had the opportunity to read such cables at various times in my life, I can testify that 95 per cent of the information essential for intelligent judgment is available to any careful reader of *The New York Times*. Indeed, the

American government would have had a much wiser Vietnam policy
had it relied more on the *Times*; the estimate of the situation supplied by newspapermen was consistently more accurate than that
supplied by the succession of ambassadors and generals in their coded
dispatches. Secrecy in diplomatic communication is mostly required
to protect negotiating strategies, techniques of intelligence collection,
details of weaponry, and gossip about personalities. One does not
require full knowledge on such points to assess a political situation.
The myth of inside information has always been used to prevent
democratic control of foreign policy; if Congress derides that myth,
it may embolden others to doubt the infallibility of Presidents and
Secretaries of State.

But the responsibility rests even more heavily on the President
than on the Congress. A President must, above all, be a man who
acts not just because he is sure about the wisdom of a course of action, but because he is responsive to the democratic process. It is not
enough for policies to be sound. In all but the most extreme cases,
that soundness must be accompanied by explanation and tested by
acceptance. The President must act on the principle of self-limitation
and live within the discipline of consent. He must understand the
legitimacy of challenges to his own authority and wisdom. He must
cherish an inner skepticism about the anointment of office, and a
constant awareness of what Whitman called "the never-ending
audacity of elected persons." He must be especially skeptical about
the unique value of information that arrives through official channels,
and about self-serving bureaucratic versions of anything. He must be
sensitive to the diversity of concern and conviction in a nation; he
must be sensitive in advance to the verdict of history; he must always
pay "a decent respect to the opinions of mankind."

No structural solutions can guarantee the choice of such Presidents, or can guarantee that, once chosen as open and modest men,
they will remain so amid the intoxications of the office. Yet, surely
the whole point of democracy is that it is not an automatic system.
It involves risks, because risks are the means of growth. Rather than
renounce the idea of an affirmative Presidency or surround the President with hampering restrictions, it would seem better to continue
to regard presidential leadership as the central instrument of American democracy, and to exercise scrupulous care in the choice of Presidents. . . .

☆

SIDNEY WARREN: *The Paradox of*
Presidential Power

For years we have been hearing that the powers of the American
Presidency have been increasing. We have come to look to the
White House for an immediate answer to any major problem that
arises. We have had warnings about the danger of too much centralization of power in the executive branch of government.

Yet it is doubtful whether anywhere in the world today is executive leadership more hemmed in, more effectively limited by
political considerations, more vulnerable to debilitating pressures
from within and without, than in the United States. Pressures from
the opposing party and from within the President's own party; pressures from Congress, with its power to enact or block presidential
programs; pressures from strongly established departments of government, like the Defense Department and the Atomic Energy
Commission; pressures from the press and various agencies of public
opinion—all these make the President's job the most difficult and
complicated balancing act in the world.

That the Founding Fathers intended to make the Presidency
"the vital place of action in the American system," as Woodrow
Wilson expressed it, is apparent from a reading of the Constitution.
In this office they combined the duties of chief executive, Commander in Chief of the armed forces, director of the nation's foreign
relations, and initiator of legislation. John Adams regarded it as of
such eminence that he wrote: "The duration of our President is

Sidney Warren is Professor of Political Science and History at California
Western University. The selection is from "How Powerful Is the Presidency?" in
The Saturday Review, July 21, 1962, pp. 12–15. Copyright © 1962 by Saturday
Review, Inc. Reprinted by permission of the publisher and the author.

neither perpetual nor for life; it is only for four years; but his power during those four years is much greater than that of an avoyer, a consul, a podesta, a doge, a stadholder. I know of no first magistrate in any Republican government, except England and Neuchâtel [a Swiss canton], who possesses a constitutional dignity, authority, and power comparable to his."

While this was an exaggeration of the President's stature at the time, considering the size and influence of the new nation, subsequent national development, the growth of governmental responsibilities, and the influence of the men who have since occupied the office have all enlarged the Presidency to an extent that could not even have been imagined by the makers of the Constitution. To the duties prescribed by the law of the land have been added such roles as party chief, custodian of the economy, and world leader.

At the same time, the world has leaped into an era so complex and in such violent contrast to either the near or distant past that it has become increasingly difficult for the President to stay "on top of events." The fact is that the chief executive of the sixties must lead his nation through global agitations that are beyond his capacity to subdue; he can only try to control them and prevent disastrous eruptions. President Kennedy was not indulging in mere rhetoric when he declared in his inaugural address: "The great work of the nation will not be finished in the first thousand days, nor in the life of this administration, nor even perhaps in our lifetime on this planet."

By contrast, within the nineteenth century, the United States was able without too much stress to achieve its national objective of preserving independence, developing its resources, expanding the continental limits, and increasing the nation's influence as a member of the international community. And the means employed was simply disengagement from the politics of European power.

Disengagement did not imply passive withdrawal from the affairs of the world. On the contrary, our Presidents were diligent and active in exploiting any circumstances that would strengthen the nation's security and increase its opportunities to develop. Jefferson's purchase of the Louisiana Territory, Monroe's Doctrine, and Polk's war with Mexico are a few examples. Contributing to the presidential ability to act were our defensive moats, the Atlantic and Pacific oceans; the preoccupation of the European powers with their own involved affairs; and our community of interests with Great Britain.

Even in our own century, as recently as the time of Theodore Roosevelt, America was still free to decide its own course. Convinced that national security would be strengthened by an Isthmian canal, Roosevelt assisted willing Panamanians to foment a revolution, thus making construction of the canal possible. Or he brandished his big stick at designing creditor nations across the Atlantic who desired to penetrate the Caribbean area, and the warning sufficed. By presidential fiat we assumed the role of policeman of the Caribbean, allocating to ourselves the right to intervene when our interests seemed to require protection.

The Cuban fiasco of 1961 offers an illustration of how infinitely more complicated was the situation which confronted President Kennedy. Communist penetration into Latin America made some response by the United States appear to be necessary and desirable. Yet the President had to consider the American-Soviet power relationship, the impact of Cuba's social revolution upon the peoples of Central and South America, and the views and reactions of the other sovereign members of the Organization of American States.

Compounding the dilemma of statesmanship was the competing and contradictory advice offered the President. One group advocated an all-out invasion backed by American military forces; the other urged no action at all. The former course, even if successful, would have won us the battle but might have lost us the war; the latter had its own risks. As it turned out, the President's solution, a middle course, proved to be the most futile of all. But, considering the possibly unhappy consequences of any action, how much power did the President have to control the situation?

Traditionally, the United States has pursued an independent course in dealing with international problems, preferring unilateralism to collaboration, freedom of action to binding commitments. The requirements of America's new leadership in world affairs, however, have necessitated a growing emphasis upon cooperation and coalition. Franklin D. Roosevelt learned how difficult it was to lead an alliance of nations even when engaged in a common military cause. His successors have discovered that in peacetime, although exercising a commanding influence over an international community, they have been subject to still greater restrictions.

At home the President has always been responsible to several constituencies: the government bureaucracy, the party, the national electorate. He has always had to balance the national interest or welfare against sectional and local interests of one kind or another. Now vast international constituencies with competing and conflicting needs have been made part of the equation.

The series of military alliances with which the United States is linked, the re-emergence of Western Europe as a vital political and economic force, the commitment of the Afro-Asian nations to a policy of nonalignment, the independent position of the Latin American republics—each factor in its own way circumscribes the Presi-

dent's authority. He is frequently impelled to consult with one or
more nations before deciding on some issues, and yet must sometimes refrain from acting after consulting; with other nations he
must collaborate even more completely.

These new constituencies far beyond our borders are influential
determinants of America's power status; and since American leadership depends upon the support that its friends are willing to give
and the respect that its enemies are compelled to acknowledge, the
President's range of free choice is narrowed. He must compromise
in view of the opposing positions among friends or the intentions
or actions of rivals.

Finally, there is the United Nations: the world's security structure, its forum, the bar of world public opinion. A President who
exercises sound and wise leadership can utilize it as an instrument
for reaching and influencing peoples all over the world. The representation which he or his ambassador makes to this body has a
direct effect on the prestige of the nation abroad. Today, when
popular reactions are a significant element in international power,
when the result of the rivalry between Communist and democratic
ideologies for the allegiances of the underdeveloped nations may be
crucial, the American image is of cardinal importance.

The obligations undertaken by the United States in subscribing
to the United Nations charter require not only joint undertakings
with other member states in a variety of political and humanitarian
endeavors, but also bind us to the decisions that are made. To win
support from the many constituent members in a particular situation involves us in a continual process of negotiation and accommodation. In other words, the kind of unilateral action President
Polk could take in 1846, in sending troops to occupy Mexican territory during a dispute with that country, or William McKinley
half a century later, in taking the country into war with Spain, is
no longer possible.

Today the President possesses terrifying military power—the right
to order the use of the nuclear bomb. Ironically, however, the existence of the ultimate weapon limits his power to well under that
of his prenuclear-age predecessors. For the first time in history the
President of the United States must consider the safety not only of
his nation but of the entire world. The nature of military technology and the entangled web of international life have drastically altered his perspective. There are no longer any simple panaceas, nor
can there be any easy or decisive victories as were possible in the
past.

When in 1917 "a little group of wilful men" in the United States
Senate filibustered to death a White House proposal to arm mer-

chant vessels, Wilson went ahead and had them armed by executive order. And though he agonized over the possibility of war with Germany, he risked involvement because he was determined to resist the assault on the nation's neutral rights. Franklin D. Roosevelt's conviction that the survival of Great Britain was essential to American security led him to assist her even to the point of war. By executive agreement he effected an exchange of destroyers for British bases and obtained from Congress wide latitude under the terms of the Lend-Lease Act.

Today President Kennedy, in attempting to strengthen the nation's security and its diplomatic position, cannot readily consider force to promote these interests. As an illustration, the direct physical confrontation between Americans and Russians in Berlin prevents the President from risking military action. He can only continue to negotiate.

That the President cannot absolutely control the Berlin situation or other international events is frustrating to the American people, whose history has taught them to regard their nation as invincible. Their inability to accept fully the fact that we live in a revolutionary age of continuing crises and that the times demand a revamping of traditional views cannot help but hamper the President's leadership. To jolt the people out of their conventional views, to make them aware of what Walter Lippmann calls "the intangible realities of international power" is far more onerous than it was for any previous President.

After he had left office Theodore Roosevelt once remarked: "People always used to say of me that I was an astonishingly good politician and divined what the people were going to think. This really was not an accurate way of stating the case. I did not 'divine' how the people were going to think; I simply made up my mind what they ought to think, and then did my best to get them to think it." The issues of his time, however, were immediate, readily comprehensible, and within a familiar frame of reference.

President Kennedy must create an awareness of the new and bewildering fact that the dichotomy between foreign and domestic policy has been all but obliterated in the postwar world. In the past, the nature of our economy was considered to be purely an internal affair, but now our economic health has direct repercussions on our ability to maintain leadership in a world where the race goes to the strongest. Full employment, gross national product, and our international trade balance directly affect our position in the world arena.

Education, which at one time was entirely a matter of local concern, is now very much the President's affair. The present competition with the Soviet Union requires an acceleration in quality and quantity of professional and technical personnel, of higher educational standards for the training of intellectual leaders.

Civil rights for our minorities have similarly become involved with our world position, and here we are perhaps most vulnerable. In the past, the wide gulf between the profession of equal rights and the performance, especially as regards the Negro citizen, may have deeply troubled thoughtful Americans and embarrassed them when they were abroad, but it did not impinge on foreign policy. Today, this internal matter is a crucial factor in our relationship with the millions of Afro-Asians whose friendship and support we must have.

The President's maneuverability is also circumscribed by the ideological conflict. The cold war has created issues that involve passionately held doctrinal convictions, and years of suspended peace have exacted a toll. Irrationalities born of fear and frustration have infected segments of the population. Individuals and groups have resorted to the shorthand of slogans and shibboleths—"soft on communism," "better dead than red," "appeasement"—as a substitute for sober discussion and calm analysis. To a considerable extent rigid views and inflexible positions have stifled free inquiry into alternative solutions to certain international problems. Assuming, for instance, that a fundamental change in our China policy would be advantageous to the national interest at this point, could President Kennedy feel politically free to advocate it? Would he not be pilloried by members of both parties in Congress, to say nothing of a large section of the population, and risk the loss of his political leadership if he did so?

To guide public opinion in our time requires the gift of a Pericles, of whom Thucydides said: "Certainly when he saw that they were going too far in a mood of overconfidence, he would bring back to them a sense of their dangers; and when they were discouraged for no good reason, he would restore their confidence." The irony of the President's situation is that while he has instruments of mass communication at his disposal that early leaders would have envied, the task of persuading the people is far greater than it was in their time.

If we live in an age of ideologies, we also live in an age dominated by science. The new military and space technology have made the government heavily dependent on the scientific experts. President Eisenhower formally acknowledged this development when he appointed a scientific adviser to the chief executive. Many of the problems which are within the purview of governmental responsibility are so technical in nature that the layman, even the layman

occupying the high office of the Presidency, must bow to the judgment of the professionals.

In this sense he is far less autonomous in arriving at a policy
than his pre-World War II predecessors, while at the same time his
power is unprecedented. The President of today cannot escape reliance upon experts, yet he alone remains solely responsible for the
great decisions of national destiny.

Since World War II the decision-making process has been further
complicated by the vast institutional apparatus which was created
by Congress to assist the President in discharging his duties. Even
before the many agencies, commissions, and councils began to pro-
liferate in Washington, Harold Laski, a careful observer of the
American Presidency, commented on the problems arising out of
the inevitable expansion of the office.

One of the fundamental qualities a President should possess,
Laski stated, is the ability to coordinate. He must also be able to
delegate and put his trust in those whom he has appointed, since,
for the most part, he can be concerned only with outlines. "The
details of the picture must be filled in by subordinates." Professor
Laski continued:

> Here certainly an art is required which must operate upon a
> scale quite different from any with which a Prime Minister is
> concerned. For the dignity of cabinet colleagues and the relative
> certainty with which he can control the House of Commons
> means that he is free, once policy in the large is settled, to leave
> its implementation alone. But a President may lose a bill in Con-
> gress if his subordinates proceed untactfully. . . . Every dele-
> gation of power is therefore a risk to be taken, and this makes
> his judgment of men a matter of supreme importance. He must
> know that the men he uses will see things through his eyes. . . .
> He must delegate, too, knowing that at best he is bound to make
> mistakes, both in men and in things. This is, above all, the
> case in matters of foreign policy.

The problem of coordination is indeed prodigious, and the
President can never be certain that the policies which he has initiated will be implemented in a way that will insure their success.

The significant place occupied today by such groups as the Joint
Chiefs of Staff, the Council of Economic Advisors, the Atomic
Energy Commission, the Central Intelligence Agency, the National
Security Council, etc., does not detract from the President's pre-
eminent position, but it places a premium upon his ability to work
out flexible formulas and to remain in control of the situation. Each

President uses the approach he considers most suitable to his own ideas of leadership. Kennedy, for example, prefers to place less formal reliance on the National Security Council than did Eisenhower. Nevertheless, the massive institution of which the President is the center will continue to restrict even as it assists.

The nation has traveled a longer distance than that represented by actual time from the point when Theodore Roosevelt kept his State Department in complete ignorance for several weeks of the delicate negotiations he was carrying on with Japan and Russia. Or when Woodrow Wilson composed on his own typewriter diplomatic protests to the German government which were of the greatest significance to both nations.

We return, then, to the paradox of presidential power. The Constitution and the force of custom have made the chief executive the most powerful figure on the domestic scene; the status of the nation has made him the most influential man in the world. But the circumstances of our age have subjected his leadership both domestically and internationally to many limitations. While he remains the pivotal figure in the affairs of mankind, he is circumscribed by the nature of the nuclear age in ways that were unknown to Presidents of simpler eras who had less power.

The American people have a right to expect leadership from the White House, leadership that is wise, imaginative, humanitarian, courageous. They can hope for a President with the capacity to perceive the direction of our time and to move the nation in that direction. But they cannot expect the Presidents of our day to surmount what has become insurmountable.

SELECTED BIBLIOGRAPHY

Abel, Elie, *The Missile Crisis* (New York: Bantam Books, 1968).

Adams, Sherman, *First-Hand Report: The Story of the Eisenhower Administration* (New York: Harper, 1961).

Allen, Roger S. and William V. Shannon, *The Truman Merry-Go-Round* (New York: Vanguard, 1950).

"The American Presidency in the Last Half Century," *Current History*, Vol. XXXIX (October 1960).

Anderson, Patrick, *The President's Men* (Garden City, N.Y.: Doubleday, 1968).

Austin, Anthony, *The President's War: The Story of the Tonkin Gulf Resolution and How The Nation Was Trapped In Vietnam* (Philadelphia, Pa.: Lippincott, 1971).

Bailey, Thomas A., *Presidential Greatness: The Image and the Man from George Washington to the Present* (New York: Appleton-Century-Crofts, 1972).

Barber, James D., *The Presidential Character: Predicting Performance in the White House* (Englewood Cliffs, N.J.: Prentice-Hall, 1972).

Bayh, Birch, *One Heartbeat Away: Presidential Disability* (New York: Bobbs-Merrill Company, Inc., 1968).

Bell, Jack, *Presidency: Office of Power* (Rockleigh, New Jersey: Allyn and Bacon, 1967).

Berdahl, Clarence, *The War Powers of the Executive in the United States* (Urbana: University of Illinois Press, 1921).

Binkley, Wilfred E., *The Man in the White House* (Baltimore: Johns Hopkins Press, 1959).

———, *The Man in the White House: His Powers and Duties* (Baltimore: Johns Hopkins, 1970).

———, *The Powers of the President* (Garden City, N.Y.: Doubleday, Doran, 1937).

———, *The President and Congress* (New York: Knopf, 1947).

Blum, John M., *The Republican Roosevelt* (Cambridge: Harvard University Press, 1961).

Borden, Morton, ed., *America's Ten Greatest Presidents* (Chicago: Rand McNally, 1961).

Brant, Irving, *James Madison*, 6 vols. (Indianapolis: Bobbs-Merrill, 1941–61).

Brogan, Denis, *Politics in America* (Garden City, N.Y.: Doubleday, 1960).

Brown, Stuart G., *The American Presidency: Leadership, Partisanship, and Popularity* (New York: Macmillan, 1966).

Brown, Stuart, *The Presidency On Trial: Robert Kennedy's 1968 Campaign And Afterwards* (Honolulu, Hawaii: University Press of Hawaii, 1971).

Brownlow, Louis, *The President and the Presidency* (Chicago: Public Administration Service, 1949).

Burns, James MacGregor, *The Deadlock of Democracy* (Englewood Cliffs, N.J.: Prentice-Hall, 1963).

———, *John Kennedy: A Political Profile* (New York: Harcourt, 1959).

———, *Presidential Government* (Boston: Houghton Mifflin, 1966).

———, *Roosevelt: The Lion and the Fox* (New York: Harcourt, 1956).

Chamberlain, Lawrence H., *The President, Congress, and Legislation* (New York: Columbia University Press, 1946).

Chester, Lewis et al., *American Melodrama: The Presidential Campaign of 1968* (New York: Viking, 1969).

Childs, Marquis, *Eisenhower: Captive Hero* (New York: Harcourt, 1958).

Christian, George, *The President Steps Down* (New York: Macmillan Company, 1970).

Clark, Keith and Laurence Legere, *The President and the Management of National Security* (New York: Praeger, 1969).

Cleveland, Grover, *Presidential Problems* (New York: Century Co., 1904).

Cornwell, Elmer E., Jr., *Presidential Leadership of Public Opinion* (Bloomington: Indiana University Press, 1965).

Corwin, Edward S., *The President: Office and Powers*, 4th rev. ed. (New York: New York University Press, 1957).

———, *The President's Control of Foreign Relations* (Princeton: Princeton University Press, 1917).

———, *Total War and the Constitution* (New York: Knopf, 1947).

———, and Louis W. Koenig, *The Presidency Today* (New York: New York University Press, 1957).

Cotter, Cornelius P. and J. Malcolm Smith, *Powers of the President During National Crises* (Washington, D.C.: Public Affairs Press, 1959).

Cronin, Thomas E. and Sanford D. Greenberg, eds., *The Presidential Advisory System* (New York: Harper and Row, 1969).

Coyle, David C., *Ordeal of the Presidency* (Washington: Public Affairs Press, 1960).

Daniels, Jonathan, *The Man of Independence* (Philadelphia: Lippincott, 1950).

David, Paul T. ed., *The Presidential Election and Transition 1960–1961* (Washington, D.C.: The Brookings Institution, 1961).

Davie, Michael, *LBJ: A Foreign Observer's Viewpoint* (New York: Duell, Sloan & Pearce, 1966).

Destler, I.M., *Presidents, Bureaucrats, and Foreign Policy: The Politics of Organization Reform* (Princeton, N.J.: Princeton University Press, 1972).

DeToledano, Ralph, *One Man Alone: Richard M. Nixon* (New York: Funk and Wagnalls, 1969).

Donald, David, *Lincoln Reconsidered* (New York: Knopf, 1956).

Donovan, Robert J., *Eisenhower: The Inside Story* (New York: Harper, 1956).

Dorman, Michael, *The Second Man: The Changing Role of the Vice President* (New York: Dell, 1970).

Eisenhower, Dwight D., *Mandate for Change* (Garden City, N.Y.: Doubleday, 1963).

———, *Waging Peace* (Garden City, N.Y.: Doubleday, 1965).

Evans, Rowland and Robert Novak, *Lyndon B. Johnson: The Exercise of Power* (New York: New American Library, 1968).

———, *Nixon in the White House: The Frustration of Power* (New York: Random House, 1972).

Fenno, Richard F., *The President's Cabinet* (Cambridge: Harvard University Press, 1959).

Finer, Herman, *The Presidency: Crisis and Regeneration* (Chicago: University of Chicago Press, 1959).

Fisher, L., *President and Congress* (Riverside, N.J.: Free Press, 1972).

Fitzsimons, Louise, *The Kennedy Doctrine* (New York: Random House, 1972).

Freeman, Douglas Southall, *George Washington*, 7 vols. (New York: Scribner's, 1948–1957).

Freidel, Frank, *Franklin D. Roosevelt*, 3 vols. (Boston: Little, Brown, 1952–1956).

Gilbert, Robert E., *Television and Presidential Politics* (North Quincy, Mass.: Christopher Publishing House, 1972).

Goebel, Dorothy B., and Julius Goebel, Jr., *Generals in the White House* (Garden City, N.Y.: Doubleday, Doran, 1945).

Goldman, Eric F., *The Tragedy of Lyndon Johnson* (New York: Alfred A. Knopf, Inc., 1969).

Graber, Doris A., *Public Opinion, the President and Foreign Policy: Four Case Studies from the Formative Years* (New York: Holt, Rinehart and Winston, Inc., 1968).

Grundstein, Nathan D., *Presidential Delegation of Authority in Wartime* (Pittsburgh: University of Pittsburgh Press, 1961).

Haight, David E., and Larry D. Johnston, *The President: Roles and Powers* (Chicago: Rand McNally, 1965).

Harbaugh, William Henry, *Power and Responsibility: The Life and Times of Theodore Roosevelt* (New York: Farrar, Straus, 1961).

Hart, James, *The American Presidency in Action* (New York: Macmillan, 1948).

Hassler, W. W., Jr., *The President As Commander in Chief* (Reading, Mass.: Addison-Wesley Publishing Co., 1971).

Heller, Francis, *The Presidency* (New York: Random House, 1960).

Henderson, Charles P., *The Nixon Theology* (New York: Harper & Row, 1972).

Herring, E. Pendleton, *Presidential Leadership* (New York: Farrar, Straus, 1940).

Hirschfield, Robert S., *The Constitution and the Court* (New York: Random House, 1962).

Hobbs, Edward H., *Behind the President* (Washington, D.C.: Public Affairs 1954).

Hofstadter, Richard, *The American Political Tradition* (New York: Knopf, 1948).

Hughes, Emmet John, *The Ordeal of Power* (New York: Atheneum, 1963).

Hyman, Sidney, *The American President* (New York: Harper, 1954).

James, Dorothy B., *The Contemporary Presidency* (New York: Pegasus, 1969).

Johnson, Donald B., and Jack L. Walker, eds., *The Dynamics of the American Presidency* (New York: Wiley, 1964).

Johnson, Lyndon B., *The Vantage Point: Perspectives of the Presidency* (New York: Harper and Row, 1971).

Johnson, Walter, *1600 Pennsylvania Avenue: Presidents and the People, 1929–1959* (Boston: Little, Brown, 1960).

Kallenbach, Joseph E., *American Chief Executive* (New York: Harper and Row, 1966).

Kennedy, John F., *Profiles in Courage* (New York: Harper & Row, 1956).

———, *The Strategy for Peace*, edited by Alan Nevins (New York: Harper and Brothers, 1960).

Keogh, James, *President Nixon and The Press* (New York: Funk and Wagnalls, 1972).

Klein, Philip Shriver, *President James Buchanan* (University Park: Pennsylvania State University Press, 1962).

Koenig, Louis W., *The Chief Executive* (New York: Harcourt, Brace & World, 1964).

———, *The Invisible Presidency* (New York: Holt, 1960).

———, *The Presidency and the Crisis* (New York: King's Crown Press, 1944).

———, *The Truman Administration* (New York: New York University Press, 1956).

Landecker, Manfred, *The President and Public Opinion: Leadership in Foreign Affairs* (Washington, D.C.: Public Affairs Press, 1968).

Larson, Arthur, *Eisenhower: The President Nobody Knew* (New York: Charles Scribner's Sons, 1968).

Laski, Harold J., *The American Presidency* (New York: Harper, 1940).

Lasky, Victor, *JFK: The Man and the Myth* (New York: The Macmillan Co., 1963).

Link, Arthur S., *Wilson*, 4 vols. (Princeton: Princeton University Press, 1956–1964).

Liston, Robert, *Presidential Power: How Much Is Too Much?* (New York: McGraw, Hill, 1971).

Longaker, Richard P., *The Presidency and Individual Liberties* (Ithaca, N.Y.: Cornell University Press, 1961).

Mailer, Norman, *Presidential Papers* (New York: G.P. Putnam's Sons, 1963).

Malone, Dumas, *Jefferson and His Time*, 3 vols. (Boston: Little, Brown, 1948–1962).

Manchester, William, *Portrait of a President: John F. Kennedy in Profile* (Boston: Little, Brown and Company, 1967).

May, Ernest R., *The Ultimate Decision* (New York: Braziller, 1960).

Mazo, Earl and Stephen Hess, *Nixon: A Political Portrait* (New York: Harper and Row, 1968).

McConnell, Grant, *Steel and the Presidency, 1962* (New York: Norton, 1963).

———, *The Modern Presidency* (New York: St. Martin's Press, 1967).

Michener, James, *Presidential Lottery* (New York: Random House, 1969).

Milton, G. R., *The Use of Presidential Power, 1789–1943* (Boston: Little, Brown, 1944).

Moe, Ronald, *Congress and the President: Allies and Adversaries* (Pacific Palisades, California: Goodyear, 1971).

Moley, Raymond, *After Seven Years* (New York: Harper, 1939).

Moos, Malcolm, *Politics, Presidents, and Coattails* (Baltimore: Johns Hopkins Press, 1952).

Morgan, Edward P., et al., *The Presidency and the Press Conference* (Washington, D.C.: American Enterprise, 1971).

Morgan, Ruth, *The President and Civil Rights: Policy-Making by Executive Order* (New York: St. Martin's Press, 1970).

Morris, Richard B., *Great Presidential Decisions* (Philadelphia: Lippincott, 1960).

Nash, Bradley D., *Staffing the Presidency* (Washington: National Planning Association, 1952).

Neustadt, Richard E., *Presidential Power* (New York: Wiley, 1960).

Nevins, Allan, *Grover Cleveland: A Study in Courage* (New York: Dodd, Mead, 1932).

Novak, Robert and Rowland Evans, *Nixon in the White House: A Critical Portrait* (New York: Random House, 1971).

"The Office of the American Presidency," *Annals of the American Academy*, Vol. CCCVII (September 1956).

Patterson, Caleb Perry, *Presidential Government in the United States* (Chapel Hill: University of North Carolina Press, 1947).

Pollard, James E., *The Presidents and the Press* (New York: Macmillan, 1947).

Polsby, Nelson W., *Congress and the Presidency* (Englewood Cliffs, N.J.: Prentice-Hall, 1964).

———, and Aaron B. Wildavsky, *Presidential Elections* (New York: Scribner's, 1964).

———, *Presidential Elections: Strategies of American Electoral Politics* (New York: Scribner, 1968).

Pomper, Gerald, *Nominating the President: The Politics of Convention Choice* (New York: Norton, 1966).

"The Presidency," *American Heritage*, Vol. XV (August 1964).

"The Presidency," *Current History*, Vol. XXV (September 1953).

"The Presidency in Transition," *Journal of Politics*, Vol. XI (February 1949).

"The Presidential Office," *Law and Contemporary Problems*, Vol. XXI (Autumn 1956).

Pringle, Henry F., *The Life and Times of William Howard Taft*, 2 vols. (New York: Farrar, Straus, 1939).

——, *Theodore Roosevelt* (New York: Harcourt, 1931).

Public Papers of the Presidents of the United States (Washington: Government Printing Office).

Pusey, Merlo J., *Eisenhower: The President* (New York: Macmillan, 1956).

Randall, James G., *Constitutional Problems Under Lincoln*, rev. ed. (Urbana: University of Illinois Press, 1964).

——, *Lincoln the President*, 4 vols. (New York: Dodd, Mead, 1945–1955).

Rankin, Robert, *When Civil Law Fails: Martial Law and Its Legal Basis in the United States* (Durham, N.C.: Duke University Press, 1939).

——, and Winfried Dallmayr, *Freedom and Emergency Powers in the Cold War* (New York: Appleton-Century-Crofts, 1964).

Reedy, George E., *The Twilight of the Presidency* (New York: World, 1970).

Richardson, James (compiler), *Messages and Papers of the Presidents* (New York: Bureau of National Literature, 1897).

Rienow, Robert, and Leona Train Rienow, *The Lonely Quest: The Evolution of Presidential Leadership* (Chicago: Follett, 1966).

Roche, John, and Leonard Levy, *The Presidency* (New York: Harcourt, 1964).

Roosevelt, Theodore, *Theodore Roosevelt: An Autobiography* (New York: Scribner's, 1920).

Rosebloom, Eugene H., *A History of Presidential Elections* (New York: Macmillan, 1959).

Rosenman, Samuel I., *Working with Roosevelt* (New York: Harper, 1952).

—— (compiler), *The Public Papers and Addresses of Franklin D. Roosevelt*, 13 vols. (New York: Random House, 1938–1950).

Rossiter, Clinton, *The American Presidency*, rev. ed. (New York: Harvest, 1960).

——, *Constitutional Dictatorship* (Princeton: Princeton University Press, 1948).

——, *The Supreme Court and the Commander-in-Chief* (Ithaca, N.Y.: Cornell University Press, 1951).

Schachner, Nathan, *Thomas Jefferson: A Biography*, 2 vols. (New York: Appleton-Century-Crofts, 1951).

Schlesinger, Arthur M., Jr., *The Age of Jackson* (Boston: Little, Brown, 1945).

——, *The Age of Roosevelt*, 3 vols. (Boston: Houghton Mifflin, 1957–1960).

——, *A Thousand Days: John F. Kennedy in the White House* (Boston: Houghton Mifflin, 1965).

Schubert, Glendon, *The Presidency in the Courts* (Minneapolis: University of Minnesota Press, 1957).

Scigliano, Robert, *The Supreme Court and the Presidency* (New York: The Free Press, 1971).

Sherrill, Robert, *Accidental President* (New York: Grossman Publishers, Inc., 1967).

Sherwood, Robert E., *Roosevelt and Hopkins* (New York: Harper, 1948).

Sidey, Hugh, *John F. Kennedy, President* (New York: Atheneum, 1963).

Silva, Ruth C., *Presidential Succession* (Ann Arbor: University of Michigan Press, 1951).

Small, Norman J., *Some Presidential Interpretations of the Presidency* (Baltimore: Johns Hopkins Press, 1932).

Smith, Malcolm J., and Cornelius Cotter, *Powers of the President During Crises* (Washington: Public Affairs Press, 1960).

Sorensen, Theodore C., *Decision-Making in the White House* (New York: Columbia University Press, 1963).

——, *Kennedy* (New York: Harper, 1965).

Spalding, Henry D., *The Nixon Nobody Knows* (Middle Village, New York: Jonathan David, 1972).

Strum, Philippa, *Presidential Power and American Democracy* (Pacific Palisades, California: Goodyear, 1971).

Sundquist, James L., *Politics and Policy: The Eisenhower, Kennedy, and Johnson Years* (Washington, D.C.: The Brookings Institution, 1968).

Sutherland, Arthur, ed., *Government Under Law* (Cambridge: Harvard University Press, 1956).

Taft, William Howard, *Our Chief Magistrate and His Powers* (New York: Columbia University Press, 1916).

Thach, Charles, *The Creation of the Presidency* (Baltimore: Johns Hopkins Press, 1922).

Thomas, Benjamin P., *Abraham Lincoln* (New York: Knopf, 1952).

Tourtellot, Arthur B., ed., *The Presidents on the Presidency* (Garden City, N.Y.: Doubleday, 1964).

———, *The Presidents on the Presidency* (New York: Russell and Russell, 1970) .

Truman, Harry S., *Memoirs*, 2 vols. (Garden City, N.Y.: Doubleday, 1958).

Tugwell, Rexford, *The Democratic Roosevelt* (Garden City, N.Y.: Doubleday, 1957).

———, *The Enlargement of the Presidency* (Garden City, N.Y.: Doubleday, 1960).

———, *How They Became President* (New York: Simon & Schuster, 1965).

Tugwell, Rexford G. *How They Became President* (New York: Simon and Schuster, 1968).

Vandenberg, Arthur H., *The Greatest American: Alexander Hamilton* (New York: Putnam's, 1921).

Van Der Linden, Frank, *Nixon's Quest for Peace* (Washington, D.C.: Luce, 1972).

Vinyard, Dale, *The Presidency* (New York: Charles Scribner's Sons, 1972).

Wann, A.J., *The President as Chief Administrator: A Study of Franklin D. Roosevelt* (Washington, D.C.: Public Affairs Press, 1968).

Warren, Sidney, *The Battle for the Presidency* (Philadelphia: Lippincott, 1968).

———, *The President as World Leader* (New York: McGraw-Hill, 1967).

Westin, Alan, *The Anatomy of a Constitutional Law Case* (New York: Macmillan, 1958).

White, Theodore H., *The Making of the President 1960* (New York: Atheneum, 1961).

———, *The Making of the President 1964* (New York: Atheneum, 1965).

———, *The Making of the President 1968* (New York: Atheneum, 1969).

White, William S., *The Professional: Lyndon B. Johnson* (Boston: Houghton Mifflin, 1964).

Wicker, Tom, *JFK and LBJ: The Influence of Personality Upon Politics* (New York: William Morrow & Co., Inc., 1968).

Wildavsky, Aaron ed., *The Presidency* (Boston: Little, Brown and Company, 1969).

Williams, Irving G., *The Rise of the Vice-Presidency* (Washington: Public Affairs Press, 1956).

Wills, Gary, *Nixon Agonistes: The Crisis of the Self-Made Man* (Boston: Houghton Mifflin Company, 1970).

Wilmerding, Lucius, *The Electoral College* (New Brunswick, N.J.: Rutgers University Press, 1958).

Wilson, Woodrow, *Congressional Government* (Boston: Houghton Mifflin, 1885).

———, *Constitutional Government in the United States* (New York: Columbia University Press, 1908).

Wise, Sidney and Richard F. Schier, eds., *The Presidential Office* (New York: Thomas Y. Crowell Company, 1969).

Wolk, Allan, *The Presidency and Black Civil Rights: Eisenhower to Nixon* (Cranbury, N.J.: Fairleigh Dickinson, 1972).

Zinn, Charles J., *The Veto Power of the President* (Washington: Government Printing Office, 1951).

INDEX

389